# Postsocialism

Social scientists did not predict the collapse of socialist systems in 1989–91 and most attempts to explain what has happened since have been flawed. Economic disintegration and political instability have been documented, but the deeper causes and consequences have often gone unnoticed. Consequently the solutions proffered, such as the promotion of non-governmental organisations as the foundations of 'civil society', have so far brought little success.

*Postsocialism* presents a range of anthropological analyses of the new social order. The view 'from below', obtained through intensive fieldwork, opens up new understanding of the postsocialist condition and the extent to which one dominant ideology has been replaced by another. The topics addressed include: the role of social and cultural capital in determining the 'winners' of rural decollectivization, the devaluation of blue collar labour, the position of Gypsies, the viability of 'multicultural' models in situations of religious difference and ethnic violence, new patterns of consumption, changing ritual practices and the healing of socialist 'trauma'.

The forcible imposition of socialist rule destroyed the integrity of many communities and individual lives; the impact of its demise has also been shattering for millions of citizens in postsocialist Eurasia. Beneath the changes, anthropological analysis brings out significant continuities, both in values and in actual behaviour. Time was not 'frozen' during the two or three generations of socialist rule. Rather, the contours of postsocialist society are being shaped by a continuous stream of evolving institutions and practices, which emerges only slowly from the valley of socialism. The term postsocialist will remain pertinent so long as the ideals, ideologies and practices of socialism are perceived to provide a meaningful (albeit increasingly mythical) reference point for understanding people's present condition.

**C. M. Hann** is Founding Director of the Max Planck Institute for Social Anthropology, in Halle, eastern Germany, which specialises in studies of postsocialist countries. His book *Socialism* was published by Routledge in the ASA Monographs series in 1993.

# Postsocialism

## Ideals, ideologies and practices in Eurasia

Edited by C. M. Hann

London and New York

First published 2002 by Routledge
2 Park Square, Milton Park, Abingdon, Oxon OX14 4RN

Simultaneously published in the USA and Canada
by Routledge
270 Madison Avenue, New York, NY 10016

Reprinted 2006, 2007

*Routledge is an imprint of the Taylor & Francis Group, an informa business*

Typeset in Goudy by Taylor & Francis Books Ltd
Printed and bound in Great Britain by MPG Books Ltd, Bodmin

*British Library Cataloguing in Publication Data*
A catalogue record for this book is available from the British
Library

*Library of Congress Cataloging in Publication Data*
Postsocialism : ideologies, and practices in Eurasia /
[edited by] C.M. Hann.
p. cm.
Includes bibliographical references and index.
1. Post-communism. 2. Social history–1970– .
I. Hann, C.M., 1953–
HX44.5. P693 2002
306~.095–dc21     2001048184

ISBN 0–415–26257–7 (hbk)
ISBN 0–415–26258–5 (pbk)

# Contents

Notes on contributors                                                      ix
Preface and acknowledgements                                               xi

1 Introduction: postsocialism as a topic of anthropological investigation   1
  CHRIS HANN, CAROLINE HUMPHREY, KATHERINE VERDERY

  Farewell to the socialist 'other'                                         1
  CHRIS HANN

  Does the category 'postsocialist' still make sense?                      12
  CAROLINE HUMPHREY

  Whither postsocialism?                                                   15
  KATHERINE VERDERY

**PART I**                                                                 **29**
**Social capital, trust and legitimacy**

2 The advantages of being collectivized: cooperative farm managers in the
  postsocialist economy                                                    31
  MARTHA LAMPLAND

3 Economic crisis and ritual decline in Eastern Europe                     57
  GERALD W. CREED

4 The social production of mistrust                                        74
  CHRISTIAN GIORDANO AND DOBRINKA KOSTOVA

PART II                                                                              93
**Dimensions of inequality: gender, class and 'underclass'**

5  Retreat to the household? Gendered domains in postsocialist Poland   95
   FRANCES PINE

6  The unmaking of an East-Central European working class              114
   DAVID A. KIDECKEL

7  Deprivation, the Roma and 'the underclass'                          133
   MICHAEL STEWART

PART III                                                                            157
**Violent histories and the renewal of identities**

8  Intolerant sovereignties and 'multi-multi' protectorates: competition
   over religious sites and (in)tolerance in the Balkans               159
   ROBERT M. HAYDEN

9  Withdrawing from the land: social and spiritual crisis in the indigenous
   Russian Arctic                                                      180
   PIERS VITEBSKY

10 Remnants of revolution in China                                     196
   STEPHAN FEUCHTWANG

PART IV                                                                             215
**Stretching postsocialism**

11 Rethinking Chinese consumption: social palliatives and the rhetorics of
   transition in postsocialist China                                   217
   KEVIN LATHAM

12 How far do analyses of postsocialism travel? The case of
   Central Asia                                                        238
   DENIZ KANDIYOTI

13 'Eurasia', ideology and the political imagination in provincial Russia 258
CAROLINE HUMPHREY


PART V 277
Democracy export and global civil society

14 Seeding civil society 279
RUTH MANDEL

15 Beyond transition: rethinking elite configurations in the Balkans 297
STEVEN SAMPSON

16 Afterword: globalism and postsocialist prospects 317
DON KALB

Index 335

# Contributors

**Gerald W. Creed**: Department of Anthropology, Hunter College and the Graduate Center, City University of New York, 695 Park Ave, New York, NY 10021, USA.

**Stephan Feuchtwang**: Department of Anthropology, London School of Economics, Houghton Street, London, WC2A 2AE, UK.

**Christian Giordano**: Institut d'Ethnologie, Universität Fribourg, Rte de Bonnefontaines 11, CH-1700, Fribourg, Switzerland.

**Chris Hann**: Max Planck Institute for Social Anthropology, PO Box 11 03 51, 06017 Halle (Saale), Germany.

**Robert M. Hayden**: Department of Anthropology, University of Pittsburgh, Pittsburgh, PA 15260, USA.

**Caroline Humphrey**: Department of Social Anthropology, University of Cambridge, Free School Lane, Cambridge, CB2 3RF, UK.

**Don Kalb**: Department of Anthropology, Utrecht University, and University College, PO Box 80145, 3508 TC Utrecht, The Netherlands.

**Deniz Kandiyoti**: Department of Anthropology, School of Oriental and African Studies, Thornhaugh Street, Russell Square, London, WC1H 0XG, UK.

**David Kideckel**: Department of Anthropology, Central Connecticut University, 1615 Stanley St, New Britain, CT 06050, USA.

**Dobrinka Kostova**: Institute of Sociology, Bulgarian Academy of Sciences, Sofia, Bulgaria.

**Martha Lampland**: Department of Sociology, University of California, 9500 Gilman Drive, La Jolla, San Diego, CA 92093-0102, USA.

**Kevin Latham**: Department of Anthropology, School of Oriental and African Studies, Thornhaugh Street, Russell Square, London, WC1H 0XG, UK.

**Ruth Mandel**: Department of Anthropology, University College, Gower Street, London, WC1E 6BT, UK.

**Frances Pine**: Department of Anthropology, University of Cambridge, Free School Lane, Cambridge, CB2 3RF, UK.

**Steven Sampson**: Department of Social Anthropology, University of Lund, Box 114, 221 00 Lund, Sweden.

**Michael Stewart**: Department of Anthropology, University College, Gower Street, London, WC1E 6BT, UK.

**Katherine Verdery**: Department of Anthropology, University of Michigan, 1020 LSA Building, Ann Arbor, MI 48109-1382, USA.

**Piers Vitebsky**: Scott Polar Research Institute, University of Cambridge, Lensfield Road, Cambridge, CB2 1ER, UK.

# Preface and acknowledgements

This book derives from a conference titled 'Actually-existing Postsocialisms', held in Halle in November 2000. Together with the meeting of specialists on the Russian North immediately preceding it, the papers from which are being published separately, this was the first major conference of the Max Planck Institute for Social Anthropology, founded in the previous year. The Institute is located in the former East Germany and investigations of the postsocialist world have high priority in our research agenda. We aim not only to show specialists in other subjects that anthropology can contribute to the study of contemporary social transformations, but also to demonstrate to anthropologists the pertinence of such studies for other concerns of the discipline. Vast regions of Europe and Asia have been relatively neglected in the dominant anthropological traditions and their integration is long overdue.

Since most of our own staff only took up their positions in 2000, it was too soon for us to present results of our new fieldwork projects concerning postsocialist property relations (for details see www.eth.mpg.de). Rather, we were treated to a feast by distinguished external scholars, who were invited to present examples of their own recent work and simultaneously to address more general themes and review the current 'state of play' across a wide range of topics and countries. All have carried out fieldwork in the postsocialist years, usually among people whom they knew well under the *ancien régime*, and they were encouraged to set this work in wider contexts. The outcome is a volume in which micro-level insights into particular processes of transformation are combined with an insistence on the more general validity of an anthropological approach, complementing the perspectives of other disciplines. The distinctive character of this approach cannot be reduced to any one body of theory or methods. The authors draw eclectically on diverse intellectual traditions, ranging from the classical sociologists to postcolonialism, from political theory to psychotherapy. The nature of their fieldwork is also extremely diverse. Yet certain themes and issues recur throughout the volume and the chapters are brought together by a common sensibility, a concern to understand how momentous social transformations affect the social relations and life-worlds of postsocialist citizens. This is often coupled with scepticism towards current 'blueprints' for change, which echoes the scepticism that many of those citizens themselves developed through their bitter experiences with the social engineers of socialism. The volume will serve as a guide to the field for many years to come, and perhaps inaugurate a new era in which the concepts of transition and postsocialism will have to be replaced by terms that are equally pertinent in other parts of the world – including the so-called developed countries.

Of course, the coverage falls short of being comprehensive. First, though the Institute is also interested in the impact of socialism elsewhere in the world, it was decided for pragmatic reasons on this occasion to restrict comparisons to Eurasia. Even so, some large countries (Vietnam and Mongolia as well as Germany and Ukraine) are regrettably missing. China does figure, though its path away from socialism has been highly distinctive. It is worth signalling that socialism, a Eurasian product, for a short period brought a remarkably uniform social organization to most parts of this landmass. This unity may now be receding; but at a time when the most powerful politicians in Western Europe are preoccupied with a very limited eastward expansion of their club, it is important that anthropologists address issues at the Eurasian level.

A second significant deficiency in our coverage is the absence of the 'local scholars', the many who practise some form of anthropological enquiry in their own country, and on whose support and cooperation most external researchers crucially depend. The Halle meeting featured a good sample of the recent work by Westerners, some of it carried out with local partners; but, again for prag- matic reasons, it was not possible on this occasion to open up to include many local anthropologists (who may or may not trade under this name), or to analyse the relations between internal and external researchers. We acknowl- edged this deficit by asking Yulian Konstantinov (Bulgaria) and Mihály Sárkány (Hungary) to lead a final, very productive session of discussion at the meeting; and we shall endeavour to do better on future occasions.

The structure of the volume differs significantly from that of the conference, and I am grateful to all contributors for their cooperation during the editorial process. Chapter 1 consists of revisions of the remarks made by myself, Caroline Humphrey and Katherine Verdery at an opening 'round table' discussion, which problematized the concept of 'postsocialist'. I have expanded my own section of this chapter to include many more references to recent anthropological work (by no means a full literature review) and to the contents of this volume. Further brief discussion of the chapters is provided at the beginning of each section.

It remains for me to acknowledge the authorities of the Franckesche Stiftungen and the Martin Luther University, who kindly allowed us to use their meeting rooms (we do not yet have suitable facilities of our own); and to thank my colleagues, students and support staff at the Institute, who have all played a huge role in the organization of the conference and in the production of this volume.

Chris Hann
Halle, April 2001

# Chapter I

# Introduction

## Postsocialism as a topic of anthropological investigation

*Chris Hann, Caroline Humphrey,*
*Katherine Verdery*

### Farewell to the socialist 'other'[1]

*Chris Hann*

The struggle between capitalism and socialism was a long drawn out contest that decisively framed the political consciousness of most of the world's population while it lasted and continues to exercise pervasive effects a decade after it was apparently won by 'the free world'. Massive changes have taken place in the former socialist countries. Many academic disciplines have addressed these changes and in some cases, notably that of economics, disciplinary paradigms have been utilized not merely to explain what is unfolding but to make changes happen in a particular way. Yet, after more than a decade, many deficits remain in social science understandings of the 'transition'. I shall argue that anthropology provides the necessary corrective to the deficits of 'transitology', and that the anthropological study of other parts of the world can also profit from attention to the emerging studies of postsocialism.[2]

For readers unfamiliar with modern anthropology, its basic aim is the documentation and analysis of human social arrangements in all their historical and geographical diversity. From its beginnings in the nineteenth century, when the prime focus was on the study of small-scale communities of 'savages', the so-called *Naturvölker*, in the course of the twentieth century anthropologists expanded their range considerably. They first extended their enquiries to include 'peasant' communities, including those of vast countries with long histories of 'civilization' such as China, India and Mexico. Following the dismantling of European colonial empires, they eventually brought their discipline to bear on European societies themselves (where the relationship between anthropologists and local specialists was sometimes problematic). They increasingly rejected the constraints of the isolated rural community and turned their attention to urban contexts, not only to 'ordinary people' and migrants, but also to the middle classes and to elites. By the end of the century, earlier disciplinary boundaries had partially broken down. The basic principle of respect for different ways of organizing society, for beliefs and practices at variance with one's own, has been retained, but the hallmark of modern anthropology tends nowadays to lie in its method, in the 'close-up' view acquired through fieldwork (ethnography). 'Qualitative' data are the main currency of this anthropological knowledge, and they sometimes lead the researcher to challenge the statistical generalizations and abstract models of other disciplines. On this basis, all human activities and institutions are equally suitable subjects for anthropological investigation, though some anthropologists continue to address distinctive themes and to work in places little frequented by their colleagues in sociology or 'cultural studies'.

Despite their obvious importance in terms of numbers and the variety of social forms they contained, anthropologists were not prominent in the study of socialist societies in Eurasia. Some of the reasons for this neglect derived from the discipline's origins and its overriding concern with 'exotic' tribal societies in regions colonized by European powers. Russia was also an imperial power and ethnographers began to document the marginal people of their peripheries in Tsarist times. Their successors after the revolution were obliged to operate within the straitjacket of Marxism–Leninism, and both Soviet and Chinese minorities policies were decisively shaped by Stalin. In some ways, however, this anthropology adhered to the paradigm that was being gradually abandoned in Western countries: the primary concern was with remote, disappearing social worlds, the antithesis of the dominant aggressive modernism of socialist ideology.

Western anthropologists were barely allowed a look-in. This began to change with the softening of socialism in a number of Eastern European countries in the 1970s. The first cohorts allowed to carry out fieldwork in socialist countries still devoted disproportionate attention to remote villages and marginal groups. These studies added valuable correctives to common social science models of socialism, by showing how it was experienced and routinized by 'ordinary people'.[3]

The dramatic events of 1989–91 created new opportunities both for established scholars and for a new generation of fieldworkers. No single scholar can possibly keep pace with the burgeoning literature and, without claiming to offer a balanced survey, the following thumbnail sketch is intended primarily to help readers to follow up topics of interest to them.[4] It goes without saying that research questions and methods necessarily reflect not only the altered nature of the research terrain but also changing concerns in the discipline, including heightened awareness of philosophical and ethical dilemmas (De Soto and Dudwick 2000). Younger anthropologists of postsocialism have paid attention to the emerging diversity of lifestyles in modern urban contexts, including capital cities; after all, this is where large sections of the population now live (Berdahl et al. 2000). Some of those nowadays undertaking 'classical' fieldwork in a village community address themes quite different from those addressed by previous village researchers: for example, Berdahl's (1999) study of an East

German community concentrates on questions of memory, consumption and identity, while themes related to agriculture and other forms of work recede into the background.

On the other hand, there have also been significant strands of continuity in the topics and locations of anthropological research into postsocialism. Several scholars have seized the opportunity to work in remote places, notably the vast regions of Siberia and Central Asia that had previously been off limits (Anderson 2000; Grant 1995; Kandiyoti and Mandel 1998; Sneath 2000). Just as many monographs of the socialist period focused on the establishment and functioning of cooperatives and collective farms, so the single most prominent theme in rural studies of the postsocialist period has been the break-up of these 'total social institutions' (for wide-ranging compilations see Abrahams 1996; Anderson and Pine 1995; Kideckel 1995). The process began earlier in China and is well documented there (Chan et al. 1992; Hann 1999; Jing 1996; Liu 2000; Nie 2001; Potter and Potter 1990; Ruf 1998; Siu 1989a; Vermeer et al. 1998). Some researchers have been able to address the balance of change and continuity by publishing updated studies of communities they first studied in the communist period. For the former Soviet Union, Caroline Humphrey has reissued her pioneering study in Buryatia (1998). In Eastern Europe, Creed's study of Bulgaria (1998) and Lampland's of Hungary (1995) present villagers' experiences of collectivization somewhat more positively than does Kideckel (1993) for the Romanian case. Postsocialist developments also vary considerably, but there seems to be a high degree of consensus that rural populations have suffered disproportionately (including, despite initial improvements, the Chinese case). Hann (1993b; 1996) found that Hungarian villagers had a sense that their 'citizenship' rights were being diminished and Hivon (1995) has described 'resistance' to widening inequalities in rural Russia. Kaneff (1996) has shown how Bulgarian villagers struggled against the odds to hold on to at least some of their collective institutions.

Processes of land privatization have been fundamental to the reconstruction of postsocialist rural society, but they are of such variety and complexity that we may have to wait for a full generation before we can specify their outcomes more adequately.[5] In Romania Katherine Verdery has documented the 'elasticity' of land that has several rival claimants, and highlighted the need to complement a focus on property rights with attention to the duties and obligations that such rights incur (1996, 1999b, 2001; cf. Cartwright 2001; Hirschhausen 1997). It is not simply that the objectives of moral justice (which might mean restoring property to former owners) and economic rationality (leaving the land in the units in which it can be farmed most efficiently) often prove incompatible. Sometimes the pursuit of private property appears conducive to neither goal, but to be the product of a new dominant ideology imposed upon the postsocialist world. The adequacy of the Western liberal distinction between public (collective) and private (individual) forms of property is called into question by the extreme fuzziness of property relations in China (Oi and Walder 1999).

Of course, the dilemmas of privatization and moral justice are not confined to the countryside. Urban settings are more complex insofar as it is usually impossible to divide up industrial means of production to create family units in the way that one can – at least theoretically – attempt to create family farmers. A comprehensive analysis of a community of workers is more daunting. The fieldworker is more likely to aim at detailed descriptions of partial networks or specific types of social interaction, or to explore more diffuse worlds of discourse (e.g. Ries 1997). However, several anthropologists have provided ethnographic studies of factory workers, including those whose workplaces were closed or radically restructured following foreign intervention (Czegledy 1999; Dunn 1999; Müller 1993, 1996, 1999). The distress is sometimes greater than that experienced in the countryside, because an entire way of life comes to an end and one is powerless to do anything about it; some redundant workers have attempted to move back to the countryside, where at least they can generate the greater part of their own food supply (see Kideckel, this volume). Social inequalities and poverty have increased in virtually all regions and economic sectors of the postsocialist countries, but only careful micro-level research can provide important information about how different groups are responding, e.g. in adjusting budgets and domestic divisions of labour and responsibility (Bridger and Pine 1998; Kandiyoti 1998). The negative implications of economic liberalization for most women have been examined in rural China by Croll (1994), Davin (1998); Jacka (1997) and Judd (1994); and in Eastern Europe by Gal and Kligman (2000a, b) and Pine (1996a, 1996b, 1998, this volume).

Other areas of economic life to attract attention from anthropologists include markets and consumption, where the explanatory models of mainstream economists are often found to be inadequate (Lampland, this volume). Whereas the latter usually assume that 'tastes' are given, anthropologists explore the social factors that shape changing consumption patterns, as Humphrey has done for postsocialist Moscow. Her wide-ranging analyses of postsocialist dynamics (2000, 2002) emphasize the 'disorderly' character of exchanges throughout the post-Soviet economy. Hann (1992b), Holy (1992), and Konstantinov (1997) have considered the impact of the 'market principle' in Eastern Europe, including the proliferation of petty-trading across state borders. Yan (1997) has described the impact of McDonald's on Beijing, where the meanings associated with American fast food are quite different from those it has in its country of origin. This global business makes a conscious effort to adapt to local conditions, because it is in its economic interests to do so. Unfortunately this point has not been grasped in many of the non-commercial interventions, notably so-called 'aid' and 'development' processes. Anthropologists have therefore contributed perceptive critiques of the practical implementation of these programmes (Bruno 1998; Mandel, this volume; Sampson 1996, this volume; Wedel 1998; Wedel and Creed 1997).

Most anthropologists have been critical of policies based on the transfer of Western models, which overlook institutional contexts and the strong threads of continuity that mark even the most dramatic of social ruptures. Most economists have tended to dismiss such points. There are, however, encouraging signs that, instead of shrill cynical comments from the sidelines, it might be possible to develop a fruitful dialogue with even the 'hardest' of the social sciences. Seabright (2000) shows how the approaches of anthropologists and sociologists can be integrated with perspectives from economics to illuminate disintegration and the prominence of barter in the post-Soviet economies. Schrader (2000) shows how a single scholar can fruitfully apply a variety of techniques, in this case to explore the changing significance of pawnshops in the strategies of poor households and new businessmen in St Petersburg.

There is scope for complementarities in many other areas. In law, for example, it is clear that at least some of the Western constitutional lawyers called upon to assist in the development of new legal codes have not considered it necessary to pay much attention to local context. An emphasis upon the legal strengthening of private property rights may be seriously misplaced if people continue to look to the state to resolve their collective action problems. In another highly contentious area of law, John Borneman (1998) has contributed an analysis of retributive justice, with a particular focus on the special case of East Germany (special because here the former socialist state disappeared). It is not necessary to accept Borneman's provocative general theory of postsocialist justice in order to welcome empirical studies that bring out further layers of socio-legal norms, which always leave their mark on the imported blueprints.

Similar points apply in the development of local administrative and political institutions, where China has been the subject of the most sustained body of research (Feuchtwang and Wang 2001; Oi 1989; Siu 1989a; Vermeer et al. 1998), Elsewhere, relatively few researchers have followed up Verdery's (1995: 230) call to investigate the 'mechanisms and arenas of state transformation'. One study that does so is that of Humphrey and Sneath (1999), whose comparative study of pastoral adaptations highlighted problems of widening income differentiation and environmental degradation in several countries of Inner Asia. In Chapter 13 of this volume, Humphrey calls for a more radical rethinking of anthropological approaches to the field of politics, since no standardized model of 'the state' can be applied to the unstable field of post-Soviet Russia.

For obvious reasons, the field of ethnicity, nationalism and 'minority rights' has attracted attention across many disciplines. The problems faced by Roma people have been well documented in the postsocialist years but, as Michael Stewart has shown (1997), they go back a long way and in some ways they were intensified under socialism. Stewart argues in this volume for the importance of detailed knowledge of the people concerned and against solutions based on the American model of a racialized 'underclass'. A more general problem with the models put forward by political scientists and 'human rights experts' is that they often fail to recognize the flexibility of collective identities over time, the possibility that persons may belong to different minorities at the same time or privilege some over others depending on context. Yet unless the context is understood and 'ethnicity' treated as contingent, rather than as primordial essence, the legislation of specific rights according to this criterion may lead to the opposite of the benign results intended. Khazanov (1995) and Tishkov (1997) have provided comprehensive accounts of developments in the former USSR. In Eastern Europe attention has concentrated primarily on the Balkans (though Kürti and Langman 1997 includes studies from other regions). Numerous scholars have shown the importance of understanding the local factors that made 'ethnic cleansing' possible in ex-Yugoslavia and continue to destabilize the wider region (Bax 2000, forthcoming; Bringa 1995; Cowan 2001; Duijzings 2000; Halpern and Kideckel 2000). A long history of 'clan' organization and vigilantism in the context of ineffective state power are certainly among the key common factors. From an appreciation of the factors on the ground, the anthropologist may move to address fundamental principles of constitutional democracy whose pertinence is by no means confined to the postsocialist countries (Hayden 1999, this volume).

The policy relevance of anthropological research and links into expanding interdisciplinary literatures on cultural and human rights are self-evident in the fields I have considered so far. Valuable work is also being undertaken in other fields where the immediate applied payoff is less obvious, such as ritual and religion. Closer inspection reveals that, here too, there are usually significant links to ongoing political and economic processes. Michał Buchowski (2001), following Zygmunt Bauman, has considered how for the current systemic transformations can be viewed as the liminal phase of a *rite de passage*. Katherine Verdery (1999a) has demonstrated the importance of rituals focused on the dead in expressing values and mobilizing people to support particular interests (cf. Kubik 1994 on late socialist Poland). Catherine Wanner (1998) has explored the new nationalist symbolism of independent Ukraine, and Bulag (1998) has explored the 'hybridities' of the new Mongolian national identity. The symbolic dimension is also prominent in Cahalen's (forthcoming) analysis of the persistence of a strong *regional* identity in Poland, despite the increased exposure of the local economy to global forces. As Creed shows (this volume), rituals also play an important role in the maintenance of highly *local*, community boundaries. They have been a prominent theme in the anthropology of post-Maoist China, where some have seen long-term continuities with presocialist customs (Potter and Potter 1990) while others have cautioned that here as in other domains the socialist past itself has also left its mark (Brandtstädter 2000; Feuchtwang 2000, this volume; Siu 1989b). Both the resurgence of traditional religious practices and the efflorescence of new sects and cults need to be understood in the context of the general loss of faith in socialism as an 'ideological system'. Increasing social instability was manifested in a variety of religious phenomena in the socialist period, an extreme example being the Marian cults at Medjugorje (Bax 1995). The demise of socialist restrictions has contributed to revivals of shamanism in large parts of the former Soviet Union, urban as well as rural (Balzer, 1996; Bellér-Hann 2001; Humphrey 2001; Vitebsky, this volume). External insistence on pluralism, on the 'open society', implies a marketplace for religions analogous to economic marketplaces, but anthropological work may caution against such a recipe – especially in countries with a dominant church, such as Poland.[6]

Many postsocialist studies have included an explicit engagement with history. This is not in itself new: Verdery's first monograph (1983) was primarily a historical study of group dynamics over several centuries of Transylvanian history. What is new is not only that anthropologists, like other scholars, have benefited from the opportunity to work in archives previously closed to them. Following the collapse of the socialist orientation to the future, they have also documented an increased concern with the past in the present. They have been at the forefront in exploring traumatic memories and recovering 'secret histories' (Jing 1996; Vitebsky, this volume; Watson 1994), in studies of postsocialist historiography and iconography (Anagnost 1997; Niedermüller 1998), and in showing how local constructions of the past establish group connections to changing national ideologies (Kaneff 2002; Lemon 2000; Schnirelman 1996). Again we see the potential for fruitful collaboration between anthropologists and other specialists, in this case oral historians as well as those working with documents. Sometimes the same scholars employ methods from all of these fields (Lehmann 2001; Skultans 1998). It is now generally accepted that ethnographic analysis can be greatly enhanced by the integration of longer time frames (Giordano and Kostova, this volume).

Non-anthropologists may still question whether such work can illuminate the macro-societal problems of postsocialism. The answer is that the insights of close-up fieldwork observation are especially valuable in periods of uncertainty and institutional instability, a point that seems to be gaining increased acceptance in neighbouring disciplines as well (Bridger and Pine 1998; Burawoy and Verdery 1999). The case studies in these two volumes reveal a high degree of overlap between the work of anthropologists and sociologists, at any rate those sociologists who, through fieldwork, come into contact with real people and their social practices. Of course, it is not easy in the space of a brief book chapter to convey a full sense of the social context, a difficulty that also applies to some of the ethnographic materials in this book. Readers inclined to dismiss such materials as unrepresentative or anecdotal are encouraged to look at more detailed work by the author in question, or indeed by any other anthropologist. We hope that the fragments presented in these brief accounts will stimulate readers to go away and seek out fuller versions.

Thus, although most anthropological work focuses on specific practices at the micro level, it invariably carries wider implications. But how does one make this explanatory leap and what are the larger units? A great deal of anthropological work has tended to extrapolate from the community study to an entity called a 'society' or a 'culture'. Often this unit is considered to approximate to a state, though large multi-ethnic states pose an immediate problem. At this point the term 'culture', widely perceived as the indispensable 'master concept' of the discipline, often slips in imperceptibly; it is prominent in this volume and in postsocialist anthropology generally (Wolfe 2000). Most of the work I have cited above could be said to be concerned with how specific cultural under-standings shape people's behaviour. If one had to sum up in a single phrase the essence of the anthropologist's critique of other social science approaches to 'the transition', the charge could be 'neglect of the cultural dimension'.

For me, however, the concept of culture raises major problems in the postsocialist context, for at least two reasons. First, the 'cultural racism'[7] that has been documented in many other parts of the world has been exceptionally trans-parent in a number of postsocialist contexts, notably where formerly federal, multi-ethnic states have disintegrated. Many postsocialist elites have drawn, implicitly or explicitly, on ideas of culture as an integrated whole to create boundaries of exclusion and, in the worst cases, to legitimize violence against those alleged to possess a different culture. Anthropologists may contest such usages and insist that their own concept of culture carries quite different impli-cations, but I am doubtful that we can succeed in correcting this popular usage – especially since some anthropologists themselves emphasize the bounded coher-ence of the 'cultures' they study.

A second, often related sense in which the culture concept is regularly abused comes when ideas such as 'Balkan mentality', 'Gypsy nature' or 'the fatalistic Orthodox soul' are invoked to explain why policies that succeed in some contexts fail entirely when transplanted to others. In these accounts, culture is a mysterious residual variable, the ultimate cause of why an entire region or 'people' may diverge from the path of development prescribed by persisting versions of 'modernization theory'. This 'black box', mystical approach to culture was fostered in many parts of the world in the twentieth century by the modern anthropologist's tendency to focus on particular units and to neglect similarities at higher regional and even continental levels. It can be corrected in this case by paying closer attention to the many features that Marxist–Leninist regimes in Eurasia shared. This opens up intriguing concep-tual problems, for it is equally clear that, in the usual sense of cultural history, socialist Eurasia was extraordinarily diverse. From Lutheran Protestants in Germany to Buddhist Lamas and Islamic Mollahs in Central Asia, from Roman Catholicism and Jewish traditions in Poland to Confucianism in China and Shamanism in Siberia, religious traditions varied enormously, often within countries as well as between them. Yet the similarities of socialist institutions imposed a layer of uniformity on top of all this diversity. This layer has been incisively analysed by Katherine Verdery (1991, 1996; cf. Hann 1994) in a general model of socialist 'allocative power' that complements her many more specialized studies of Romanian case materials. She does not speak of a culture of socialism but emphasizes instead institutions and the logic of bureaucratic centralism. She has argued powerfully against the teleology of 'transition', the assumption that the future condition of the former socialist countries can be read off from the development path followed by Western capitalism (1996).

But we must not privilege the common distinctive features of the socialist countries to the extent that we lose sight of the many features shared all along with other parts of the world, including the most developed industrial societies of the West. There was a tendency in much of the social-science literature on socialism to construct an 'other', corresponding to the 'savage other' of colonial anthropology. Anthropological work began to subvert simple models of 'totalitarianism' while the Cold War was still very much under way; the anthropology of postsocialism can perhaps go a step further. The central concepts used here are no less applicable in other parts of the world. The clearest example is the concept of 'civil society', which was rediscovered in the last years of socialism, in opposition to the 'totalitarian' state (Gellner 1994; Hall 1995; Hann 1990). Because of its normative attractions, civil society has been invoked in many programmes of Western aid (Kalb, this volume; Mandel, this volume; Sampson 1996, this volume; Wedel 1999); but often it, too, has remained an elusive, black-box category. Some scholars in other disciplines have tried to operationalize it by counting the number of 'non-governmental organizations' and treating this as an index of the health of the society (Cellarius and Staddon 2002). Anthropologists studying postsocialism are likely to be sceptical of such approaches, since a proliferation of 'autonomous' associations is likely to be small consolation to people suddenly deprived of jobs and public goods. Pursuing a simplistic Western definition of civil society can in some postsocialist conditions lead directly to heightened incivility (Hann 1998). The concept therefore needs to be broadened, relativized and adapted to local conditions (Brook and Frolic 1997; De Soto and Anderson 1993; Hann 1992a, 1995; Hann and Dunn 1996; Kligman 1990). If this is done, 'civil society' can remain a useful general term to designate a broad flow of social activity, the study of which has always been central to anthropology, between the domestic sphere on the one hand and the state on the other, but not sharply separable from either of these.

Another concept that the postsocialist settings invite us to reconsider is 'embeddedness', the metaphor adapted by Karl Polanyi from Richard Thurnwald to convey what the early substantivist economic anthropologists felt to be the unique way in which modern capitalist economies had ruptured the traditional integration of economic activities into other sectors of life. Are the postsocialist market economies more 'disembedded' than their predecessors, and if so how? What other terms might better capture the current character of economic relationships in postsocialist countries? Anthropologists have pioneered investigations of the economy variously described as 'informal', 'second' or 'underground', showing that these activities are always tightly connected to the 'official' economy, and that allegedly impersonal spheres of market and contractual relations are always mediated by personal contacts. Socialist central planning spawned rich varieties of economic sociality, some of which have collapsed completely, while others have experienced efflorescence in postsocialist conditions (Wedel 1992). The nexus of gifts, 'connections' and trust is especially well documented for China (Kipnis 1997; Yan 1996; Yang 1994). Contributors to this volume (see especially Part I) take up these and related concepts that have been prominent in postsocialist studies, but which are no less pertinent elsewhere.

Terms like 'civil society' and 'trust' immediately betray their normative loading. So too does the concept of *legitimacy*, which is broached by several contributors to this volume (see especially Giordano, who follows Weber, and Latham, whose approach derives more from Foucault). Communist systems collapsed because they had evidently lost political and moral legitimacy. Much fine writing at the time, both by local intellectuals and by Westerners connected to such 'dissidents', was premised on the assumption that an intellectual author could speak up for a whole society or a people, oppressed by an authoritarian regime. A decade later Vaclav Havel used the occasion of a World Bank meeting in Prague to call for a 'restructuring of the entire system of values which forms the basis of our civilization today'. At the same time he urged the Bank to pay more attention to the views of the people – as if this were the easiest thing in the world to do.[8] Many Eastern European social scientists and the few Western anthropologists who worked in the region knew of complicating circumstances when Havel and others formulated their critiques of communism 'in the people's name'; but few objected to simplifying intellectual discourses about a 'return to Europe' or the 'rediscovery of civil society'. Now, a decade after the Cold War ended, anthropologists are well positioned to move the moral debates to another level by showing how terms like 'private property' and 'market economy' connect to social realities for the citizens of today's democracies. Are these still lofty ideals, or are they merely key slogans in the new ideologies? Have Western elites, supported by the dominant disciplines of transitology, systematically promoted models for the postsocialist countries that bear little connection to the social realities of their own countries?

I suggest that postsocialist anthropology necessarily engages with both a political and an ethical dimension. Unlike other analysts who deploy terms like 'civil society', our close-up scrutiny of practices allows us to assess a changing moral climate where it matters most, in everyday life. From this perspective it is striking that the dissidents' diagnoses of a 'moral vacuum' are turning up again in characterizations of postsocialism. Neither the new ideological slogans nor the efflorescence of religious phenomena seem able to fill this new social void. The *everyday moral communities* of socialism have been undermined but not replaced. Nor does lacing capitalist consumerism with increased doses of national sentiment seem to produce the desired results. In socialist times, many citizens were uncomfortable with their rulers; some tuned in to Radio Free Europe whenever they could. Some lived in a climate of fear at the workplace and suspicion in the neighbourhood; but this has perhaps been exaggerated in the Western literature. Some of those who grumbled most in the old days now share the nostalgia of the less articulate, for an age when they had fewer and less secure rights in a legal sense, yet their needs were more adequately fulfilled than is the case a decade later. And they often bring a moral dimension into their comments, regretting the shrinking of the public sector and articulating a strongly held sense that the new regimes do not respect entitlements to which they had become accustomed under socialism (Pine, Kandiyoti, this volume).

For some of us, who knew these places when they were more isolated but safe, cheap and somehow unspoiled, the new inequalities make painful viewing. The influx of multinational businesses, property developers and advertising agencies is painful to behold. The consumer consolations are inadequate and not available to all, while the sordid aspects of the new market economy (e.g. prostitution) go uncontrolled. Of course, the distress experienced by some outside observers may exceed that felt by local people, among whom traces of nostalgia are usually dissipated when they reflect on the squalid and sordid aspects of their daily lives under socialism. Even so, there were plenty who *believed* in that system to some degree. Among those who rejected it, many did so on well thought out moral grounds. As for the majorities in the middle, those who simply took their social system for granted as most people do, all were exposed to an ideology that, even when it was patently collapsing, never abandoned its claim to ethical superiority. Whatever one thinks about this claim, my point is that the market and pluralist democracy have not, at the level of everyday practices, ushered in new moral forces comparable to those that have been displaced. Postsocialist corruption, criminality and social disintegration are constant topics of moral commentary. When all the evils and iniquities of socialism have been recognized (and many are documented in this volume), it remains important to note this register. At any rate, anthropologists are professionally obliged to recognize the moral complexities, to respect as well as critique the world that has now (almost everywhere) disappeared; those socialist ideals shaped the lives of the millions who lived in that world and, indirectly, of all the rest of us as well. We need shed no tears as we bid farewell to the 'socialist other' but, as Don Kalb points out in his 'Afterword' to this volume, it would be arrogant and myopic to imagine that global capitalism offers a universal panacea or moral yardstick.

Continuing anthropological explorations of the interplay between diverse histories, belief systems and practices may eventually render the concept 'postsocialist' redundant; but it seems to me that the experience of Marxist–Leninist socialism, the reproduction of a common layer of socialist institutions, ideology and moral purpose over two generations or more, will continue to have decisive effects on this interplay everywhere in Eurasia for many years to come.

## Does the category 'postsocialist' still make sense?

*Caroline Humphrey*

The category 'postsocialist' rests on what seem to me a number of reasonable assumptions. First, there never can be a sudden and total emptying out of all social phenomena and their replacement by other ways of life. Second, what Rudolf Bahro called 'actually existing socialism' was a deeply pervasive phenomenon, existing not only as practices but also as public and covert ideologies and contestations. A third assumption, more disputed perhaps, is that 'actually existing socialism' had a certain foundational unity, derived in its public ideology from Marx and in its dominant political practice from Lenin. Even if the shared features of actually existing socialism were very unevenly distributed and moulded in diverging ways in different countries, those structures still had more in common than actually existing capitalisms – and 'capitalism' is a category that people go on using profitably, without qualms. So while 'postsocialism' is certainly a construct of the academy, it is not ours alone, and it does correspond to certain historical conditions 'out there'.

This is not to argue that 'postsocialist studies' should constitute a subdiscipline in the sense outlined by Strathern (1981). Strathern argued against an 'anthropology of women' precisely on the grounds that it was beginning to look like the manufacture of a closed subdiscipline, defined by specific values and interests. The study of formerly socialist societies must remain open, with possibilities of privileged insight from various different positions, both from inside and outside. It should not be separated off from other analytical concerns in anthropology, such as comparative studies of imperialism and colonialism, post-imperialism or political anthropology more generally.

Having asserted the basic unity of the field of investigation, it is very obvious, if we scan across from Eastern Europe to Vladivostok, that divergences between the former socialist countries have been accentuated over the last decade. In particular, there seems to be a growing gap between Central and Eastern Europe (including the Baltic states) on the one hand, and the Russian Federation and the Central Asian countries on the other, not to speak of the Caucasus and China. Differences in crucial matters such as the way 'democracy' is operated, attitudes to private property in land, the relation of the individual to the state, and the role of law, seem to be widening as each year goes by. Yet it makes sense, at least for the time being, to keep the category of 'postsocialism' in order to maintain the broadest field for comparison. I have three main reasons for saying this.

The first is that we still have not worked out what the heritage of actually existing socialism is. To give an example, in the recent presidential elections in Kyrgyzstan the incumbent, Akayev, was returned to power with 75 per cent of the vote, and journalists rushed to pronounce this a sad day for democracy and a return of communist political habits. In other parts of Inner Asia, with which I am more familiar, there have been even more overwhelming electoral victories, such as the 88 per cent of the vote won by the singer and mafia-boss Kobzon in the Aga Buryat district in Russia. Kobzon's victory too was attributed by Russian journalists to 'Soviet mentality' among local Buryats. But what grounds do we have for concluding that these electoral results have anything to do with the previous conduct of politics under socialism? Other explanations might start from an examination of local patronage systems or vote-rigging – we cannot know until we make on-the-spot historically informed studies and also look comparatively at why regions with more or less the same formation of 'actually existing socialism' have followed diverging paths in recent years.

This brings me to my second point: how can we most profitably conduct comparison? It's not much good describing two different situations and then totting up, 'There is X here, but not there; there's Y here, but not there' and so on. Rather, by investigating broadly while we are in the process of trying to understand any one situation, this can inform our analysis of that very situation. In other words, comparison should inform description, not the other way around. One needs a relevant field for comparison, and for us this will very often be the wide field of 'postsocialisms'.

Third, it is important to recognize that changes in postsocialist countries are not simple and unidirectional (Burawoy and Verdery 1999). There have been twists and unexpected reversals. In many countries there is a rather unpredictable propensity to 'turn back', or at least a resolute refusal to abandon values and expectations associated with socialism among sectors of the population. We do not see this everywhere to the same degree, but in one form or another it seems very common. For example, in Mongolia the previous revolutionary (i.e. 'communist') party has just been re-elected by a staggering majority (only three among over seventy seats in the parliament are held by other parties). This party has been very much transformed, and indeed advocates a 'Third Way' with echoes of Britain's Tony Blair. Nevertheless, what Mongolians say is that its appeal really rests on its previously established legitimacy of having provided for substantive 'needs', such as regular wages, health and free education, during the socialist period. The resurgence of communist parties in this way is temporal evidence that we are in a period of postsocialism. It would be perverse not to recognize the fact that people from East Germany to Mongolia are making political judgments over a time span that includes the socialist past as their prime reference point, rather than thinking just about the present trajectory to the future.

This point cannot, however, retain its force indefinitely. Sooner or later, as the generations brought up under socialist regimes disappear from the political scene, the category of postsocialism is likely to break apart and disappear. I have the impression that many younger people across a wide swathe of the region are already beginning to reject the term, which can be seen as a constricting, even insulting, label, something imposed from outside that seems to imply constraints on the freedom of people in these countries to determine their own futures. If people themselves reject the category, we as anthropologists should not cling to it, but pay attention to whatever other frameworks of analysis arise from within these countries themselves. In any case, another aspect of the generational problem is that the anthropologists who knew those societies under socialism, the 'old-timers' like me, are being replaced by younger scholars with their own agendas and interests. They are likely to focus on new issues, like the integration of Europe, globalization, or new communications technologies, that have little to do with the socialist past.

Finally, let us reflect further on some of the salient 'objective' processes and events ongoing in the vast space of 'postsocialism'. In the western regions we have the spread of NATO, and preparations for entry into the European Union are well advanced in a number of countries. Less well known is what is happening further east. For some years now, many writers and politicians in Russia have been debating what a non-Western-oriented, even an 'anti-Atlanticist', future would look like. They have been debating the historical identity of Russia and the nature of the Federation in relation to the imperial and Soviet heritage. Central to this have been discussions about 'Eurasianism', in which the political traditions of Asian cultures within the Federation are held to make a creative synergy with that of the Slavs. Some of the Asian peoples concerned have rejected Eurasianism, seeing it as a mask for domination by Moscow. Others have welcomed it because it seems to give value to their own cultures. Now as far as I can see, these 'Asian values' are something new and not resurrections of pre-Soviet forms, often concern religion, reinterpretations of history or the overturning of past humiliations, and in many cases they also respond to current global alignments. At the same time, they are indigenous, by which I mean that they are positioned, and come out of regional experience.

The more extreme Russian nationalist forms of Eurasianism will present a challenge to anthropology similar in some ways to that posed by irredentist movements in Western Europe. One difference is that the political structure of Russia, with its eighty-nine federated polities, may provide locales where such ideologies could become dominant, in combination with regional vested interests. We may be witnessing in parts of Russia and Central Asia the emergence of the legitimation of a style of authoritarian government that could have no comparable purchase in East-Central Europe. Furthermore, it seems to me probable that the way this is experienced internally is very different from the face put on it externally, for the benefit of international relations – and hence the need for anthropological studies. There is a most complex relationship between the pragmatic attempt by Moscow to verticalize power all the way down to the level of the district, the pacts between local resource-holders, and the attempts by people of different cultures to register publicly their own ways of conceiving political relations. With the growing popularity of an overarching Eurasianism, the potential is there for a new kind of rhetorically anti-rational authoritarianism, validated by mystical ideological notions which coexist uneasily with the hard facts of who controls and monopolizes resources and who is reduced to economic destitution. The challenge will be two-fold: first, how to understand and interpret such situations without prejudging them from a Euro-American set of values, and here it seems to me that collaboration between regional and outsider anthropologists must be essential. Second, as Verdery argues below, the vision of Western societies from Eurasian perspectives will inform our own self-understanding.

I examine this new ideology of Eurasianism in more detail in Chapter 13. The current situation in the provinces that promote such and idea may have certain significant links to aspects of Sovietism as a style of government, but even so privatization and the new electoral politics have made a decisive break with the past structures. These new formations seem set on trajectories that will take them ever further from socialism, and in a quite different way from the processes under way in East-Central Europe. If we see a growing gulf between two broad paths, if socialist values come to be rejected in several entirely different ways in different regions of the former socialist zone, and if 'actually existing socialism' comes to be relegated into a largely forgotten past of yellowing newsprint, then it will be time to lay the category 'postsocialist' finally to rest.

## Whither postsocialism?

*Katherine Verdery*

If the two preceding contributions show us the variety of ethnographic work being done since 1989 and inquire how long the term 'postsocialist' will remain meaningful for research in the region, this final essay turns away from the ethnographically concrete to speculate about the future.[9] Whether under the rubric postsocialist or not, where should scholarship on the former socialist bloc be heading? Chris Hann's essay has shown some of the first steps, which include efforts to understand the transformation process and 'legacies' of socialism, practices and dilemmas of 'daily life', and problems that had not arisen in the earlier literature (such as tourism, nostalgia, and prostitution).[10] Becoming historians and continuing to study socialism through newly opened archives has been another option.[11] But from a decade of such writing, no clear direction for postsocialism and the study of 'transition' has emerged. To orient our research, it seems time to seek a new angle of vision on processes of the socialist and postsocialist periods.

One possibility is to create a parallel with postcolonial studies, inviting that body of work to open itself to insights from a rather different quarter while also turning postsocialist studies in new directions.[12] The parallel makes a certain sense: not only were Eastern Europe and much of the former Soviet Union under a form of colonial domination, but numerous other countries – Cuba, Mozambique, Ethiopia, Yemen, Laos, etc. – entered into the Soviet orbit, often as part of establishing their independence from one or another Western colonial power. In this essay I will point to what I see as some of the more productive moves in postcolonial studies so as to explore their analogues for work on postsocialism.

Just as postcolonial studies examines the colonial pasts that shaped societies in present-day Africa, Latin America and Asia, so we might now explore these same processes for Soviet imperialism. Such an exercise would enable several things, among them analyses of kinds of empire. The Soviet empire was not organized like those of Great Britain, France and other capitalist countries. Although both involved complex combinations of conquest, infiltration and annexation to the projects of the imperial centre, those projects differed: 'Moscow Centre' aimed to integrate its dependencies into a process of accumulating not capital but, as I have argued elsewhere, allocative power through accumulating means of production (see Verdery 1991). Integral to this goal was building a wall that would *insulate* it and its dependencies from processes of capital accumulation. Thus, security was an obsession, and part of the point of expanding the empire westward was to create a safety zone (Eastern Europe) so that imperial territory would not be contiguous with that of the European capitalist centres. The Soviet empire was more self-consciously invasive and ambitious than West European empires: its instruments were generally more blunt, and its plans for ideological transformation emphasized different routes to that end.

One objective of postsocialist studies, then, might be to examine more fully through newly accessible archives how the Soviet empire functioned. How did the colonial connections work, as compared with those of Western Europe's empires?[13] What was the difference among the 'inner tier' of Soviet Republics, the 'second tier' of East European satellites, and the 'outer tier' of client states in Africa, Asia and the New World? How might explorations of this kind modify postcolonial theory? And might both bodies of work be enhanced by comparing the routes out of empire – the differential insertions of colonies or satellites into global capital flows, the effects of varying the speed of decolonization?

A second possible analogue for postsocialism from postcolonial studies is the latter's questions about how the interactive field uniting colony and metropole helped to constitute and transform the imperial centre. Thus, how did the Soviet Union's relations with its various satellites constitute and transform 'Moscow Centre' itself? One could argue that these relations helped to bring the system down altogether, as debts in the satellites caused a drain on the centre (Bunce 1985) or as Soviet concern about the implications of Poland's Solidarity movement fuelled the emergence of a reformist faction in the Soviet leadership; by supporting reformists in Eastern Europe, this faction brought about the 'revolutions' of 1989. But aside from these kinds of economic and political relations, postcolonial studies might encourage us to ask further how the very mechanisms of domination rebounded against the imperial centre. One obvious way was through the party's instrumentalization of national identities; a second might be reactions against its technologies of intimacy;[14] we should look for others.

Yet another parallel would be with postcolonial studies' emphasis upon the role of knowledge and representation in colonial rule. These were also fundamental, though in a different way, in the world of the Cold War. In fact, that war was nothing if not an organization both of the world and of images and knowledge about it (Verdery 1996: 4). The Cold War organized the world around a dichotomy different from that of postcoloniality – not colonies and metropole, 'the West' and 'the Rest', but East and West, communism and capitalism. And it organized knowledge both by underscoring other aspects of capitalism than colonial relations and by grouping places and states differently from the centre–colony groupings of European imperialism. Such a perspective indicates that we are talking about a scholarly orientation much broader than simply 'postsocialism', and one that incorporates study of the Cold War as well. Perhaps we should speak, then, not of *postsocialist* but of *post-Cold War studies*. Let me elaborate on the above thoughts.

Just as postcolonial studies examines the representations of 'self' and 'other' in the colonial encounter, we might further explore the history of such representations in the socialist and capitalist worlds – each holding up the other as its nemesis, the image of all that can be evil. This imagery has some postcolonial parallels in Western Europe's 'Orientalist' constructs and images of the 'savage'. We need to understand better how reciprocal images of 'the West' were made and propagated in both the communist and the colonial environments (one agenda of the subaltern school of postcolonial studies, for example). Literature has been an important site for that, in the colonies but not in socialist contexts; there, it might be that the image of the Western other was constructed mainly through negations of how socialist officialdom presented its own virtues.

Concerning the organization of knowledge, postcolonial studies generally contrasts colonial areas with the imperial centres – what we have come loosely and problematically to call the First World, with the Third. Studies of socialism and postsocialism, on the other hand, have emphasized the First and Second Worlds, aligning parts of the Third as clients of these. The knowledge sought in each body of scholarship has differed as well. Most area-studies work on the socialist bloc during the Cold War focused on excessive political control ('totalitarianism') and the absence of consumption and markets – features opposite to basic features of our own Western identity, just as much scholarly effort since 1989 has gone to studying the rectification of these 'lacks'.[15] Postcolonial studies emphasizes, rather, *practices of domination*, such as techniques of evangelizing, manipulations of time and space, modes of inscribing the colonial system on the bodies of its subjects, etc. To adopt this broader rubric, along with some of its insights, would give an alternative kind of coherence to postsocialist studies.

So far it appears that I am merely calling for the application to the formerly socialist bloc of lessons learned from a postcolonial tutor. I have in mind, however, something rather more ambitious. I want to suggest that postsocialist or post-Cold War studies, whatever broader term we might adopt for it, should both amplify and incorporate postcolonial studies – or, less imperialistically, we should integrate these separate areas of inquiry into a single field. If the Third World gave us postcoloniality, then the Second World should be giving us something even more comprehensive, for the very concept of a Third, non-aligned World itself emerged from the Cold War. The presence of the Soviet system gave a very particular shape to global politics, with proxy wars, battles for client states, and clients playing the two superpowers off against one another – Yugoslavia is a prime, and sobering, example. That is, the global order that gave rise not only to neocolonialism but to *postcolonial studies itself* was an order structured by the Cold War, whose very existence compelled Western states to struggle for pieces of countries and regions that were not directly part of the Soviet bloc.

We should go further than merely integrating the 'worlds' to ask why studies of colonialism and socialism have been so separated from one another. What has that separation been accomplishing? There are fascinating insights to be gained from refusing that separation, insights such as Frank Costigliola's findings about the numbers of ex-colonial officers who moved into Cold War posts in the 1950s, bringing with them ideas about 'otherness' they saw no problem in transferring to their new socialist contexts.[16] What might this finding imply for the failures of Western intelligence to understand what was actually going on in those countries?

The more comprehensive frame I am proposing would lead to research that deals with colonialism in all its many forms: not only the European empires of previous centuries, not only the Soviet colonies in Eastern Europe and the numerous client-states in the Third World, but also the full incorporation of both the former colonies *and* the former socialist bloc into a global capitalist economy. To organize research in this way is to position the Third World differently from the way postcolonial studies does. Moreover, it affords us a rather different view of questions concerning Western identity by asking how not just the colonies but the *existence of socialism itself* affected the constitution and becoming of 'the West', often simultaneously with processes involving the colonies, postcolonies and neocolonies. The larger aim of this way of organizing knowledge would be to revise our understanding of twentieth-century capitalism, to which the socialist system posed a fundamental challenge. What were the effects of that challenge, and how can we find those effects historically or ethnographically?

To begin with, it seems likely that increased state intervention in Western European economies was a response to the danger that was perceived in the socialist alternative – as well, of course, as a response to working-class self-organization and social democracy. It is possible, in addition, that the organization of socialist political economies made them powerful competitors in a way that Western propaganda about the 'inefficiencies' of socialism served to obscure. For example, party-states regularly did what democratic ones rarely did until the 1970s: they bailed out failing enterprises – and they did it with 'taxpayers' money but without the political fall-out occasioned, for instance, by the US government's bail-out of the savings and loan industry. Party-states began early to protect firms against risk, through their practice of soft budget constraints; it was only later that their Western counterparts would begin to serve explicitly as cushions against risk (cf. Maurer 1999). Moreover, organizing property in a system of devolving use-rights rather than ownership rights, these states showed how enterprises might successfully shuck costs and liabilities precisely because they did *not* own. We increasingly see this insight at work both among property-rights theorists and in contemporary practices involving intellectual property, in which not owning but *leasing* and other temporary arrangements sustain profits.[17] It begins to seem that socialism was perhaps less outmoded than we were told.

We might go further. Is it also possible that the 'flexible specialization' so much analysed in the past two decades is in part a result of the challenge posed by socialism? Capitalist growth depends on consumption, in order to absorb the products it creates and generate the profits upon which accumulation depends. With the expansion of socialism not just in Europe but elsewhere as well, a staggering proportion of the world's people was hindered from consuming Western goods. Although the 1970s saw a gradual seepage of such products into socialist economies, they never flowed in at a rate that might have prevented the crisis into which global capitalism entered during the late 1960s and to which flexible specialization emerged as a solution. The crisis began when consumer markets for the output of mass production became saturated – that is, when *available* markets were saturated, those not embedded in the socialist sphere of exchange. The solution was to develop new techniques for expanding demand and consumption. Without socialist autarky, would this solution have arisen precisely when it did? Would 'niche markets', just-in-time manufacturing, and the tremendous speed-up of contemporary capitalism have been precluded – at least for a time? Post-Cold War studies would encourage us to ask this kind of question.

What I have said so far indicates some of the ways in which a new post-Cold War studies might illuminate the very constitution of colonial studies. It might also, more modestly, illuminate some of the problems that latter body of work addresses. For example, a common theme in writings on postsocialism is transferring Western institutions (markets, democracy, etc.) to non-Western settings. This work offers fascinating grounds, then, for comparison with those interested in how colonialism involved something similar.[18] Putting the two together, we could ask comparatively about the timing of this 'transfer' process (during/after colonialism versus primarily after it); the participation of NGOs and other international organizations in it; the significance of attempting it in the heart of Europe as opposed to at a far remove; and the continuing question of how such transfers of Western outcomes (forms of economy and polity, nation and state) – common to all these situations – are expected to 'take' without the usual origins and supports these forms had in their Western development. For this problem it actually *makes sense* to divide the world into the 'West' and the 'Rest' and to subdivide the Rest further into different *kinds* of colonial/neo-colonial experience. The comparison could be highly instructive.

How might this sort of orientation shape the anthropology of postsocialism? First, it offers a new mandate for research in historical anthropology, comparable to the work being done in postcolonial studies. Were it to choose the Foucauldian approach of much of that work, it would afford us a very broad field for asking about the multiple technologies, including especially those involving race and gender, through which modernity in its many guises – fascist, socialist and capitalist – was produced.[19] Students of postsocialism would thus have substantial room for theoretical development concerning varieties of modernity. Their efforts might, incidentally, include judicious revival of a materialist perspective, this time unencumbered by its ossified, institutionalized Marxist–Leninist forms.

Second, like postcolonial studies, the framework I propose would bring together scholars from many disciplines and countries – far beyond the 'core' socialist states – who might not otherwise communicate much with one another. Instead of carving up the world into students of politics and economics and literary studies, it would compel a multi-disciplinary effort, but not one beholden to the old 'area studies' paradigm. The effects of the Cold War were not confined to any single world area: they were wholly pervasive throughout most of the twentieth century. It is time to liberate the Cold War from the ghetto of Soviet area studies.

Third, like postcolonial studies, the orientation I am advocating would give voice to the 'natives' as analysts of their own condition. Although it is not yet clear who would be the Franz Fanon of this corpus, his or her forerunners surely include the East European dissidents and other scholars – people like Rudolph Bahro, Pavel Câmpeanu, György Konrád, János Kornai, István Rév, Jadwiga Staniszkis and Iván Szelényi[20] – whose writing spurred us to seek an understanding of socialism different from that offered by Cold War categories, even if we now perceive deficiencies in their view of it. Yet for both postsocialist and postcolonial studies, as anthropologists we ought to insist on broadening the category of 'native' to incorporate the understandings of people who have less privileged positions in their societies than do those I have just mentioned.[21] Intellectuals, after all, often hold to radically different ideals and ideologies from those of other sorts of people – as the history of Bolshevism itself confirms.

The Cold War is not over; its influence is felt even now. How else to understand the importance accorded by both scholars and policy-makers alike to 'privatization', 'marketization' and 'democratization' – that troika of Western self-identity so insistently being imposed on the ex-socialist 'other' as a sign that the Cold War *is* over? Is the emphasis on these features driven by the ideological goal of compelling 'them' to be like our outdated image of 'us'? Here is one task for postsocialist ethnography: to ferret out the self-representations that are emerging on both sides with the collapse of socialism. Others would be to discover and analyse the processes less driven by Cold War ideology (the sex trade, transformations of space and time) as well as those still governed by it (property relations, ideas about money, gender roles). This kind of research will provide a new body of work, built upon but not hostage to the analysis of socialism, that will cast new light upon the world of twentieth-century empires and their twenty-first-century successors.

## Notes

1 This is an expanded version of the notes prepared for the Halle meeting. My warm thanks to Caroline Humphrey, Katherine Verdery and my colleagues in the Max Planck Institute for Social Anthropology.
2 I prefer this term to 'postcommunism', though the latter is perhaps more commonly employed, both externally and internally. Most of the states concerned claimed to be socialist rather than communist, and the latter is coloured in many places by its frequent use as a term of political abuse.
3 For reviews of studies of Eastern Europe in the socialist period see Halpern and Kideckel 1983, Hann 1993a. The bias towards the rural sector could be justified on the grounds that not only this sector was less visible to other investigators, but in most socialist countries until comparatively recently the bulk of the population lived in the countryside.
  In China the opening came roughly a decade earlier, but work on China is rarely cited by those studying postsocialism elsewhere, and vice versa. Despite improved conditions for fieldwork, Eurasian postsocialism as a whole attracts less attention from anthropologists than from other social scientists. It is not significantly harder to obtain funding and authorization for field research than in most other parts of the world, but linguistic and other barriers remain, inhibiting the rapid emergence of a new research community. Thus, both in Britain and in America, many more PhD students work in Western Europe and in the Mediterranean than embark on projects further east.
4 In addition to the items mentioned in the following very partial literature review, those wishing to explore a wider range of recent anthropological contributions should consult *The Anthropology of East Europe Review* – http://Las1.depaul.edu/Aeer/ – and a number of journal special issues: *Anthropological Journal of European Cultures* vol. 2, nos 1–2 (1993); *Etudes Rurales* nos 138–40 (1995); *Cambridge Anthropology* vol. 18, no. 2 (1995); *Central Asian Survey* vol. 17, no. 4 (1998); *Ethnologia Europaea* vol. 28, no. 2 (1998); *Focaal* no. 33 (1999).
5 This topic is the principal focus of the postsocialist research team at the Max Planck Institute in Halle in the period 2000–3.
6 The enormous expansion of religious activity in postsocialist conditions has attracted relatively little attention from anthropologists to date and we therefore plan to make this a focus for projects at the Max Planck Institute in the years ahead. For sociological work see Borowik and Babiński 1997; see also Hann 2000.
7 See Stolcke 1995. Cultural racism is a continuation of the tradition of regarding certain categories of people as inherently inferior to others, but the cause is now said to lie in culture rather than the (pseudo)biological concept of race.

8  Address by Vaclav Havel at the Opening Ceremony of the Meetings of the International Monetary Fund and the World Bank Group (Prague, 26 September 2000). Source: http://www.hrad.cz/president/Havel/speeches/index_uk.html.
9  I am deeply grateful for conversations with Elizabeth Dunn, who stimulated me to think about the issues raised in this essay, and to Valerie Bunce and Ann Stoler, who greatly improved an earlier version of it with their suggestions.
10  See, for example, papers in Berdahl et al. 2000; compare with Kideckel 1995, Burawoy and Verdery 1999.
11  For example, Martha Lampland is carrying out archival research on Stalinism and the economic history of forms of remuneration used in the socialist economy. Similarly, Gail Kligman and I are engaged in a project concerning the effects of collectivization upon the transformation of persons, *Transforming Property, Persons, and State: collectivization in Romania, 1948–1962.*
12  A similar proposal appears in Burawoy 2001; see also Deniz Kandiyoti's paper in this volume.
13  See Jowitt 1987. For an illuminating discussion of how we might think about the very notion of 'comparison', see Stoler 2001.
14  For one possible model see Kligman 1998. See also Stoler 2001.
15  Anthropologists, by contrast, investigated other kinds of topics earlier, such as rural life, ritual, and national identity. The papers in this volume offer excellent illustrations of what anthropologists of the region are up to now.
16  See, for example, Costigliola 2000. I am grateful to Ann Stoler for informing me about this body of work.
17  For example, agricultural economists raise questions about whether land privatization was actually such a good idea and whether leasing arrangements are not preferable (e.g. Hagedorn 2000). At the same time, intellectual property rights are sought less in ownership of *objects* than in capturing *revenue streams* from them.
18  The example comes from Valerie Bunce.
19  Thanks to Ann Stoler for this phrasing.
20  We also have several examples of fruitful collaborations involving 'outsiders' and 'natives' (e.g. Burawoy and Lukács 1992; Stark and Bruszt 1998).
21  Thanks to Chris Hann for rightly insisting on this point.

## References

Abrahams, Ray (ed.) (1996) *After Socialism: Land Reform and Social Changes in Eastern Europe*, Oxford: Berghahn.

Anagnost, Ann (1997) *National Past-times: Narrative, Representation, and Power in Modern China*, Durham: Duke University Press.

Anderson, David G. (2000) *Identity and Ecology in Arctic Siberia: the Number One Reindeer Brigade*, Oxford: Oxford University Press.

Anderson, David G. and Frances Pine (eds) (1995) *Surviving the Transition: Development Concerns in the Postsocialist World*, special issue of *Cambridge Anthropology*, 18(2).

Balzer, Marjorie Mandelstam (1996) 'Flights of the sacred: symbolism and theory in Siberian shamanism', *American Anthropologist* 98(2): 305–18.

Bax, Mart (1995) *Medjugorje: Religion, Politics and Violence in Rural Bosnia*, Amsterdam: VU University Press.

——(2000) 'Planned policy or primitive Balkanism? A local contribution to the ethnography of the war in Bosnia-Herzegovina', *Ethnos* 65(3): 317–40.

——(forthcoming) *Priests and Warlords: the Dynamics of Processes of State Deformation and Reformation in Rural Bosnia-Herzegovina.*

Bellér-Hann, Ildikó (2001) 'Solidarity and contest among Uyghur healers in Kazakhstan', *Inner Asia* 3: 73–98.

Berdahl, Daphne (1999) *Where the World Ended: Re-unification and Identity in the German Borderland*, Berkeley: University of California Press.

Berdahl, Daphne, Matti Bunzl and Martha Lampland (eds) (2000) *Altering States: Ethnographies of Transformation in Eastern Europe and the Former Soviet Union*, Ann Arbor: University of Michigan Press.

Borneman, John (1998) *Settling Accounts: Violence, Justice and Accountability in Postsocialist Europe*, Princeton: Princeton University Press.

Borowik, Irena and Grzegorz Babiński (eds) (1997) *New Religious Phenomena in Central and Eastern Europe*, Kraków: Nomos.

Brandstädter, Susanne (2000) 'Taking Elias to China (and leaving Weber at home): post-Mao transformations and neo-traditional revivals in the Chinese countryside', *Sociologus* 50(2): 113–44.

Bridger, Sue and Frances Pine (eds) (1998) *Surviving Postsocialism: Local Strategies and Regional Responses in Eastern Europe and the Former Soviet Union*, London: Routledge.

Bringa, Tone (1995) *Being Moslem the Bosnian Way: Identity and Community in a Central Bosnian Village*, Princeton: Princeton University Press.

Brook, Timothy and Michael Frolic (eds) (1997) *Civil Society in China*, Armonk: M.E. Sharpe.

Bruno, Marta (1998) 'Playing the co-operation game: strategies around international aid in postsocialist Russia', in Sue Bridger and Frances Pine (eds) *Surviving Postsocialism: Local strategies and Regional Responses in Eastern Europe and the Former Soviet Union*, London: Routledge, pp. 170–87.

Buchowski, Michał (2001) *Rethinking Transformation*: an anthropological perspective on post-socialism, Poznań: Wydawnictwa Humaniora.

Bulag, Uradyn E. (1998) *Nationalism and Hybridity in Mongolia*, Oxford: Clarendon Press.

Bunce, Valerie (1985) 'The empire strikes back: the evolution of the eastern bloc from a Soviet asset to a Soviet liability', *International Organization* 39: 1–46.

Burawoy, Michael (2001) 'Neoclassical sociology: from the end of Communism to the end of classes', *American Journal of Sociology* 106: 1099–120.

Burawoy, Michael and János Lukács (1992) *The Radiant Past: Ideology and Reality in Hungary's Road to Capitalism*, Chicago: University of Chicago Press.

Burawoy, Michael and Katherine Verdery (eds) (1999) *Uncertain Transition; Ethnographies of Change in the Postsocialist World*, Lanham, MD: Rowman and Littlefield.

Cahalen, Deborah (forthcoming) *Being Góral*, Albany: State University of New York Press.

Cartwright, A.L. (2001) *The Return of the Peasant; Land Reform in Post-Communist Romania*, Aldershot: Ashgate.

Cellarius, Barbara and Caedmon Staddon (2002) 'Environmental non-governmental organizations, civil society and democratization in Bulgaria', *East European Politics and Society*.

Chan, Anita, Richard Madsen and Jonathan Unger (1992) *Chen Village under Mao and Deng*, Berkeley: University of California Press.

Costigliola, Frank (2000) '"I had come as a friend": emotion, culture, and ambiguity in the formation of the Cold War', *Cold War History* 1(1.1): 103–28;

Cowan, Jane (ed.) (2001) *Macedonia: the Politics of Identity and Difference*, London: Pluto.

Creed, Gerald (1998) *Domesticating Revolution. From Socialist Reform to Ambivalent Transition in a Bulgarian Village*, University Park, Pennsylvania State University Press.

Croll, Elizabeth (1994) *From Heaven to Earth: Images and Experiences of Development in China*, London: Routledge.

Czegledy, André (1999) 'Corporate identities and the continuity of power', in Birgit Müller (ed.) *Power and Institutional Change in Post-Communist Eastern Europe*, Canterbury: CSAC.

Davin, Delia (1998) *Internal Migration in Contemporary China*, Basingstoke: Macmillan.

De Soto, Hermine and David G. Anderson (eds) (1993) *The Curtain Rises: Rethinking Culture, Ideology and the State in Eastern Europe*, New Jersey: Humanities Press.

De Soto, Hermine and Nora Dudwick (eds) (2000) *Fieldwork Dilemmas: Anthropologists in Postsocialist States*, Madison: University of Wisconsin Press.

Duijzings, Ger (2000) *Religion and the Politics of Identity in Kosovo*, London: Hurst.

Dunn, Elizabeth (1999) 'Slick salesmen and simple people: negotiated capitalism in a privatized Polish firm', in Michael Burawoy and Katherine Verdery (eds) *Uncertain Transition Ethnographies of Change in the Postsocialist World*, Lanham: Rowman and Littlefield, pp. 125–50.

Feuchtwang, Stephan (2000) 'Religion as resistance', in Elizabeth Perry and Mark Selden (eds) *Chinese Society: Change, Conflict and Resistance*, London and New York: Routledge, pp. 161–77.

Feuchtwang, Stephan and Wang Mingming (2001) *Grassroots Charisma: Four Local Leaders in China*, London and New York: Routledge.

Gal, Susan and Gail Kligman (2000a) *The Politics of Gender after Socialism*, Princeton: Princeton University Press.

——(eds) (2000b) *Reproducing Gender: Politics, Publics, and Everyday Life after Socialism*, Princeton: Princeton University Press.

Gellner, Ernest (1994) *Conditions of Liberty: Civil Society and its Rivals*, London: Hamish Hamilton.

Grant, Bruce (1995) *In the Soviet House of Culture: a Century of Perestroikas*, Princeton: Princeton University Press.

Hagedorn, Konrad (2000) 'Privatisation', lecture presented at the symposium *Understanding Transition of Central and Eastern European Agriculture*, Humboldt University, Berlin, November.

Hall, John A. (ed.) (1995) *Civil Society: Theory, History, Comparison*, Cambridge: Polity Press.

Halpern, Joel M. and David A. Kideckel (1983) 'Anthropology of Eastern Europe', *Annual Review of Anthropology* 12: 377–402.

——(eds) (2000) *Neighbours at War: Anthropological Perspectives on Yugoslav Ethnicity, Culture and History*, University Park: Pennsylvania State University Press.

Hann, C.M. (ed.) (1990) *Market Economy and Civil Society in Hungary*, London: Frank Cass.

——(1992a) 'Civil society at the grassroots: a reactionary view', in Paul G. Lewis (ed.) *Democracy and Civil Society in Eastern Europe*, London: Macmillan, pp. 152–65.

——(1992b) 'Market principle, market-place and the transition in Eastern Europe', in Roy Dilley (ed.) *Contesting Markets: Analyses of Ideology, Discourse and Practice*, Edinburgh: Edinburgh University Press, pp. 244–59.

——(1993a) 'Introduction: social anthropology and socialism', in C.M. Hann (ed.) *Socialism; Ideals, Ideologies and Local Practice*, London: Routledge, pp. 1–26.

——(1993b) 'From production to property: decollectivization and the family–land relationship in contemporary Hungary', *Man* 28(3): 299–320.

——(1994) 'After Communism: reflections on East European anthropology and the transition', *Social Anthropology* 2(3): 229–49.

——(1995) 'Philosophers' models on the Carpathian Lowlands', in John A. Hall (ed.) *Civil Society: Theory, History, Comparison*, Cambridge: Polity Press, pp. 158–82.

——(1996) 'Land tenure and citizenship in Tázlár', in Ray Abrahams (ed.) *After Socialism: Land Reform and Social Changes in Eastern Europe*, Oxford: Berghahn, pp. 23–49.

——(1998) 'Postsocialist nationalism: rediscovering the past in South East Poland', *Slavic Review* 57(4): 840–63.

——(1999) 'Peasants in an era of freedom: property and market economy in southern Xinjiang', *Inner Asia* 1(2): 195–219.

——(2000) 'Problems with the (de)privatization of religion', *Anthropology Today* 16(6): 14–20.

Hann, C.M. and Elizabeth Dunn (eds) (1996) *Civil Society: Challenging Western Models*, London: Routledge.

Hayden, Robert M. (1999) *Blueprints for a House Divided: the Constitutional Logic of the Yugoslav Conflicts*, Ann Arbor: University of Michigan Press.

Hirschhausen, Béatrice von (1997) *Les Nouvelles Campagnes Roumaines: paradoxes d'un 'retour' paysan*, Paris: Belin.

Hivon, Myriam (1995) 'Local resistance to privatization in rural Russia', *Cambridge Anthropology* 18(2): 13–22.

Holy, Ladislav (1992) 'Culture, market ideology and economic reform in Czechoslovakia', in Roy Dilley (ed.) *Contesting Markets: Analyses of Ideology, Discourse and Practice*, Edinburgh: Edinburgh University Press, pp. 231–43.

Humphrey, Caroline (1998) *Marx Went Away but Karl Stayed Behind*, Ann Arbor: University of Michigan Press.

——(2000) 'How is barter done? The social relations of barter in provincial Russia', in Paul Seabright (ed.) *The Disappearing Rouble: Barter Networks and Non-Monetary Transactions in Post-Soviet Societies*, Cambridge: Cambridge University Press, pp. 259–97.

——(2002) *The Unmaking of Soviet Life: Everyday Economies in Russia and Mongolia*, Ithaca: Cornell University Press.

Humphrey, Caroline and David Sneath (1999) *The End of Nomadism? Society, State and the Environment in Inner Asia*, Cambridge: White Horse Press.

Jacka, Tamara (1997) *Women's Work in Rural China: Change and Opportunity in an Era of Reform*, Cambridge: Cambridge University Press.

Jing, Jun (1996) *The Temple of Memories: History, Power and Morality in a Chinese Village*, Stanford: Stanford University Press.

Jowitt, Ken (1987) 'Moscow "Centre"', *East European Politics and Societies* 1: 296–348.

Judd, Ellen R. (1994) *Gender and Power in Rural North China*, Stanford: Stanford University Press.

Kandiyoti, Deniz (1998) 'Rural livelihoods and social networks in Uzbekistan: perspectives from Andijan', *Central Asian Survey* 17(4): 561–78.

Kandiyoti, Deniz and Ruth Mandel (eds) (1998) *Market Reforms, Social Dislocations and Survival in Post-Soviet Central Asia*, special issue of *Central Asian Survey*, 17(4).

Kaneff, Deema (1996) 'Responses to "democratic" land reforms in a Bulgarian village', in Ray Abrahams (ed.) *After Socialism: Land Reform and Social Changes in Eastern Europe*, Oxford: Berghahn, pp. 85–114.

——(2002) *Who Owns the Past? The Politics of Time in a 'Model' Bulgarian Village*, Oxford: Berghahn.

Khazanov, Anatoly M. (1995) *After the USSR: Ethnicity, Nationalism and Politics in the Commonwealth of Independent States*, Madison: University of Wisconsin Press.

Kideckel, David A. (1993) *The Solitude of Collectivism: Romanian Villagers to the Revolution and Beyond*, Ithaca: Cornell University Press.

——(ed.) (1995) *East European Communities: the Struggle for Balance in Turbulent Times*, Boulder: Westview Press.

Kipnis, Andrew B. (1997) *Producing Guanxi: Sentiment, Self and Subculture in a North China Village*, Durham: Duke University Press.

Kligman, Gail (1990) 'Reclaiming the public; a reflection on creating civil society in Romania', *East European Politics and Societies* 4(3): 393–438.

——(1998) *The Politics of Duplicity: Controlling Reproduction in Ceausescu's Romania*, Berkeley: University of California Press.

Konstantinov, Yulian (1997) 'Patterns of reinterpretation: trader-tourism in the Balkans (Bulgaria) as a picaresque metaphorical enactment of post-totalitarianism', *American Ethnologist* 23(4): 762–82.

Kubik, Jan (1994) *The Power of Symbols against the Symbols of Power: The Rise of Solidarity and the Fall of State Socialism in Poland*, University Park: Pennsylvania State University Press.

Kürti, László and Juliet Langman (eds) (1997) *Beyond Borders: Remaking Cultural Identities in the New East and Central Europe*, Boulder: Westview Press.

Lampland, Martha (1995) *The Object of Labor: Commmodification in Socialist Hungary*, Chicago: Chicago University Press.

Lehmann, Rosa (2001) *Symbiosis and Ambivalence: Poles and Jews in a Small Galician Town*, Oxford: Berghahn.

Lemon, Alaina (2000) *Between Two Fires: Gypsy Performance and Romani Memory from Pushkin to Postsocialism*, Durham: Duke University Press.

Liu, Xin (2000) *In One's Own Shadow: an Ethnographic Account of the Condition of Post-Reform China*, Berkeley: University of California Press.

Maurer, William (1999) 'Forget Locke? From Proprietor to Risk-Bearer in New Logics of Finance', *Public Culture* 11: 47–67.

Müller, Birgit (1993) 'The wall in the heads: East–West German stereotypes and the problems of transition in three enterprises in East Berlin', *Anthropological Journal on European Cultures* 2(1): 9–42.

——(ed.) (1996) *A la Recherche des Certitudes Perdues ... anthropologie du travail et des affaires dans une Europe en mutation*, Berlin: Centre Marc Bloch.

——(ed.) (1999) *Power and Institutional Change in Post-Communist Eastern Europe*, Canterbury: CSAC.

Nie, Lili (2001) *Liu Village: Lineage and Change in Northeastern China*: Oxford: Berghahn.

Niedermüller, Peter (1998) 'History, past, and the postsocialist nation', *Ethnologia Europaea* 28: 169–82.

Oi, Jean C. (1989) *State and Peasant in Contemporary China: the Political Economy of Village Government*, Berkeley: University of California Press.

Oi, Jean C. and Andrew Walder (eds) (1999) *Property Rights and Economic Reform in China*, Stanford: Stanford University Press.

Pine, Frances (1996a) 'Naming the house and naming the land: kinship and social groups in highland Poland', *Journal of the Royal Anthropological Institute* 2(3): 443–60.

——(1996b) 'Redefining women's work in rural Poland', in Ray Abrahams (ed.) *After Socialism: Land Reform and Social Changes in Eastern Europe*, Oxford: Berghahn, pp. 133–55.

——(1998) 'Dealing with fragmentation; the consequences of privatization for rural women in central and southern Poland', in Sue Bridger and Frances Pine (eds) *Surviving Postsocialism: Local Strategies and Regional Responses in Eastern Europe and the Former Soviet Union*, London: Routledge, pp. 106–23.

Potter, Sulamith Heins and Jack M. Potter (1990) *China's Peasants: the Anthropology of a Revolution*, Cambridge: Cambridge University Press.

Ries, Nancy (1997) *Russian Talk: Culture and Conversation during Perestroika*, Ithaca: Cornell University Press.

Ruf, Gregory A. (1998) *Cadres and Kin: Making a Socialist Village in West China, 1921–1991*, Stanford: Stanford University Press.

Sampson, Steven L. (1996) 'The social life of projects: importing civil society to Albania', in Chris Hann and Elizabeth Dunn (eds) *Civil Society: Challenging Western Models*, London: Routledge, pp. 121–42.

Schnirelman, Victor A. (1996) *Who Gets the Past? Competition for Ancestors among Non-Russian Intellectuals in Russia*, Washington: Woodrow Wilson Center Press.

Schrader, Heiko (2000) *Lombard Houses in St. Petersburg: Pawning as a Survival Strategy of Low Income Households*, Münster: LIT.

Seabright, Paul (ed.) (2000) *The Disappearing Rouble; Barter Networks and Non-Monetary Transactions in Post-Soviet Societies*, Cambridge: Cambridge University Press.

Siu, Helen F. (1989a) *Agents and Victims in South China: Accomplices in Rural Revolution*, New Haven: Yale University Press.

——(1989b) 'Recycling rituals: politics and popular culture in contemporary rural China', in Perry Link, Richard Madsen and Paul G. Pickowicz (eds) *Unofficial China: Popular Culture and Thought in the People's Republic*, Boulder: Westview Press.

Skultans, Vieda (1998) *The Testimony of Lives: Narrative and Memory in Post-Soviet Latvia*, London: Routledge.

Sneath, David (2000) *Changing Inner Mongolia: Pastoral Mongolian Society and the Chinese State*, Oxford: Oxford University Press.

Stark, David and László Bruszt (1998) *Postsocialist Pathways: Transforming Politics and Property in East Central Europe*, Cambridge: Cambridge University Press.

Stewart, Michael (1997) *The Time of the Gypsies*, Oxford: Westview Press.

Stolcke, Verena (1995) 'Talking culture: new boundaries, new rhetorics of exclusion in Europe', *Current Anthropology* 36: 1–24.

Stoler, Ann (2001) 'Tense and tender ties: intimacies of Empire in North American history and (post)colonial studies', *Journal of American History*, 106 (5).

Strathern, Marilyn (1981) 'Culture in a netbag: the manufacture of a subdiscipline in anthropology', *Man* 16(4): 665–88.

Tishkov, Valery (1997) *Ethnicity, Nationalism, and Conflict in and after the Soviet Union: the Mind Aflame*, London: Sage.

Verdery, Katherine (1983) *Transylvanian Villagers: Three Centuries of Political, Economic and Ethnic Change*, Berkeley: University of California Press.

——(1991) 'Theorizing socialism: a prologue to the transition', *American Ethnologist* 18: 419–39.

——(1995) 'Notes toward an ethnography of a transforming state: Romania, 1991', in Jane Schneider and Reyna Rapp (eds) *Articulating Hidden Histories: Exploring the Influence of Eric R. Wolf*, Berkeley: University of California Press, pp. 228–42.

——(1996) *What Was Socialism and What Comes Next?* Princeton: Princeton University Press.

——(1999a) *The Political Lives of Dead Bodies: Reburial and Postsocialist Change*, New York: Columbia University Press.

——(1999b) 'Fuzzy property: rights, power and identity in Transylvania's decollectivization', in Michael Burawoy and Katherine Verdery (eds) *Uncertain Transition: Ethnographies of Change in the Postsocialist World*, Lanham: Rowman and Littlefield, pp. 53–81.

——(2001) 'The obligations of ownership: restoring rights to land in postsocialist Eastern Europe', Wenner-Gren Foundation Conference paper.

Vermeer, Eduard B., Frank N. Pieke and Woei Lien Chong (eds) (1998) *Cooperative and Collective in China's Rural Development: Between State and Private Interests*, Armonk: M.E. Sharpe.

Wanner, Catherine (1998) *Burden of Dreams: History and Identity in Post-Soviet Ukraine*, University Park: Pennsylvania State University Press.

Watson, Rubie S. (ed.) (1994) *Memory, History and Opposition under State Socialism*, Santa Fe: School of American Research Press.

Wedel, Janine R. (ed.) (1992) *The Unplanned Society: Poland during and after Communism*, New York: Columbia University Press.

——(1998) *Collision and Collusion: the Strange Case of Western Aid to Eastern Europe, 1989–1998*, New York: St Martin's Press.

Wedel, Janine R. and Gerald Creed (1997) 'Second thoughts from the second world: interpreting aid in post-communist Eastern Europe', *Human Organization* 56(3): 253–64.

Wolfe, Thomas C. (2000) 'Cultures and communities in the anthropology of Eastern Europe and the former Soviet Union', *Annual Review of Anthropology* 29: 195–216.

Yan, Yunxiang (1996) *The Flow of Gifts: Reciprocity and Social Networks in a Chinese Village*, Stanford: Stanford University Press.

——(1997) 'McDonald's in Beijing: the localization of Americana', in James L. Watson (ed.) *Golden Arches East: McDonald's in East Asia*, Stanford: Stanford University Press, pp. 39–76.

Yang, Mayfair Mei-hui (1994) *Gifts, Favors and Banquets: the Art of Social Relationships in China*, Ithaca: Cornell University Press.

# Part I

# Social capital, trust and legitimacy

What do social scientists mean when they speak of 'social' and 'cultural' forms of capital and how can these be investigated empirically? Why have scholars looked increasingly to the peculiarities of local institutions and their histories to explain the outcomes not predicted in their models? In what circumstances does the introduction of market economy destroy sources of capital? What happens to the legitimacy of powerholders when their policies contradict both basic laws of economics and everyday practices?

Concepts of trust and social capital have been theorized and put into operation in various disciplines in recent decades and, although not specifically invented for the study of postsocialist transformation, they have been prominent here. In the opening chapter Martha Lampland provides a wide-ranging theoretical critique of the way a narrow focus on rational choice-making makes many economists blind to the importance of historical and social complexity. Although some strands of institutional economics and political sociology do better, developing ideas such as 'path-dependency', Lampland finds the most satisfactory elaboration of social capital in the work of Pierre Bourdieu. Economic blueprints must not be decontextualized: it is essential to integrate the analysis of *practices*, what people actually do, and to explore how this is shaped by the beliefs they hold and the social relationships they maintain. In the empirical part of her chapter she applies this perspective to the former cooperative farm officials in Hungary, whose economic successes can be best explained in terms of the practices, skills and networks of trustworthy contacts that they built up in the socialist period.

The existence of strong personal networks was well documented under the old conditions of central planning, when the 'second economy' was often seen by external commentators as a corrupt, corrosive influence. Yet even forms of sociability forced upon people by the 'economy of shortage' of the socialist period, such as queuing, had their positive aspects, and they are sorely missed today. Gerald Creed has shown in previous publications how ordinary Bulgarian villagers managed to 'domesticate' the principles of collective planning. In his contribution to this volume he shows how the imposition of the market and privatization policies has undermined local cohesion, which in socialist times supported an ebullient ritual life, intimately related to household self-provisioning. This has been severely attenuated in recent years due to the collapse of the socialist agricultural synthesis. Creed interprets this 'ritual retrenchment' as a diminution of the villagers' social capital. The implementation of Western development advice has paradoxically hindered potential entrepreneurs from responding to the demands of the new market economy. In a similarly vicious circle in the political realm, culture is depolitizised, financial support is withdrawn, and, stronger forms of ethnicity and nationalism seem to be replacing the celebration of more local forms of identity. Democratic elections may also be seen as a new form of ritual; participation rates have declined, because many people no longer see any possibility of improving their lot. (Turnout rose slightly in the election of 2001, as this volume went to press; it remains to be seen if the coming to power of the country's former King will now remould party politics and perhaps intensify the ritual dimension.)

Rural Bulgaria also provides the setting for the third chapter of this section, in which Christian Giordano and Dobrinka Kostova show how, in the historically and ecologically distinctive region of Dobrudzha, decollectivization has led to the emergence of a new 'awkward class' of entrepreneurs. The elites of the capital imagined that they could restore smallholder agriculture as it had existed half a century previously, but local people saw the economic absurdity of this aspiration only too clearly. The successful *arendatori* resemble the ex-managers identified in Hungary by Lampland, and the majority of new landowners have little option but to rent out their land to them. The authors emphasize the political dimension of these developments, which they view as the latest manifestation of a gulf of mistrust of urban powerholders that originates in the centuries of Ottoman rule. As a result of their attempts to impose policies that take no account of local economic and demographic realities, the new elites have squandered their legitimacy.

# Chapter 2

# The advantages of being collectivized

## Cooperative farm managers in the postsocialist economy[1]

*Martha Lampland*

Collectivization has gotten a bad rap. Like so many of the other policies of the socialist regimes of Eastern Europe, the manner of its implementation has overshadowed the social and economic benefits the policy provided rural communities. The Hungarian case is instructive. From the 1970s onward – that is, from the final consolidation of large-scale, mechanized agriculture – social observers regularly lauded party officials and agrarian specialists for having worked out a reasonable compromise with villagers. For many commentators, the key to success was a thriving 'second economy' in agricultural production (Rév 1987; Swain 1985). Less often mentioned, but crucial to this success, was the thriving cooperative sector, which was a crucial player in facilitating the ease of private production and ensuring the wealth of second economy agriculture. Once decollectivization became a possibility, what happened to the rosy picture of the Hungarian agricultural economy? The assessment of collectivized agriculture has been hijacked by property rights enthusiasts, whose interests in private property have eclipsed questions about the actual character of production. Socialist collectivization has been decried, and rightly so, for taking away families' land under duress, forcing villagers to become dependent upon the state for a job and benefits. Yet cooperative production is not a problematic form *per se*, only when the participation of members of a cooperative enterprise is restricted politically, as was the case in socialist countries. On the other hand, collectivization modernized agricultural production in positive ways: amalgamating lands to create better economies of scale, mechanizing production to reduce the physical toil of workers, and improving the access of producers to up-to-date scientific research. During the period of collectivized agriculture in socialist Eastern Europe, many countries, not least the United States, underwent comparable processes of modernization in agriculture. So the question arises: just what aspects of cooperative agriculture were irremediably socialist, and what features are shared more widely in modernized, capitalist economies? More to the point, understanding the dynamics of the postsocialist agricultural landscape requires a close attention to distinctions between property relations, modernized production and cooperative management practices. If these simple differentiations are not made, then we will be ill-equipped to analyse the current transformation of economic practices.

The purpose of this investigation is to criticize a prominent view of the transition in Eastern Europe. In this perspective, a simple change in the structure of institutions would be necessary to transform these economies, removing barriers to participation in international commerce (Åslund 1994; Brada 1993). Missing from this view is the simple but crucial insight that institutions are peopled by local actors, for whom the patterns of thought and action characteristic of the previous regime are normal and routine. The difficulties aid agencies and other frontline organizations have encountered in Eastern Europe are not due to intransigence, ignorance or incompetence, as some would have it, but to the very simple problem that learning new ways of doing business takes time. It is difficult to alter habits, ideas, opinions people hold of themselves, of others and of the world around them in short order. Moreover, people live within complex social relations: ties of affection, respect, obligation and reciprocity. A radical change in economic activity requires not only a change in thinking, but a restructuring of the larger social world of which one is a part. Actually, refiguring one's social relationships is far more difficult than learning new habits. In contrast to the views of liberal economists (and ironically, their Marxist–Leninist predecessors), I do not believe that attitudes and practices change quickly or easily, even when much effort is expended in altering the institutional context. It takes years of altered circumstances and new experiences to change the way people think and act. We are witnessing this transformation in Eastern Europe, but must recognize it for what it is: a slow yet thorough transformation of social community and social thought.

Advocates for radical and rapid social change tend to disregard the complex social and cultural worlds in which people live. Perhaps more importantly for the current analysis, these advocates disregard what people *have been doing* in the recent past. For 'big bang' theorists, what preceded the transition is irrelevant. More accurately, the past is anathema and must be eradicated. The tendency to dismiss the consequences of local socialist history is problematic, and arises from two misconceptions. The first is a general point about why history matters, or what otherwise might be called the constitutive power of social action. Socialism was not simply a package of bad economic policies, but a complex social and cultural world in which people lived and worked. No matter how much people resisted or rejected principles promoted by the Communist Party, they lived in a world which was transformed by the socialist project over time. Late Hungarian socialism bore little resemblance to Hungary *circa* 1945: millions of impoverished peasants, far fewer skilled workers and a smattering of déclassé aristocrats. Attitudes to work, to business, to property and to leisure have been altered in the course of building socialism. Without a clear theoretical understanding of the way actions and ideas combine into a complex social process of being and becoming, analysts will reinforce – either explicitly or implicitly – the political agendas of those who argue that we can simply return to the 'proper' trajectory of capitalist development, abandoned in 1948. This zero-sum game thinking – they lost, we won – might be a good way to mount a political campaign, but it is a very poor means of analysing social history. It also justifies the restoration of *particular* social and cultural elites. The rush to bring counts and countesses back home seemed rather comical in the early 1990s; the larger point, about who has a right to lead society and why, is a political question for today's society, not yesterday's. Furthermore, the kind of thinking which suggests that we can turn back the clock, or at least return Eastern European societies to a 'normal' economic foundation, is based on an analogy with the transition to Stalinism in the late 1940s. This is the second misconception which underlies much work in the present transition, and is related to the first. It has long been assumed that the transition to Stalinism entailed a rapid and dramatic change. Nationalization of schools, banks and industry was followed in short order by the collectivization of agriculture. Private property was appropriated by the state, unreliable bureaucrats were replaced with loyal party cadres, and production was organized according to national economic plans. In fact, the image of a simple model and an omnipotent state bears little resemblance to the actual process whereby Stalinism was implemented. Our assumptions about the radical departure of socialist economics have been fed by years of Cold War politics, and the political restrictions on scholarship. History is now being rewritten, showing that the Stalinist transition took many years, and was fraught with obstacles, compromise and occasional failure (Krementsov 2000; Lampland 1997, 2000; Péteri 1997; Pittaway 1999). It is precisely the quicksand of politicized conceptions of historical change – be they Marxist–Leninist or Western triumphalist – which should be avoided. Working from a theoretically informed understanding of social action, anthropology and social history prods us to eschew superficial readings, and consider in more rigorous fashion just how such transitions occur, and why.

This chapter considers the new agrarian elite in the first half of the 1990s.[2] It represents a portion of a larger project designed to investigate how social relations and cultural views influence the process of economic transition.[3] How do ideas about how the world works, and should work, affect state policies and private initiatives in periods of economic transition? How do professional and personal networks play a part in structuring new institutions? Here I shall discuss the social conditions which facilitated the acquisition of properties by former managers of cooperative farms since 1989, and examine the advantages that former socialist managers commanded in running capitalist businesses, advantages which, I argue, are based on their experiences in the late socialist economy.

Initial studies of decollectivization in Eastern Europe have provided us with stimulating analyses of land reform, a process wracked with far more difficulties than many of their proponents would have imagined (Creed 1995; Hann 1996; Kideckel 1995; Kovács 1996; Swain 1994). Years of collective production have substantially altered the landscape, making restitution of family properties nigh on impossible. The intricacies of local governments, the questionable actions of land restitution committees, confusing legislation and the nightmare of resolving irreconcilable legal claims has made what to many seemed a simple process of getting their land back into a long and embittered battle (Verdery 1994). The danger, however, is that in the all too understandable focus on the legal revolution in property rights under way in Eastern Europe, the actual practices of new farms would be obscured. As skirmishes over property claims subside (or at least fester), we must turn our attention to the actual activities of managing post-collective farms to understand in what direction the economy is going. After all, the transition depends on a revolution in business practices as much as anything else. Indeed, I would argue that a serious understanding of 'transition economies' depends on a clear picture of how managers are transforming former cooperative farms into viable capitalist businesses.

## Domains and relations in the social world

In the first several years of the transition, there were fears that Communist elites would transform their political advantages into economic ones. Initial fears had much basis in fact; all of those working in the region can recite tales of brazen appropriation and rapid enrichment by former party elites. Concerns about pernicious alliances within the economy – often referred to as mafias to underscore their insidious techniques – were also frequently discussed (Wedel 1998). These fears were based on more than concerns with social justice, a goal many held dear in their struggles against the socialist state in years past. Specialists worried that these new conglomerations would seriously deform the economy, preventing the development of a free market and hampering the transition to a truly capitalist economy (Staniszkis 1991; Stark 1990; see also Verdery 1996: 168–203). Accordingly, a number of analysts threw themselves into studies of elites, in order to determine to what degree brute power and malfeasance among politicians would explain the reconstitution of elites, and what other, more subtle and powerful mechanisms might be at play. The results of these studies demonstrate that political position is an insufficient explanation; a more complex and theoretically satisfying interpretation lies in the role of social and cultural capital in the Eastern European transition (Czakó and Sik 1995; Grabher and Stark 1997; Kuczi 1996; Róna-Tas and Böröcz 2000; Szalai 1997). My work builds on these studies, focusing specifically on the agricultural sector.

There are two major strains in the social analysis of the economic transition. These are, first, studies considering the role of social capital, trust, knowledge and experience, and second, studies which consider the role of formal and informal structures within the economy. The approaches overlap in important ways, but I wish to distinguish them analytically. In both strands, the primary question is to what degree new economic activities are constrained by socialist practices, often referred to as the 'legacies' problem (Jowitt 1992; Comisso

1995). In the first approach, attention is paid to the character of social relations within the economy, generally distinguished as formal or institutionalized relations and informal connections. In the second approach, the nature of economic activity is at issue, rather than the specific social relations which give form to economic patterns. Hence the focus is on sectors of the economy, e.g. the formal and informal domains of economic practices and everyday interactions. It should be obvious that institutionalized relations are correlated with the formal economy, whereas informal relations are found in the informal sector. Although these two approaches dominate the field, they fall short in the social analysis of postsocialism. The problem lies in analytic categories being too narrowly or arbitrarily restricted. The world is broken up into seemingly exclusive domains such as formal and informal sectors or socialist and capitalist practices, which do little to illuminate the form and character of social processes.

## Social capital and experience

Scholarship on social capital analyses the role of social relations as assets which complement other, more traditionally recognized economic benefits, such as financial resources, access to desired market position, and timing or first-mover advantage. The study of social capital has grown rapidly over recent years, being taken up by analysts committed to different theoretical traditions and for different purposes (Portes 1998). There are three main strands of scholarship, approaches we may distinguish as that of the rational choice school, exemplified by Coleman, the community-centered approach of the political scientist Robert Putnam, and the insistently sociocultural approach of Bourdieu.

One may define social capital in the simplest terms as the value of significant social connections to one's career in school, business or politics.[4] The manner in which analysts understand how social capital is deployed by social actors, and its analytic purchase in social analysis, differs among the various schools. Coleman, who works with a theory of rational action, cleaves to an economistic subject, who calculates self-interest and manipulates resources. The advantage of social capital, Coleman states, is as 'an aid in accounting for different outcomes at the level of individual actors and an aid toward making the micro-to-macro transitions without elaborating the social structural details through which this occurs' (1988: 19).[5] In Robert Putnam's work (1995), social capital resides in the community as a whole, an emergent quality that arises from the participation of community members in various activities, foregrounding the role of trust in community relations. The notion that communities need a counterbalance to intensely individuated and self-interested actors is based on the vision of a rational actor, a feature Putnam shares with Coleman. This approach reinforces the common tendency in the sociological literature to evaluate social capital only in positive terms, overlooking its negative consequences (Portes 1998). Bourdieu's approach is different, since he examines the dynamics of capital in a world inhabited by essentially *social* actors, made through practices and embodied in *habitus*. Enduring cultural ideas and a history of practice constitute the foundation of Bourdieu's analysis; they are not an afterthought or remedy to an insufficient model, as is the case for those working with rational choice theories.

Studies of social capital in the East European transition have drawn inspiration from the work of neo-institutionalists or evolutionary economists (e.g. Murrell 1992, 1993; North 1992; Stark 1992, 1996). This approach constitutes a direct challenge to the neo-classical or neo-liberal approach to economics generally, and the transition in particular (Przeworski 1993). The central disagreement between evolutionary or neo-institutional economics and their neo-classical colleagues is found in their contrasting understandings of human motivation, notions which have implications for building institutions in the postsocialist economy. In a neo-classical world, people act according to their immediate interest, situated within the present (and future) decision-making context. Thus, the past is irrelevant, since one is free to act according to one's perceived interests. Moreover, a swift transition is desirable precisely because it eliminates incentives for inefficient and costly behavior associated in the minds of these scholars with the world of socialism. New institutions can and should be built quickly, depriving elites tied to the past political and economic system of the ability to live off the state. Any intransigence to new ideas would be a sure sign of corruption and rent-seeking.[6]

Evolutionary economists, in contrast, are far more sanguine about the nature of social relationships in economic activity, and look to past actions as a means of explaining behaviors to be anticipated in the present. They are thus less apt to consider malfeasance or intransigence to be the cause of difficulties in the transition and more apt to see that learning new ways of doing business takes time and effort. Murrell criticizes shock therapists for their technocratic hubris, identifying in their work two crucial, but faulty assumptions: we know how capitalism works; and 'the technocrat's creations will have a powerful and salutary influence' (1993: 118). Murrell offers a historically nuanced understanding of modern economies, proposing that there are a variety of capitalisms, evolving from historically divergent and culturally complex circumstances. This perspective rejects the simplistic models of neo-liberal theorists, recognizes both the diversity and complexity of economic systems, and sees these systems as products of historical processes.

### Formal and informal domains

Neo-institutionalists are often grouped with evolutionary economists, although the emphasis is somewhat different. Neo-institutionalists, such as North (1992), focus on the role of ideologies and institutions in economic action. This perspective presumes the significance of historical processes, insofar as there is an understanding that formal rules do not exist in a vacuum but within a world of informal rules and subjective views. North distinguishes between formal rules and informal constraints, in order to emphasize the disparity between how organizations have been designed and how people may act, sometimes disregarding the rules of the game. North's discussion of ideology and informal constraints is intended to correct a central weakness in neo-classical economics. 'It would be little exaggeration to say that while neoclassical theory is focused on the operation of efficient markets, few Western economists understand the institutional requirements essential to creating such markets, because they simply take them for granted' (478). His approach is compatible with that of the evolutionary economists, though he appears far less concerned with the systemic consequences of economic forms, such as the possibility of multiple capitalisms, than with figuring out how formal rules, informal patterns and subjective elements interact in particular contexts.

Much work in the study of economics by anthropologists has been a direct critique of economism, utilitarianism and the rational individual (Polanyi 1968; Sahlins 1972, 1976). Accordingly, the analytic conceptions of economists – even those attempting to understand social change from a more historical perspective – have little credence among anthropologists. David Stark, who has written extensively on the transition (1990, 1992, 1996), differs from North and other, more economistically inclined neo-institutionalists by building on the work of Bourdieu in analysing institutional *practices*. This brings us far closer to the conceptual world of anthropological inquiry. Nonetheless, Stark does share with North a simple division between formal and informal components of the economy. He posits that in the postsocialist transition formal institutions (practices) will expire, while informal practices will continue.

> The existence of parallel structures (however contradictory and fragmentary) in these informal and interfirm networks that 'got the job done' means that the collapse of the formal structures of the socialist regime does not result in an institutional vacuum. Instead, we find the persistence of routines and practices, organizational forms and social ties, that can become assets, resources, and the basis for credible commitments and coordinated actions in the postsocialist period ... In short, in place of disorientation, we find the metamorphosis of sub-rosa organizational forms and the activation of preexisting networks of affiliation.
>
> (Stark 1996: 994–5)

Stark's discussion of parallel structures refers to much work, his own included, which analysed the significance of informal structures, second economy economic activities – indeed, the whole concept of a second society in late socialism (e.g. Gábor 1979; Hankiss 1988; Róna-Tas 1997; Stark 1986, 1989; Wedel 1986).

Is this division between formal structures and informal networks, routines and practices a helpful one in analysing the historical impact of socialism? The notion of the second economy and second society was a powerful one in Eastern European societies, not only because it captured important components of economic activity outside the state sector, but also because it corresponded to a deep desire on the part of many socialist citizens to distance themselves from the socialist project. Yet, as I have argued elsewhere (1995: 332–3), the quick and easy division into first and second, public and private, repugnant and moral domains of social life may tell us much about how people wished to live their lives, but not in actuality about how their lives were lived. In other words, the concept of second society, which resurfaces here as the informal, was a deeply ideological stance among the region's inhabitants (Hann 1990; Lampland 1995). Escaping the public for the private world was considered the right moral choice for socialist citizens; engaging in or, worse yet, promoting public ends was a sullied, disreputable activity. Hence the recurring emphasis upon the significance of the informal sector or second society was as much an argument for the integrity of socialist citizens in the face of a repressive state apparatus as it was a description of *some* of their daily affairs. It is not a useful, or even adequate, *analytic* tool for describing how people's actions and their ideas took form over time. The impact of socialism cannot simply be parsed into ephemeral public activities and enduring private or informal practices.

Let me illustrate my discomfort with the formal/informal division for analysing the transition with two examples. The practices of planning budgets for enterprises were complex and convoluted. Costs of production had to be calculated, machinery amortized, various taxes and insurance costs figured; all this had to be coordinated with the current state of legislation and edicts concerning enterprise management. We associate these kinds of innovations with the development of agro-business. The accounting procedures of socialist planning were a far cry from the management practices of manorial estates, much less family farms prior to 1948. Since 1989, new accounting practices have been advocated to correct for the discrepancies between enterprises working toward brute growth in a socialist model, and working toward bottom-line profits in a capitalist model. Presumably the new accounting procedures being introduced would be an example of a change in formal rules. Does that mean that knowing how to manage a complex book-keeping system is an informal practice? Or would we define it as an experience, learned over years of running a farm, as an evolutionary economist might? In what sense is the complex set of assumptions about prices, costs, calculation, utility a less formal-ized set of practices than a particular subset of cost accounting procedures advocated to improve the calculation of profit? Stark classifies informal prac-tices and routines as those activities which 'got the job done', implying that these were the myriad ways people managed despite the enormous difficulties of the socialist economy.[7] These sorts of clever machinations were well known in socialism; János Kenedi's book, *Do it Yourself*, is a comic masterpiece retelling the convoluted procedures required to build a private house in late socialist Hungary (1981). Is the ability to work around the law a practice which will continue in capitalism, while the ability to manage a set of books will not? Running a Hungarian business today assumes a world in which value is calculated in numbers and codified in record books, even if some citizens are less able to do this task than others. Figuring value in a far more volatile market environment may be new, but the techniques of calculation are not.

Another example. The transition to socialism has entailed a substantial shift in everyday temporal practices. Prior to 1948 the large majority of Hungarian citizens had been employed in agriculture, where the work day was defined as beginning at sunrise and ending at sunset. Thus, the change to workplaces with new temporal registers – hourly wages and, more commonly, norms which tied activity to smaller units of time – was a major transformation. We know full well that the introduction of finely calibrated wages and time-clocks did not ensure a steady flow of work throughout the day, or even throughout the year, as factories were plagued with shortages and then forced to engage in storming when materials became available. Government bureaucrats were also known to pace their work in creative ways, straying from their offices during the paid work day to take care of personal affairs. No doubt the work pace in the new capitalist enterprises is more intense than was characteristic of most socialist factories; I have been told so on more than one occasion. So the pace of activity in capitalism will be greater; will the conceptual pairing of money and effort be irrelevant to the capitalist workplace? Will workers stop arriving on time, or forego lunch and other breaks as legitimate employee rights?

I am arguing that the cultural world of former socialist citizens has been profoundly altered by socialism. These changes have affected a wide range of practices and routines, which influence the character of economics in a direct way: concepts of time, practices of calculation, routines of production. In the rush to condemn the entire socialist enterprise, a wide range of practices have been demonized as poorly designed and unnatural products of Soviet statism. Yet many of the techniques of the socialist economy – productivity norms, long-term budgeting strategies, anti-inflationary measures, to list only a few – were commonly deployed elsewhere in the capitalist world, with more or less success. 'Transitologists' have a narrow conception of institution, even in Stark's more nuanced understanding of practices and routines. The bounded character of economic domains implicit in this work excludes consideration of the complex cultural world in which they are embedded. This no doubt derives from the tendency in much social science research to take European modernity for granted, rather than seeing it as a cultural revolution of recent origin. Accordingly, significant transformations that accompany socialism are ignored, even though they are direct products of this era. To recover the particularities of Eastern European history, we must expand our vision of the social world to encompass the cultural beliefs and practices many of us have long taken for granted. It also requires us to shift our perspective from one of exclusive domains – such as the formal and informal, or public and private – to one of overlapping, interdependent realms of activity. By analysing the tos-and-fros of social interaction, the mutually reinforcing conceptions of time, effort, money and goods implicated in a wide range of activities, we will be better able to judge analytically how to parse the world into socialist and capitalist, past and present, lingering and emerging.

## *Bourdieu*

Let us return now to the work of Bourdieu, the richest and most provocative theorist among the holy trinity of social capital theorists I evoked. Bourdieu emphasizes how sociocultural relations are built, lived and embodied. He does not simply point to the value of connections between actors, but to how these relations take on a particular form, correlated with, but not reducible to, economic capital. His critique of economism is trenchant, and of particular value here. Moreover, he specifies that these relations are created in the mundane activities of everyday interactions and the more ritualized forms of family parties and school celebrations. In this way, he highlights the importance of time. The vibrancy of a network depends upon its constant renewal and the subtle exchanges which take place in these repetitive encounters (cf. Williams 1977). Finally, Bourdieu points to the inequalities that are generated by the disproportionate distribution of capital within society. He thus combines a subtle analysis of the relations which create social capital over time with a sustained analysis of the inequalities within society that such practices of exchange create and reproduce. For virtually all the analysts of the transition, the question of inequalities – of the past, and emerging in the future – are of central concern. Yet Bourdieu extends his analysis of the way in which economic, social and cultural capital build on each other to examine how these privileges are masked, making the on-going process of building and retaining privilege less visible.

> A general science of the economy of practices, capable of reappropriating the totality of the practices which, although objectively economic, are not and cannot be socially recognized as economic, and which can be performed only at the cost of a whole labor of dissimulation, or, more precisely, *euphemization*, must endeavor to grasp capital and profit in all their forms and to establish the laws whereby the different types of capital (or power, which amounts to the same thing) change into one another.
>
> (1985: 242–3)

It is to Bourdieu's credit that he states the obvious point that capital is about power, an element in the study of inequalities which is strangely missing from the other theorists discussed. This general theoretical oversight in the literature on social capital is paralleled by a similar neglect of class in the Eastern European transition.[8]

Practices of euphemization are not restricted to publicly undervaluing the significance of social contacts. Cultural capital is manifested not only in material objects, but also in embodied states. This concept is not only useful for grasping the complex dynamics of *habitus*, but also for evaluating claims about character or personhood which justify inequalities. Explanations for success and failure in capitalism are often framed within a world view which emphasizes personal achievement of the successful and major failings of the less so. The ability of certain citizens to wrest goods and opportunities from others is deftly explained by the inherent abilities of the actor, rather than by the complex social processes of social and cultural capital which ensure success. This Horatio Alger mentality is not new, however. It was one of the most striking features of late socialism in Hungary, so at odds with what one would have assumed to be the dominant theory of effort and inequality in socialist society.

In the case to which I now turn, the social capital of former socialist managers is complemented by their educational training, knowledge, skill and experience of managing large farms. Long experience in running a farm and the extensive contacts developed in the socialist period appear to be more crucial than education in enabling managers to operate successfully in the new market economy.[9] Furthermore, I shall argue that neither qualifications nor friendships from the socialist period are sufficient to ensure success in the ever-shifting agrarian market. The advantages he[10] enjoyed in the immediate postsocialist years must be renewed and enhanced, if success is to be maintained.

## Land reform

Legislation governing land redistribution and the restructuring of cooperative farms was passed in 1991–2. In a complex process, cooperative lands were divided among former land owners, cooperative farm members and former employees (Swain 1993). The mechanism for returning land to former owners was strongly influenced by the Smallholders' Party, one of the three coalition parties in the government elected in 1990 (Comisso 1995). The plan to convert socialist enterprises into small, independent family farms did not make much sense, since small farms are not suitable for the large-scale grain production on which the country had come to depend. Indeed, it was rejected by the large majority of those working in agriculture.[11] The anachronistic vision of the Smallholders was explicitly intended to disenfranchise former socialist managers, the so-called Green Barons, who personified the evils of collectivization. This was so despite the fact that most managers were elected in the last years of the regime (Swain 1993: 3). The attempt to eliminate the Green Barons foundered, however, because the Smallholders overestimated the villagers' commitment to an old-fashioned view of agriculture, and did not appreciate the skills the Green Barons commanded to run large-scale enterprises. The entire strategy backfired, easing rather than preventing socialist managers' appropriation of property and assets.

Hungary implemented a voucher system for restituting land claims. Families were not given their land back directly, but in the form of vouchers for the value of land once owned. Each cooperative farm was required to set aside land for restitution claims, and portions of former state farms were also appropriated for distribution. Distribution was then decided at auctions, where anyone in possession of vouchers could participate. The hesitation many expressed in dismantling cooperatives also made itself felt in people's ambivalence toward the auctions themselves, not to mention the confusion surrounding the bidding process (Swain 1994). It was easy for a minority of participants to manipulate the auction for their own purposes. Those who held back in the first round of auctions, either because they didn't understand what was going on or because they disagreed with the principles of the policy, soon realized their mistake. As one villager explained to me, those who missed this first opportunity were obliged to spend a lot of time coaxing fellow villagers to help them consolidate small strips into a plot large enough to form a viable farm.

The second phase of land redistribution was initiated with the process of 'naming': that is, allocating cooperative land and assets to the membership. Cooperative farm members and their heirs, as well as former employees, were able to apply for lands in the cooperative. (It is important to underscore the fact that corporations or other legal entities could not legally buy land in the initial auctions and subsequent sales.) The continued existence of cooperative farms has depended upon former cooperative farm members renting their land to the cooperative farm, thus transforming what had been the fiction of cooperative farm members' ownership of land into a reality. Cooperative farm managers in the mid-1990s were wont to complain that the anti-cooperative farm slant of the 1992 legislation put them at a disadvantage, preventing them from acquiring lands on behalf of the cooperative. Potentially viable units of production have been undermined in some cases by their lack of adequate lands; this is particularly true for dairies, which require extensive pasturage. Although one can sympathize with the managers' concerns about sustaining a viable farm, it is clear that if current cooperative farms had been able to acquire lands, it would have further enhanced the financial advantages farm managers wielded over the membership. As it is, they are forced, for the first time, to consider the interests of their membership in developing the farm.

In addition to these legal means of acquiring land, a third, very common option was the so-called 'pocket contract' (*zsebszerződés*). This informal but binding contract enabled people who had obtained land which they could not use to obtain cash instead. Elderly villagers, unemployed workers and other vulnerable parties were easy targets for potential buyers, who paid substantially less than would have been the case if owners had waited until the legal restriction on land purchase was lifted and a more open market in land came into being. For this reason, statistics present a very misleading picture: a large percentage of land has already devolved from the registered owners to other parties, either in the local community or elsewhere.

## Post-collective farms

Farms range from plots of several hectares worked by family members and equipped with little more than a horse-drawn plough to fully mechanized farms of up to 1,000 hectares worked by a couple of hired hands. Many are the successors of previous units of the cooperative, such as the dairy or the pig farm, or simply the rump left over after the initial redistribution. These smaller cooperatives still employ many of their former members, often because of their need to maintain access to lands. Some cooperatives and state farms have evolved into service units which specialize in maintaining machinery and renting it out to the new private farmers. In other cases, similar businesses are expansions of a successful second economy business that started out with a single tractor. The process by which some farms transmogrified into capitalist agro-business while others fragmented or became bankrupt was replete with contention and struggle (Andor 1996; Kovács 1996; Swain 1995). Decollectivization was an enormous scramble for collective assets, but the emerging pattern of farming is remarkably consistent. Most people are not interested in farming the land they own and rent it to whomever they can. One to ten families per village have farms which cover more than subsistence, and three to four families at most per village are embarking on large-scale commercial farming. If the cooperative no longer exists, successor companies have been established which farm roughly the same acreage of land and look after roughly the same quantity of livestock, but with far fewer staff (Swain 1995: 76).

What were the factors which allowed former socialist farm managers to stay in positions of authority and privilege? How did they circumvent the Smallholders' legislative tactics meant to dispossess them? To determine just how decollectivization was proceeding, Mihály Andor and Tibor Kuczi mounted a study, conducting a series of case studies and compiling statistical information to augment the picture they gathered locally.[12] Andor's work in particular offers valuable insights into the various strategies former socialist managers followed to maintain their farm, or to preserve some semblance of a large-scale farm following decollectivization.[13]

The strategies former socialist managers have followed to improve the viability of their farms and related businesses do not differ substantially from the strategies of new businesses in other sectors: reducing staff and restructuring the dimensions of the enterprise to enhance efficiency. The devolution of cooperative farms into smaller units with a specialized profile follows the pattern of large industrial conglomerates in the early years of privatization. In industry, new managers pruned former factories, forging smaller, more efficient businesses out of the constituent parts of the enterprise. While the construction of specialized functional units such as a dairy farm makes business sense, it is often also motivated by the desire among aspiring managers to escape debt burdens accumulated in the socialist period. Selling off viable units of mammoth factories, leaving the inefficient and indebted remainder in the hands of the state, has been a common tactic in the process of the privatization of industry. In cooperative farms, at least, the success of this maneuver depends on the foresight of a manager able to sneak out from under the debt looming over the farm, and leaving his former, less insightful colleagues with a quickly deteriorating farm (see Kovács 1996). It often also depends on the manager's ability to convince a portion of the former cooperative membership to ally with him in his new business venture.

Initially the size of cooperative farm membership was reduced with the migration of former members into independent farming. After the initial drop in membership, however, cooperative farm management was left with the task of reducing the staff further, in order to rid itself of workers long deemed unqualified or unreliable. This has not been as easy as it would be in other businesses, such as state farms or non-agrarian companies where management could simply fire as many workers as possible to reach a reasonable staff size. Cooperative farms rely entirely upon the goodwill of their membership to continue farming, since they must now rent the land they once farmed with legal impunity. While not all the land post-collective farms rent belongs to their employees, managers are aware of the dangers of alienating segments of the village community by harsh personnel policies, the results of which could easily be the withdrawal of lands from their control. It is thus extremely important for postsocialist cooperative farm managers to be able to convince segments of the local community to support their efforts. In this context it becomes clear why long-term ties developed in the socialist period between managerial elites and their manual workforce can be deployed in classically paternalist fashion to accrue to the manager's benefit.

The alienation of state properties by private businessmen has been a contentious process throughout Eastern Europe in the postsocialist period, raising all sorts of questions about the constitution of new elites and the rejuvenation of old patterns of privilege and power. This is as true in Hungary as anywhere else. I would argue, however, that the process of restructuring agrarian businesses – in the case of outright appropriation by private interests, or in milder cases in which cooperative farms are simply reconstituted – has some special features which distinguish it from the process of privatizing industry or service companies. Both the social location of farm businesses – that is, a close and observant village community – and the requirements for successful business – that is, access to land – have constrained management decision-making in the course of the transition to new business forms differently from other sectors of the economy. Since at the time of the research land could still not be bought and sold legally, the range of options open to managers was limited.

Former socialist managers have succeeded in maintaining their authority and position within the agrarian sector, either as fully private farm owners, as cooperative farm managers or as managers of successor businesses. The degree of their success, however, was not always in line with their ambitions, as their strategies for retaining control over property and assets could be stymied by opponents within the community and beyond. Management success, or the ability of villagers to frustrate their plans, depended not only on features of the socialist farm prior to decollectivization but also upon features of the community to which it belonged.[14] By features of the socialist cooperative farm I have in mind, first of all, the degree to which farm members were able to influence decision-making during the socialist period. After amalgamations in the 1970s, the daily management of cooperative farms often took place in farm centers far away from the village, making it difficult for villagers to keep a close eye on managerial activities. This concentrated greater power in the hands of management, a factor which managers could use to their advantage during decollectivization. A second factor was the development of forms of commodity production in the socialist second economy, e.g. vineyard cultivation. This gave farm members more autonomy, but also kept them at a distance from the farm's daily workings, so it tended to strengthen management's control over the cooperative's fate. Third, a record of management success in the 1980s increased the probability that farm members would go along with managers' strategies for reorganizing the farm in the 1990s. If managers encountered resistance, they could use the loyalty of some members to put pressure on those who wished to break with the farm. Membership composition was a fourth significant factor. Managers were more likely to achieve their aims if their membership was, on average, older, poorer, less educated and had a higher proportion of women. Such members were less apt to take an interest in decision-making generally and more apt to defer to the authority of managers. Finally, there is the 'missing generations' factor. In more industrialized regions, one or two generations have abandoned agricultural production entirely, leaving no one to make claims on agricultural properties. In this context, managers could often acquire commercial assets with little resistance. A history of commuting to employment in nearby or distant towns made it harder for villagers to exercise significant control over local institutions.

The extent to which management could benefit from decollectivization was also determined by current circumstances in the community. If a former socialist manager lived outside the community in which the cooperative farm was located, it was easier for him to engage in shady dealings than if he were subject to the censure and moral pressure of his neighbors. Second, management's hand was strengthened if the community was located in a region of limited employment possibilities. Third, the proximity of markets for farm goods influenced decisions to leave the cooperative to farm privately. The final factor we need to consider is the extended history of the community. Management may have faced an easier task if the community traditionally lacked strong representative institutions (Andor 1996). It is interesting that both sociologists and villagers themselves tend to explain the passivity of former cooperative farm members in terms of pre-war labor relations. Communities inhabited by former sharecroppers, manorial estate employees and day laborers are seen to be apathetic and lacking entrepreneurial spirit, while communities of self-sufficient peasants are understood to be more active politically and commercially.

I remain skeptical of these claims for the simple reason that they ignore the intervening forty years of socialism, in which workers were regularly prevented from having a say in politics in general, or in the policies of their workplace in particular. Second economy activities were perhaps more widespread and ingenious in some types of community than in others, correlated with pre-war patterns of property ownership. Nonetheless, the second economy remained dependent upon cooperatives and state farms for cheap sources of grain and livestock, advice from agronomists and marketing assistance. Rather than consider these activities to have been incipient capitalist businesses, it would be more accurate to describe them as adjuncts to production in the socialist sector. Thus it is unnecessary to reach back to the pre-war period to explain the lack of an entrepreneurial attitude. As is true in any capitalist economy, there are those who simply are unwilling, or in some cases unable, to become a manager. Among these one finds those who were themselves restricted to certain kinds of employment which their ambition would shun but their abilities dictate. Then there are those who chose the nine-to-five job, preferring a low-key lifestyle to one fraught with the anxiety and stress of management. Nonetheless, there *were* former cooperative farm members and state farm workers who would have enjoyed the prospects of running a large farm, and would even have been good at it. But as various local studies of decollectivization demonstrate, a number of factors determined whether one succeeded in acquiring the sorts of assets necessary to run a large farm, not least the ability to defeat others in their bid for land, machinery and managerial control.

My skepticism about the role of personal or family history in explaining the success of certain villagers over others is fed by a concern about emerging ideologies of success and failure in the current transition. Managers represent their success in appropriating farms, and their various assets, in light of what they see to have been the inability of former workers to mount a significant resistance. They would talk about former cooperative farm workers as having a 'socialist worker attitude'. This intransigence was juxtaposed to their own abilities to adapt to the situation, to learn new tricks and discard the old. Such self-flattery is an example of euphemization (Bourdieu 1985), masking the very complex, and sometimes quite shady dealings the present managers engaged in to assure their own success. The *social* process of acquisition and the *social* character of the managers' advantages (social capital, pragmatic experience) are ignored, while the personal characteristics of the manager are heightened.

Managers spout self-aggrandizing accounts; villagers counter with charges of corruption and theft. Feelings of powerlessness and despair among the less fortunate find their expression in the near universal assumption that management is well situated and inclined to steal and cheat. This perception is not new; during the socialist period, one also heard these claims. Rancor has increased, however, since the stakes are much higher than before. In the early 1990s, villagers were sanguine about the political and economic transition, not expecting much change from the new government or new economy. Comments during successive elections have affirmed this view. Villagers gave voice to this notion when explaining why voting for the incumbent party was preferable to electing a new set of leaders. After all, incumbents had already lined their pockets and wouldn't need to raid the coffers, as a new government coalition would. Numerous scandals surrounding the activities of governing coalitions have simply reinforced villagers' views. In a village I know well, villagers' distrust has even turned on a once well-respected cooperative farm manager, whose attempts to acquire land within the village have prompted frequent comment. While he could easily have been elected mayor in 1990, and only refused the post because he thought the work did not warrant a full-time salary, he is now regularly maligned by his former supporters, who consider him to have fallen lower than his notorious boss in the socialist period. This radical shift in attitude has been the most surprising turn of events for me in the transition, one I would never have anticipated. My surprise reveals the extent to which I underestimated how angry villagers have become at their continued impoverishment and disenfranchisement. Thus, the individuation of success promoted by managers finds its corollary in villagers' vilification of accomplishment. Euphemization in this context also overlooks social process, although here the practices of managing are ignored in favor of essentialist claims of greed and depravity.

I now wish to examine the crucial attributes former cooperative and state farm managers possessed at the moment of decollectivization. I argue that the combination of social ties, expert knowledge and extensive experience gave agrarian elites a disproportionate advantage in the transition (cf. Kuczi 1996). Successful entrepreneurship depends in the first instance on a variety of social relations, often including relations with kin. For example, the financial resources of one's family could be vital in a context in which bank loans in agriculture were difficult to obtain, due to uncertain property rights. Defining one's business obligations within the boundaries of family can also be a useful way of deflecting demands made by friends and former colleagues as one's business grows, although the flip side – strong pressures from family members for a share of the wealth – are also well known.

It is equally important to consider long-standing paternalist relations between managers and the cooperative farm workforce. During the socialist period, cooperative farms played an important role as channels of social goods and services, e.g. organizing holidays for the children, subsidizing local day-care facilities, providing cheap means of transport for the second economy or helping a family in need with funeral costs. The habit of seeking out the cooperative farm president in times of need has persisted in the postsocialist era and it is, of course, a two-way street: managers can call in their debts and exercise diffuse moral suasion. If villagers find the activities of new entrepreneurs suspicious – because they are aware of the chicanery involved or are wary of commerce in general – then downward leveling norms may constitute a barrier to growth (Portes 1998: 15).[15] Ethnic hostilities and lingering political hostilities can also impair business success. A manager complained to me about former cooperative farm members refusing to rent their land to the now much smaller cooperative, simply because they resented having been forced to transfer their lands to the cooperative in the early 1960s.

The most valuable form of social capital former cooperative farm managers possess for building a business is an extensive network of county-wide and national contacts in the agrarian economy. These contacts range from simple friendships to complex bureaucratic and commercial connections. Fellow agronomists and agrarian managers at cooperatives and their successor businesses rely on each other for information and assistance. Agrarian managers formed long-lasting relationships while still in school, or when attending refresher courses or other classes designed to advance their training. The frequency of county-level and other regional meetings and conferences created a large and valuable network of advisors and friends. Some of the meetings in which relations were forged were political in nature, such as county party organizational forums, but that would not detract from one's ability to use these contacts to further one's business ambitions. Finally, many of the valuable ties former cooperative managers held were with communities in the commercial sector, such as personnel at local processing factories or agents for seed companies or fertilizer companies.

The central feature of these relationships is trust. In all of these various transactions, the players can rely upon each other to deliver goods in time, to offer a decent price, to provide valuable information, to make the right decision on one's behalf. The dependability of these relationships diffuses the uncertainty of the new market economy, and gives entrepreneurs an edge on their competition. Used in the right ways, such relationships can enhance the viability of one's enterprise. Used poorly, they can undermine one's profitability and signal future losses. This was illustrated to me in the case of one cooperative president, who consistently refused to sell his produce to strangers, even when they offered him a higher price than his regular customers. He found the transaction with strangers uncertain. 'He's not a sure buyer (*Nem biztos vevö*),' he has claimed. Villagers attributed this reluctance to engage in transactions to his fear of losing control and the bribes with which he had lined his own pocket. His intransigence had pushed the farm to the edge of bankruptcy, in contrast to a neighboring farm, where management had established a positive reputation by reorganizing the cooperative into an agricultural service station.

A crucial strategy deployed by former socialist managers in their transformation into capitalist businessmen has been the use of their extensive contacts in the agrarian sector, as noted above. The advantages that former cooperative managers had in terms of social networks cannot be underestimated. It should be noted, however, that the means of negotiating a good contract, of getting a fair price for one's goods, cannot be attributed to personal contacts alone. Simple economic laws play an enormous role in these transactions, an issue which may be overlooked in the hurry to emphasize the significance of social relations. Economies of scale strongly influence one's position in contractual negotiations. One of the greatest problems the push to small family farms created was the loss of economies of scale. It was simply wrongheaded to think that small farmers would flourish in a new economy which no longer has any form of marketing cooperatives to guard them from exploitation by middlemen and commercial agents. (Such marketing cooperatives existed in the pre-1948 period, and lived on in altered form in the socialist period, playing an important role in buying up produce from the second economy.) It is clear that many cooperative farms will take on the role of clearing agents for the produce of local farmers; their interests and that of the community are to enhance their bargaining power with commercial agents.

Possessing good social and economic contacts is insufficient if one has not learned to run a business effectively. The knowledge and experience of running a large-scale farm has also helped to facilitate the success of the former socialist elite in agriculture. From the mid-1960s, cooperative farm managers enjoyed fewer supports from the state than their colleagues in industry or at state farms. Forced to scramble for scarce resources, such as sources of credit to see them through the growing season, cooperative managers had to learn to cajole county officials, bending the rules and cooking the books when necessary. While this did not always lead to the most efficient use of resources (Lampland 1995: 247–72), it did teach managers that having privileged access to information, well-cultivated contacts and good leverage can make all the difference in one's career. These sorts of elaborate machinations were not specific to agriculture. As the work of János Kornai has shown (1959, 1992), the planned economy depended on regular negotiations – finagling, manipulating, reworking plans – to achieve an overall plan which suited actors at different levels of the party, state and enterprise hierarchies. The absence of monopolies in agriculture enhanced the significance of these everyday negotiations. More than 3,000 cooperative farms across the country regularly competed with each other in a difficult economic environment for attention and resources. Managers were able to build on this experience in the new economic environment of the 1990s. Knowing how to write up a budget, how to plan investments, where and how to cut corners if necessary: these traits have long been the stock-in-trade of the socialist farm manager.

Managers of socialist enterprises learned to take *risks*. It is true that state and party agencies constrained decision-making and prevented a lively market from developing in many sectors. Yet the fragility of state supports and the chaos of planning schedules accustomed them to coping in an environment of high uncertainty. Playing against the legal edifice has honed the skills of former cooperative managers in knowing how and under what conditions to move forward, to hesitate, to diversify, to scramble.[16] This is precisely the quality non-managers lack. Admittedly, not all former socialist managers will be as skilled in weathering the difficult waters of the new market economy (just as not all were equally adept in the socialist economy). The cooperative farm president who only sells to friends will soon find this a dead-end strategy. But many others will learn, and already have learned, to build upon their extensive managing skills to extend and strengthen their businesses.

## Conclusion

The ability of former socialist managers to slide into positions of authority (or outright ownership) in successor businesses is well documented. Just how successful these managers will continue to be is an open question. I have argued that former cooperative farm managers wielded significant advantages over other villagers adjusting to the new economic environment in the first half of the 1990s. I would hasten to add, however, that those advantages are not necessarily long-lasting. Changes in the law on property ownership may influence investment policies of agrarian businesses. Changes in the ruling coalition of the government have had a number of consequences, unforeseen in 1997, on the agrarian business environment. And certainly, accommodations to EU policies – particularly if the view of these policies as discriminatory to Hungarian businessmen is accurate – will have significant consequences for the viability of agrarian enterprises. Finally, the shift in the overall economic environment is bound to influence the way managers run their businesses. If managers do not continue to keep informed of possible innovations in techniques and new varieties of seeds and animal stock, do not continue to reach out to and expand valuable contacts in the business sector, research community and government bureaus, then they are bound to suffer. In short, while social and cultural capital are important resources, they must be sustained and enhanced over time. Otherwise, their strength and value lessen. This is a lesson former cooperative managers will have learned by now.

I would hope that there is a lesson here for theorists of the postsocialist transition. Economists and economic sociologists have dominated the study of the transforming economy in Eastern Europe. They are wedded to a series of concepts – such as the formal and informal or private and public – which establish artificial boundaries between domains of social life long intertwined in important and complex ways. As a consequence of disciplinary divisions they are less interested in cultural issues, but this blinds them to significant elements of the economic world which should be examined: beliefs, perceptions, motivations and moral principles. Anthropologists, on the other hand, bring important tools to the study of the transition. They see economics to be as deeply cultural as any other human activity. Their discomfort with reductionist assumptions about utility or simplistic notions of rational individualism allows them to question anachronistic formulations and culturally bounded conceptions. The culturally bounded categories of postsocialist European economies just so happen to include those social scientists deploy analytically: formal and informal sectors, social and financial capital, states and markets. The strength that anthropologists bring to the study of transitions lies precisely in their willingness to play local cultural categories against their analytic stepchildren, i.e. to use local categories (and their conceptual relatives) as grist for analysis. In so doing, they study how social domains are thought, how they are lived and, perhaps most crucially, how and why these two may diverge. The task of interrogating theoretical categories is a hallmark of any rigorous social analysis, but it should be even more central in the study of communities actively seeking to transform central organizing features. Studying the grand capitalist ascension on the heels of the socialist experiment in Eastern Europe offers social scientists of all stripes an opportunity to appraise the value of their analytic repertoire. The unique approach anthropologists bring to this exercise can contribute productively to our combined efforts.

## Notes

1 The work leading to this article was supported in part from funds provided by the National Council for Eurasian and East European Research, for which I am grateful. The Council, however, is not responsible for the content or findings of this report. I also wish to thank the International Research and Exchanges Board and the American Council of Learned Societies for their support of my research. I am indebted to Chris Hann, Joanna Goven, Ákos Róna-Tas and Carlos Waisman for extensive discussions over the issues in this paper. My title invokes a famous article by István Rév (1987). While he focused on the significance of peasant resistance to the state's project of collectivization, here the point is to demonstrate the advantage that cooperative farm management has enjoyed in the post-collectivized farming sector. Despite my ironic use of Rév's title, I do believe our studies complement each other in important ways.

2 The research for this component of the project was conducted in 1996 and 1997. The data include: interviews with farm managers and with specialists in service industries associated with agriculture, statistical materials on land ownership and the social profile of the farming population since decollectivization, studies of decollectivization in various communities, and historical analyses of cooperative farming in the country as a whole.

3 The other component of this project concerns the transition to Stalinism in 1948–56, focusing specifically on the role of agrarian economists trained in the interwar period in crafting new cooperative wage forms (work units or *munkaegység*) during the early 1950s. While it has long been assumed that these forms were adopted from the Soviet Union, I demonstrate that the complex calculations of value and organizational structures necessary for work units were entirely developed in the field of Hungarian agrarian work science of the interwar period, whose primary influence was German business science.

4 Granovetter's work on embeddedness bears similarities to these views, as it attempts to highlight the role of informal relations within formal hierarchies such as organizations and institutions such as the market (1985, 1993).

5 Coleman does consider the role of norms as social capital, moving his analysis beyond crass economism. Yet this move simply remedies the theoretical weaknesses of rational choice theory, not substantially altering Coleman's conception of the social actor.

6 A central concern in the debate over the rapidity of economic reforms centers on the role of citizens in crafting public policy. Åslund clearly thinks a radical change

may not be democratic, but would be expeditious. He believes, as does Brada, that in the long run citizens will benefit (see also Shearmur 1993). Przeworski, among others, is concerned that setting policies in an undemocratic fashion undermines the sovereignty of these countries and endangers the integrity of a renewed politics of democratic inclusion.

7  I would hazard to guess that learning to make the best of – or even slide out from under – onerous state regulations, is a common phenomenon in capitalist economies as well. While reading materials on the transition from socialism, I am often reminded of Burawoy and Lukács's caution to avoid comparing actual socialist practices with idealized capitalist models (1985).

8  While I appreciate the discomfort former socialist citizens may have with the analytic baggage associated with the study of class relations, I do not comprehend the silence about class in what would presumably be its natural home: studies of emerging capitalist relations of property and production. For two prominent exceptions to this trend, see Clarke 1994, 1998; Ost 1997, 1999, 2000.

9  An important component of the shift in the Hungarian socialist economy to a technocratic elite during the 1970s was dependent upon an ideology of training and expertise (Szelényi 1982). The abuse of a technocratic model of managerial authority, however, seriously contributed to the disenfranchisement and disillusionment of workers under socialism (see Lampland 1995: 223–31).

10  Managing socialist farms was a highly masculine profession (Lampland 1995: 185). While women often worked in socialist farm offices, as lawyers, accountants or secretaries, they were far less represented among the technocratic and managerial elite, i.e. as agronomists, machine-shop managers or farm presidents. This disproportionate representation of men among the agrarian elite continues into the post-collective period.

11  In a poll conducted in 1993, 'over ninety per cent of coop members said that they would not opt for a breakup of the cooperatives into small-sized individualized holdings' (Agócs and Agócs 1994: 33).

12  This study was part of a larger study of decollectivization in Hungary, the Czech Republic and Poland, led by Nigel Swain at the Centre for Central and Eastern European Studies of the University of Liverpool (cf. Swain 2000).

13  I am indebted to Mihály Andor for providing me with an unpublished version of the results of his study (1996).

14  My analysis here follows the nine factors identified by Andor (1996: 5–8).

15  For Portes this is one of four negative consequences of social capital. The others are exclusion of outsiders, excess claims on group members, and restrictions on individual freedoms.

16  The success of former Communist Party leaders in electoral and parliamentary politics since 1989/91 has surprised many observers east and west, who had come to view Communist Party activists as ignorant hacks. This neglects the long history of party politics in the socialist period. We can surmise that party politics, albeit invisible to the general public, was no less dependent on skilled politicking, machiavellian strategizing and judicious compromises than any other political process. Indeed, one might suspect that the absence of a multi-party system and lack of transparency may have intensified the stakes of interparty politics.

# References

Agócs, Péter and Sándor Agócs (1994) '"The change was but an unfulfilled promise": agriculture and the rural population in post-Communist Hungary', *East European Politics and Societies* 8(1): 32–57.

Andor, Mihály (1996) 'A magyar mezögazdaság 1990 után (háttértanulmány) [Hungarian agriculture after 1990. A background essay]', manuscript.

Åslund, Anders (1994) 'Lessons of the first four years of systemic change in Eastern Europe, *Journal of Comparative Economics* 19: 22–38.

Bourdieu, Pierre (1985) 'The forms of capital', in J.G. Richardson (ed.) *The Handbook of Theory and Research for the Sociology of Education*, New York: Greenwood, pp. 241–58.

Brada, Josef (1993) 'The transformation from Communism to capitalism: how far? how fast?', *Post-Soviet Affairs* 9(2): 87–100.

Burawoy, Michael and János Lukács (1985) 'Mythologies of work: a comparison of firms in state socialism and advanced capitalism', *American Sociological Review* 50: 723–37.

Clarke, Simon (1994) 'Is there room for an independent trade unionism in Russia? Trade unionism in the Russian aviation industry', *British Journal of Industrial Relations* 32(3): 359–78.

——(1998) 'Trade unions and the nonpayment of wages in Russia', *International Journal of Manpower* 19(1–2): 68–94.

Coleman, James (1988) 'Social capital in the creation of human capital', *American Journal of Sociology*, Supplement (94): 95–120.

Comisso, Ellen (1995) 'Legacies of the past or new institutions? The struggle over restitution in Hungary', *Comparative Political Studies* 28(2): 200–38.

Creed, Gerald (1995) 'An old song in a new voice: decollectivization in Bulgaria in East European communities', in David Kideckel (ed.) *The Struggle for Balance in Turbulent Times*, Boulder: Westview Press, pp. 25–46.

Czakó, Agnes and Endre Sik (1995) A hálózati töke szerepe Magyarországon a rendszerváltás elött és után [The role of network capital in Hungary before the regime change and after] *2000*, February: 3–12.

Gábor, István (1979) 'A második (másodlagos) gazdaság [The second (secondary) economy]', *Valóság* 1: 22–36.

Grabher, Gernot and David Stark (1997) 'Organizing diversity: evolutionary theory, network analysis, and postsocialism', in Gernot Grabher and David Stark (eds) *Restructuring Networks in Postsocialism*, Oxford: Oxford University Press, pp. 1–32.

Granovetter, Mark (1985) 'Economic action and social structure: the problem of embeddedness', *American Journal of Sociology* 91(3): 481–510.

——(1993) 'The nature of economic relationships', in Richard Swedberg (ed.) *Explorations in Economic Sociology*, New York: Russell Sage Foundation, pp. 3–41.

Hankiss, Elemér (1988) 'The second society: is there an alternative social model emerging in contemporary Hungary?', *Social Research* 55: 13–42.

Hann, Chris (ed.) (1990) *Market Economy and Civil Society in Hungary*, London: Frank Cass.

——(1996) 'Land and citizenship in Tázlár', in Ray Abrahams (ed.) *After Socialism: Land Reform and Social Change in Eastern Europe*, Providence: Berghahn Books.

Jowitt, Ken (1992) *New World Disorder: The Leninist Extinction*, Berkeley: University of California Press.

Kenedi, János (1981) *Do It Yourself: Hungary's Hidden Economy*, London: Pluto Press.

Kideckel, David (1995) 'Two incidents on the plains in southern Transylvania: pitfalls of privatization in a Romanian community', in David Kideckel (ed.) *East European Communities: the Struggle for Balance in Turbulent Times*, Boulder: Westview Press, pp. 47–64.

Kornai, János (1959) *Overcentralization in Economic Administration: a Critical Analysis Based on Experience in Hungarian Light Industry*, translated by John Knapp, Oxford: Oxford University Press.

——(1992) *The Socialist System: the Political Economy of Communism*, Princeton: Princeton University Press.

Kovács, Katalin (1996) 'The transition to Hungarian agriculture 1990–1993. General tendencies, background factors and the case of the "Golden Age" ', in Ray Abrahams (ed.) *After Socialism: Land Reform and Social Change in Eastern Europe*, Providence: Berghahn, pp. 51–84.

Krementsov, Nikolai (2000) 'Lysenkoism in Europe: export-import of the Soviet model', in Michael David-Fox and György Péteri (eds) *Academia in Upheaval: Origins, Transfers, and Transformations of the Communist Academic Regime in Russia and East Central Europe*, Westport: Bergin and Garvey, pp. 179–202.

Kuczi, Tibor (1996) 'A vállalkozók társadalmi tökéi az átalakulásban [Entrepreneurs' social capital in the transition]', *Századvég* 1 (új folyam): 29–51.

Lampland, Martha (1995) *The Object of Labor: Commodification in Socialist Hungary*, Chicago: University of Chicago Press.

——(1997) 'The social constraints on economic transitions. State wage policy in the transition to Stalinism', paper written for the National Council for Eurasian and East European Research.

——(2000) 'Making science work: scientific management and the Stalinist state in Hungary', paper delivered at the Science Studies Colloquium, University of California, San Diego, 1 May.

Murrell, Peter (1992) 'Conservative political philosophy and the strategy of economics transition', *East European Politics and Societies* 6(1): 3–16.

——(1993) 'What is shock therapy? What did it do in Poland and Russia?', *Post-Soviet Affairs* 9(2): 111–40.

North, Douglas C. (1992) 'Institutions, ideology, and economic performance', *Cato Journal* 11(3): 477–88.

Ost, David (1997) 'Can unions survive communism?', *Dissent* 44(1): 21–7.

——(1999) 'Unionists against unions: toward hierarchical management in post-communist Poland', *East European Politics and Societies* 13(1): 1–33.

——(2000) 'Illusory corporatism in Eastern Europe: neoliberal tripartism and postcommunist class identities', *Politics and Society* 28(4): 504–30.

Péteri, György (1997) 'New course economics: the field of economic research in Hungary', *Contemporary European History* 6(3): 295–327.

Pittaway, Mark (1999) 'The social limits of state control: time, the industrial wage relation, and social identity in Stalinist Hungary, 1948–1953', *Journal of Historical Sociology* 12(3): 271–301.

Polanyi, Karl (1968) 'Primitive, archaic and modern economies', in George Dalton (ed.) *Essays of Karl Polanyi*, Boston: Beacon Press.

Portes, Alejandro (1998) 'Social capital: its origins and applications in modern sociology', *Annual Review of Sociology* 24: 1–24.

Przeworski, Adam (1993) 'The neoliberal fallacy', in Larry Diamond and Marc F. Plattner (eds) *Capitalism, Socialism, and Democracy Revisited*, Baltimore: Johns Hopkins University Press, pp. 39–53.

Putnam, Robert (1995) 'Bowling alone: America's declining social capital', *Journal of Democracy* 6(1): 65–78.

Rév, István (1987) 'The advantages of being atomized: how Hungarian peasants coped with collectivization', *Dissent* 34: 335–50.

Róna-Tas, Akos (1997) *The Great Surprise of the Small Transformation: the Demise of Communism and the Rise of the Private Sector in Hungary*, Ann Arbor: University of Michigan Press.

Róna-Tas, Akos and József Böröcz (2000) 'The formation of new business elites in Bulgaria, the Czech Republic, Hungary and Poland: continuity and change, pre-communist and communist legacies', in John Higley and Gyorgy Lengyel (eds) *Elites after State Socialism*, Oxford: Rowman and Littlefield.

Sahlins, Marshall (1972) *Stone Age Economics*, Chicago: Aldine.

——(1976) *Culture and Practical Reason*, Chicago: University of Chicago Press.

Shearmur, Jeremy (1993) 'In defense of neoliberalism', in Larry Diamond and Marc F. Plattner (eds) *Capitalism, Socialism, and Democracy Revisited*, Baltimore: Johns Hopkins University Press, pp. 69–75.

Staniszkis, Jadwiga (1991) 'Political capitalism in Poland', *East European Politics and Societies* 5(1): 127–41.

Stark, David (1986) 'Rethinking internal labor markets: new insights from a comparative perspective', *American Sociological Review* 51: 492–504.

——(1989) 'Coexisting organizational forms in Hungary's emerging mixed economy', in Victor Nee and David Stark (eds) *Remaking of the Economic Institutions of Socialism: China and Eastern Europe*, Stanford: Stanford University Press, pp. 115–46.

——(1990) 'Privatization in Hungary: from plan to market or from plan to clan?', *East European Politics and Societies* 4(3): 351–92.

——(1992) 'Path dependence and privatization strategies in East Central Europe', *East European Politics and Societies* 6(1): 17–54.

——(1996) 'Recombinant property in East European capitalism', *American Journal of Sociology* 101(4): 993–1027.

Swain, Nigel (1985) *Collective Farms which Work?*, Cambridge: Cambridge University Press.

——(1993) *The Smallholders versus the Green Barons: Class Relations in the Restructuring of Hungarian Agriculture*, Working Papers, Rural Transition Series no. 8, Liverpool: Centre for Central and Eastern European Studies.

——(1994) *Getting Land in Central Europe*, Working Papers, Rural Transition Series no. 29, Liverpool: Centre for Central and Eastern European Studies.

——(1995) 'Decollectivising agriculture in the Visegrad countries of Central Europe', *Labour Focus on Eastern Europe* 51: 65–85.

——(2000) *The Rural Transition in Post-Socialist Central Europe and the Balkans*, Working Paper no. 9, Halle/Saale: Max Planck Institute for Social Anthropology.

Szalai, Erzsébet (1997) 'Political changeover, economic transformation, elites', paper prepared for the workshop on 'Elites and New Rules of the Game' at Budapest University of Economic Sciences, 25–7 April.

Szelényi, Iván (1982) 'The intelligentsia in the class structure of state socialist societies', in M. Burawoy and T. Skocpol (eds) *Marxist Inquiries*, Chicago: University of Chicago Press, pp. 287–326.

Verdery, Katherine (1994) 'The elasticity of land: problems of property restitution in Transylvania', *Slavic Review* 53(4): 1071–109.

——(1996) *What Was Socialism, and What Comes Next?*, Princeton: Princeton University Press.

Wedel, Janine (1986) *The Private Poland*, New York: Facts on File.
——(1998) *Collision and Collusion: the Strange Case of Western Aid to Eastern Europe, 1989–1998*, New York: St Martin's Press.
Williams, Raymond (1977) *Marxism and Literature*, Oxford: Oxford University Press.

# Chapter 3

# Economic crisis and ritual decline in Eastern Europe

*Gerald W. Creed*

After more than a decade of expanding research, the anthropology of postsocialist Eastern Europe exhibits a curious lacuna: ritual analysis. The absence is not absolute (e.g. Verdery 1999), but compared to most other topics ritual has been neglected. This is especially peculiar given earlier attention to socialist ritual (Binns 1979, 1980; Humphrey 1983; Kideckel 1983; Kligman 1981; Lane 1981; Mach 1992; Roth 1990), continuing attention to ritual in parts of Europe not undergoing 'transition' (Badone 1990; Boissevain 1992; Dubisch 1995; Gilmore 1998) and the attention paid to ritual in other 'postsocialist' contexts, notably China (Yang 2000; Feuchtwang this volume). The silence on a topic foundational to the discipline tends to separate current East European research both from mainstream anthropology and from indigenous ethnography, in which ritual continues to figure prominently.

There is an obvious explanation: anthropologists' lack of interest in contemporary East European ritual reflects the changed position of ritual in postsocialist conditions and its relative insignificance in the lives of East Europeans trying to survive under difficult existential conditions. This was brought home to me in February 1997 when I canvassed villages in Bulgaria's Rose Valley with a colleague to determine if and when certain carnival-like rituals associated with the beginning of Lent, known generically as *kukeri*, would be performed. In the village of Turlichene, I did not even have to ask because a large invitation to the festivities beckoned from one of the few remaining windows of the abandoned village grocery store. Stores such as this one throughout the country had met a similar fate in the 1990s as their administering cooperatives folded and impoverished villagers stopped buying goods. Still, this battered shell was more dismal and depressing than most. The fact that the town hall, the administrative heart of the village, operated from the second floor of the same building made the impact even worse, and there was no redeeming evidence of other commercial activity at the village square. In the face of such economic prostration I felt buoyed by the villagers' apparent commitment to the ritual and made a note to return on the appointed day. As we prepared to move on to the next village, I overheard one of the villagers with whom we had discussed the event mumble in disgust, 'We're starving here and he wants to know if there will be *kukeri*. Never mind the *kukeri!*'

I had never subscribed to the idea that ritual and belief can be understood apart from political economy and my work heretofore had focused exclusively on the latter, so I did not accept the foundation or logic of this complaint. Still, I appreciated the emotions involved and it bothered me. This essay is an effort to use my personal discomfort as a foil to facilitate a general assessment of the field. My goal is to suggest ways in which attention to ritual can contribute to a better understanding of seemingly more pressing topics in contemporary Eastern Europe, such as economic development and democratic empowerment. One contribution of anthropology to the analysis of postsocialism may be to bring these connections to the attention of other disciplines and transitologists. To make this case I cite research that has demonstrated the significance of ritual in other cases of capitalist and democratic transition, then draw upon case material from both my own research in Bulgaria and ethnographic work elsewhere in Eastern Europe to explore similar connections. Space prevents me from analysing the connections in detail, but I hope to demonstrate the potential of such an analysis. I am especially concerned with the extent to which declining ritual activity in parts of Eastern Europe erodes the social relations on which villagers depend to survive difficult economic circumstances and to exert effective political influence.

## Economy and ritual

Mayfair Yang (2000) describes a Chinese case in which economic success led to an explosion of ritual activities, the logic of which subverts both capitalist and state socialist principles. Money is burned and food and goods given away in exaggerated displays, which she likens to post-contact Kwakiutl potlatch. In her view,

> this ritual economy cannot be seen merely as the result of economic development for ritual life has also *fueled* economic growth (it often provides the organizational apparatus, site, and motivation for economic activity) and *constrained and channeled* it through the deployment of ritual consumption against capital accumulation. Thus, to understand the Chinese peasant economy we must widen the frame of our analysis to see how economy and production are part of the ritual and religious system.
>
> (2000: 480, emphasis in the original)

Whether or not one accepts her use of the term 'economic hybridity' to capture this interaction, Yang provides a compelling illustration of one possible relationship between ritual and economic transitions.[1] Bulgaria's trajectory is somewhat different. In many villages rituals expanded under late socialism, especially weddings and christenings but also landmark birthdays, retirements, soldier sendoffs and family reunions. Weddings were the most spectacular events, often spanning three or more days; the engagement festivities, usually preceding the wedding by many months, were also extensive. In an earlier description of Bulgarian village weddings I used the same potlatch analogy invoked by Yang (Creed 1998: 203–4). While Bulgarian events lacked the purposeful destruction evident in post-contact northwest coastal societies and post-Mao China, here too it was impossible to consume all the food and drink bounty provided (although some leftovers were recycled as animal food). Both the bride's and the groom's families as well as their ritual kin bestowed an avalanche of gifts. Whenever my village neighbour was working hard on his subsistence plot or doing extra work elsewhere for others, the justification was always that he had two daughters to marry soon. Certainly, wedding expenses were not the only or even the primary motivation for his labor, but the fact that he and others invoked them as *the* explanation testifies to the significance of extravagance on this occasion. High levels of investment are also evident in wedding descriptions in Romania (Kligman 1988) and Macedonia (Rheubottom 1980).

Christenings followed weddings on the scale of ritual expenditure. As with weddings, only close relatives and ritual kin attended the official ceremony, usually a secular one at the village town hall, but the banquet that followed was a massive affair. Hundreds of relatives, neighbors and friends would give money to the new parents as they moved around the restaurant toasting each guest in turn, much as newlyweds do at wedding banquets. The large banquet in which guests were wined, dined and entertained in exchange for gifts of money and goods was a core component of all the rituals discussed here. I participated in one soldier sendoff with well over 200 guests. Obviously, the cost of such events was substantial. In addition to providing all the food, wine, beer and soft drinks that guests could consume, there were fees for use of the restaurant or cooperative canteen and for the mandatory musicians, who according to Donna Buchanan (1996: 203–4) often commanded 'outrageously high sums of money'. It was also usual to present all guests with a token gift.

At all these galas the honorees received gifts and/or money from the guests, but the events cannot be reduced to a monetary calculation on the part of the organizers. In weddings and soldier sendoffs the gifts go to the couple and soldier respectively while the expenses are borne by their parents, so there is a generational transfer of resources. One might still view ritual expenditure as an investment strategy of parents for their children, or as part of a broader family strategy whereby the external gifts, though designated for an individual or couple, are in fact made available for extended-family use. For example, at one wedding I attended the extravagant gifts presented by a godfather were in fact items received by his mother at her recent retirement party. Similarly, accumulated cash was often used as partial payment for large purchases such as a car, which could then be requested to chauffeur other family members. Still, such claims are not extensive or secure enough to support a strictly economic calculus. It is in practice impossible to calculate profitability since so many of the resources for ritual events were produced in the subsistence sector or acquired through personal and kin relations. Moreover, the close family members who contributed the most to the capital and labor requirements of the banquet were the very people expected to make the largest gifts. Although villagers often highlighted the total amount of money received by a couple at a wedding or christening, they talked more about the expenses incurred. Overall, the complex transactions constituted a 'total social fact' in the sense of Marcel Mauss (1990).

In the socialist context, this Maussian gift economy can be interpreted as a demonstration of family wealth and a form of social capital (Bourdieu 1985).[2] Rituals were not only a context to collect money and gifts but also a forum to display them ostentatiously. Money was often collected in transparent plastic bags, so everybody could marvel at the quantity. Cash was sometimes pinned to the bride's dress or transformed into a necklace which the bride, groom or new soldier had to wear. At one christening the baby received a parasol adorned with cash, which the parents carried around during the festivities. Midway through this event, all the other gifts the child had received were displayed on an improvised clothes line strung across the restaurant. When it became apparent that the line could not hold all the gifts, they were taken down to make room for more. Unlike potlatches, these were demonstrations of what people had received; but they testified to a family's wealth in social relations, which in an economy of shortage with limited consumer options could be more important than money. Villagers demonstrated their financial capital by extravagant entertaining, and their social capital by accepting gifts. The exchanges helped to reproduce these extremely important relationships. For the system to work, however, families had to have sufficient resources to sponsor a mass event, and guests had to be able to provide significant gifts.

Villagers located the efflorescence of this gift economy in the period of late socialism. While celebrations had sometimes been longer and more elaborate in the past, many of the gifts were then handmade. By the 1980s older villagers regularly commented on how much more was given and received compared to the past. The difference is verified by Irwin Sanders' (1949) description of weddings in the village of Dragalevsty in the 1930s, when much of the trousseau a girl had acquired was given away to numerous relatives of both families at the wedding in return for a 'small sum of money from each person she honored' (1949: 86; see also Ivanova 1984).

Ritual expansion was also evident in the use of the banquet model for new purposes in the 1970s and 1980s, notably retirement parties and family reunions. The concept of retirement only emerged in rural Bulgaria during the socialist period, when peasants became *de facto* state employees as a result of collectivization and subsequent rural industrialization. Pensions became one of the legitimizing benefits of socialism and were celebrated accordingly. Socialist economic developments also form the background to the practice of family reunions which developed in the 1980s.[3] At these banquets the money collected went towards the banquet expenses, so the event testified to economic possibilities of all the families involved, but especially those who had to finance travel from distant locations. The phenomenon can be traced to the massive out migration of villagers in the 1960s (Creed 1998: 123–8), which dispersed families to a degree previously unknown. Out migration was subsequently curtailed but it continued on a smaller scale. By the 1980s early migrants had children and even grandchildren, some of whom had little opportunity to visit with cousins and other relatives, even if they returned to visit village grandparents periodically. The family reunion developed at a time of expanding discretionary income in response to an increasing sense of temporal and spatial separation, in a context where family connections remained emotionally significant and potentially of instrumental use.

The same demographic factors that inspired family reunions also help explain ritual inflation more generally. Fertility decline since the 1920s and massive out migration of the younger generation following collectivization resulted in fewer children to christen, marry and send off to the army. The reduced number of these events allowed families to invest more in each one and to participate in a wider circle of ritual relations within the village, enlarging these events beyond the family into quasi-village rituals. Villagers' domestication of the socialist system, most evident in reform processes since the 1960s, put increasing amounts of produce and money at their disposal (Creed 1998). At the same time the system limited what people could do with these resources, owing to continued neglect of the consumption sector and limitations on other private investments. Much of the resulting excess was funneled into ritual elaborations.

The opposite development – ritual retrenchment – has been reported by Tone Bringa (1995) for the Bosnian village she studied in the late 1980s, where 'fictive elopements' were practiced by Muslim villagers in order to minimize wedding costs, even though villagers were growing richer. Bosnians, however, had more economic alternatives facilitated by the country's more open economy, dating back to the 1960s when labor migration to northern Europe and the massive introduction of consumer goods began. So while Bulgarians with expanding resources and few investment options indulged in ritual *faute de mieux*, their Bosnian counterparts with more economic options invested elsewhere. This formulation, however, implies a familiar 'modernization' theory of changes in family economy that deserves closer scrutiny. According to Bringa the trend towards a less public wedding ritual was the 'result of increased access to wage labor, work migration, and education. This had reduced the importance of extended kin groups and the local neighborhood as a source of mutual obligations and help' (1995: 131). The traditional wedding feast, designed to enhance the cohesion of the extended kin group and the community as 'bound together by mutual obligations, common interests and understandings' (*ibid.*) was no longer appropriate or necessary. The ensuing rational choice echoes the common evolutionary view of family and kinship, according to which economic development goes hand in hand with smaller, increasingly autonomous families. But this trajectory seems to contradict the continued importance of community, which Bringa documents among Muslims in the rest of her book. Moreover, she reports that gift exchanges between the families involved in elopements still amounted to 'a major economic burden on most households' (1995: 138). If this expense was a burden, how could a large feast even be considered? It seems preferable to view the decline in wedding celebrations as the result of an inability to do more elaborate rituals in the face of new economic demands, rather than a positive benefit of an inevitable individualization of choices. The results may then reflect not so much the virtue of liberal economic policy as an early version of what Bulgaria came to experience in the 1990s.

Most of the production underlying ritual extravagance took place in the informal sector under family control. Rituals were important motivations shifting informal activity into overdrive (Creed 1998: 202–4). In this respect they formed part of a complex economy that was simplified after 1989. The socialist collapse removed the structures that made the informal and subsistence sectors so productive and decimated the alternative sources of income that allowed villagers to consume much of their personal agricultural production. For the few villagers with expendable resources after 1989, new avenues of consumption or exit have attracted what had been village ritual expenditures, much as Bringa found in Bosnia. In contrast to Yang's example, then, the expansion of market economy in rural Bulgaria has eroded rather than expanded ritual activities.

This erosion has major implications for social capital. Daphne Berdahl (1999) has applied this concept to describe differentiation in socialist East Germany, and I find her analysis a useful point of departure. She uses it to counter both naive views of socialism as classless and the crude class-based alternatives. The use of this term challenges the modernization perspective, in that it turns what is usually viewed as a negative heritage of traditional society, thought to inhibit development, into an economic resource potentially valuable for capitalist progress.[4] Ethnographically informed research confirms the economic utility of these social relations. Stark and Bruszt (1998) verify the value of enterprise networks forged under socialism for postsocialist economic development. Bruun (1993) suggests similar possibilities for post-Mao China. Martha Lampland (this volume) outlines the value of social capital in explaining the success of Hungarian cooperative farm managers in the postsocialist economy. Contrary to modernization views, this research suggests that the social relations of socialism can be useful in postsocialist development.

According to Berdahl (1999) this potential is not realized in East Germany because the society shifted after 1989 from one based on the social capital of connection to one based on the acquisitive power of economic capital and the symbolic capital of taste. But her own material shows not simply a reversal in the value of types of capital concomitant with systemic shift, but also the decimation of social capital which might have been useful and valuable had it not been eroded. She describes numerous changes that have diminished social capital, such as the elimination of the public address system which drew people out of their houses to listen and discuss news, and the decline in church activities, which regularly brought people together. In rural Bulgaria the consumer practices of socialism dictated comparable interactions, as villagers waited together daily in line for bread and queued weekly for the scheduled delivery of meat or fish. The collective nature of these quotidian activities was even greater at ritual times, when everyone needed large amounts of goods for their galas. This is not to say that people bemoan the end of shortage, but simply to point to a decline in an important forum for sociability. More important than the shared frustration of consumption were relations at the workplace, and these too have been greatly diminished through mass unemployment (cf. Kideckel, Pine, Stewart, this volume). The village where I worked in 1987–8 had numerous industrial work sites including a motor assembly plant, textile enterprises and a biscuit factory, most of which closed in the early 1990s. Co-workers were one of the most significant avenues of social relations beyond family connections during the socialist period, so the decline of both ritual and work connections is devastating to social networks. With diminishing social capital, villagers end up with no capital of any type: like rustic people everywhere they are excluded from the symbolic capital of taste by evolutionary theories of civilization, while the combination of prior socialist limitations on investment and subsequent capitalist structural adjustment policies makes it extremely difficult for them to acquire economic capital.

Of course, postsocialist economic changes *have* affected the utility of village social networks. The social capital derived from village social relations was less useful in the 1990s than it was in the 1980s, but this was not because the system had switched to a rational market mentality alien to network considerations. Quite the contrary, networks remain essential for success in Bulgarian capitalism; it is just that villagers have dropped out of these networks. In the integrated socialist system villagers were connected to people and administrative units with distributive power; this meant that relations with co-villagers could deliver at least some desired goods, and they might be an important first step in a hierarchical chain that linked friends of friends. Some villagers had direct access to higher levels through family members who had migrated to towns and 'made good'. Nowadays, however, few villagers can plug into the new system of strategic relationships. Thus, it is erroneous to conclude that the lack of social capital is the cause of economic difficulties. Villagers' personal relations did constitute valuable social capital during the socialist period, and the decline in their value is due to other changes, not the lack of social relations.

Even now, social relations offer one of the few avenues for rural economic development. With limited financial resources and political emphasis on local initiative, cooperative activities may be the only way to finance or support entrepreneurial activity. However, the diminished exchange rate of rural social capital in the larger economy combines with declining economic resources to reduce the ritual investments that produce social capital, inhibiting self-organization for the limited range of tasks that rural social capital could still potentially achieve. The systemic connections that rendered village social relations highly valuable as a socio-economic resource under socialism have been dismantled. The reduced value of village social relations then combines with economic difficulty to depress ritual activity, and this brings about a vicious circle. Villagers have social capital developed in the socialist economy, but it is diminishing and ritual decline contributes to that trajectory. Their remaining social capital is not as useful in the larger society as it was previously, but it is still potentially valuable for local economic activity from subsistence to cooperative organizing, so this decline must be a cause for concern.

This interpretation of rural social relations differs from those which emphasize the 'atomization' of village life under socialism, whereby individual households withdrew from the intrusive state and became increasingly autonomous at the cost of village cooperation (e.g. Kideckel 1993 on Romania; Rév 1987; Lampland 1995 on Hungary). While I recognized this tendency in Bulgaria in the 1980s, it was not as extreme as described for Hungary and Romania. Of course, this may reflect empirical differences in the places involved, but attention to ritual activity suggests that there is more to it. In Bulgaria, family-based events motivated most of the extensive ritual activity described above, much as one would expect in a society of atomized families. Indeed, non-family ritual events showed little inflation, apart from state investments. Elaborate family festivals, however, were also occasions for generating and reaffirming broader networks within the village. Robert Minnich's (1979) description of pig slaughter as a sort of practical family ritual integrating autonomous households in Slovenia makes this point clearly, and its significance is magnified with ritual inflation. In Bulgaria an extravagant celebration required mobilization well beyond family limits. Attendance integrated large numbers of village families and the numbers became measures of the success of the ritual, encouraging wider incorporation. Family rituals were in many ways village demonstrations and even those who were not invited to a banquet might join the festivities when the orchestra stepped outside the crowded restaurant to accompany other dancers in the village square. These family activities ironically redressed atomization! Changes in such rituals are bound to impact on both the village and the larger society.

While ritual is clearly implicated in economic change, the connections are not limited to those discussed here. Economic development can lead to the proliferation of ritual activity, which can drive economic expansion in the sectors of the economy that provide ritual paraphernalia but operate as a break on capitalist development if it diverts resources away from more profitable avenues of investment. Conversely ritual retrenchment might operate as a fuel to development if the conserved resources are redirected to more profitable venues. The role of social capital and networks is strongly implicated here: if social capital plays a prominent role in the economy, the investment in ritual is likely to translate into other capital forms; if the role of social capital is more constrained, the investment in ritual is unlikely to have spin-off effects conducive to economic development. The final options are the ones that follow from underdevelopment. Rituals may be continued or expanded under conditions of economic privation, for example when they articulate with objectives such as reclaiming territory or nationalist struggles, or when they are underwritten by privileged classes. However, the decline in ritual activity documented here is the more common outcome. Activity can be redirected toward more ascetic practices that still produce needed social networks, but this requires major change in traditional notions of exchange and solidarity, which throughout the Balkans are undergirded by material exchanges. Protestant conversion offers one evident avenue for such a change, but it has not yet shown mass appeal.

The links between economy and ritual can also be explored in the urban context, where conspicuous consumption has helped the newly rich to establish new networks of relations among those who can afford to sponsor and attend their ceremonies. This was already evident during my visits to Sofia in the late 1990s. Ironically, a resource of rural villagers under socialism is now serving urban capitalists. In the countryside, ritual extravagance persists primarily where villagers commute to work in more economically privileged towns. In the village where I overheard the fateful comment about people starving, ritual activity on the prescribed day was anemic. Only a few friends of the woman who had organized the event were in costume and the village children provided their only audience for much of the day. At one point, I overheard the organizer say in disgust, 'They won't come out. What can I do, drag them out of their houses?' Eventually a few more participants arrived in costume and danced around the village square, but one young man in elaborate costume stood on the sidelines and subsequently returned home without participating, because the ritual activity was so 'weak'. Overall, the experience had the opposite of the intended impact and most people went away depressed. In contrast, similar festivities in a smaller village in the same part of the country attracted a very large number of participants. The events started with a bang (literally the firing of guns) in the morning and continued all day, culminating in a ritual battle on the village square and collective bathing in the freezing village stream. This village had a stronger *kukeri* tradition than the previous one and, more importantly, it was economically integrated with the district capital and had not been as devastated by the economic crises of the 1990s. Many of the other thriving ceremonies I witnessed were in similarly situated villages. Buchanan (1996: 226) reports that the agriculturally wealthy region of Dobrudzha was the only area of the country where villagers could still afford to host large weddings in the mid-1990s. So ritual decline is not a universal phenomenon in rural Bulgaria but a pervasive one that correlates closely with economic difficulty. Ethnographic descriptions from Poland (Pine 2000) and Romania (Kideckel, this volume) support this correlation. To the degree that ritual relations produce social capital useful in new economic organizations and activities, decline operates as part of a positive feedback loop accentuating economic differentiation both between town and country, and between villages differentially situated geographically and economically.

## Politics and ritual

Of course, the value of social capital is not limited to the economy and must also be explored in the domain of politics. In his analysis of Italy Robert Putnam (1993) suggested that social capital is crucial to the success of democracy, which works best where people have social capital acquired through years of extensive civic engagement. The social capital that Eastern European citizens developed under socialism did not derive from civic engagement. Most networks depended on kinship or on state-sponsored groupings such as the workplace and activities organized by cultural workers at the local level. The system itself created social capital by forcing citizens to initiate and maintain relationships for acquiring basic objects and objectives. For this reason, ethnographers have tended to be critical of the focus on civic or civil society for obscuring more pertinent forms of sociability, including the avenues that East Europeans had to influence socialism (Creed 1991; Hann and Dunn 1996). The socialist state largely monopolized formal organizational activity and the means of mass communication, but it also created an extremely integrated populace with its own ways of spreading information, and even some potential for political mobilization when such activities became more feasible (see e.g. Wedel 1992). How can societies move towards democratization when the social capital and community engagements available to them are being undermined by economic changes? From this perspective, it is not the socialist gutting of civil society which limits democratization, but the postsocialist diminution of the prior bases of social relations and engagement.

Michelle Bigenho (1999) has explored ritual influence on democratization in highland Bolivia, where the state has tried to decentralize political power through the Law of Popular Participation. This law established the concept of local Territorial Base Organizations (OTBs in the Spanish acronym), to be constituted out of prominent local organizations, which would then have major input into municipal spending plans. The ideal was that existing highland indigenous organizations known as *ayllus* would play a new bureaucratic role, but this rarely happened. By looking at one of the ritual contexts in which indigenous organizations were central – carnival – Bigenho is able to suggest why these units were incompatible with the characteristics prescribed for OTBs. The latter were supposed to be fixed entities, enduring continuously through time within boundaries designated by the state. Carnival, however, reveals indigenous organizations as defined temporarily by movement and sound, with no continuous existence outside the carnival context. In short, studies of indigenous social groups through their ritual can help explain why state democratization efforts often do not proceed as intended.

I do not see close East European parallels with the Andes, but this case can provoke us to think about the role of ritual in the construction and definition of communities and the extent to which they articulate with various dimensions of democratization. The micro-practices of rituals in Eastern Europe were crucial to defining villages as communities of significance, despite household atomization and national homogenization. Local identification, in turn, is crucial to efforts at local empowerment and political participation. Democratization depends not only on participation but also on a sense that the units of representation are meaningful and valid. Indeed, this was a major limitation on local interest in agricultural administration under socialism from the point at which the state defined farm units larger than single villages. Decline in ritual erodes village and other group identifications that form the basis of electoral structures. This in turn may have implications for larger imagined communities of identification, notably the nation. The socialist states of Eastern Europe pursued ritual homogenization to enhance national sentiment (Silverman 1983); the current decline of local variants may serve to heighten this sense of ritual unity, which anyway continues to be promoted by the postsocialist state.

Diversity of ritual practice is an important feature of multi-ethnic or plural communities, confirming and reinforcing divisions within villages by creating communities of participation. Bringa's description of what she calls the 'Muslim community in a [Bosnian] village of Muslim and Catholic inhabitants' is illustrative (1995: 6). Without postulating a direct link to the subsequent war, she shows that ritual events and activities constitute a clear boundary. It was ritual practice that defined the Muslim community as distinct from the larger village and the Yugoslav 'nation' in which villagers (especially men) participated daily. Conversely, in some cases ritual operates to connect ethnic and religious groups. In Bulgaria, for example, the spectacle of some Roma celebrations attracted Bulgarian co-villagers. While such events hardly erased the ethnic divide, even during the event (as conveyed by the common Bulgarian commentary, 'nice work, but it's gypsy'), it did provide a forum for interethnic interaction, as did Bulgarian ritual events in which Roma performed, notably as musicians (Buchanan 1996). Village celebrations connected to local or national holidays such as May Day also formed contexts for mutual celebration and interaction, irrespective of ethnic or political diversity. Such intergroup participation declines with ritual retrenchment and rituals across ethnic or religious lines may be the first casualties. Where rituals separate ethno-religious communities, their demise is unlikely to translate automatically into better relations. The impact will depend on the degree of mutual participation and the alternative avenues for social exchange within communities. My point is simply that ritual activity is critical to understanding ethnic relations in Eastern Europe. At the very least, it provides a barometer of shifting relations, as Hayden demonstrates in his contribution to this volume: in both the Balkans and South Asia, ritual practices and sites that had acquired meaning for different ethno-religious groups were re-segregated when relations worsened in other spheres.

In defining communities, death rituals are often especially significant. Gail Kligman's (1988) descriptions of mortuary practices in Romania and Loring Danforth and Alexander Tsiaras's (1982) study of Greece both illustrate how these rituals maintain village social relations (cf. Stewart, this volume). Funeral rites perpetuate the kindred and personal network of the deceased after death and they usually reinforce connections between mourners from different families. Death rituals can also be readily adapted to sustain imaginary relations between members of a nation, as Katherine Verdery (1999) has demonstrated in her study of postsocialist reburials. Understanding the resonance of nationalist and political activities requires an appreciation not only of the material interests behind them but also of why they are compelling to the people involved, which requires an analysis of the ritual forms invoked.

The appeal of nationalism to rural people in much of Eastern Europe since 1989 may be traced indirectly to the use of rural ritual by socialist governments to help construct the nation. As happened elsewhere and earlier (Swedenberg 1990; Kisbán 1989), villagers tended to be cast by the socialist state as the embodiment of the nation, which was embellished with images drawn from folk ritual practice, along with folk music, dance and crafts (Lass 1989). However anachronistically negative this association of the peasant with an ancient period of ethnogenesis, to the degree that nationalism was touted by political leaders the association brought positive connotations and villagers accepted validation wherever they could find it. As their economic avenues of influence dried up, nationalism seemed to many the only source of value or influence they had left. To recognize such possibilities we must appreciate the history of ritual activity in the past and see how those practices and beliefs articulate with new political and economic efforts.

In Sofia in the winter of 1997 I was able to observe this articulation directly. I arrived on the day that protesters stormed the parliament building, ushering in weeks of massive public demonstrations intended to force the socialist government to resign. Strikes and barricades spread throughout the country and eventually had the desired effect. A significant component of this movement was the activity of the students, who staged daily demonstrations prior to the mass marches organized by the opposition. Popular sentiment was already on the side of the demonstrators, due largely to worsening economic conditions, but Sofia residents commented repeatedly on the compelling impact of the student protests, and the way these drew upon old ritual themes (see also Benovska-Săbkova 1998). One day they staged a mock funeral for the 'Communist Party',[5] complete with wailers and laments especially composed for the occasion. Another day they donned the costumes of Bulgarian *kukeri* and enacted the associated rituals for driving away evil, identified with 'the

Communists'. They mobilized masses to lug rocks to a major traffic circle where the rural ritual of cursing an errant villager by piling stones at the scene of the crime was metaphysically transformed to pillory the criminal 'Communist Party'. These ritual forms provided potent resources for political action.

The contemporary political potential of ritual is greatly influenced by former socialist practice. In keeping with the quality that I have termed 'conflicting complementarity' (Creed 1998), characteristic of socialism generally, rituals in the 1980s were often ambivalent statements of both support for the state and resistance to it. The same ritual could incorporate state prescribed elements such as the state marriage rite and the official swearing in of new military recruits, while its most elaborate aspects – the gifting and banquets – remained beyond the state's reach. The extravagant displays of consumption ran counter to state redistribution priorities, but at the same time they testified to the productivity and abundance of the socialist system and became extremely important in legitimating socialist rule. The comparison that older villagers drew between the extravagant weddings of the 1980s and the spartan ones of the past was often issued as an explicit validation of socialist development. Soldier sendoffs were prohibited by the state in the 1980s as occasions of drunkenness and violence, but they continued anyway, a challenge to the very state the soldiers swore to serve and defend! State efforts to homogenize and nationalize folk culture led to prohibitions against Turkish, Roma and Serbian songs (Buchanan 1996), which emerged nonetheless in the repertoire of orchestras at nearly all celebrations I attended. Ritual practices thus became a forum for state resistance, much as Kligman (1983, 1988) described for Transylvanian ritual poetry. In the postsocialist context, however, the decline in ritual activity or ritual commitments diminishes such possibilities.

During the 1980s many ritual activities, in fact most of those not associated with the family life cycle, were underwritten to some degree by the state. Local cultural workers organized ritual activities as part of their job. The state also provided cultural funds to villages and municipalities that could be used for financing the costs of ritual activities and/or ensuring participation by offering awards. Municipalities sponsored festivals which provided a chance for folklore groups to travel and compete against those from other villages. Such opportunities were very popular and participants recounted many stories of the good times they had at these festivals. This sponsorship encouraged the continued practice of the rituals in the village itself (although many villages sent folklore groups to festivals to perform rituals that no one in the village still practiced). As a result of general economic difficulties and subsequent structural adjustment policies the state has slashed such funds for municipalities. In one village I visited in 1997, the lack of funds for awards was cited by the village librarian as a major depressant on ritual participation. Where festivals were attempted, organizers complained about the lack of subsidies and especially about the high travel costs facing participants. Ritual decline in the 1990s became a symbol of state lack of interest and withdrawal, complementing political exasperation and economic disillusionment.

One can of course view the decline as a desirable depoliticization of culture. The socialist state certainly attempted to direct and control cultural expressions for political purposes, notably in ways that enhanced the resonances of national identification and socialist ideology. But the politicization of culture also turned it into a political tool that the population could use to resist and subvert power-holders. The depoliticization of culture may have contributed to ritual's declining appeal or political utility. Unfortunately, it has yet to be replaced by effective democratic avenues of participation. For many Bulgarians even voting has lost its political efficacy, becoming an empty ritual, apparently with the same fate as other rituals discussed here.

## Prospects

Attention to ritual, I have argued, should not be approached as an alternative to investigations of privatization and democratization in Eastern Europe but as complementary to these investigations. Ritual demands and objectives in rural Bulgaria still influence investments in subsistence farming. Ritual extravagance has become difficult, if not impossible, but ritual desires and expectations, the sociability that defines humanity around food and wine, continue to motivate both economic activity and political opinion.

The decline of ritual can help us better understand the contradictions that pervade contemporary Bulgarian economic reports. Since the late 1990s the world financial institutions that shape its economy have issued positive macro-economic assessments that contradict depressing reports from the countryside. The decimation of the rich ritual life of villagers is part of a perceived deterioration of village life that is not captured in comparative economic statistics about village production. Ritual decline is not simply a barometer of economic and political difficulty, but itself contributes to rural dissatisfaction and disappointment. For Bulgarian villagers in the 1980s, as for the Buryats described by Humphrey (1983), a rich ritual life was part of what constituted living well; it was built into their national and local identities. Socialist emphasis on folklore enhanced the affiliation between ritual and national identity, while resilient local differences in ritual practice maintained local identifications. Ritual excess represented one of the few arenas in which rural life could demonstrate its superiority over the otherwise privileged urban sector; it was a legitimation of village life and of the socialist system itself. From a village point of view then ritual decline produces a sort of disemia (Herzfeld 1987) in which recollections of past ritual glory coexist with a ritually depressed present. This lens colors perceptions and interpretations of other changes in the transition. Ritual decimation is both a result and a cause of political and economic difficulties. It entails a loss in dignity and self-worth, a decline in the quality of life, and a change in notions of village identity. For these reasons, ritual analysis should not be confined to the political and economic dimensions on which I have concentrated in this chapter. However, as anthropologists of the transition it is imperative that we highlight the potential economic and political consequences of ritual change. In many parts of rural Bulgaria ritual retrenchment is diminishing the social capital villagers might use to pull themselves from the current morass and contributing to a spiraling sense of dislocation and helplessness.

## Notes

1 Although not strictly a case of 'transition', see Vertovec (1992) for discussion of a similar expansion of ritual among Hindus in Trinidad during the oil boom of the 1970s.
2 I use the term 'social capital' here to highlight the economic utility and convertibility of social relations and to render associated ritual activity relevant to transitologists currently deploying the concept. However, I sympathize with arguments against forcing all aspects of life into a capitalist grid of intelligibility and do not advocate it more generally.
3 These were more sporadic events, but one occurred in the village where I was conducting fieldwork in 1988 and I was told of several others.
4 This very possibility has provoked devotees of modernization theory to exclude East European social networks from the category of social capital or define them as a 'negative' manifestation. In this view the personal relations important to East Europeans do not constitute social capital but rather an exaggerated personal/family sector which is anathema to capitalist development. When joined with the still bloated state sector it constitutes an 'hour-glass society' in which the 'positive' social capital linking the two is limited and restricted (Rose 1995).
5 Their use of the term 'Communist' was an intentional effort to equate the Socialist Party with its Communist predecessor.

## References

Badone, Ellen (ed.) (1990) Religious Orthodoxy and Popular Faith in European Society, Princeton: Princeton University Press.
Benovska-Săbkova, Milena (1998) 'The signs of protest: January 10–February 5, 1997', Ethnologia Bulgarica 1: 67–77.
Berdahl, Daphne (1999) Where the World Ended: Re-unification and Identity in the German Borderland, Berkeley: University of California Press.
Bigenho, Michelle (1999) 'Sensing locality in Yura: rituals of carnival and of the Bolivian state', American Ethnologist 26: 957–80.
Binns, Christopher A.P. (1979) 'The changing face of power: revolution and accommodation in the development of the Soviet ceremonial system: part I', Man 14: 585–606.
——(1980) 'The changing face of power: revolution and accommodation in the development of the Soviet ceremonial system: part II', Man 15: 170–87.
Boissevain, Jeremy (ed.) (1992) Revitalizing European Rituals, London: Routledge.
Bourdieu, Pierre (1985) 'The forms of capital', in J.G. Richardson (ed.) The Handbook of Theory and Research for the Sociology of Education, New York: Greenwood, pp. 241–58.
Bringa, Tone (1995) Being Muslim the Bosnian Way: Identity and Community in a Central Bosnian Village, Princeton: Princeton University Press.

Bruun, Ole (1993) *Business and Bureaucracy in a Chinese City: an Ethnography of Private Business Households in Contemporary China*, Berkeley: Institute of East Asian Studies.

Buchanan, Donna (1996) 'Wedding musicians, political transition, and national consciousness in Bulgaria', in Mark Slobin (ed.) *Retuning Culture: Musical Changes in Central and Eastern Europe*, Durham: Duke University Press, pp. 200–30.

Creed, Gerald W. (1991) 'Civil society and the spirit of capitalism: a Bulgarian critique', paper presented at the 90th Annual Meeting of the American Anthropological Association, Chicago, Illinois, 20–4 November.

——(1998) *Domesticating Revolution: From Socialist Reform to Ambivalent Transition in a Bulgarian Village*, University Park: Pennsylvania State University Press.

Danforth, Loring and Alexander Tsiaras (1982) *The Death Rituals of Rural Greece*, Princeton: Princeton University Press.

Dubisch, Jill (1995) *In a Different Place: Pilgrimage, Gender, and Politics at a Greek Island Shrine*, Princeton: Princeton University Press.

Gilmore, David D. (1998) *Carnival and Culture: Sex, Symbol and Status in Spain*, New Haven: Yale University Press.

Hann, Chris and Elizabeth Dunn (eds) (1996) *Civil Society: Challenging Western Models*, London: Routledge.

Herzfeld, Michael (1987) *Anthropology Through the Looking Glass: Critical Ethnography in the Margins of Europe*, Cambridge: Cambridge University Press.

Humphrey, Caroline (1983) *Karl Marx Collective: Economy, Society and Religion in a Siberian Collective Farm*, Cambridge: Cambridge University Press.

Ivanova, Radost (1984) *Bulgarska Folklorna Svatba*, Sofia: Bulgarskata Akademiya na Naoukite.

Kideckel, David A. (1983) 'Secular ritual and social change: a Romanian example', *Anthropological Quarterly* 56(2): 69–75.

——(1993) *The Solitude of Collectivism: Romanian Villagers to the Revolution and Beyond*, Ithaca: Cornell University Press.

Kisbán, Eszter (1989) 'From peasant dish to national symbol: an early deliberate example', *Ethnologia Europaea* 19(1): 95–102.

Kligman, Gail (1981) *Căluş: Symbolic Transformation in Romanian Ritual*, Chicago: University of Chicago Press.

——(1983) 'Poetry as politics in a Transylvanian village', *Anthropological Quarterly* 56(2): 83–9.

——(1988) *The Wedding of the Dead: Ritual, Poetics and Popular Culture in Transylvania*, Berkeley: University of California Press.

Lampland, Martha (1995) *The Object of Labor: Commodification in Socialist Hungary*, Chicago: University of Chicago Press.

Lane, Christel (1981) *The Rites of Rulers: Ritual in Industrial Society – the Soviet Case*, New York: Cambridge University Press.

Lass, Andrew (1989) 'What keeps the Czech folk "alive"?', *Dialectical Anthropology* 14(1): 7–19.

Mach, Zdzisław (1992) 'Continuity and change in political ritual: May Day in Poland', in Jeremy Boissevain (ed.) *Revitalizing European Rituals*, London: Routledge, pp. 43–61.

Mauss, Marcel (1990 [1924]) *The Gift*, London: Routledge

Minnich, R.G. (1979) *The Homemade World of Zagaj: An Interpretation of the 'Practical Life' among Traditional Peasant Farmers in West Haloze Slovenia, Yugoslavia*, Bergen: University of Bergen.

Pine, Frances (2000) 'Kinship, gender and work in socialist and post socialist rural Poland', in Victoria Ana Goddard (ed.) *Gender, Agency and Change: Anthropological Perspectives*, London: Routledge, pp. 86–101.

Putnam, Robert (1993) *Making Democracy Work: Civic Traditions in Modern Italy*, Princeton: Princeton University Press.

Rév, István (1987) 'The advantage of being atomized: how Hungarian peasants coped with collectivization', *Dissent* 34: 335–50.

Rheubottom, D.B. (1980) 'Dowry and wedding celebrations in Yugoslav Macedonia', in J.L. Comaroff (ed.) *The Meaning of Marriage Payments*, New York: Academic Press, pp. 221–49.

Rose, Richard (1995) 'Russia as an hour-glass society: a constitution without citizens', *East European Constitutional Review* 4(3): 34–42.

Roth, Klaus (1990) 'Socialist life-cycle rituals in Bulgaria', *Anthropology Today* 6(5): 8–10.

Sanders, Irwin T. (1949) *Balkan Village*, Lexington: University of Kentucky Press.

Silverman, Carol (1983) 'The politics of folklore in Bulgaria', *Anthropological Quarterly* 56(2): 55–61.

Stark, David and L. Bruszt (1998) *Postsocialist Pathways*, New York: Cambridge University Press.

Swedenburg, Ted (1990) 'The Palestinian peasant as national signifier', *Anthropological Quarterly* 63(1): 18–30.

Verdery, Katherine (1999) *The Political Lives of Dead Bodies: Reburial and Postsocialist Change*, New York: Columbia University Press.

Vertovec, Steven (1992) *Hindu Trinidad: Religion, Ethnicity and Socio-Economic Change*, London: Macmillan.

Wedel, Janine (ed.) (1992) *The Unplanned Society: Poland During and After Communism*, New York: Columbia University Press.

Yang, Mayfair Mei-hui (2000) 'Putting global capitalism in its place: economic hybridity, Bataille, and ritual expenditure', *Current Anthropology* 41: 477–510.

# Chapter 4

# The social production of mistrust

*Christian Giordano and Dobrinka Kostova*

## Introduction: transition, consolidation, and mistrust

The unexpected and sudden fall of the Berlin Wall in November 1989 gave rise to an impressive surge of enthusiasm and optimism in both Eastern and Western Europe. During the somewhat millenarian atmosphere of this first phase, the visions of the future which emerged and proliferated assumed a swift and painless shift from socialist totalitarianism to liberal democracy, and from the planned economy to the market. With this spirit of confidence, transitology, as it came to be labelled, with a touch of irony, spread out into other social sciences. In one way or another, almost all authors predicted swift and essentially unilinear change. This is not the place to judge transition's teleology. It is enough to note that the original enthusiasm has given way to disillusionment, scepticism, apathy and in some cases even anger.

This recalcitrant reality has affected the vast majority of the population in the ex-socialist countries and led some social scientists to revise their interpretations of social, political and economic changes in postsocialist societies. The concept of transition, though it has not disappeared completely, has been increasingly replaced by less teleological terms such as 'transformation' and 'consolidation'. This latter notion, with its geological connotations, evokes complex social processes with uncertain outcomes. It has been used especially to emphasize the laborious importation of public structures (parliamentary institutions, bureaucratic administration, etc.) and political practices from Western democracies (Linz and Stepan 1996: 235 ff.). Claus Offe and his colleagues have demonstrated that the 'democratic system' in Western Europe has been established and subjectively internalized for over a century, whereas in Eastern Europe it is largely alien, the outcome of a more or less opportunistic strategy to find favour with the winners of the Cold War (Elster *et al.* 1997). The general conclusion is that democracy in Western Europe is well established and fully consolidated, while in Eastern Europe it has yet to be consolidated at all.

For an anthropologist the term 'consolidation', as it is now being employed by the orphans of transitology, is infected by ethnocentric or 'Orientalist' associations. It rests on a dichotomy between East and West which is grossly over-drawn. The study of democratic consolidation nonetheless highlights a crucial issue for the anthropological analysis of postsocialist societies. In Weberian terms, the issue pertains to the precarious legitimacy of legal power and its representatives. Many of the new post-totalitarian states have encountered serious problems in imposing a 'monopoly of force and violence' (Weber 1956: vol. 2, 832) within their territory. Even in countries where violence has not been a prime concern, such as Bulgaria, a lack of confidence in the state and limited trust towards its institutions are salient problems. Trust between citizen and state is confined to those situations in which the citizen is certain to achieve personal benefit. In terms of the distinction between trust and protection (Tilly 1985: 170; Gambetta 1992), it seems undeniable that many postsocialist citizens consider being part of a highly personalized network based upon the principle of protection more reliable, more effective and therefore more rational than reliance upon the state. This should not be interpreted from a culturalist viewpoint that would reduce them to the expression of a presumed 'Balkan asociality', or an improbable 'Magyar temperament'. The precariousness of legal power, the prevalence of personalized protection structures, and the resulting gulf between *pays légal* and *pays réel*, are better approached as indicators of the *social production of mistrust*. This is a system of representations and rational strategies that actors follow when a state repeatedly fails to perform its fundamental duties, particularly the responsibility of creating the conditions to guarantee a 'pacified space', in which they can trust each other through the 'rule of law'.

The social production of mistrust is based on specific practices that necessarily stem from past negative experiences, which are reactivated in the present through the group's collective memory. In this article we shall apply this perspective to rural Bulgaria and show how the land reform and land restitution laws have in substance maintained centuries-old patterns of mistrust. We shall illustrate how the legal instruments devised by the Bulgarian state to give back land and privatize the agricultural sector have once more highlighted a lack of communication between the political elite and citizens of rural extraction. This lack is the outcome of two different views on what the country's postsocialist agricultural structure could and should be. From the powerholders' point of view, reflected in the 'spirit of the law', the goal was to establish a private agricultural sector based on small peasant property, which is explicitly or implicitly deemed to be the 'cradle of national virtues'. It is an abstract view that aspires to reinstate an imaginary past and overlooks, willingly or otherwise, the undeniable social changes that took place during the socialist era. Though not questioning the denationalization principle, subordinate groups in the agricultural sector have a far more pragmatic attitude towards reality. Bulgarian rural society's changes over the past fifty years are taken for granted by the ruled; they are considered an evident and ineffaceable fact. The ruled have reacted to the rulers' projects by following an intuitive sociology of their own, which has led to strategies quite unlike those expected by the legislators. The ruled voice their mistrust openly, often in a lapidary phrase that was the *Leitmotiv* of most of our interviews: 'Politicians are all alike; you can't trust them.'

In this article we shall link several aspects of this misrecognition which at first may not seem interrelated. First, we discuss the ideological contents of the 'reversibility of events' myth, which has guided the ruling elites in their legislative action. Second, we explore the reaction of different rural groups, including strategies, that were often extra-legal if not illegal, but more in line with the realities of the new social structure. Finally, it will be shown that this significant divergence between legal framework and social practices is more than an indication of socially produced mistrust between public institutions and society; it will be interpreted as one of several circumstances that strengthen the persistence of a centuries-old divide between state legality and the legitimacy of norms, institutions and social actions.

Case material was collected in Dobrudzha, a fertile agrarian area in the country's northeast region with a socio-economic structure distinct from that of the rest of Bulgaria. Within present-day Bulgarian boundaries it is, for geomorphologic and geological reasons, the most suitable region for large-scale agriculture. This was well understood during Ottoman domination which, in this area of the country more than others, resolutely applied the model of 'prebendal feudalism' based on the *timar* and later on the *chiflik* system (Weber 1956: vol. 2, 635; Tonev 1995: 73–6). However, for over four hundred years the region was sparsely populated, land was tilled extensively rather than by intensive methods, and output was geared more to the needs of the local economy (Tonev 1995: 74). Much later, socialist planners realized Dobrudzha's potential and strove, quite successfully, to transform this area into Bulgaria's granary through collectivization and investing in large cooperative enterprises. Dobrudzha was deemed the ideal location to implement the policy of centralization and concentration in gigantic agro-industrial complexes, which between the early 1970s and the mid-1980s replaced the former cooperatives (Crampton 1997: 202 ff.; Giordano and Kostova 1995: 166). Dobrudzha has long been a borderland region, the theatre of endless contention between major powers and bordering states (Castellan 1991: 201 ff., 319 ff., 374 ff.). The area has been difficult to control because of its remoteness. The state has always had difficulties in imposing itself, and rebellion and smuggling have been historical constants. These circumstances combine to make Dobrudzha an excellent location to study the social production of mistrust.

Our research diverged in its methods from those of the standard anthropological monograph. In the first place, data were not gathered during a lengthy stay in a single village. We conducted in-depth interviews and also focused discussion groups outside a strictly agricultural context. In our view, a monographic research is not the best way to explore a phenomenon like postsocialist land reform and its repercussions on the social structure of a complex society. If this type of research had been employed, many of the actors affected by the reform process, who for various reasons have little or nothing to do with the strictly local reality, would have gone unnoticed. As in other countries, the land reform in postsocialist Bulgaria has been a nationwide process that has touched the entire society, both rural and urban. If the research had focused on the rural and local reality, centred on one or more villages of Dobrudzha, the population would have largely limited to old and/or lowly qualified people, a statistically small proportion of the regional agricultural sector. Most of the entrepreneurs presently doing business in Dobrudzha's agriculture are not to be found in the villages. The population that can truly be defined as rural, i.e. those who dwell, work and socially interact predominantly within the village context, coincides only partially with those who have benefited from the land reform. For all these reasons, it was clear for us that the social impact of land reform in a region of large-scale agriculture such as Dobrudzha could not be adequately addressed through traditional fieldwork in the village context. Consequently, employing a 'translocal' and 'de-territorialized' point of view, we have deliberately transcended the narrow spaces of the locality (cf. Hannerz 1998a: 246 ff., b: 93).

## The past in the present: actualizing history under postsocialism

For most anthropologists, history is above all 'actualized history'; in other words, it refers to a past that is more or less intentionally 'mobilized' in the present (Giordano 1996: 99). This actualization or mobilization of the past helps one to find one's bearings in everyday life. It signals a sense of belonging or identity, and it transmits a symbolic or metaphorical message to other social actors. It may serve to stabilize power relations or, in other cases, to protest against conditions deemed unacceptable. But how do specific actors use past events in the present? In what ways is history reinterpreted, manipulated and even reinvented? What are the reasons underlying such processes? In actualized history the problem of linear time is not crucial, since the metaphors, metonyms and allegories it employs do not respect chronology. The 'mathematical', 'naturalistic' and therefore 'exogenous' time of history, as defined by Fernand Braudel and Norbert Elias (Braudel 1977: 77; Elias 1988: ix), is at least partially erased. The time of actualized history is much more 'endogenous' and 'condensed' in the individuals as social actors. However, this immediately reveals its selective aspect. The past in the present may be likened to a huge quarry, where each person can extract the stones that they consider appropriate.

We suggest that two distinctive forms of the actualization of history have been characteristic of socialisms and postsocialisms between 1917 and today: 'annihilation of the past' and 'reversibility of events'. The former refers to the systematic elimination of past facts, symbols and social practices that are believed to be the heritage of eras labelled 'barbaric', 'obscurantist' or 'degenerate'. The latter refers to the project of restoring matters 'as they were before', thus leaving behind a recent past now exposed as a fatal mistake. The first strategy has been well described by Predrag Matvejevic, who has shown how the socialist regimes that seized power in Central and Eastern Europe almost without exception attempted to propel history forward and were ruthless in pursuit of their futurist goal (Matvejevic, 1992: 38). This haste implied a definite break with the past and the disavowal of its legacy. The party functionaries and intellectuals who promoted this utopian acceleration of social processes annihilated reminders of previous corruption and despotism, poverty and alienation. Many examples of urban reconstruction, from Stalinist Moscow in the 1930s to Ceauşescu's Bucharest in the 1980s, illustrate this iconoclast frenzy towards history. Socialist triumphalism was built on the ruins of Orthodox churches, bourgeois neighbourhoods and aristocratic mansions. This 'annihilation of history' had less sensational, apparently banal aspects. In Dobrudzha, after the 1946 land reform and the subsequent land collectivization, local functionaries destroyed many land register records. Convinced that the sinister era of landed property was definitely over, the local functionaries organized rallies in which these documents were burned. The intention of these symbolic public bonfires, which peasant smallholders actively supported, was to erase the legacy of an unacceptable past, now forever vanquished.

The 1989 revolution radically altered this view of history. The socialist interpretation of the past was suddenly declared to be a tissue of 'lies' that had merely served the regime's interests. Socialism itself was denounced as a fatal 'historical' mistake. Thus, while socialist history was based upon the past's selective destruction, postsocialist history stems from an assumption of the reversibility of events. One narrative is 'prospective' while the other is 'retrospective', implying that the postsocialist future can begin by returning to a *status quo ante*. According to the logic of this representation, it is necessary and desirable to recreate the conditions of the pre-socialist era as if socialism had never existed – or as if it existed only outside the 'correct flow of history'. The spate of name changes after the fall of the Berlin Wall shows this logic. Thus the renowned Bulgarian resort of Druzhba, which means friendship (among the people), was renamed Sveti Konstantin i Helena (St Constantine and Helena). Within cities, 'revisionist' enthusiasm has affected many local landmarks, including streets, bridges and underground stations. The same tendency is evident everywhere in state and national symbolism: from flags and monuments to national anthems, uniforms, banknotes and passports. The 'exhumation' of the pre-socialist order takes an extreme form when earlier constitutions are re-enacted in almost identical form, as in Estonia and Latvia. These examples in the first phase of postsocialism are attributable to a political class bent on sweeping away every possible trace of the previous regime. However, the subsequent electoral successes of neo-communists in many countries call into question the notion of reversibility. A stalemate tantamount to political paralysis can be observed in certain cases, when the antagonism between two structurally inverse forms of 'restorationism' or 'revivalism' is exacerbated. On the one hand, deeply anticommunist nationalists rely on neo-liberal economic doctrines and give credence to a notion of 'reversibility' in the hope of bolstering their claim to a political genealogy reaching back to the 'glorious era' before socialism. On the other hand, the new generations of 'red' politicians prominent in the state apparatus, while finding themselves compelled to exhibit a 'non-ideological' pragmatism and to accept postsocialism symbology, maintain the socio-political networks of the old apparatus. The myth of 'reversible history' preserves a certain ideological relevance, with practical consequences for all competing groups.

## 'Reversible history' and 'actual boundaries' in rural Bulgaria

Land decollectivization was one of the main concerns of each postsocialist government, but the course of this process varied greatly from country to country. Most Eastern European countries implemented restitution as an 'act of justice' towards people portrayed as the victims of a 'non-legitimate power'. In several cases, this meant the restoration of pre-socialist property relations, often with the explicit intention of making family-run farms the bedrock of the rural society. Behind the wish to 'make history reversible' lies more than the official idea of rightful compensation for damages suffered. There is also the covert project to reinstate the 'traditional' peasant society, envisioned as the depository of the nation's most genuine values and virtues. Some politicians have overtly promoted a 'ruralist ideology' based upon peasant smallholders. Consciously or unconsciously, a fraction of the urban political and bureaucratic elites, supported by Western experts, adopted the policies of pre-war agrarian populism. The resulting 'paysannerie pensée' was quite unlike the 'paysannerie vécue' of mature socialism, but it was the former which served as a reference point in drawing up land reform acts.

The case of Bulgaria fits this pattern well. The essence of the land reform of 1991 evoked the pre-socialist past of a 'small nation of small peasants'. 'Rurality' as celebrated by writers, artists and the Bulgarian Agrarian National Union, the pre-war populist party led by the charismatic Alexandar Stamboliiski, was a myth that socialism had not erased. The legislation of 1991 (amended in 1992 and 1995) provided for the liquidation of cooperative farms and the restitution of land based on the boundaries of 1946. The legitimate owner was expected, according to the land reform's philosophy, to reassume the ideal role of the smallholder who owned the plot in 1946. This nostalgic view of the postsocialist agricultural social structure was articulated by numerous politicians and intellectuals turned politicians. For example, in 2000 we had an opportunity to interview a member of the Centre–Right coalition, which had enacted the crucial land reform law amendments. When we raised the issue of the land reform, our enquiry produced bewilderment and dismay. At first, this renowned poet and ex-minister asked why anthropologists would be interested in such a topic, since Bulgaria offered far more interesting and attractive subject matter. Finally, after an embarrassing silence, she answered: 'Catastrophic ... the land reform law has turned out to be an utter catastrophe. It has not been able to efface socialism from the agricultural sector and has not fostered the rebirth of the true Bulgarian peasant. Give up this research, since it will not show you what our country is really like.'

This attempt to incorporate the past into the present by reversing history and reviving the Bulgarian peasant myth has proven highly problematic. To begin with, there were formidable practical problems. The total lack of land registers, as in the villages studied in Dobrudzha, or the faulty organization of registration in the general land offices in other parts of the country, made the reconstruction of the actual boundaries of 1946 extremely arduous. In many cases the local land commissions deemed it sufficient to ask the older members of the community to reconstruct the size and location of peasant holdings. Given memory's proclivity to select and manipulate (Candau 1996: 72 ff.), it is not surprising that this has given rise to countless objections, appeals and disputes both between state and citizens and among the new owners themselves. Controversial cases were referred to the courts, but these were understaffed, unfamiliar with the new rules, and therefore unable to reach prompt decisions. Consequently the land commissions have been stigmatized as biased and dishonest, if not downright corrupt, while the institutions of the law have confirmed their reputation for unreliability and inefficiency.

The second major problem is that restitution within the actual boundaries of 1946 re-established conditions of extreme property fragmentation. Up until independence, attained in 1878 after almost five hundred years of Ottoman domination, neither customary law nor Ottoman law provided for the division of landholdings among heirs. Independent of the legal category (*timar*, *chiflik*, tenancy or other), the holding was a unit and it was bequeathed as such from generation to generation. A land market was practically non-existent. After 1878, Bulgaria rapidly imported the practices of Western Europe. This Europeanization affected the entire apparatus of public administration and government. The new legal system required land to be divided among the lineal descendants, and this brought about a progressive fragmentation of property, with alarming social and economic consequences (Bell 1977: 13). Alexandar Stamboliiski outlined a reform project to achieve land consolidation but he was assassinated in 1923 and the problem persisted (Mollov 1930: 180 ff.; Giordano and Kostova 1995: 159). The 1934 statistical data indicated that the situation was getting worse. Over 80 per cent of the land was held in the form of holdings smaller than 10 ha, and only three per cent of all farms were larger than 20 ha (Minkov and Luzov 1979: 12). The peak of extreme fragmentation was reached in 1946 when over 92 per cent of all farms were smaller than 10 ha and less than one per cent were larger than 20 ha (Giordano and Kostova 1995: 159). Thus land restitution according to the actual boundaries of 1946 meant reviving minifundism within postsocialism. Those actually engaged in the agrarian sector perceived this manoeuvre as an absurdity contrived by politicians in the capital who, due to their urban upbringing, were unable to update their abstract and bucolic notion of a 'paysannerie pensée' and unable to tackle agrarian problems.

The third problem is that restoring land property within the actual boundaries of 1946 means giving land to people who have not tilled it for years, or have never done so. The rapid industrialization upon which Bulgaria embarked in the late 1940s resulted in a high degree of rural urban migration, indeed the highest rural population decrease anywhere in socialist Eastern Europe. Between 1950 and 1990 the rural population dropped from 72.6 per cent to 34.1 per cent. In comparison, over the same period Hungary had only a 14.7 per cent decrease, Poland 21.6 per cent, Czechoslovakia 24.4 per cent, and Romania 31.0 per cent (Eberhardt 1993: 35). This massive urbanization also meant deep changes in social structure, values and lifestyles. These immigrants formed a petit bourgeois social stratum, now highly visible in the rapidly decaying tenement blocks on the outskirts of urban centres. In some cases they would commute back to the village cooperatives where they were employed from nine to five, as if they too were industrial factory workers. The routine differed totally from that of a peasant, whose working practices were determined primarily by the seasons and the climate. In some regions, such as the highly mechanized grain-producing region of Dobrudzha, the countryside was almost literally deserted, with only the old and the unskilled remaining in the villages.

## Unexpected outcomes: new social agents in rural Dobrudzha

For all the above reasons, a revival of the family-run enterprise based on private smallholdings has caused considerable consternation in Bulgaria. Land reform based on the 'paysannerie pensée' as conceived by the political class has been put into practice, and land has been redistributed according to the boundaries of 1946. The people directly involved (new owners, leaders of the disbanded production cooperatives, employees and agronomists), deeming the law wrong rather than unfair, have responded with extra-legal initiatives in accordance with their peasant savoir-faire. Deftly taking advantage of the land reform law's loopholes, they have established new social agents (individual and collective), who represent specific interests and economic strategies. These new agents can be seen very clearly in the region of Dobrudzha, where in the years before 1989 many villagers, including those who remained active in the agricultural sector, had moved to Dobric, the most important city of the region. Negative opinions of the power elite, depicted as a distant and alien clique run by string-pulling lawyers, are widespread. In this region, due to geographic as well as technical considerations, the transformation of large collectivized enterprises into thousands of privatized minifundia seemed nonsensical to most people concerned, and the prelude to an economic disaster. These new social agents are seen by the dominant faction of the postsocialist ruling elite as acting contrary to the 'spirit' of the land reform and, in effect, forming a new 'awkward class' (Shanin 1972). Five new social agents can be observed in Dobrudzha's agricultural sector.

## New owners

A large number of new owners, though profiting from the land reform, have no intention of embarking on an agricultural venture on the land which they have received. These are mostly the heirs of people who moved from the countryside to the cities during socialism. These citizens of rural origin no longer want to be what they or their fathers once were and what the authors of the policy for the re-establishment of peasant smallholdings wanted to reinstate. During ten years of postsocialism, most of these new owners have suffered a sharp decline in the standard and quality of their lifestyle. Many have lost their jobs, many have to subsist on meagre pensions. Land restitution has allowed them to alleviate their chronic economic straits by leasing much of their land to persons who are more enterprising, while cultivating up to 1 ha of the restored land for their own subsistence. Rather than becoming full-time peasants, the new owners have preferred playing the role of small-scale *rentier* capitalists.

## Arendatori

The second social agent that has emerged from the land reform process is the *arendatori*, the agricultural entrepreneurs who, especially in Dobrudzha and in the country's other fertile and level regions, lease the land that the new owners have no intention of tilling themselves. Many *arendatori* belonged to the local political and economic elite during socialism. They began their careers as functionaries of the now disbanded cooperatives – the TKZS – and made a strikingly swift transformation into rampant capitalists. Although the cooperatives were liquidated and all employees dismissed, the land reform did not oust the former leaders economically. The goal to 'decommunize' the countryside was not achieved, because, after a brief period of confusion, the rural *nomenklatura* quickly adapted and succeeded in appropriating the best equipment. At the same time they were able to use their networks to lease the best cultivable lands from the beneficiaries of the land restitution. The *arendatori* were able in a short time to accumulate holdings in Dobrudzha of up to 15,000 ha. Using the former members and employees of the disbanded cooperatives as hired labourers, these new entrepreneurs have engaged in highly speculative private agricultural ventures. Their strategies are analogous to those that Max Weber formulated in his notion of pre-rational capitalism (Weber 1956: vol. 2, 834), and they are readily explicable in view of the short duration of the leases (one to three years). The *arendatori* have concentrated on high-productivity annual crops and not concerned themselves with land improvement or ecological balance. Some of them have prospered and would now be willing to buy the land they farm, if the Bulgarian state were able to guarantee a more effective 'rule of law' and, in particular, a clear and indisputable definition of property rights. So long as economic difficulties and legal uncertainties persist, however, *arendatori* say that it makes no sense to pursue ownership. In any case, the present owners do not want to part with their land, since many still depend on their landholdings for subsistence food production. It is important to note that the economic success of the *arendatori* derives in part from their genuine agricultural expertise as well as from their network of privileged relations, which is crucial for marketing.

Nedko was a typical *arendator* in Dobrudzha, whom we got to know well between 1992 and 1999. We were introduced to him by an official of the regional section of the farmers' labour union in Dobric in January 1992, a few months before the passage of the first amendment to the land reform. With the rise to power of the Centre–Right coalition, there was turmoil because public opinion sensed the impending threat to the socio-economic structure of Dobrudzha. In a region traditionally labelled 'red', there were expectations of resistance if not of open rebellion against the new government's intention to enact the reformulated 1991 land reform, which until then had remained a dead letter. In this climate of dissent, which was marked by sloganeering against decollectivization and the restitution of land to the former owners, we had our first meeting with Nedko, who was reputed to be a staunch advocate of the cooperatives. We travelled to the village of O., about fifteen kilometres from Dobric, where the cooperative had its seat; it had not yet been liquidated and was still under Nedko's supervision. We had a long interview in which he explained the management policy of the cooperative in detail. According to him, its economic prosperity was due both to his expertise as an agronomist and to his loyalty to the party's directives. He went on to explain the advantages of collectivized agriculture in Dobrudzha and consequently the senselessness of the denationalization and restitution policy. At the end of the interview and in the presence of his staff, he stated that 'the members of this cooperative, with me in the lead, will never come to terms with the denationalization of agriculture. We shall carry on doing what we have done until now.'

We met him again about six months after the amended land reform had been passed. In the meantime, he had been fired, and by law the cooperative had been placed under the control of a liquidation committee, which comprised a small group of people very close to the new Centre–Right government. This second interview was held in a plain and narrow room at the former labour union headquarters' building in the centre of Dobric. There was no trace of the collectivistic triumphalism that had characterized our previous meeting. This interview was briefer than the first and much more dramatic. Nedko admitted with dismay that he was now just another unemployed person in search of a job, obviously in the agricultural sector. He was not too worried about financial problems since his wife was a teacher, but he was nonetheless determined to contrive an occupation with prospects. He did have some plans, he said, but these were not yet well defined. He stressed that the situation in Dobrudzha after the amendment of the land reform was so unsettled that he could only live day by day, that planning for the longer term was impossible. When we deliberately pressed him on the immediate consequences of denationalization in Dobrudzha, Nedko suddenly broke down, shaking his head, and declared between sobs, 'What a catastrophe ... all is lost ... they [the politicians and the liquidation committees] have destroyed everything we accomplished in years and years of work.' At the end of the interview Nedko declared dejectedly, 'Probably the only prospect is to begin an activity in the market economy (*pazarna ikonomia*).'

A few years later, in May 1996, Nedko surprised us by arranging our meeting at his former cooperative, which had been liquidated in the meantime. He greeted us in his former manager's office and we realized immediately that his spirits had improved greatly since our last meeting. He was affable and paraded his self-assurance as never before. We had barely entered the room when he began to tell us of his achievements. He explained that he had started to lease plots from the new owners to build up an acreage sufficient for a profitable agricultural enterprise. 'In Dobrudzha,' he added, 'agriculture can only work on a large scale, but those in Sofia don't understand this, so we have to organize things our own way.' As before, he went on to complain about 'politicians in the capital'. What could you expect from those who 'have never seen the countryside'? According to Nedko, this explained why obtaining financial support to buy seeds and machinery, and to pay wages, was so difficult. Notwithstanding these problems, he emphasized that he had been able to buy out cooperative property, since its successor organization lacked the means to manage it. He had also hired the best qualified workers he had known during his management of the old cooperative, together with many unskilled. At the end of our meeting, he insisted that we have lunch together at the private *mechana*, which had been recently opened in the village. The regular customers greeted him with overt respect and deference, which is unusual for Bulgarians, who generally prefer to assert their egalitarianism. We concluded that Nedko had brought us to this restaurant in order to demonstrate that he had recovered the prestige that he had enjoyed at the time of our first meeting. Of course, it was also an opportunity for him to show the owner and his customers that he had an important visitor from abroad.

We met Nedko again in 1998. He was a couple of hours late for our appointment and we had time to notice, from the increased number of employees, that the enterprise was flourishing. When Nedko arrived, he reported an acreage of 3,500 ha; business was quite good, but he had to beware of speculators from the main cities, who were trying to fix their own prices. We asked him whether he wanted to buy the land he had leased. Smiling slyly, he answered, 'The situation is still too uncertain; this is a future goal.' He then suggested that we should see how he had managed to avoid pressure from speculators and proudly took us over to the cooperative's old granaries, now restored and augmented with brand-new metal silos. We congratulated him and he remarked, 'You need good storage to avoid having to agree to the speculators' terms, as many *arendatori* and above all the cooperatives have to do.' At the end of our meeting, he asked us whether we could invite him to Switzerland (at his expense, 'of course', he stressed) because there he would be able to refine his knowledge of 'how to be a capitalist'.[1] At this point we understood that Nedko had graduated from a member of the local *nomenklatura* into a capitalist.

Nedko's career is representative. His success as an *arendator*, as he occasionally concedes, has a lot to do with the wide social network he possesses at national and at local level. After the breakdown of the socialist regime, he remained on good terms with old functionaries, some of whom managed to retain key positions in the Ministry of Agriculture while others acquired important jobs in the new banking system. Nedko professed disdain for the ruling class in the capital, but this did not inhibit him from using his connections to obtain credits at lower interest rates and important information about agricultural policy and market conditions. Meanwhile, at the local level his patronage ties to members of the old cooperative gave him the opportunity to recruit the best technicians and workers for his new enterprise. In short, the strategic position he held as a broker or 'gatekeeper' before 1989 brought him even more payoffs in the first postsocialist decade; it also brought him envy and criticism from the less fortunate, though many admired his energy and praised his loyalty to former colleagues.

By no means all ex-chairmen have been as successful as this. Spas P. represents another type, a quiet, calculating man who chose to proceed more cautiously on the basis of his kinship and family ties. When he lost his position as chairman of the regional cooperative Trade Unions in 1992, he was asked to become leader of the new cooperative in his village, 40 km from his home in Dobric, the regional capital. Declining this offer, he set about cultivating only the land he and his own family members were allocated. Later he opened a bakery, using primarily his own wheat, but his acreage was clearly insufficient. At this point he began to rent land from his neighbours, expanding to about 200 ha. To diversify production he launched a chicken farm, employing his own son-in-law as a vet. He continued to follow a step-by-step strategy: though he wanted to enlarge his acreage, when we last met him in 1998 he was afraid to take a bank loan due to high interest rates. Until his death in a car accident in summer 2000 his success was unspectacular but unbroken; this is the kind of entrepreneurialism, based on strong family links, that is less likely to attract the envy and opprobrium of others.

The career of Georgi G. is different again. When we met him for the first time in 1992 he was still chairman of the village cooperative in K. After being fired he began, helped by his brother, to rent land in and around his village of origin; he still lived in Dobric, though it was a long way from his new farmland. Many former colleagues in the cooperative of K. view Georgi as an adventurer, using all the means at his disposal to enrich himself. He is suspected of plundering the bank accounts of the cooperative just before its liquidation in order to start his *arendator* activity, and the extreme variability of his farming strategies has confirmed his reputation as an inveterate speculator. He began by renting over 1,000 ha for growing cereals but, in search of higher profit margins, soon switched into water melons with the intention of manufacturing a special kind of *rakia* spirit. This undertaking failed, the *rakia* was undrinkable and therefore also unmarketable. After this unsuccessful experience he returned to cereals and, when we last had contact in 1998, he was trying to work together with some *akuli* in order to export (probably through illegal channels) this produce to Macedonia. Unlike Nedko and Spas, this *arendator* seems to treat market economy (*pazarna ikonomia*) largely as a game of chance. Such jovial charlatanism could bring dividends in the first years of postsocialism but it was no recipe for business consolidation. The biggest obstacle to success for Georgi is his bad reputation, for his behaviour has flouted all the norms of Dobrudzhan moral economy.

On the whole, however, the *arendatori* are the clear winners of the land reform process for the time being. For the postsocialist ruling class, particularly for the political elite in power after 1997, they are an 'awkward' group that emerged unexpectedly from the dissolution of collectivized agriculture. They attract widespread antipathy, and some parliamentarians would like to eliminate them by imposing legal limits on the area of land that can be leased by a single farmer. Locally, however, some *arendatori* enjoy a more positive image, due either to a hard-working entrepreneurialism based on family labour or to a continuation of the paternalistic methods they used when they controlled the socialist cooperatives.

## Cooperatives

The cooperatives established after the land reform are based upon both the equivalent Western European institutions and the Bulgarian cooperative tradition before World War II (Giordano and Kostova 1999: 20). In practice, however, they have shown more continuity with the former socialist model. Members entrust their land to a 'presidential committee', which determines the crops to be cultivated. There is almost no participation from below in management decision-making. The fact that managers stress this point might lead us to suspect a pretext to legitimize their paternalistic control of the association, but it is hard to see how this might change. Members evidently have not grasped the 'one man, one vote' principle (Hettlage 1987), and many do not attend the general assemblies. In March 1998 we went to the village of P. where the annual general assembly was supposed to begin at 10.00 a.m. in the local culture house (*narodno chitalishte*, Kaneff 2000: 3 ff.). The attendance was so low that the meeting was cancelled as inquorate. Even members of the presidential committee failed to show up. 'Assemblies always turn out this way anyhow,' the president later reassured us.[2]

Most cooperative members are elderly retired people who were unskilled workers in the socialist cooperatives, when their jobs were secure and relatively well remunerated. Thus, they often say that 'we were better off when matters were worse'. Therefore, few of them have been affected by the urbanization process and they have remained in the villages. As Creed has noticed in a very different region (Creed 1998: 246), the main reason for choosing a cooperative is economic: lack of capital to set up a private business and insufficient property. Their decision to join a cooperative and to entrust their land to it implies a refusal to comply with the capitalist rules of the game; the Dobrudzha region is renowned for being 'red', for which their age and experience made them completely unqualified. The new cooperatives have faced formidable economic, technical and management problems. Their functionaries are unfamiliar with the new practices of market economy and have lost the battle with the *arendatori* to appropriate the best equipment of the old socialist institutions. As the managers of the cooperatives have repeatedly told us, relations with the *arendatori* are not easy, especially when buying up the new owners' land is the issue. Moreover, there is competition with the *arendatori*, although the cooperative executives are realistically aware of their technical-economic inferiority. One need only visit the cooperatives' sites to realize that these associations are inadequately qualified in every respect: rudimentary business management and accounting, ramshackle buildings, rusty and ineffective machinery, lack of storehouses, etc. However, the attitude of cooperators and functionaries towards the *arendatori* is ambivalent: on the one hand, they stand in awe and admire them for their success, but at the same time the *arendatori* are considered unreliable, dangerous and above all opportunists. Their sudden conversion to capitalism is often sarcastically stressed. The very fact that they are cooperatives is sufficient to give these organizations a bad reputation with the new owners of land, for whom they evoke the worst associations of the *ancien régime*. For many new owners, especially those of urban origin who are hardly familiar with the countryside, joining a cooperative is tantamount to wanting to be robbed all over again. Finally, the government tends to treat the cooperatives as a relic of the past and does not support them with credit or fiscal incentives. They are therefore the clear losers in the land reform process to date.

## Akuli

The success of private *arendatori* in Dobrudzha depends largely upon good relations with commercial intermediaries. These represent the fourth major social agent in contemporary Bulgarian agriculture, a group commonly labelled *akuli*, the Bulgarian term for sharks. Urban speculators have developed devious strategies for acquiring produce at low prices from cooperatives and less knowledgeable *arendatori*. Taking advantage of the inadequate storage infrastructures, these 'cell phone and Mercedes' entrepreneurs negotiate skilfully. They can afford to wait for crop deterioration to set in, in order to strike a deal at the lowest price.[3] The *akuli* control most of the major markets (Sofia, Plovdiv, Varna), and this virtual monopoly enables them to reap high profits. They have also engaged in lucrative smuggling of foodstuffs into Serbia (via Macedonia) during the UN trade embargo against that country, and into Greece, where produce is illegally 'Europeanized' before being sold on to other countries of the European Union without taxes or import duties. This illegal trafficking of cereals has caused shortages and exorbitant price rises for basic goods within Bulgaria. The ensuing public discontent was directed, however, not at the *akuli* but at the ruling political class, which was accused once again of inefficiency and dishonesty. The political class in turn considers them to be another 'awkward' group, though some members of the power elite probably profit from its illegal activities. The *akuli* tarnish Bulgaria's image by confirming the sinister stereotype of a country at the mercy of the mafia.

### Foreign entrepreneurs

Foreign entrepreneurs from Western Europe have so far played only a marginal role in Bulgarian agriculture, and in Dobrudzha so far a single British company is the only foreign presence. The low degree of transparency characterizing the land reforms, the lack of a real market for land and the risks of economic and political instability, both nationally and in the wider region, have deterred foreign investors. Those who have nonetheless entered the new market have done so in ways resembling the *arendatori*: in other words, by taking short-term leases for large tracts of land. Thus Rainbow Farming has amassed over 3,500 ha. It is viewed with suspicion both by cooperatives and *arendatori*, who dread the competition, and by the dominant political class, which does not favour the transfer of land to non-Bulgarian citizens. One reason is the fear that land market 'deregulation' could lead to a return of the 'ethnic Turks' expelled during the repressive campaign in the 1980s.

## Conclusions: legacies from the past and today's mistrust

This brief outline of the strategies employed by the new social agents in rural Dobrudzha reveals how the abstract societal project of land reform, as conceived by the political elite, diverged from the expectations and behaviour of the actors on the ground. This can be viewed in terms of the distinctions drawn by Victor Turner between 'ideology', 'situational adjustment' and ultimately 'performance' (Turner 1986). The clash between 'paysannerie pensée' and 'paysannerie vécue' takes shape in the discrepancy between legal framework and social practices, a gap which challenges the Weberian assumption that legality and legitimacy belong indissolubly together (Weber 1956: vol. 1, 124). For Weber, authority in a rational state is grounded in acceptance of the rule of law and the political and moral capacities of the state and its agents to enforce it

(Weber 1968: 151 ff.). The Bulgarian land reform and its unexpected outcomes reveal a critical divide between legality and legitimacy, because the new legal framework is constantly circumvented via social practices that agents deem more appropriate to their circumstances. In other words, legal norms and institutions coexist with other norms and social conduct regarded locally as legitimate but extra-legal or even illegal. Competition between the two is prevalent and in everyday life gives rise to misinterpretations, tensions and conflicts between the state on the one hand and citizens on the other. Many citizens in the Dobrudzha countryside perceive state laws as restrictions imposed by incompetent and dishonest politicians and bureaucrats. At best, the state and its representatives are perceived as 'distant' and 'alien' to the population's real problems. At worst, the public institutions are a foreign body, an obstacle to be avoided if at all possible. In the eyes of the new power elite and functionaries, the citizen is a person of dubious loyalty, scarcely aware of the public interest and always about to infringe the law. He or she must therefore be kept in check, and be treated more as a subject than a citizen.

Such a rift between legality and legitimacy allows the social production of mistrust to thrive in the form of negative representations and activities outside the law. The agents – whether they are owners, *arendatori* or the members of cooperatives – defend their practices as 'weapons' of the weak without which they cannot withstand the 'strong' (cf. Scott 1985). Similar processes proliferating mistrust can be found elsewhere in Bulgaria, in other postsocialist countries, and indeed in quite different contexts altogether. Such mistrust is always historically rooted and depends on what Reinhart Koselleck called the 'space of experience' shaped by history (1979: 349 ff.; cf. Ricoeur 1985: vol. 3, 301 ff.). Although this space is primarily individual, it becomes the 'cognitive capital' of many due to their shared life experiences. This cognitive capital allows people to get their bearings in the present and to plan their future. It is necessarily intersubjective, i.e. social. In the particular case of the social production of mistrust in postsocialist Bulgaria, the problem is compounded by relations of mutual suspicion between society and state throughout the centuries of Ottoman domination which in Dobrudzha took an extreme form in the *chiflik* system. Independence in 1878 did not substantially alter this relation, since up until 1944 the country was ruled by elites who largely pursued their own clientelistic strategies (Bell 1977: 8 ff.). The gap between the power elite and the citizens remained enormous in the socialist variant of paternalist cronyism. Indeed, the gap between legality and legitimacy widened in the later socialist years, as the informal economy, black market and interpersonal networking were increasingly tolerated by the ageing elites (cf. Ledeneva 1998).

All this 'real' history feeds into the 'space of experience' and the 'cognitive capital' of the new social agents. In this context it is not surprising that the land reform law has been interpreted by most of those concerned with agriculture as the project of an illegitimate state. The social production of mistrust, well tested in past performances, seems to be the fitting response to the pernicious effects of the new public institutions.

## Notes

1   Obviously, for him this country represented the epitome of the market economy, but he wasn't aware that Swiss 'peasants' are an 'endangered species' protected by federal financial assistance from the harsh laws of supply and demand.
2   In fact we were not surprised, since we had had similar experiences in Sicily (Giordano and Hettlage 1979: 192 ff.). This experience in Dobrudzha reconfirmed the hypothesis that if the basic structures of trust in the public sphere are missing, it is unrealistic to expect a true participation in cooperatives.
3   The mafia adopt the same strategy on the food and agriculture market in Sicily (Giordano and Hettlage 1975: 39 ff., 1979: 180 ff.).

## References

Bell, John D. (1977) *Peasant in Power, Alexandar Stamboliiski and the Bulgarian Agrarian National Union, 1899–1923*, Princeton: Princeton University Press.

Braudel, Fernand (1977) 'Geschichte und Sozialwissenschaften. Die "longue durée"', in Claudia Honegger (ed.) *Schrift und Materie der Geschichte. Vorschläge zur systematischen Aneignung historischer Prozesse*, Frankfurt a. M.: Suhrkamp Verlag, pp. 47–85.

Candau, Joël (1996) *Anthropologie de la mémoire*, Paris: Presses Universitaires de France.

Castellan, Georges (1991) *Histoire des Balkans XIV–XX siècle*, Paris: Fayard.

Crampton, Richard J. (1997) *A Concise History of Bulgaria*, Cambridge: Cambridge University Press.

Creed, Gerald W. (1998) *Domesticating Revolution: From Socialist Reform to Ambivalent Transition in a Bulgarian Village*, University Park: Pennsylvania State University Press.

Eberhardt, Piotr (1993) 'Depopulation processes in rural areas of East-Central Europe', *Eastern European Countryside* 0: 31–40.

Elias, Norbert (1988) *Über die Zeit*, Frankfurt a. M.: Suhrkamp Verlag.

Elster, Jon, Claus Offe and Ulrich K. Preuss (1997) *Institutional Design in Post-Communist Societies: Repairing the Ship at Sea*, Cambridge: Cambridge University Press.

Gambetta, Diego (1992) *La mafia siciliana. Un'industria della protezione privata*, Torino: Einaudi.

Giordano, Christian (1996) 'The past in the present: actualized history in the social construction of reality', in Don Kalb, Hans Marks and Herman Tak (eds) 'Historical anthropology: the unwaged debate', *Focaal, tijdschrift voor antropologie* 26/7: 97–107.

Giordano, Christian and Hettlage, Robert (1975) *Mobilisierung oder Scheinmobilisierung? Genossenschaften und traditionelle Sozialstruktur am Beispiel Siziliens*, Basel: Social Strategies, Monographs on Sociology and Social Policy, vol. 1.

——(1979) *Persistenz im Wandel. Das Mobilisierungspotential sizilianischer Genossenschaften. Eine Fallstudie zur Entwicklungsproblematik*, Tübingen: J.C.B. Mohr, Paul Siebeck, Heidelberger Sociologica 17.

Giordano, Christian and Dobrinka Kostova (1995) 'Bulgarie, une réforme agraire sans paysans', in Edouard Conte and Christian Giordano (eds) 'Paysans au-délà du mur', *Etudes Rurales* 138/39/40: 157–71.

——(1999) 'The crisis of the Bulgarian cooperatives in the 1990s', *Journal of Rural Cooperation* 27(1): 17–29.

Hannerz, Ulf (1998a) 'Transnational research', in R.H. Bernard (ed.) *Handbook of Methods in Cultural Anthropology*, Walnut Creek, London and New Delhi: Altamira Press, pp. 235–56.

——(1998b) 'Of correspondents and collages', *Anthropological Journal on European Cultures* 7(1): 91–109.

Hettlage, Robert (1987) *Genossenschaftstheorie und Partizipationsdiskussion*, Göttingen: Vandenhoeck and Ruprecht.

Kaneff, Deema (2000) *Property, Work and Local Identity*, Working Paper no. 15, Halle/Saale: Max Planck Institute for Social Anthropology.

Koselleck, Reinhart (1979) *Vergangene Zukunft. Zur Semantik geschichtlicher Zeiten*, Frankfurt a. M.: Suhrkamp Verlag.

Ledeneva, Alena V. (1998) *Russia's Economy of Favours: Blat, Networking and Informal Favours*, Cambridge: Cambridge University Press.

Linz, Juan J. and Alfred Stepan, (eds) (1996) *Problems of Democratic Transition and Consolidation: Southern Europe, South America, and Post-Communist Europe*, Baltimore and London: Johns Hopkins University Press.

Matvejevic, Predrag (1992) *Otvorena Pisma*, Zagreb: publisher unknown.

Minkov, Mihail and Luzov, I. (eds) (1979) *Pojava i razvitie na kooperativnoto zemedelie v Balgarija (The Appearance and Development of Collective Cultivation in Bulgaria)*, Sofia: Zamizdat.

Mollov, Jordan (1930) 'Dnechnoto sastojanie na Balgarskoto zemedelie i meroprijatija za negovoto podobrjavane (The present development of Bulgarian agriculture and the mechanisms to better it)', *Spisanie na balgarskoto ikonomicesko druzestvo* 19(4): 181–212.

Ricoeur, Paul (1985) *Temps et récit*, Paris: Editions du Seuil, 3 volumes.

Scott, James C. (1985) *Weapons of the Weak: Everyday Forms of Peasant Resistance*, New Haven: Yale University Press.

Shanin, Teodor (1972) *The Awkward Class: Political Sociology of Peasantry in a Developing Society: Russia 1010–1925*, Oxford: Clarendon.

Tilly, Charles (1985) 'War making and state making as organized crime', in P.B. Evans, D. Rüschemeyer and T. Skocpol (eds) *Bringing the State Back In*, Cambridge; Cambridge University Press.

Tonev, Velko (1995) *Balgarskoto Chernomorie prez vazrazhdaneto (The Bulgarian Black Sea during the Renaissance)*, Sofia: Marin Drinov.

Turner, Victor (1986) *The Anthropology of Performance*, New York: Paj Publications.

Weber, Max (1956) *Wirtschaft und Gesellschaft*, Tübingen: J.C.B. Mohr und Paul Siebeck Verlag, 2 volumes.

——(1968) *Soziologie – Weltgeschichtliche Analysen – Politik*, Stuttgart: Alfred Kröner Verlag.

# Part II

# Dimensions of inequality

## Gender, class and 'underclass'

How does one measure the widening social inequalities of the postsocialist years? What gender differences are left out of statistical analyses of aggregate income distribution? Is the concept of class still helpful? Are inter-ethnic differences also widening, e.g. through the emergence of new ghettos?

Socialism was supposed to destroy earlier forms of hierarchy, which ideologists usually labelled feudal (except in those parts where capitalist classes had already appeared on the scene). Political pressure and coercion imposed levelling and high rates of both geographical and social mobility, although these began to decline in the later decades of socialism. The impact of the market economy plunged millions into poverty. Postsocialist regimes, increasingly constrained by international forces, have curtailed state redistribution, restored privileges to churches and other bodies, promoted private education, and generally contributed to a climate in which many citizens feel excluded from their national society, which they perceive to be institutionalizing unfamiliar inequalities.

Gender inequalities certainly existed under socialism, since women always bore the brunt of domestic burdens, but they were also given considerable support in the 'public' domain. Drawing mainly on her fieldwork in industrialized central Poland, Frances Pine shows that postsocialist redundancies have disadvantaged women and obliged them to turn instead to small-scale farming. More generally, households survive by turning 'inwards' and expanding the activities of their 'private' sphere. This sphere was important under socialism (in other, less industrialized regions it was dominant), but it has of necessity become much more visible lately. Pine shows that different 'gendered spaces of work' penalize women; farming, for them, is not separable from 'kin work', it cannot be a 'job' in the way it is for men. Her interviewees express their anger that their state is not meeting its basic obligations, that it is propelling its 'children' backwards. There is 'ambiguity' towards some of these developments, since people may also take pride in their creative accomplishments in the domestic domain. However, anger, resignation and selective nostalgia for the socialist era seem more significant in defining the new subjectivities. In an ironic shift from the days when the private domain was defined in opposition to an alien socialist state, it is the seductive consumerism of 'the West' that is increasingly imagined as a threatening 'other'.

David Kideckel's contribution outlines the on-going 'sub-alternity' of former chemical workers and miners in Romania, a country which has experienced both socialist industrialization and postsocialist deindustrialization in their most crude and cruel forms. Kideckel compares the current 'neo-capitalism' to the 'neo-serfdom' experienced by this region in the past: once again, Eastern Europe has to endure an oppressive, inhumane variant of a system that is subject to quite different norms in the West. Some of those made redundant have tried unsuccessfully to return to their villages; some have become labour migrants to Italy. The position is marginally less bleak for the former chemical workers, where household support networks function better; but levels of psychological distress are everywhere high, workers are starved of information, exploited in the black market and scapegoated in the new 'open' media. Workers' symbols have been rendered worthless and are now turned against them. They have become the demons of a new ideology.

Finally in this section Michael Stewart addresses the problems of another group commonly demonized in postsocialist Central and Eastern Europe. There is no doubting the extreme social deprivation experienced by many Roma, but Stewart goes against the grain of much social science analysis by rebutting 'underclass' approaches. In his view, such approaches have been too easily distorted for dubious political purposes; they only distract attention from the specifics of Roma social relations. To view Roma as an underclass or *lumpenproletariat* has the effect of distancing them and reinforcing exclusionary practices. Eastern European Roma are not, according to the available ethnographic evidence, perceived by their neighbours as an alien, 'racialized' group. Policies based on such assumptions – widely shared both by external observers and concerned local intellectuals – could therefore be dangerously counterproductive, creating racism where it does not exist. Stewart suggests that Roma creativity and ingenuity, including behavioural patterns typically condemned by outsiders, can provide group members with the social capital they need to prosper in the new forms of economy.

Chapter 5

# Retreat to the household?

Gendered domains in postsocialist
Poland

*Frances Pine*

## Introduction

The rapid and often quite brutal 'shock therapy' implemented in Poland after
1989 radically altered both the shape of public life and the domestic relationships and sense of private personhood of much of the population.[1] In the
highly industrialized region in and around the city of Łódź, the effects of
deindustrialization were immediate and highly visible. By 1991, when I began
to do research in this region, many of the old textile factories were operating
with severely curtailed labour forces, or were shut down altogether; the buildings had a deserted, neglected and decrepit appearance, far removed from the
hubs of activity and productivity of socialist times. The *Biuro Pracy* (employment centre), where the unemployed went to register and to claim benefits,
was full to overflowing. Indeed, this often seemed to be the only public space
bustling with people and motion. Old women and mothers carrying young
children could be seen begging on the streets, something unimaginable under
socialism. A plethora of small shops and fast food outlets, selling Western
and Western-style goods and products, sprang up almost overnight. The
contrast between these chic retail outlets, the huge empty state department
stores and the open markets and street corners, where rural women and
'Russian' traders sold their fruits and vegetables and their small and often
shoddy wares, created a striking and evocative symbolic mapping of the new
local economy.

Men and women employed in industry or in the service sector found themselves suddenly without work, while those still working were living with the
threat of unemployment, for the first time in their lives. In the face of this
change and uncertainty, women in particular appeared paralysed by a kind of
shocked trauma (cf. Vitebsky, this volume). Many of those I interviewed in
1991 and 1992 talked about being prescribed 'tablets' for depression. Some
spoke of sitting at home all day, seeing no one other than their immediate
family members, crying all the time; others said that they had to stay strong for
their children and their mothers, but they had no one to talk to and felt they
were coming apart, silently, inside.

When they described their situations, women separated their worlds into that of work and that of home and family. When they talked about their work and the experience of becoming unemployed, they mourned their workplace friendships and their sense that work was the space where they were able to act as individuals, away from the routine demands of motherhood and domestic responsibility. Their stories were couched in terms of loss: loss of income, loss of self-esteem, an incredible sense of loss of the sociality and close relations of the workplace. These were personal stories, stories of the individual self. When the same women moved on to talk about their situations at home, they used quite a different voice, which was, I think, that of kinship and kin obligation and responsibility. All perceived their homes and families to be threatened; they were terrified that they would be unable to provide for their children or to care for their aged parents. They feared being unable to pay utility bills and rents, or even being unable to buy groceries. Those who were receiving unemployment benefits, family assistance or pensions maintained that such income was barely enough to buy shoes for their children, let alone cover the family's subsistence.

By the mid-1990s, the tone of women's stories was changing. Loss, anxiety and betrayal were still topics frequently discussed and mulled over, but in both interviews and kitchen table conversations other themes were becoming more dominant. Women talked at length about food: where to get good, cheap, local food, and how they were suspicious of foreign, imported produce; how home-grown food and home-made things were the best, and which particular recipes for canning, bottling and preserving were the most satisfactory. Among themselves, they exchanged plant cuttings and seeds, swapped home remedies for common and chronic ailments, and pooled information about sewing patterns, recipes and other home-based activities. It seemed as if, having been excluded from the public domain of production, they were consciously rejecting the world of consumption (particularly of foreign goods) and in its place building complicated structures and networks for subsistence production within and around the household. For these women, the gendered nature of work, space and time had been drastically altered by the new economic order, perhaps irrevocably.

It is clear from the existing work on postsocialist countries that gender is a critical issue in the period of 'transition', not only because it penetrates and affects almost every aspect and level of social and cultural process and practice, but also because the move from socialism to the market economy and new political forms has particular consequences both for gender construction and for gender inequality.[2] In this chapter I focus primarily on women, and on some of the implications of what appears to be a growing exclusion of women from the public domain. Similar themes arise in the research literature on both gender and on women throughout the postsocialist world, from Germany to Central Asia, and from remote rural areas to central urban spaces. Most analyses paint a bleak portrait of current trends and future possibilities and focus on women's exclusion and privation in the emerging political economies. They stress the exclusion of women from civil society and full citizenship (Einhorn 1993; Watson 1993, 1996), their disproportionate unemployment in formal terms and their over-representation in part-time, *ad hoc* and badly paid work (Bridger *et al.* 1996), their increasing association with subsistence rather than market-orientated farming (Pine 1996a), their responsibility for types of care previously provided by the socialist state (Haney 1999) and their vulnerability in terms of domestic violence and personal safety (Atwood 1997). A lot of attention has been paid to the sexualization of the workplace, and the way that this serves as a barrier to the employment of middle-aged and older women (Bridger *et al.* 1996; Kay 1997; Pine 1996a, 1998). The growth of pornography and what seems to be an ever expanding arena for sex work has been discussed, particularly in the context of debates over censorship on the one hand and survival strategies on the other (Shreeves 1992; Baban 2000). New discourses of motherhood and what can best be termed patriarchy, and the extent to which these are implicated in everything from loss of reproductive rights to new nationalisms, have also been examined (Pinnick 1997; Haney 1999; Maleck-Lewy and Ferree 2000; Wolchik 2000; Zielińska 2000; Pine 2001). Not a cheerful picture, any of this.

But it strikes me that out of this rather untidy list we can see several themes emerging. When I look at material from my own work in rural Poland, I am constantly struck by the depth and breadth of regional variation, even within this one country, in ideas and ideologies about gender, gendered domains, and what we might call work practices and practices/production of the self. However, in some critical senses there are remarkable similarities between regions and across countries; these are particularly clear in relation to the structural constraints facing men and women in the context of deindustrialization, unemployment and the collapse of collectivized agriculture, but there are also common threads which are harder to separate and define, concerning senses of loss and uncertainty, fear of chaos, and impending danger from the outside – danger which may take the form of 'mafia', the army or police, or random drunks and thieves, or which may be represented in less embodied ways, as arising from pollution of the environment, poisonous food or hazardous commodities. Some of these fears and senses of loss are obviously well grounded in the reality of lived experience, 'of actually existing postsocialism'. They tend, however, to be exaggerated, blown up and dwelt on as metaphors expressing a more general sense of unease with and in the world. Further, it seems that these ways of seeing are linked to gender in particular ways, and gender is often a critical part of the form that they take. Here I have in mind, for example, ideas that food from the outside is dangerous, while *nasza* (our) food, which is also maternal/mother's food, is safe (see Haukanes 2001). Or we might consider what people are obliquely expressing about their sense of personal security when they talk about their fears of being unable to care for and feed their children (Pilkington 1997; Pine 1998), or their anxiety about the negative effects of dangerous chemicals, contacted through piecework done at home (Pine 1997). In his article for this volume, Vitebsky writes about the loss that parents in northern Russia experience when giving away their children; this abandonment of children, of the next generation, can be seen as the starkest statement of lack of faith or belief in the future. In all of these conversations, it seems to me, what is being addressed implicitly is a pending or present sense of total despair: despair about loss of fertility, threat to reproduction, failure to care for, and hence abandonment and loss of, children. In this paper I want to consider ways in which people attempt to deal with such loss and fear, and with the situations that give rise to them.

It is often in the context of gender and kinship practices that concepts concerning morality, entitlement and trust, and ideas about labour, the meaning of work and the negotiation of working lives, are brought together. The ways in which the conceptual spaces feed into each other, and how the state/the outside world/the wider economy impinge upon both, are integral pieces of the puzzle of gender construction, gendered experience and gendered practices in rural areas. Here it is particularly important to explore which particular forces and struc-tures, both internal and external, make redefining work and work practices so difficult and painful for some people, in some regions, while others, in other contexts or other regions, are proving to be adept at all sorts of entrepreneurial activities and different types of work.[3]

I shall consider three topic clusters that highlight basic issues around gender, particularly in rural areas, in the actually existing post-1989 world. The first is concerned with the changing nature of work and labour, and with ways in which local understandings of work in relation to the gendered person affect practice. Connected to this is a new division between public and private, or public and domestic, or inside and outside. Renegotiations of work, entitle-ments and production and reproduction are generating new sorts of relatedness, in both rural and urban spaces. Finally, both of these themes link directly to the spread of, and sometimes the opposition to, Western ideas and practices pertaining to the market and consumption. In the postsocialist world, particu-larly, any discussion of continuity and change is complicated by the fact that many social and economic processes, which appear to be quite new, demon-strate under closer scrutiny a marked similarity to older relations and practices, while others which appear to be continuities are taking place in contexts which are drastically different from any which previously existed. More than a world moving forwards, or even a world turned upside down, we seem to have before us a world moving sideways and backwards, simultaneously and often skewed. The ways that people talk about the past and the present, and their ambiva-lence about both 'modernity' and 'tradition', reflect this confusion.

## Work practices and ambiguous modernity

I would make two initial points here. First, it is clear that age and generation are inextricably linked to gender in moulding the processes which are now emerging in terms of work, access and eligibility. Other factors, primarily class (for lack of a better word), and place (city/country, east/west, central/periph-eral) and, connected to both, mobility, also continue to constrain the choices available to both women and men. Second, gender relations are being negoti-ated not only in the current context of post-1989 change, but also in relation to the memory of, and often the leftovers from, half a century of socialism. The inequities of gender relations in this period, particularly the double and triple burdens shouldered by women, are well known (Corrin 1992; Rai et al. 1992). However, the fact that legislation existed in nearly all of the socialist states to safeguard the reproductive rights of women, to guarantee employment to all, male and female, and to place various aspects of social caring, including child-care and care of the ill and the elderly, under the umbrella of the state, meant that ideas and ideologies about gender equality were present and visible in public discourse. While these were often inefficient or deficient in their imple-mentation, at a very basic level such rights and provisions were taken for granted as part of daily life and entitlement (like electricity or running water, which were similarly there, or at least planned even when they didn't always work in practice). The retraction of the state has either left a void in these areas, or it has replaced universal *entitlement* with new criteria, often market driven, of individual *eligibility* (Einhorn 1993; Bridger et al. 1996; Kay 2000; Gal and Kligman 2000). In rural areas particularly, what this retraction of state institutions and influence seems to lead to is not a filling of that empty public space with the associations of civil society, as many Western commentators and observers anticipated, but rather an expansion of household production and kinship obligations.

In one sense what appears to have happened in rural areas, very crudely, has been a retreat into subsistence production – i.e. *back* into the old-style peasant farm. However, rather than a straightforward reversion to old household production forms, this has been accompanied by a simultaneous drive towards new or more elaborate forms of consumption, urban values and exchanges, highly individualistic entrepreneurial activities, movement and mobility. In other words, things appear concurrently to be going back to a former time – feudal and pre-industrial are the ages most frequently evoked – and entering the chaotic and fragmented post-Fordist industrial globalism of the twenty-first century. At first glance, this may seem like an uneasy voyage into not-so-parallel universes, but perhaps the two are not as incompatible as they seem.

Here it is useful to look at the ways that the people who are experiencing acute change and upheaval in their daily lives themselves talk about and respond to this. During the initial period of economic uncertainty, right across the former socialist bloc, two quite different responses seemed to be common. One was anger at being forced back, from a position of modernity, to one which was seen as backward, and *pre*-modern. In Myriam Hivon's work on early decol-lectivization in Russia, she refers to the protests of milkmaids that they had been highly skilled workers, but now they were being pushed out of their work back into the household (Hivon 1995). In rather a different context, Hilary

Pilkington (1997) describes the disappointment and anger expressed by returning 'Russian' migrants, who had been relatively affluent and well established in their working lives in Central Asia, and suddenly found that on their 'return' they were seen as backward and expected to live in barely renovated cowsheds in remote rural areas. Again, people had the feeling of being pushed back into what seemed to them to be the past. In Poland, there was a dramatic episode involving Jacek Kuroń, the then Minister of Social Services, who had engineered the first set of postsocialist social benefits and was generally regarded as highly sympathetic to workers and peasants. When he visited a former collective farm and was asked by the laid-off workers what they were supposed to do now, he replied in effect that with a cottage, a piece of land and a cow, they should be all right. The workers were furious, shouted that they were not peasants and had no intention of 'returning' to the backward way of life of smallholders, and proceeded to subject Kuroń to an onslaught of abuse, threats and flying objects.

It is clear from all of these and many similar accounts that people valued their 'modern' life/work and had no intention of being shoved in a direction they saw as backward, at least not quietly and not without protest. However, other accounts from the same period reported a growing emphasis on taking up 'traditional' skills, on producing on a very small scale within the house or the community, and on emphasizing the superiority of home production and the shoddy nature of Western imports (see Humphrey 1995; Hivon 1995; Pine 1998). What people seem to be expressing is an ambivalence about both modernity and tradition, because both have particular political and social connotations: if they are forced back into the traditional household, they will lose what made them modern; conversely, if they choose to go back to the household, they will rediscover the value of their own traditions. I shall return to this ambivalence and the ambiguity it produces below.

In Łódź and the towns and villages around it I collected stories and work histories from women who had lost their jobs in the textile trade and other state enterprises as a result of restructuring, forced redundancies and factory closures. I have discussed this process, and the strategies developed by women to attempt to cope, elsewhere (Pine 1996a, 1998). Here I am concerned with ways in which space, work and ideas about morality or entitlement informed, and were informed by, gendered ideas and practices during the socialist period, and what the repercussions of the post-1989 restructuring have been for this.

The textile industry developed in the Łódź region, on the western borders of the Russian Partition, in the nineteenth century, and from that time on provided employment for workers from both the towns and the surrounding countryside. Here, as elsewhere in the world, textile production relied heavily on female labour. Agriculture was primarily associated with men, as both landholders and heads of farming households, despite the fact that women were responsible for a large proportion of the actual labour.[4] This meant that, whereas masculinity and male value in rural areas were constructed around provision and visible agency through farming, through being a productive, often skilled and always hard-working member of the farming community, femininity was more fragmented, divided between a domestic (kinship) self and a public (productive) self. Men could farm or work in waged labour and industry, and could move between the two sectors, quite visibly, with a highly integrated sense of self or personhood. Women's labour occupied different gendered spaces, a sphere (domestic/private) concerned with household provision, kinship, what could be considered reproduction, and a sphere (public) centred around production, waged labour and strong social ties outside kinship. As I have argued elsewhere (Pine 1996a), although they were essential members of the agricultural labour force, and worked exceedingly long hours in the farm yard and the fields, their labour was masked by kinship. Farming for women was a part of, and not separable from, kin work and kin obligations generally; it was simply part of what a woman, as the wife, mother or sister of a farmer, did.

Unemployment had serious repercussions for both men and women, in terms of loss of earning and attached 'perks'; it also brought about a loss of status, in the eyes of the community or as a perception of self or both. For women this latter aspect was often more intense, because the alternatives open to them were more limited than those available to men, and because work in the public sector had provided them with a whole range of ways of making relatedness which were not automatically present in their farm and home work (see Pine 1996a). Relations on the factory floor, what might be considered the social relations of work ranging from mutual help and support in both emotional and economic terms, to teaching and sharing skills between generations of workers, covering for and protecting each other at work, and socializing outside work were immensely important in women's daily lives; in the stories they told, and in their accounts of their working lives, they repeatedly stressed their skill and strength, their intimate friendships with other women, and their completeness as social beings. Anna Pollert (1981) has described the feminization or domestication of the factory workplace in the cigarette factory she studied in Bristol; in similar ways, the women to whom I spoke had transformed their workplace into a particular kind of social space. For women, there was usually no equivalent social space located in farming. Hence, unemployed rural women took little account of the hours they spent milking cows, tending chickens, planting potatoes, raking hay and weeding, and described themselves as 'sitting at home' and as 'not working'; their male equivalents were far more likely to say that they were now working in agriculture, or running the farm.

Insofar as they had ready access to food, rural women acknowledged themselves to be more secure than their urban friends and kin, but in the face of falling prices for local produce, they too feared that they would be unable to pay for their children's clothes, for family healthcare and medication, for their children's most basic school books. Unlike their accounts of work, their reflections on their current situations stressed motherhood and other close kin relationships, the importance of maternal nurture, and their fears of being unable to provide for their families. They spoke of their own futures as a blank, with no possibility of further work, and no option other than sitting at home. Their dreams, tellingly, were for their children. 'It's not going to get better. Not in my lifetime. I won't work again,' said Kasia, an unemployed seamstress, but immediately qualified this with: 'Of course I have hopes and dreams – not for myself, you understand, but for my children. We have to believe and dream for our children don't we? Or we have nothing.'

As this material indicates, the ideological and emotional importance placed on women as mothers is enormous. In this ideology, motherhood is about nurturing and feeding, both in the sense of the individual mother feeding her own child and of the nation as mother feeding the people. The images that I evoked at the beginning of this chapter – of fear of dangerous (outside, polluted) food, of risk posed to maternal fertility and children's wellbeing from (outside) pollution, of being unable to provide even the basics for one's children – all refer to the threats to children which the postsocialist order is seen either as creating or as failing to prevent. Children in this sense seem to me to refer both to actual children – the future, the next generation – and by extension to the family and the entire society and *its* future. The emphasis is on governmental betrayal of the future: by failing to protect mothers and children, and by selling off the nation's inheritance. In other words, the state is seen as failing to fulfil an implicit reciprocity in which it repaid production with care and protection, especially of women and children. Two comments made to me in the early 1990s make these accusations explicitly. Janka, a grandmother in her seventies, spoke angrily about the proposed legislation to curtail abortion: 'I remember what it was like before the war. Women can't afford to have more children. They are going to go to old witches [i.e. backstreet abortionists] again, and they are going to die.' Ewa, a middle-aged unemployed weaver, expressed her fear and uncertainty about whether she could meet the costs of private medicine and school books which were no longer being provided by the state: 'My mother has had a heart attack and the doctor has given her a prescription for foreign medicine. It would cost everything we earn from milk sales. And then I have to buy my daughter's books. I can't do both. There's simply not enough money.' In the eyes of both women, the state had reneged on its obligation to provide and protect.

## Domains of work

It is important to bear in mind that gender is not the only factor implicated in the changing social order, and women are not the only ones adversely affected. I would argue, however, that the claim which has been made by various feminist analysts that the new democracy is a 'masculinist' democracy (Einhorn 1993; Watson 1993; Gal and Kligman 2000) is correct in two important senses. First, regardless of individual successes or failures, many of the structures and mechanisms associated with building the privatized, market economy favour what are established male practices and prerogatives and limit those of women. Second, the division between public and private, which pre-dates socialism as an ideological construct but was exacerbated under socialism, is being reformulated in ways which exaggerate the established tendency to associate women with domestic and household activities and production, and which, conversely, make it easier for men than for women to move horizontally within the public domain.[5] While both women and men experienced immediate and immense losses as a result of restructuring in the Łódź region, one aspect of this was a relocation of female activities – from waged work in the public, state sector to caring for children, the ill and the elderly in the domestic, household sector. In other words, the gender order itself shifted, and in a way which effectively excluded many women from full public participation and over-emphasized their domestic participation.

Anthropologists have frequently argued that under socialism the private domestic world of intimate, face-to-face relations was the site of resistance to the state and the centre of the moral economy (Kligman 1988; Wedel 1992; Pine 1996b; Yurchak 1997; Ledeneva 1998). However, as I have suggested elsewhere (Pine 1998, 1999), the morality and obligations of kinship tend to emphasize collective good; it was often only in their work outside the domestic domain that women, particularly, were able to realize a sense of individual autonomy. Under socialism, the balance between what might be considered the labour of kinship and the labour of the individual citizen produced two rather different senses of self for women: the mother/daughter/wife and the productive individual.[6] The reciprocal obligations of kinship might provide the moral core of relatedness, but they are also the ties that bind. In their work relations and activities in the state sector women were able to realize a kind of individual value which transcended, without excluding, the prescriptions of kinship and gender located in the domestic domain. As skilled weavers and seamstresses, they were able to bring earnings into the household, which fulfilled their obligations as mothers and wives. They were also able to define themselves positively, as individuals, in terms of their work.

> [Waged] work is important because of the earnings. We needed my earnings, and it is difficult to cope without them. But work also means more than that to women. Perhaps some women are happy sitting at home playing with their children, but it's not enough for me. Work is necessary for me. I need to go away from the house. I need adult company, something of my own. I am a weaver. That's what I do.

Here, Barbara, who had worked in the same textile factory from the time she left school at 17 until she lost her job in her mid-thirties, clearly located her social and personal identity both in the household/family and in her individual work and personal relationships around work. In my interviews with unemployed women, these same sentiments, and even the same phrasing, kept recurring.

In Poland in the early 1990s, in conjunction with additional economic hardship resulting from rising consumer prices and a massive increase in availability of expensive and other, cheaper, consumer goods from countries such as Turkey, China and Vietnam, there was an expansion (efflorescence) of the domestic domain. This can perhaps best be understood in terms of the different types of moralities and entitlements associated with the world of public/state sector work and the world of kin or domestic-based production. Under socialism, work generally was couched in terms of strongly ingrained ideas about legitimacy and entitlement and (public) value. Loss of work in the public domain also implied loss of certain kinds of relations and of ways of being related – those mediated through shared space, daily experience and labour not based specifically on kinship and family. Danka, a woman of 40 who had lost her factory job the previous year, talked to me about her work and what losing it had changed for her:

> Oh, we had fun at work. We laughed a lot together. That is to say, the work was really hard, physically hard, you know? But we looked after each other. If one girl was ill, we others would cover for her, do her work, so the directors wouldn't know. Oh, and we went out together after work – sometimes for tea and cakes and sometimes – you know? – for vodka. Now? No, I don't see any of them any more. It costs too much to go into town. And I have no money to go out. And what would we talk about now? I'm embarrassed.

Hence, I argue, rather than turn to other institutions in the public domain, or work towards creating new ones, as theories of civil society might anticipate, people like Danka frequently turned away from the 'outside', into the 'inside'; through this process, the domestic domain and kinship and family came to carry an enormous and expanded load in social, economic and emotional terms. In both moral and practical terms, the legitimacy of the public domain, including the state in both an abstract sense and a practical one, was seen to be damaged if not destroyed altogether by its failure to meet its side of an implicit social contract.

Underlying the frequently told stories of enormous loss was a strong sense of outrage about moral entitlement under siege: people who had worked all their lives, with the belief that labour entitles the worker to subsistence and support from the state, now found themselves relying on state support which was barely adequate for survival, or simply plummeting into poverty. In equal measure they blamed the new state – as Jurek, a middle-aged mechanic still in work, put it to me in the early 1990s, 'Wałęsa has betrayed Poland; he has sold our inheritance (*majatek*) to the West!' – and those who, without working themselves, were profiting from the privatization process – foreign speculators, new *biznes* men, former party directors and *nomenklatura* turned new private owners, Roma, mafia, etc. These are Jurek's sentiments again:

I've always worked, always been hardworking. But look at my own tiny flat. And the *biznes* men and the gypsies, they do no honest work, they steal, and deal, and they have those huge houses. And look at their cars!

Despite their very bleak view of their place in the new order, many people I spoke to were from the beginning of postsocialism exercising considerable, often imaginative agency in developing strategies to fill the economic gaps left by loss of work. Rural women became involved in informal marketing of farm produce, in complicated kin networks of exchanges of food, childcare and information. Some were able to get *ad hoc* part-time or temporary work in small private sweatshops which were built up in private houses. These activities were, however, rarely seen as productive or valuable in the way that full-time employment in the state sector had been. The networks of trade and exchange which developed were part of the private, hidden world of home and kinship. Even paid labour in private sweatshops, because it was often for kin and because it took place not in appropriate work space, a factory, but in an inappropriate one, domestic space, was seen as falling into this category.

Because of the structure of agriculture in this region, for men the farm often *was* the workplace, in a visible and recognized sense.[7] On the one hand, this meant that for men involved in farming, a retreat to the household was not initially an issue: as I have already suggested, the public/private boundary did not have the same implications for them as it did for women. (By the mid-1990s, however, as I shall discuss below, an increasing emphasis on household production by both men and women was becoming apparent.) On the other hand, the situation of men who had been full-time industrial workers, and who were not also farmers, was very similar to that of women. They lost their ability to provide adequately. For such men, the worst outcome of unemployment was seen as being forced to depend on state benefit or on working for kin with farms. I heard many accounts of men reacting to unemployment by drinking excessively; domestic violence was also often linked in people's accounts to unemployment and hardship. Others, rather than retreating to the household, left it, either temporarily as economic migrants, or permanently.

However, men also had more options than women in terms of casual work, in areas such as driving and building. Although the socialized side of agriculture underwent a process of privatization similar in some senses to that in the factories, men who were already involved in farming were able to transfer their skills and statuses more easily. So, when the agricultural cooperative in the village I lived in was closed down, three men managed to build up private businesses by buying up the combines and other big machines and hiring them out, with their labour, to their neighbours.[8] Others bought land formerly owned by the cooperative, and set themselves up as specialist dairy or poultry farmers. This is a very similar process to that which took place in the auctioning off of factory equipment; for some people, primarily men, such moves provided the productive means to enter into the new private market economy. For various structural reasons (lack of collateral, inability to secure loans or financial backing, lack of connections and insider knowledge), there was little if any scope for women to make this kind of investment, although they may often have been invisible contributors in terms of both labour and decision-making.[9]

By the mid-1990s, a noticeable shift had taken place in the responses and strategies of both women and men. By then it had become clear that unemployment, deindustrialization, failing markets for local produce and a new world of consumption to which few could afford access were not temporary adjustments but had become entrenched. Many farms in the area, particularly the smaller, non-specialist ones, were scaling down their enterprises and moving away from production for sale towards subsistence or semi-subsistence farming. It is at this point that a more general retreat to the household set in, manifested in terms of both production and consumption practices. Increasing time and energy were spent on producing in the household, to provide for needs that would previously have been met partly or completely by the market. Throughout the summer months, all members of extended family households, often joined by urban kin, would spend their time bottling, canning and preserving the fruits and vegetables they had harvested for the winter. Many made their own wine. Clothes were sewn at home, rather than purchased, and kitchen haircuts, permanents and colouring replaced visits to the hairdresser. This was clearly presented as a highly politicized rejection of consumerism. Metaphors of danger and pollution from the outside abounded: foreign foodstuffs sold in the shop were said to be full of dangerous chemicals, past their sell-by date or simply inferior. People lamented the lack of cheap, good Polish food and commodities; when an item could not be produced at home but had to be purchased, they would spend hours and even days searching the shops and marketplaces for the best, cheapest, Polish goods. Where foreign goods had previously been a source of prestige and a sign of affluence, they were now conspicuously rejected. Goods and produce spoken of as *nasza*, meaning either produced in the household or Polish, depending on the context, were shown off to visitors.[10] This coincided with a more general pride in the home and an emphasis on DIY transformations, often based on images in the growing number of 'home and garden' magazines, which also tended to stress 'Polish' rather than 'foreign' style.

## Westernization and new subjectivities

The associations here between economic hardship, anti-Western sentiment, and a kind of domestic, small manifestation of nationalism are clear. However, I think these practices can also be seen as a new way of demonstrating labour and skill – a kind of reclaiming, primarily but by no means exclusively by women, of domestic and farming space as a place where people can be and are visibly productive. Secure employment and stable farming with a safe market, supported by the state, to which everyone was entitled, had all been lost. What people remember about socialism is a pride in production and in their labour and also a sense of being part of a project that was *modern* and directed towards the general good. When people speak angrily about Poland being turned into a 'Third World' country, their anger is both about economic decline, about what they see as a two-sided coin of dependency and exploitation, and about being transformed not into the (even more modern) capitalist future but back into a pre-socialist past. The traumas of the initial period of deindustrialization were enormous, for both men and women. The more gradual erosion of farming has been less obvious and dramatic, but equally difficult. Some people, the real tragedies and victims of this new world, have fallen off the social map. Alcoholism, drug abuse and homelessness are the clearest manifestations of this, but other, more ordinary patterns are both more insidious and more common. The feminization of poverty, particularly in the case of lone unemployed mothers, is one such. Other casualties of change are middle-aged women unable to enter any of the new types of work which call for computer and IT skills, languages and, all too often, a 'young, attractive' appearance. All of these women rely on social security, which is never enough to live on, and on 'help' from kin. The obvious success stories in this region are the few, mostly men, who have been able to benefit from the dismantling of state industrial and agricultural enterprises and set themselves up as businessmen or entrepreneurs. For most people, the retraction of the state has resulted in the development of diversified survival strategies, many of them rooted in subsistence and in *ad hoc*, multiplex forms of work, including home-work, trade and marketing.

Under socialism, the domestic domain was constantly juxtaposed to, and positively judged in relation to, the state. In the ideological battles of the Cold War, the West may have been the official 'enemy other', but at a local level, within Poland, that 'other' was far more frequently imagined as Soviet Russia and, closer to home, as the Soviet-backed Polish state. Because of the corruption and inefficiency of what was often perceived as an occupying state, people felt morally entitled to take what they felt was owed to them, and to generate their own economic networks (Pawlik 1992; Firlik and Chłopecki 1992). Even in areas such as Łódź and its surrounds, where support of socialism was and continues to be strong, people felt that they had the right to reprimand the state when it failed in its duty to the people. Hence, political protest, factory occupations and strikes in Łódź from the 1950s onwards focused on the failure of the state to look after the nation. People worked to feed the nation; it was the responsibility of the state to feed and care for those people. Mothers and their children were vital to the future of the nation. During socialism, opposition to the state reached a critical point when food prices, particularly of that most symbolic of staples, bread, were raised suddenly, or when shift structures were changed so that mothers could no longer easily spend time with their children (Reading 1992; Long 1996). These discourses reverberate with metaphors of gender and kinship. The State, as father, should provide for the nation. The Nation, as mother, should nurture and protect. Each works to protect and feed the other, and both to protect and feed the children. When the state fails, or reneges on its obligations, people are morally entitled to make their own provisions, political, economic or social. Although by necessity hidden from the scrutiny of the state, the informal economy was often presented as the 'real' economy, which operated in terms of trust (a quality rarely extended to the state) and favours, through the medium of, and between, kin and close friends. In terms of local understandings, activities which were officially subversive, like strikes, or dishonest, like stealing from the workplace, were morally legitimate. In order to be so, they were routinely 'naturalized': that is, situated within discourses of kinship and gender. These patterns have continued after socialism, but the context is different. The safety net of the welfare state has been eroded, and consequently what were under socialism 'alternate strategies' have for some people become the central or sole keys to their survival.

In contrast to the socialist state, the postsocialist state represented itself, and was initially seen, as independent, led by Poles for the good of Poland. Very soon, however, the severe measures taken by Minister of Finance, Leszek Balcerowicz, to restructure the national economy in line with the demands of the IMF led to high rates of unemployment and retraction of social services. Gradually the new Polish state came to be seen in a negative light similar to that of the old socialist one – in fact, socialist times were often recalled, and remembered as a good and stable period, when the state cared for the people.[11] Once again, in rural areas and in regions with high industrial unemployment, the state and the public domain came to carry connotations of the oppressive 'other', this time in conjunction not with Russia but with the 'West'.

## Conclusion

Gender is only one strand, albeit a very important one, in the processes through which new economies and social relations are emerging in postsocialist conditions. Class, rural or urban place, age and generation, and sometimes, as in the case of Roma, ethnicity, all cross-cut gender in significant ways. In the rural area that I have discussed in this chapter, the withdrawal of state structures and supports is perceived as a betrayal and a reversal. None of the strategies I have discussed is new – household production, informal economic dealings, reliance on extended kin networks were all parts of the socialist world. However, then they were largely hidden, unacknowledged and above all part of a private, domestic world which people attempted to keep from the intrusive gaze of the state. The institutions of the state – industrial production, separate workplaces, regulated markets and a tightly organized agricultural system – were the visible and publicly acknowledged spaces. When they collapsed, what was left was this private, domestic, invisible or hidden world. The gap left by this collapse of state industry, regulated, institutionalized agriculture, and social institutions is being filled less by the emergence of new institutions of civil society than by the expansion of that domestic, private world which was formerly quite carefully protected from public scrutiny. Recent research by rural sociologists in central

Europe (Kaleta *et al.* 2001) suggests that this may be symptomatic of a wider pattern. Pluskota, for instance, argues that

> In ... central Europe ... there is a relatively low political, social and economic activity among rural inhabitants – a low percentage of people belong to formal organisations.
>
> [This] correspond[s] with the so-called social void observed over the past decade. The social void is a feeling of lack of identity with average sized groups, institutions or associations, and rather identifying with small groups, such as family ... The intensification of this phenomenon carries many negative consequences, such as diminished feeling of responsibility for matters beyond the area of privacy.
>
> (Pluskota 2001)

Similarly, Kaleta notes that, in the case of Poland,

> most rural inhabitants do not trust political, administrative or economic institutions and ... feel they have no influence on the course of events in their own country ... The influence of political parties has dropped radically and so has the role of paracooperative organisations serving the countryside and agriculture. The lack of developed voluntary organisations and consequently the absence of various forms of expression of public opinion seems to indicate that the order of a pluralistic society is practically non-existent in rural communities.
>
> (Kaleta 2001)

If the retraction of the state is not accompanied by a successful growth of other institutions and associations with which people can identify and through which they can realize some form of public agency, informal relations and transactions and the direction of resources back into the domestic domain offer one kind of alternative. This domestic domain, I have argued, was under socialism a highly gendered space, one that disguised production and highlighted reproduction. Increasingly, as it expands to fill those emptying places where the state used to be, it is becoming both more visible and more explicitly associated with new, or perhaps newly recognized, forms of production. While women have suffered most from exclusion from the public domain, this new space builds upon types of reciprocity and cooperation which have long been associated with kinship, and female kinship particularly.

All of this raises questions about what kind of society, and what kind of economy, is emerging under postsocialism. One possibility is that this retreat to the domestic is a temporary phenomenon, and that as members of the new generation who have no memory of socialism move into economic prominence, they will have the skills and the opportunities to participate more fully in the global economy. Accession to the European Union, increased mobility across international borders, and investment by global manufacturing bodies in the country are factors that make this scenario more likely than it seemed a decade ago. It remains to be seen whether these processes will result in a retreat *from* the household and more equity in gender relations, or in a growing polarization between these regions which are incorporated into the global economy and others which have no choice but to turn more and more inwards into small-scale local production and exchange.

## Notes

1  I am grateful to the ESRC for funding the research upon which this paper is based, from 1988 to 1990 (R0002314) and from 1991 to 1995 (R000233019). I also thank Chris Hann and Deema Kaneff for reading the original draft and making many helpful suggestions about organization.

2  See Einhorn 1993, Gal and Kligman 2000, for discussion of these issues in the post-socialist countries; Watson 1993, 1996 for discussion of gender, civil society and the new 'masculinism'; and Bridger *et al.* 1996 for an analysis of women and the market in Russia.

3  See Pine 1996a, 1998, for discussion of regional differences, specifically for comparison between the Lodz region and the Podhale of southwestern Poland, the home of the Gorale.

4  In this region, as in Poland generally, although there were a few state farms, most agriculture was carried out on privately owned small family farms.

5  Yuval-Davis (1997: 78–84) and others have discussed the problems with conflating the private and the domestic, correctly pointing out that domestic relations are not private in the sense of individual autonomy, but involve power relations, conflicting interests, inequality and negotiations between members. This is an important distinction; however, 'private' also took on a particular set of meanings during socialism, which included both the sense of the private individual and the sense of private (economic and social) as opposed to state. I have discussed this distinction between *prywatny* and *panstwowy* elsewhere, and also the ways in which the meanings of *prywatny* change with postsocialism. In the latter context, private comes to mean both private as in non-state, and private as in capitalist or entrepreneurial. A third category, *domowy*, domestic or 'of the house' then comes to encompass some of the social and economic meanings ascribed to private during socialism. See Pine 1996a, 1998.

6  I have described a similar division between the kinship 'ties that bind' and the individualistic work outside the demands of kinship for the Górale in the Podhale region of southwestern Poland where I have been doing research since the late 1970s. For the Górale, however, state sector employment tended to represent oppression, and it was in marketing, trading and economic migration that women realized this sense of self (Pine 1999).

7  In the Podhale region, there is far less emphasis on the gendered nature of work, and both men and women are associated first and foremost with the domestic economy and with any kind of work which helps to support it. This means, in effect, that both men and women can be absent if they are working for the house economy, and that motherhood is not dependent upon physical presence any more than fatherhood is. See Pine 2001.

8  Although most village land was owned privately, the agricultural cooperative owned some fields as well the large machines such as combines.

9 For a discussion of gender aspects of agricultural decollectivization in Kazakstan highlighting similar processes, see Shreeves nd.
10 Humphrey (1995) documents a similar trend in Moscow, and more recently Haukanes (2001) discusses this in the context of the Czech countryside.
11 Rather than a case of collective amnesia or even nostalgia, I think this should be taken partly as an invocation of a past order to contrast it with, and thereby criticize, the present. Social memory is selective and contextual. When people evoked the 'good' socialist past, they were not denying the corruption, the shortages, the queues and the endless intrusions and infringements by the state; rather, they were choosing to emphasize other aspects: economic security, full employment, universal healthcare and education.

# References

Atwood, L. (1997) '"She was asking for it": rape and domestic violence against women', in M. Buckley (ed.) *Post-Soviet Women: From the Baltic to Central Asia*, Cambridge: Cambridge University Press.
Baban, A. (2000) 'Women's sexuality and reproductive behaviour in post-Ceausescu Romania: a psychological approach', in S. Gal and G. Kligman (eds) *Reproducing Gender: Politics, Publics, and Everyday Life after Socialism*, Princeton: Princeton University Press.
Bridger, S., R. Kay and K. Pinnick (1996) *No More Heroines? Russia, Women and the Market*, London: Routledge.
Corrin, C. (1992) *Superwoman and the Double Burden*, London: Scarlet Press.
Einhorn, B. (1993) *Cinderella Goes to Market*, London: Verso.
Firlik, E. and J. Chłopecki (1992) 'When theft is not theft', in J. Wedel (ed.) *The Unplanned Society: Poland During and After Communism*, New York: Columbia University Press.
Gal, S. and G. Kligman (eds) (2000) *Reproducing Gender: Politics, Publics, and Everyday Life after Socialism*, Princeton: Princeton University Press.
Haney, L. (1999) 'But we are still mothers: gender, the state and the construction of need in postsocialist Hungary', in M. Burowoy and K. Verdery (eds) *Uncertain Transition: Ethnographies of Change in the Postsocialist World*, Lanham, Boulder, New York and London: Rowman and Littlefield.
Haukanes, H. (2001) 'Women as nurturers: food and ideology of care in the Czech Republic', in H. Haukanes (ed.) *Women after Communism: Ideal Images and Real Lives*, Bergen: Centre for Women's Studies and Gender Relations, University of Bergen (in press).
Hivon, M. (1995) 'Local resistance to privatisation in rural Russia', *Cambridge Anthropology* 18(2): 13–22.
Humphrey, C. (1995) 'Creating a culture of disillusionment: consumption in Moscow, a chronicle of changing times', in D. Miller (ed.) *Worlds Apart: Modernity through the Prism of the Local*, London: Routledge.
Kaleta, A. (2001) 'The Polish countryside during the system transformation', in A. Kaleta, N. Swain and G. Zabłocki (eds) *Rural and Agricultural Transformation in Central Europe*, Wrocław: Ossolineum.
Kaleta, A., N. Swain and G. Zabłocki (eds) (2001) *Rural and Agricultural Transformation in Central Europe*, Wrocław: Ossolineum.

Kay, R. (1997) 'Images of an ideal woman: perceptions of Russian womanhood through the media, education and women's own eyes', in M. Buckley (ed.) *Post-Soviet Women: from the Baltic to Central Asia*, Cambridge: Cambridge University Press.

——(2000) *Russian Women and their Organizations: Gender, Discrimination and Grassroots Women's Organizations 1991–96*, Basingstoke and London: Macmillan.

Kligman, G. (1988) *The Wedding of the Dead: Ritual, Poetics and Popular Culture in Transylvania*, Berkeley: University of California Press.

Ledeneva, A. (1998) *Russia's Economy of Favours: Blat, Networking and Informal Exchange*, Cambridge: Cambridge University Press.

Long, K. (1996) *We All Fought for Freedom: Women in Poland's Solidarity Movement*, Boulder: Westview.

Maleck-Lewy, M. and E.M. Ferree (2000) 'Talking about women and wombs: the discourse of abortion and reproductive rights in the G.D.R. during and after the *Wende*', in S. Gal and G. Kligman (eds) *Reproducing Gender: Politics, Publics, and Everyday Life after Socialism*, Princeton: Princeton University Press.

Pawlik, W. (1992) 'Intimate commerce', in J. Wedel (ed.) *The Unplanned Society: Poland During and After Communism*, New York: Columbia University Press.

Pilkington, H. (1997) '"For the sake of the children": gender and migration in the former Soviet Union', in M. Buckley (ed.) *Post-Soviet Women: from the Baltic to Central Asia*, Cambridge: Cambridge University Press.

Pine, F. (1996a) 'Redefining women's work in rural Poland', in R. Abrahams (ed.) *After Socialism: Land Reform and Social Change in Eastern Europe*, Oxford: Berghahn.

——(1996b) 'Naming the house and naming the land: kinship and social groups in the Polish highlands', *Journal of the Royal Anthropological Institute* 2(2): 443–59.

——(1997) 'Pilfering culture: Gorale identity in postsocialist Poland', *Paragraph* 20(1): 59–74.

——(1998) 'Dealing with fragmentation: the consequences of privatisation for rural women in central and southern Poland', in S. Bridger and F. Pine (eds) *Surviving Postsocialism: Local Strategies and Regional Responses in Eastern Europe and the Former Soviet Union*, London: Routledge.

——(1999) 'Incorporation and exclusion in the Podhale', in S. Day, E. Papataxiarchis and M. Stewart (eds) *Lilies of the Field: Marginal People who Live for the Moment*, Boulder: Westview.

——(2001) 'Who better than your mother? Some reflections on gender in postsocialist Poland', in H. Haukanes (ed.) *Women after Communism: Ideal Images and Real Lives*, Bergen: Centre for Women's Studies and Gender Relations, University of Bergen (in press).

Pinnick, K. (1997) 'When the fighting is over: the soldiers' mothers and the Afghan madonnas', in M. Buckley (ed.) *Post-Soviet Women: from the Baltic to Central Asia*, Cambridge: Cambridge University Press.

Pollert, A. (1981) *Girls, Wives, Factory Lives*, London and Basingstoke: Macmillan.

Rai, S., A. Phizacklea and H. Pilkington (eds) (1992) *Women in the Face of Change: the Soviet Union, Eastern Europe and China*, London: Routledge.

Reading, A. (1992) *Polish Women, Solidarity and Feminism*, London and Basingstoke: Macmillan.

Shreeves, R. (1992) 'Sexual revolution or "sexploitation"? the pornography and erotica debate in the Soviet Union', in S. Rai, A. Phizacklea and H. Pilkington (eds) (1992)

*Women in the Face of Change: the Soviet Union, Eastern Europe and China*, London: Routledge.

——(nd) 'Gender issues in the development of rural areas in Kazakstan', PhD in process, University of Wolverhampton.

Watson, P. (1993) 'The rise of masculinism in Eastern Europe', *New Left Review* 198: 71–82.

——(1996) 'Civil society and the politics of difference in eastern Europe', in J. Scott, C. Kaplan and D. Keates (eds) *Transitions, Environments, Translations: Feminisms in International Politics*, New York: Routledge.

Wedel, J. (ed.) (1992) *The Unplanned Society: Poland During and After Communism*, New York: Columbia University Press.

Wolchik, S. (2000) 'Reproductive policies in the Czech and Slovak Republics', in S. Gal and G. Kligman (eds) *Reproducing Gender: Politics, Publics, and Everyday Life after Socialism*, Princeton: Princeton University Press.

Yurchak, A. (1997) 'The cynical reason of late socialism: power, pretence and the *anekdot*', *Public Culture* 9: 161–88.

Yuval-Davis, N. (1997) *Gender and Nation*, London: Sage.

Zielińska, E. (2000) 'Between ideology, politics and common sense: the discourse of reproductive rights in Poland', in S. Gal and G. Kligman (eds) *Reproducing Gender: Politics, Publics, and Everyday Life after Socialism*, Princeton: Princeton University Press.

Chapter 6

# The unmaking of an East-Central European working class[1]

*David A. Kideckel*

## Blaming the victim – workers in East Europe's neo-capitalism

When the proprietor of a restaurant in the Romanian Jiu Valley mining town of Petroşani asked me to his table to introduce me to two of his former teachers, one of the elderly men wanted to know my purpose in the valley. As I told him about my interest in labor, miner working conditions, the health of miners and the impact of unemployment, he cocked one eyebrow and looked at me quizzically. 'What are you,' he said, 'a Communist?'

This anecdote reveals the attitudes of many in East-Central Europe to the postsocialist working classes. Concern for workers' conditions is marginalized and delegitimized, and many branches of industry are scorned as socialist survivals. Under socialism industrial workers were the privileged recipients of higher wages and supplementary state services and perquisites, in accordance with the ideology that stressed the role of the working class. The change from elevation to denigration has been especially sharp in Romania. Public opinion identifies many culprits for the country's economic and political difficulties, including corrupt politicians, rapacious business people, and allegedly anti-Romanian foreign agencies such as the World Bank, but workers are always among those most reviled. They are said to hold the country down and set back reform due to the bad habits they learned during 'the time of Ceauşescu', which included a questionable work ethic with a resulting lack of productivity, generalized dishonesty, and the expectation of getting something for nothing.

Criticism is extended to unions and their leaders, who are said to be uninterested in the general welfare, more involved in politics than in protecting workers, excessively militant, and often complicit in the destruction of enterprises. Even the unemployed are not spared. They are said to collect unemployment benefit while working 'under the table', or to work for as long as it takes to qualify for the dole and then quit. They are accused of refusing to train for new positions, or to move to regions where jobs are available, or to spend the proceeds of their severance packages extravagantly, and then have the gall to demand their former jobs back.

Thus, the victims of economic downturn are held to blame for that same downturn, even as those who cast the blame – media, new entrepreneurs, parliamentarians, some state functionaries – reap the lion's share of benefits in the new political economy.

This wholesale denigration of labor dividing workers from other social sectors contains a more general message about the nature of postsocialism in East-Central Europe. Postsocialism is an amorphous concept that defines societies by something they are not, instead of what they are. In this sense it shares much with the increasingly discredited concept of 'transition'. 'Transition' is increasingly recognized as teleological, ethnocentrically triumphalist and disrespectful of cross-national variation (Blanchard and Froot et al. 1994; Offe 1997; Pasti 1997; Verdery 1996; Wedel 1998; Snyder and Vachudova 1997; Berdahl 2000). To the extent that it implicitly assumes that the current conditions are temporary and about to be consolidated into some new system, the notion of postsocialism is similarly problematic, though remaining silent about what the new system will be. Postsocialist theorists thus fail to acknowledge East-Central Europe's headlong rush to adopt some variant of world capitalism as a basic organizing principle.

In this respect, transition theory is quite right and may indeed underestimate the pace of capitalist development in East-Central Europe. I shall argue that the region's problematic is not too slow a movement to capitalism (as 'transition' would have it) but too fast; not too little capitalism, but too much. Rather than postsocialist, it is better understood as 'neo-capitalist', a social system that reworks basic capitalist principles in new, even more inegalitarian ways than the Western model from which it derives.

Like neo-serfdom in the so-called 'long sixteenth century', neo-capitalism involves the re-working of a Western prototype so as to establish a dependent hinterland in Central and Eastern Europe. As with neo-serfdom, under neo-capitalism the pace and extent of class differentiation exceeds the Western experience. When capitalism was first extended east, the numerically dominant peasants were never granted the social benefits that came to characterize Western capitalism and no strong middle class ever emerged. Under neo-capitalism we again see how narrow elites have been able to appropriate public resources and prevent their transparent, equitable distribution. There have been some exceptions. Some joint ventures with enterprises of the developed capitalist world have given workers reasonable wages and job security. The dominant trends, however, have been to sanctify individualized ownership at the expense of social equity, to pursue inappropriate loan policies, and to facilitate a corrupt bargain between owning and political classes at the expense of labor. Industrial workers have fallen to near the bottom of the economic and social scale, there is still no effective middle class, and class boundaries are further solidified (Słomczyński and Shabad 1997).

East-Central Europe is thus caught up in a system whose basic characteristics are capitalist, but clearly not of the Euro-American variety. The new principles of property and governance appear to be the same, but the conditions and identities of the working classes are shaped by their rapidly diminishing access to resources – material, social and symbolic – in neo-capitalist society. Worker jobs and wages decline both absolutely and relative to the cost of living. Worker social networks implode under such pressures. Worker symbolic supports in society are removed in reaction to the socialist past and response to the globalist present. And nearly everywhere stress translates into threat to psychological and physiological health.

By placing workers at or near the bottom of new national political economic and cultural categories, neo-capitalism manufactures social structures with which workers engage either as degraded supplicants or as alienated antagonists. It produces exchange relationships in which workers both define themselves and are defined by others as unequal. In so doing, this neo-capitalism is creating a kind of 'durable inequality' for the region's workers, i.e. an inequality which 'last[s] from one social interaction to the next ... [and tends to] persist over whole careers, lifetimes, and organizational histories' (Tilly 1998: 6). Such inequality is best understood if we begin with a consideration of the domination of labor in socialism, from which contemporary actualities ensue.

## The ethnographic basis of neo-capitalist assumptions

The assumptions and conclusions of this essay are based on three years of inter-mittent fieldwork, 1998–2000, among two populations of declining Romanian workers, along with related research on changes in and perceptions of Romanian labor unions in contemporary society (Kideckel 1999). The workers examined, both active and unemployed, include the hard coal miners of the Jiu Valley, located in southwest Romania at the intersection of the historic regions of Banat, Oltenia and Transylvania, and the chemical workers of the Făgăraş region, in south central Transylvania.

On the surface, the Jiu Valley and Făgăraş regions share many similarities throughout socialism and neo-capitalism. In the socialist years both regions prospered from a concentrated mono-industrial production base. Their successes drew labor from other Romanian regions. However, today, because of that same concentration of industry, both regions have been targeted for extensive economic restructuring, the results of which have now produced devastating unemployment and active labor movements.

Today the Jiu Valley mining industry (*minerit*) is reeling from two rounds of mass lay-offs spurred by worker 'contract buy-outs' (*disponibilizare*) that offered lump-sum severance to miners of twelve to twenty months of pay in addition to regular unemployment benefits (Government of Romania 1997). The buy-outs enabled closure of two of thirteen mines, threaten an unspecified additional number today, and have decreased *minerit* employees from roughly 42,000 in 1997 to 18,216 today.[2] The majority of the unemployed miners now sit idle in the Jiu Valley towns, their benefits running out in December 1999. Many idled miners who previously immigrated to the region used part of their severance to return to their areas of origin, chiefly Moldavia. However, they returned to the Jiu when their prospects did not pan out. They were rejected by their families for their lack of jobs and seen as interlopers on family inheritances by siblings. Similarly, in the three factories of the Făgăraş region where we carried out research[3] the number of employees declined precipitously from a total of 17,239 in 1989 to 5,636 today. While many of these laid-off workers have immigrated to Italy, both legally and illegally, most remain in the region in a constant scramble to seek other sources of livelihood, but with little success.

High unemployment and steep rises in the cost of living have galvanized labor's anger in both regions. Jiu Valley miners are, of course, infamous for their periodic actual and threatened marches on Bucharest.[4] Despite the renown this brings, these actions have been eclipsed by miner grievances against local mine administrations. Făgăraş factory unions and workers have also participated in labor actions at both national and local levels, but in that region labor actions have been more motivated by poor-quality city services.

In part to stem such actions and address economic needs, the Romanian government passed the Law on Disfavored Zones (Government of Romania 1998) that offers economic advantages to regions meeting certain criteria.[5] This law ostensibly shows the country's concern about the conditions of workers. However, closer study shows it to be more an attempt to neutralize labor's voice, providing little in return. Thus, according to many, the Disfavored Zones law was mainly passed specifically to dampen the political volatility of the Jiu Valley, the first region to receive this designation. More to the point, application of the law has been especially spotty. Taxes and customs are levied where they should be excused. New businesses bring in workers from elsewhere instead of hiring unemployed miners. Job training programs are of little relevance. Meanwhile the petition for 'Disfavored' status for the Făgăraş region had been denied twice as of summer 2000, though the region satisfies most of the law's criteria.

As seen from their troubled circumstances, the Jiu Valley miners and Făgăraş chemical workers are representative of the extremes of decline suffered by Romanian workers. This essay, consequently, is offered more as a polemic about the sorry state of East-Central European workers than an indication of variation in such populations. Nonetheless their conditions are redolent throughout the region. The situation among working people from Varna to Gdańsk is clearly dire, though increasingly marginal to the concerns of regional governments and international organizations. Everywhere workers suffer severe social dislocation and equally must contend with falling standards of living and declining physical health (Bobek and Marmot 1996; Stone 2000; Watson 1995). And everywhere East-Central European workers face declining respect and limited prospects. It is for such reasons that the experiences of the Jiu Valley miners and Făgăraş chemical workers bear witness to the unmaking of regional working classes and the conditions of sub-alternity they face in neo-capitalism.

## Sub-alternity then and now: the disempowerment of labor under socialism and neo-capitalism

Sub-alternity was the concept used by Rudolf Bahro (1977) to explain workers' location at the bottom of a knowledge-based division of labor in socialism (cf. Konrád and Szelényi 1979). Structurally, labor's position deprived workers of voice and power and relegated them to the role of theatrical prop in the legitimating discourses and rituals of socialism. In Romania, for example, the 'Cult of Labor' (*Cultul Muncii*) portrayed work as the source of all value and lauded workers as responsible for Romanian cultural and scientific achievement (Hoffman *et al.* 1984; Kideckel 1993: 189). Socialist literature and journalism were full of heroic, stalwart, socially conscious workers (Bârgău 1984; Kideckel 1988; Pospai 1978). Labor-related events were prominent in the ritual calendar, like celebrations surrounding the ambiguous 1929 miners' strike from Lupeni in the Jiu Valley. Socialist historiography portrayed this as the murder of twenty-two miners due to the anti-worker policies of the right-wing Peasant Party governments of the time (Oprea 1970: 486; see also Țic 1977).

Celebration of worker images in socialist ritual and state policies promoting working-class types into positions of authority and requiring a modicum of attention to worker material needs provided workers a degree of symbolic and social capital. Lampland (this volume) defines social capital as the 'value of significant social connections to one's career in school, business, or politics'. Though socialist society doled out such capital in measured doses, it nonetheless softened and masked the sizable differences between social strata that were institutionalized under socialism.

Other structural principles of socialist political economy also encouraged senses of worker power, even if they were limited. Thus, 'soft budget constraints' (Kornai 1980) and labor hoarding gave workers some suasion over managers. Full employment guaranteed regular incomes, supplemented by pensions and other benefits. Consumer shortages forced people of all social backgrounds into protracted 'second economy' relationships (Sampson 1987). Worker and peasant social mobility moderated class distance in the workplace, especially in the first years of socialist power. There was little residential segregation and pay and 'lifestyle' differences were modest, except at the highest levels of factory directors and state officials. Workers and supervisors shopped at the same stores, went to the same resorts and attended each other's weddings, baptisms and funerals.

In Ceaușescu's last decade material deprivation linked workers with other classes in common suffering and the *Cultul Muncii* discourse was partially replaced by the discourse of nation and ethnicity. However, though the 'nation as trope' discourse promulgated unity between Romanians, it especially eroded labor's social capital in the last decade of socialism. Workers of different ethnic identities were alienated from each other and resources were distributed by an increasingly ethnic calculus (Verdery 1994), further ensuring labor's impotence and division in socialist political economy.

The fall of Romanian socialism in 1989 and the transformation of Romanian political economy have deepened the subalternization of labor. Once again, related to the vast structural transformations of neo-capitalism, the basis of worker subalternity is their and their representatives' declining access to all manner of resources. This includes limitations on access to knowledge and information, decline in the availability of jobs related to processes of privatization, and a decrease in training and education opportunities. Furthermore, each of these processes places downward pressure on the valorization of labor in society and the efficacy of its diverse social ties. Eight key factors appear with different intensities and combinations across the regions to explain renewed and reinvigorated worker subalternity and its social decline:

1   limited knowledge of and access to the labor market, which conduces to higher unemployment, and sometimes to aggressive labor activism, perceived negatively by other social groups;
2   limited information about privatization processes, which increases the sense of being excluded from economic transformation and of being victims of pervasive corruption;
3   segmentation and intra-class rivalry, accentuated by falling standards of living and undermining labor's solidarity and the close relationships of the 'second economy';
4   ineffective representative institutions, notably unions, whose leaders are also deprived of information regarding social and economic transformations;
5   increased dependency due to expansion of the black market for labor and manipulation of working conditions by unscrupulous employers;
6   the devaluation of industrial work and loss of symbolic capital due to the expansion of the information society and globalized culture;
7   widespread societal rejection of socialism and socialist categories, thus facilitating half-hearted state policies and practices for labor protection, remediation, and training;
8   the general dissolution of worker social networks, encouraging their loss of energy and physical incapacity.

Some items on this list overlap, and it is by no means comprehensive. Furthermore, some points, including information issues and unfavorable images of labor in the media and education, are by no means unique to Central and Eastern Europe (Castells 1996). Nonetheless, the specific circumstances in which socialism has been replaced by neo-capitalism have certainly intensified the differentiation of workers from other class groups and also the alienation of workers from each other. Let us now turn to the Romanian case in more detail, beginning with the structural changes in workers' lives and moving on to consider symbolic and social dimensions.

## Information and contemporary Romanian class transformations

Since the fall of the socialist state, the most dramatic structural changes in Romanian society have included massive unemployment and huge increases in the cost of living. Unemployment rose from 12 per cent in 1998 to 16 per cent by the end of 2000. The figure has been inflated by state employee labor contract 'buy-outs', termed *disponibilizare*, which offer workers a relatively generous severance package.[6] Typically the unemployed are workers with high school and trade school education, the former backbone of the socialist economy. Unemployment is less prevalent among white-collar professionals and the college-educated. Unemployment has pitted workers against each other, notably when the 'streamlining' of production involves the closure of some sections of a factory, while others are spared.

The informational basis of internal competition is especially clear in the recent labor buy-out programs. In the Jiu Valley, for example, looking back on the 'buy-out', many former miners spoke of coercive manipulation and the lies and half-truths they were told to get them to accept the inducement. According to one, who chose to reject the buy-out:

> The idea circulated that anyone charged more than three times with unmotivated work, or those who drank, would be kicked out … I heard a rumor about a list with the names of unmotivated workers scheduled to be made redundant … and people were constantly checking you out. Later this list changed. I don't know why, because there were also good guys [i.e. hard workers] on it.

Others were led to believe, incorrectly, that they could regain their jobs at a later date. When this turned out not to be the case, anger and suspicion were directed at those who had retained their positions, further undermining the close relations that were the basis of miner identities.

In the recent buy-out at the Viromet Chemical Company in Victoria City, Braşov County, a number of information issues also proved controversial. While state regulations now discourage lump sum payments, these were still legally available to workers capable of drawing up a business plan in order to pursue a private investment opportunity. However, this was not explained to the workers, who were first told that no buy-out at all was planned, and then misinformed about the possibility of receiving their severance in a single sum. Those who retained their jobs were mainly the relatives of senior management at the factory, who blatantly used their relationships to hold on to their jobs.

Women workers are doubly subaltern (Watson 1993). Neo-capitalism has accentuated the gendered realities of industrial production. Throughout the country, women were generally among the first workers to be dismissed and the last to be re-hired. Women comprise 44 per cent of Romania's workforce (Comisia Naţionala Pentru Statistica 1996: 152), but make up nearly 50 per cent of the unemployed, and are even more conspicuous among the long-term unemployed (Bacon and Pol 1994: 55–6; Rompres 1998). There are few women union leaders and women's domestic responsibilities tend to exclude even those who are union members from the all important networks to share information.

Given that so many workers have either lost their jobs or need to supplement their salaries, a large black market (*la negru*) has developed that has further adverse effects on workers' lives and their images in society (Birtalan 1999: 8).[7] Formerly proud skilled workers can be hired and fired for unskilled tasks, while women, especially good-looking ones, are prominent in small-scale commerce and service occupations. Many are harassed by their employers for sexual favors and threatened if they refuse, not only in the black market, but also in the legal, 'formal sector'. 'Black' work is always insecure and unscrupulous employers often pay black market workers less than agreed, knowing that they have no means of redress.

The rapid emergence of a wealthy class of owners, especially in commercial sectors, highlights and makes direr the poverty that many workers now experience. Not only has privatization been accompanied by massive collusion between political and business classes but many state factories have been allowed to wither and die as a deliberate strategy on the part of their managers, who siphon off their resources to parasitical firms (*firme capuşe*, literally 'tick firms') controlled by relatives and/or clients. As the host firm dies, those involved in unproductive work grow wealthy at the expense of working people.

Workers accept income inequality in the new privatized economy. However, they decry the speed with which some fortunes have been made, the corruption this implies, and also the conspicuous nature of wealth consumption patterns that stand in stark contrast to their own declining circumstances. For example, huge numbers of lavish luxury homes and vacation *cabanas* have seemed to spring up overnight in the hills and mountains surrounding Jiu Valley towns. The unemployed and threatened miners point them out and speak of how they sit in the same areas where the miners used to go together on outings, long since stopped in the decline of the mine industry.

Other groups besides state-sector industrial workers have also suffered under neo-capitalism. Nonetheless these professionals and white-collar wage-earners, such as clerks, teachers and health workers, distance themselves from workers, since they have somewhat better job security and positions that attract more respect in the new economic system. They know their salaries are not commensurate with their education but they are also conscious of professional responsibilities and, unlike their industrial counterparts, seldom inclined to militancy.

In fact, the Romanian union movement itself is a riot of competing sectors and interests that paradoxically encourage its high visibility, but questionable efficacy (Bush 1993; Ockenga 1997; Rodina 1994; Synovitz 1997). At the same time, such visibility causes it to be viewed suspiciously, not only by workers but also by society in general. Romanian labor unions are some of the most militant and active throughout the formerly socialist countries. However, as I analysed elsewhere (Kideckel 1999, 2001a, b), this activity is mainly a finger in the dike of the neo-capitalist deluge. Romania's workers continue to fall further behind in salary levels, job protection, increases in illegal non-contractual black market labor, and the like. The union movement is especially divided by professional or worker status. Thus, general strikes planned for spring and autumn 1999 fizzled when teachers and health workers failed to sign on in sufficient numbers. The comment of an over-worked, under-paid Braşov doctor about industrial workers is not atypical:

> Many workers are to blame for their own problems. People are lazy and those who aren't are able to get all they need. There are jobs available if one wants to work. As we say in Romania, 'Seek and you will find.'

## Symbolic dimensions of labor's decline

Structural transformations in the position of the working classes are insufficient to account for worker subalternity. It is also important to consider how the new dominant classes use symbolic manipulation, to consolidate their power by the denial and denigration of worker symbolic and social capital. In this the meaning of the workers' lives and concerns are dismissed and the very category 'worker' or 'industrial worker' is made almost invisible in public discourse, even though industrial workers are still numerically predominant in most countries. The new media often project (and deride) their image as the favored class of the socialist state, the 'heroic working class', as a ruse to justify ignoring the realities. As a Bucharest journalist said to me, 'Workers, workers, workers. People are sick of hearing about workers.' As a result the real lives and concerns of workers are absent from the new Romanian print and broadcast media. If represented at all, it is likely to be in the context of industrial accidents (whether as cause or victim), or of theft and familial abuse. The implication is often that somehow workers' lives are less worthy than others.

Coverage of strikes and union activities in general often insinuates attempts by labor to maintain their alleged past privileges. Romanian worker protests have been more frequent and intense than those of most other ex-socialist countries (Brehoi and Popescu 1991; Bush 1993; Ockenga 1997).[8] They have ranged from mass invasions of Bucharest to periodic planned walkouts by the major union confederations and countless spontaneous protests at the grass roots. The more extreme the conflict, the more likely it is to attract negative airplay. Media discussions of threatened incursions into Bucharest by Jiu Valley miners were especially one-sided. In the *mineriade* of January and February 1999, the miners marched in protest at the closing of three mines, a series of broken promises by political leaders, and the prosecution of union leader Miron Cozma for 'undermining state authority' during the miners' 1991 march on Bucharest, when they toppled the government of Prime Minister Petre Roman.[9] Though the economic issues were real enough, the entire spectrum of the Romanian press, from left-leaning *Revista 22*, *Sfera Politicii* and *Adevărul*, to mainstream *România Libera*, and even the humor weekly *Academia Caţavencu*, focused on the threat to the security of the capital and dwelt at length on the Cozma question. Press analysis either vilified the miners or portrayed them as homogenous innocents, manipulated by Cozma or by former and current President Ion Iliescu.

In fact there was considerable diversity in the opinions and responses of miners, whose economic predicament has been even more troubled than other Romanian workers. Mining families generally have only a single source of income. Work in the mines does not leave time or energy to hold additional jobs, and miners' wives generally do not work due to lack of other employment opportunities. Many miners originate in poorer regions such as Moldavia: their families are unable to provide assistance, and emigration is seldom an option. Individual decisions, including the decision to join a strike, depend on a range of factors, including kin and family relations. Some were coerced into participating in strikes by their union. Most participated voluntarily, but explained that in addition to their economic complaints they were against corrupt politicians and the bias of the media. As one man at Lonea Mine, to great assent from his colleagues, said to me in an interview:

> They arrested [Cozma] because he tried to help us, the people. He wants to re-open factories, so that they would need coal for power. People in Bucharest weren't afraid of us. We went there peacefully in 1990, but they shot at us. We feel 60 per cent of Romanians are for us, including all other workers, but the press turns the people against us. *Adevărul* is like a foreign newspaper. They know the truth, but when the stories come out on TV it is completely different. Why should we even pay our taxes for TV when they lie like this?

During my fieldwork, virtually every worker I interviewed in four factories in the cities of Cluj-Napoca and Făgăraş said that miner actions were mainly legitimate. As one respondent put it, 'The miners were right to march since they were trying to maintain their workplaces. They were only criticized for political motives. I'd march for them if I was asked.' Most professionals, on the other hand, held that the miners had set back economic reform and blamed them for contributing to anti-democratic sentiment and scaring away foreign investors.

In contrast to their critique of worker actions, Romanian media present new forms of employment and material culture in a very positive light. Newspaper and television advertisements portray middle-class professionals engaged in 'clean' activities with high-tech products such as cell phones and computers that have no symbolic connection to the 'working classes'. Worker concerns are also increasingly shunned in education, where business studies, foreign languages and law have displaced disciplines related to the industrial workplace, notably engineering. Workers' opinions are not canvassed and academic researchers do not collect data on the physical and psychological pressures under which they and their households operate.[10]

The neglect and denigration of industrial labor is reflected in parliament and government actions such as the imperfect application of the Law on Disfavored Zones discussed above. Rarely have Romania's government, even that headed by Victor Ciorbea, former head of the National Confederation of Free Romanian Trade Unions (CNSLR), placed workers' concerns at or near the tops of their agendas. Some political groups, like Ion Iliescu's Romanian Party of Social Democracy (PDSR), call for industrial jobs protection, but are restricted by the realities of Romania's World Bank loans and EU accession strategies, which lead to further job losses. Furthermore, there are few other political avenues to which workers can turn. Romanian labor does not vote in a bloc. Its legions are cross-cut by so many different affiliations, interests and internal contests for power that avowedly pro-labor political parties, such as the Socialists (PS) and the Socialist Labor Party (PSM), have been without sufficient support to enter parliament.

The alienation of rank-and-file workers from politics is thus assured even as unions and union leaders are steeped in political maneuvering and relationships.[11] Workers decry politicians of all stripes, and see the whole process as designed to keep workers down. The growth of a dynamic and prosperous stratum of entrepreneurs is attributed solely to political influence-peddling and collusion between government, the state privatization agency and enterprise managers. Reacting against the increased class divisions and insecurities of neo-capitalism, many workers long for a return to the security and predictability of socialism. Like miners and workers elsewhere in Russia and East-Central Europe, from the best case of the Czech Republic (Pollert 1999), through war-torn Serbia (Arandarenko 1999), to prostrate Russia and Ukraine (Ashwin 1999; Crowley 1997), declining economic circumstances encourage a turn to socialist nostalgia, nationalist cant or frustrated inaction. In Romania some workers even display portraits of Ceauşescu on lathes, lockers and workbenches. When they are asked what is needed to put Romania right, they say 'an iron hand', 'a six-month military dictatorship', or 'Hitler, Stalin, and Vlad the Impaler rolled into one'.

The symbols deployed by workers during strikes and other protest actions retain the nationalist flavor of the Ceauşescu years and illustrate their perceived sub-alternity. The raw emotion of the miners' repeated incursions into Bucharest emphasized the ritual-like quality of these events. During the national strike in 1997, protesters in Revolution Square shouted, 'Down with the government!' 'Resignation!' 'We don't need reform that leads to the poverty!' 'We voted for you – you betrayed us!' 'Freedom for Cozma!' 'Miners will survive this government!' One group was draped in a black cover decorated with skeletons, to symbolize the death of the Romanian economy. Many protesters carried crosses bearing the names of Romanian enterprises closed down due to the intervention of the International Monetary Fund.

During the wreath-laying in 1999 in honor of the twenty-two miners shot dead in the August 1929 Lupeni strike, the strongest applause went to the most aggressive union leaders and the representative of the extremist right-wing nationalist, Coreliu Vadim Tudor, and his Greater Romania Party (PRM). Delegations from centrist groups were met with silence and catcalls.

## The decline of worker social networks and physical prowess

Worker alienation and subalternity have been intensified by further social and existential changes, including isolation from other groups and erosion of their own internal social supports. Connections have undoubtedly been important in the strategies of elites, but networks do not necessarily function well for other social groups. Most owners and managers of private firms with whom I spoke said hiring kin was no longer automatic. One said, 'It is better to hire people who are not related, since responsibilities to family complicate business.' Another said that he would prefer to trust close family with the handling of large sums of money, but otherwise he too preferred his staff to be unrelated. Workers themselves were adamant that network ties were no longer effective to secure employment or improve their working conditions. A few elderly people suggest a comparison with the turbulence of the inter-war period, when similar stresses and uncertainty resulted in high divorce, out-migration and a variety of adaptations at household level. Multi-family households often fissure over issues of money, and virtually everyone has had to develop more stringent budgets. The restructuring of households always affects the identities of members and intensifies their experience of subalternity.

Such experience is often reflected in local social relations, which are just as important in the erosion of workers' social capital and the production of sub-alternity as are patterns of incomes and information. Among Jiu Valley miners the incidence of intra-familial conflict has risen directly with unemployment. For example, the number of divorces increased from 463 in 1993 to 473 in 1998, and even more people would divorce, miners say, were it not for the high legal costs and long delays. More significantly, local statistics showed 63 cases of family abandonment in 1998–9 alone compared to 67 cases in the previous four years, and 27 cases of violent crime in 1998–9 compared to 32 cases in the previous five years. Prostitution and procuring are new categories in the recent regional statistics (Judecătorie Petroşani 1999) and spousal abuse has also increased, though there is only anecdotal evidence for this.

There is less statistically evident distress at the level of the family in the

Făgăraş region, despite its failing chemical industry and widespread unemployment. Families stay together as both husbands and wives seek to find whatever bit of gainful activity they can. Families here also have somewhat greater access to village social relations and income. Consequently, in Făgăraş divorce and family abandonment have actually declined in recent years, while the number of marriages has remained stable (Judecătorie Făgăraş 1999).[12] This stability comes at a price, however, for the high rate of male labor migration places great pressure on Făgăraş networks and on women in particular. They are expected to find jobs, and when none are available in the formal sector they are forced into the black market, with its attendant exploitation. As one Făgăraş woman said:

> Even if I only make 400,000 lei a month, that still helps us to do a little extra for the family. It pays for the telephone or the school field trip for one of the kids. It helps make life a little better, even though my work schedule takes me away from home all the time, even when the children come home from school.

There are also heavy emotional costs with subalternity. In the Jiu Valley miners' wives valorized themselves by maintaining standards of consumption, encouraging children's schooling and representing the family in the public sphere, but not through earning cash. They budgeted and conspicuously spent the money earned by their husbands. These role expectations have been threatened by the changed economic context, since declining disposable income has forced women to retreat into their homes. Their resulting depression is evident in the rising incidence of emotional illness.[13] Men have lost their pride in their work and few see any alternative to a further decline in their standard of living. The patriarchal household that supported their authority and relegated women and children to dependent roles under socialism is waning. One Făgăraş chemical worker, who tried unsuccessfully to find illegal labor in Germany, attributed his divorce directly to loss of his job. Unemployment 'was my great shame. Because of the stress of having no work, I lost my family.'

The subalternity of industrial workers also impacts on their collegiality. Though they may still express sentiments of collectivity and mutual support, the lack of money gives them little opportunity to operationalize these relationships. Few work groups socialize outside their workplace, as was common in the past. Neo-capitalist conditions have generally narrowed the range of contacts and limited the exchanges on which Romanian social life is predicated. Here is the account of a Făgăraş worker:

> We had friends until just a few years ago, but now we mainly stay at home on our own. People can't afford to have friends these days. We can't afford vacations either. Before we went to the Black Sea all the time, but we haven't since 1990. The last wedding we attended was five months ago and we had to save for three months to buy the present. Last year we were

godparents (*naş*) for my wife's cousin, which cost us 7 million lei in last year's prices. To be asked to be *naş* is a double-edged sword. If you refuse, it is shameful, but if you accept you set yourself back monetarily. We were the third family that the couple asked, and are hardly even related to them. At least these godchildren (*fini*) are in better shape than us. They are from a village and have a tractor and a brandy distillery.

Mass unemployment and the contract buy-outs also undermined miners' solidarity and sense of professional identity. As one former Lonea miner said:

> After I left my work I was no longer one of the guys (*ortaci*). Your *ortaci* were like your wife. We would share everything and we would always reciprocate. Now you're alone; it's like you don't have a family.

Taking the buy-out also often induced a sense of shame (*ruşine*), a consequence magnified by the fact that most of those affected were recent migrants from rural environments where labor is the central value (cf. Lampland 1995). If they returned to their natal communities they were stigmatized because job loss was seen as loss of personhood and gainful well-remunerated employment was the basic criterion that conferred social capital. Thus, the wife of an unemployed miner said that he

> hadn't gone back to his village since he left work. You'd think he wasn't even [his parents'] child any longer. We go back to my parents' place often, but my parents don't know he took the buy-out.

In contrast, in Făgăraş established international networks have made it more feasible for men to migrate to Italy and Germany. Consequently, when the contract buy-outs first began many were only too happy to accept them, and many who wanted to quit were even prevented from doing so. This also led to jealousy and competitiveness, which again isolated and alienated workers from each other. Later, as the economic crisis deepened, the buy-outs came to be seen more as a threat, to be avoided by any means possible, including the use of bribes and connections. In the midst of the recent Viromet buy-out I interviewed a machinist with over twenty years' seniority whose entire section was to be closed. Some of his co-workers were able to use their connections to sign on in other sections. But he was not in the in-group and was threatened with the prospect of loss of his job in a month. During the interview he broke down and wept as he described his situation, which was even direr since his wife, a school secretary in a nearby village, was also faced with loss of her job in a national education reorganization.

A final indicator of the consolidation of workers' subalternity is the dramatic decline in health and life expectancy, especially among middle-aged men. This is one of the hallmarks of neo-capitalist East-Central Europe (Watson 1995;

Weidner 1998). The precise mechanisms involved are partly understood, but formative work suggests that one over-riding condition shaping declines in worker health is stress (Cockerham 1999; Sapolsky 1997; Stone 2000; Straussner et al. 1999). This word was used constantly in the interviews I conducted with Jiu Valley miners and Făgăraş chemical workers. It is induced by all the conditions outlined above and has the consequence that workers' subalternity is reinforced by their own torpor and physical responses, above all the stress of alienation.

## Conclusions

Clearly, the position of workers in Romanian and East-Central European society has declined precipitously in the last years. They are the prime losers of post-1989 changes. Though other social groups experience similar threats to their wellbeing, none are so negatively viewed by the general public. This is a partial consequence of an ideologically distorted perception of workers' position under socialism and the manner by which workers articulate with the new political economy. In this chapter I have documented a process of class differentiation and subalternization, which amounts to a unique regional variant of world capitalism. The popular image of workers as angry anachronisms shows the successful dissemination of a new ideology. While many people (not only workers) believe that the movement toward a market economy has been beset with abuses and brought benefits primarily to the old elite and to the dishonest, nonetheless it is workers who are either blamed or shunned.

They have been denied their history and their subjective realities, and their basic human dignity is threatened at every turn, all tarnished by the stain of socialism. They are the new 'other', best kept under wraps for fear that their otherness and decline will also tarnish and discomfort the passage to neo-capitalist, globalized reality.

## Notes

1 The research for this essay was mainly supported by the US National Council for Eurasian and East European Research with funds provided under authority of a Title VIII grant from the US Department of State, the International Research and Exchanges Board, with funds provided by the US National Endowment for the Humanities and Title VIII, the Wenner-Gren Foundation for Anthropological Research, and the Connecticut State University. None of these organizations nor the US government are responsible for views expressed here. Research assistance for this project was provided by Bianca Botea, Raluca Nahorniac and Vasile Şoflâu.

2 At the time of the Romanian 'revolution' in 1989, there were 53,446 people employed in the minerit.

3 These include the Nitramonia Chemical Company and the UPRUC Chemical Outfits company from Făgăraş and the Viromet Chemical Company from Oraşul Victoria.

4 The miners have threatened Bucharest seven times since the 1989 revolution. These marches and attacks are known in Romanian as mineriade, a name based on Homer's

*Iliad, Iliade* in Romanian, and thus evoking the quest-like character of these actions. I owe this interpretation to Katherine Verdery.

5 On the basis of the Romanian government's Ordonanţa de Urgenţa, 24/1998, a disfavored zone meets at least one of the following conditions:

1 mono-industrial production profile which employs at least 50 per cent of the labor force;
2 mining zone where workers are released by collective termination of their work contract;
3 collective termination of the work contract affects at least 25 per cent of the local workforce;
4 an unemployment rate at least 25 per cent higher than the national rate;
5 a poor communications and transportation infrastructure.

6 See Government of Romania 1997. Each buy-out offers workers who apply a large severance payoff based on their seniority. For Jiu Valley miners, Ordinance 22/1997 established that those who worked more than fifteen years could receive a severance package worth twenty-two monthly salaries, a sum of money averaging about 44 million lei or over US$3,000 in 1997 exchange rates. For other workers, severance packages totaled less than one year's salary.

7 State regulations impinge significantly on the costs of hiring labor legally. Employers typically have to pay an additional 40 per cent of a worker's salary for various benefits, which leads many to hire at least some of their workers illegally.

8 Parliament passed Law 15 in 1991 to regulate the process by which strikes are to be called and implement a mechanism to punish unlawful actions (Bush 1993; Parliament of Romania 1991); this brought only limited success.

9 The miners first marched on Bucharest in January 1990 and again in June 1990 at the behest of then acting president Ion Iliescu. In January they threatened the opposition building against the FSN and Iliescu. In June, they broke up a tent encampment of protesters in Bucharest's University Square (Abraham 1990; Beck 1991).

10 Officials at the Ministry of Labor and Social Protection, Ministry of Health, and the National Agency for Professional Formation (devoted to training the unemployed) therefore expressed great interest in my research, for the possible insight into workers' thoughts it offered. The dearth of studies of worker opinions, in fact, is common throughout the formerly socialist countries (Gardawski *et al.* 1999).

11 Recent public opinion polls show that unions are held in very low regard in Romania (Center for Urban and Regional Sociology 1997: 29–30; Muntean 1997: 21).

12 Many marriages are now held in August when young emigrants return from West European countries, mainly Italy, to marry local girls before returning to continue their work.

13 Făgăraş women also appear to be suffering increased incidences of abuse, mental illness and suicide. According to one informant, women in this region have higher rates of mental illness than anywhere else in the country (Maria Eşan, personal communication).

# References

Abraham, Dorel (1990) 'Post-revolutionary social phenomena in Romania: "The University Square" and the violent collective behavior of June 13th to 15th', *Romanian Journal of Sociology* 1(1–2): 121–30.

Arandarenko, Mihail (1999) 'Labour quiescence in Serbia', *Emergo: Journal of Transforming Economies and Societies*, 6(2): 75–83.

Ashwin, Sarah (1999) 'Redefining the collective: Russian mineworkers in transition', in Michael Burawoy and Katherine Verdery (eds) *Uncertain Transition: Ethnographies of Change in the Postsocialist World*, Lanham: Rowman and Littlefield, pp. 245–71.

Bacon, Walter M. Jr and Louis G. Pol (1994) 'The economic status of women in Romania', in Nahid Aslanbeigui, Steven Pressman and Gale Summerfield, *Women in the Age of Economic Transformation: Gender Impact of Reforms in Postsocialist and Developing Countries*, London and New York: Routledge, pp. 43–58.

Bahro, Rudolf (1977) *The Alternative in Eastern Europe*, London: NLB.

Bârgău, Valeriu (1984) 'Oamenii Subpămîntului', in Gligor Haşa (ed.) *Planeta Cărbunului*, Bucharest: Editura Eminescu, pp. 115–70.

Beck, Sam (1991) 'Toward a civil society: the struggle over University Square in Bucharest, Romania, June, 1990', *Socialism and Democracy* 13: 135–54.

Berdahl, Daphne (2000) 'Introduction: an anthropology of postsocialism', in Daphne Berdahl, Matti Bunzl and Martha Lampland (eds) *Altering States: Ethnographies of Transition in Eastern Europe and the Former Soviet Union*, Ann Arbor: University of Michigan Press, pp. 1–13.

Birtalan, Laura (1999) 'Munca la negru atinge dimensiuni fărabreve; precedent', *Adevărul*, 26 July: 8.

Blanchard, Olivier Jean and Kenneth A. Froot *et al.* (1994) 'The transition in Eastern Europe', Chicago: University of Chicago Press.

Bobek, Martin and Michael Marmot (1996) 'East–West mortality divide and its potential explanation: proposed research agenda,' *British Medical Journal* 312: 421–5.

Brehoi, Gheorghe and A. Popescu (1991) *Conflictul Colectiv de Muncă şi Grevă*, Bucharest: Forum.

Bush, Larry (1993) 'Collective labor disputes in post-Ceauşescu Romania', *Cornell International Law Journal* 26(2): 373–85.

Castells, Manuel (1996) *The Rise of the Network Society*, Cambridge, MA: Blackwell.

Center for Urban and Regional Sociology (1997) *National Public Opinion Poll*, Bucharest: CURS.

Cockerham, William C. (1999) *Health and Social Change in Russia and Eastern Europe*, London: Routledge.

Comisia Naţionala Pentru Statistica (1996) *Anuarul Statistic al României 1996*, Bucharest.

Crowley, Stephen (1997) *Hot Coal, Cold Steel: Russian and Ukrainian Workers from the End of the Soviet Union to the Post-Communist Transformations*, Ann Arbor: University of Michigan Press.

Gardawski, Juliusz, Barbara Gąciarz, Andrzej Mokrzyszewski and Wlodzimierz Palków (1999) *Rozpad Bastionu? Związki zawodowe w gospodarce prywatyzowanej*, Warsaw: Institute for Public Affairs.

Government of Romania (1997) *Ordonanţa privind unele măsuri de protecţie ce se acordă personalului din industria minieră şi din activităţile de prospecţiuni şi explorări geologice*, României: Monitorul Oficial al României.

Hobsbawm, E.J. (1984) 'Man and woman: images on the left', in E.J. Hobsbawm, *Workers: Worlds of Labour*, New York: Pantheon, pp. 49–65.

Hoffman, Oscar, Simona Raşeev and Dinu Ţenovici (1984) *Clasa Muncitoare din România în Condiţiile Revoluţiei Tehnico-Ştiinţifice*, Bucharest: Editura Academiei.

Judecătorie Făgăraş (1999) *Dosarele de statistica a le Judecătoriei Făgăraş 1976–1999*.

Judecătorie Petroşani (1999) *Dosarele de statistica a le Judecătoriei Petroşani, 1989–1999*.

Kideckel, David A. (1988) 'Economic images in the Romanian socialist transformation', *Dialectical Anthropology* 12(4): 399–411.

——(1993) *The Solitude of Collectivism: Romanian Villagers to the Revolution and Beyond*, Ithaca: Cornell University Press.

——(1999) 'Storm and stasis: the paradox of labour in post-socialist Romania', *Emergo: Journal of Transforming Economies and Societies* 6(2): 24–46.

——(2001a) 'The un-dead: the death and rebirth of Nicolae Ceauşescu and patriarchal politics in post-socialist Romania', in John W. Borneman (ed.) *Death of the Father: an Anthropology of Closure in Political Authority*, Princeton: Princeton University Press, forthcoming.

——(2001b) 'Winning the battles, losing the war: contradictions of Romanian labour in the post-Communist transformation', in David Ost and Stephen Crowley (eds) *Class Dismissed: Labour Quiescence in Post-Communist Transformations*, Lanham: Rowman and Littlefield (in press).

Konrád, George and Ivan Szelényi (1979) *The Intellectuals on the Road to Class Power: a Sociological Study of the Role of the Intelligentsia in Socialism*, New York: Harcourt, Brace, Jovanovich.

Kornai, János (1980) *Economics of Shortage*, Amsterdam: North-Holland.

Lampland, Martha (1995) *The Object of Labour: Commodification in Socialist Hungary*, Chicago: University of Chicago Press.

Muntean, Georgeta (1997) *Atitudini Politice, Civice, şi Morale ale Populaţiei României Faţă de Procesul de Tranziţiei: Fază Unică*, Bucharest: Research Group Romania.

Ockenga, Edzard (1997) 'Trade unions in Romania', *Transfer: European Review of Labour and Research* 3(2): 313–28.

Offe, Claus (1997) *Varieties of Transition: the East European and East German Experience*, Cambridge, MA: MIT Press.

Oprea, Ion (1970) *Istoria Românilor*, Bucharest: Editura Didactică şi Pedagogică.

Parliament of Romania (1991) *A Law on the Settlement of Collective Labor Conflicts*, Springfield: National Technical Information Service.

Pasti, Vladimir (1997) *România în Tranziţia: Căderea în Viitor*, Bucharest: Editura Nemir.

Pollert, Anna (1999) 'Class dismissed? Labour and trade unions in the Czech Republic, 1989–1999', *Emergo: Journal of Transforming Economies and Societies* 6(2): 6–23.

Pospai, Mircea (1978) *Amintiri din Valea Luminii: Viaţa şi Activitatea Minerilor din Oltenia*, Craiova: Scrisul Românesc.

Rodina, Vladimir (1994) 'Romania: unions running out of steam', *Warsaw Post*, 26 June, cited in Lexis-Nexis European News Service.

Rompres (1998) 'Women make up nearly 50 per cent of unemployed in Romania', BBC Summary of World Broadcasts, Part 2, Central Europe, 8 October.

Sampson, Steven (1987) 'The informal sector in Eastern Europe', *Telos* 66(Winter): 44–66.

Sapolsky, Robert M. (1997) *The Trouble with Testosterone and Other Essays on the Biology of the Human Predicament*, New York: Simon and Schuster.

Słomczyński, Kazimierz and Goldie Shabad (1997) 'Systemic transformation and the salience of class structure in East Central Europe', *East European Politics and Societies* 11(1): 155–89.

Snyder, Tim and Milada Vachudova (1997) 'Are transitions transitory? Two types of political change in Eastern Europe since 1989', *East European Politics and Societies* 11(1): 1–35.

Stone, Richard (2000) 'Stress: the invisible hand in Eastern Europe's death rates', *Science* 288: 1732–3.

Straussner, Shulamith, Lala Ashenberg and Norma Phillips (1999) 'The impact of job loss on professional and managerial employees and their families', *Families in Society* 80(6): 642–8.

Synovitz, Ron (1997) 'The East: labour leader says unreformed unions fail workers', *RFE/RL Newsline*, 2 December.

Ţic, Nicolae (1977) *Roşu pe Alb*, Craiova.

Tilly, Charles (1998) *Durable Inequality*, Berkeley: University of California Press.

Verdery, Katherine (1994) *National Ideology under Socialism: Identity and Cultural Politics in Ceauşescu's Romania*, Berkeley: University of California Press.

——(1996) *What Was Socialism and What Comes Next?*, Princeton: Princeton University Press.

Watson, Peggy (1993) 'The rise of masculinism in Eastern Europe', *New Left Review* 198: 71–82.

——(1995) 'Explaining rising mortality among men in Eastern Europe', *Social Science in Medicine* 41: 923–34.

Wedel, Janine R. (1998) *Collision and Collusion: the Strange Case of Western Aid to Eastern Europe, 1989–1998*, New York: St Martin's Press.

Weidner, Gerdi (1998) 'Gender gap in health decline in East Europe', *Nature* 395 (29 October): 835.

Chapter 7

# Deprivation, the Roma and 'the underclass'

*Michael Stewart*

## Introduction

The plight of the Romany peoples or *Roma* of Eastern Europe has been inten-
sively addressed since the 'changes' of 1989, mainly in Anglo-American
NGO-speak.[1] The tide began to rise with a memorable series of reports by
various wings of Human Rights Watch in the early 1990s, followed by many
further reports and briefings on the often intolerable position of Romany
minorities (see, most recently, Zoon 2001). The migration of thousands of
Roma to Western Europe and North America has highlighted in the West the
view, first articulated by liberals in the East, that the treatment of this group is a
litmus test for the 'new democracies'. For the time being at least, it is a test that
consistently shows an unpleasant hue. More recently, sociological surveys have
also painted an almost unremittingly dismal picture of the fate of Romany
people in the contexts of employment, education and health. These two streams
of data-gathering from Human Rights observers and social scientists offer alternative models of the source of the plight of the Roma and divergent solutions.
Curiously, however, both apply metaphors drawn from Western societies and,
more specifically, North American folk discourse. Thus in modelling post-
communist deprivation, social scientists have taken over the image of an
'underclass', segregated from the rest of society and discriminated against in
such a way that 'those in the underclass have almost no chance of finding roles
in the new division of labour or of having "normal" jobs, income, housing,
social security, or access to better education for their children' (Ladányi 2000:
71). The activists, by contrast, talk of racial discrimination and evoke a 'civil
rights' tradition drawn in large measure from 1960s North America.

I shall argue that the position and opportunities of the 'deprived' of postsocialism are misleadingly characterized in both these models. I begin by
comparing and contrasting postsocialist economic collapse with the Great
Depression as a means to measure one aspect of the plight of the Roma. Though
this may seem an exaggerated contrast, seen from the inside the shift in
economic activity has been as great in 1989–96 as it was in 1929–36 (Milanovic
1998: 23–39). However, since the socialist economies did not have major

trading partners in the capitalist world, the external world has not noticed (*ibid.*: 28). Milanovic distinguishes between two patterns, exemplified by Poland and Russia. Whereas Poland between 1987 and 1995 experienced a rapid fall in GDP followed by recovery, rather similar to the pattern of the US and Germany in 1927–35, the fall of Russian GDP over the same period was deeper and it did not begin to recover until much later.[2] Hungary and the Czech Republic resemble Poland, while Romania and Bulgaria fall closer to the Russian model (for Romania see Biró and Biró 1997). The most interesting parallel for understanding the place of the Roma lies in the relationship between real wages and unemployment rates. Real wages in all the postsocialist countries have fallen, but unemployment has not risen to the levels of the Great Depression, when the entire brunt of restructuring was born by those pushed out of work and the real wages of those in work remained stable (Milanovic 1998: 29–30). In other words, the postsocialist governments of Eastern Europe and the former Soviet Union have – in classic Keynesian fashion – kept employment up, but at the cost of rising inflation and falling real wages, thus in effect spreading the 'social costs' of economic restructuring at the possible cost of prolonging its negative features.

In contrast to this general picture, postsocialist Romany unemployment rose across the region in the early 1990s to the level attained in Germany in 1932 and has stayed near there till the present day.[3] Whereas under socialism the employment rates for Romany and non-Romany males were virtually identical, in the 1990s a cleavage developed (see Ringold 2000 for analysis of the Czech and Hungarian cases). The disproportionate number of unemployed Roma is not attributable to direct discrimination in the sense of Roma losing jobs when non-Roma, in structurally similar positions, retain theirs. Rather, it is the consequence of the broom of 'efficiency' sweeping through the dead undergrowth of the socialist economy (Kertesi 2000). The fundamental causes lie in the socialist regimes' educational policies towards the Roma, which were an unmitigated disaster. Even at the end of the communist period, Roma were disproportionately employed in low-skill, labour-intensive jobs which only existed because of the redistributive, egalitarian logic of the socialist economy. These people were inevitably the first to lose their jobs under the rationalization programmes of new property owners. For example, in a factory which I first investigated in 1985, only one semi-skilled Romany employee held on to his job, and the unskilled were made redundant after 1989. There is little evidence of racial discrimination *per se*, although there is a tendency among employers to use Romany ethnicity as a marker for lack of schooling and other negative attributes. Kertesi (2000: 442–5) estimates that 30 per cent of Romany unemployment in Hungary results from this kind of 'over-generalization' of an ethnic stereotype. However, Milanovic's data indicate a broader exclusion of the Roma. As he shows, 'non-profitable' economic activities have been sustained through hidden subsidies, tardy changes to bankruptcy laws and all kinds of manoeuvres to 'buy time', but the benefits of such policies only extend 'down' to the level of the semi-skilled – the latter have been allowed to fall out of the Keynesian job-protection net. It is also evident that the Roma have not benefited from appropriate targeting of social benefits to meet their needs – on the contrary, some aspects of social and welfare policy seem designed to make it harder for Romany people to receive benefits.[4]

Unemployment has halted the reduction in relative deprivation of the Roma that the socialist period instigated (see Stewart 1990). Residential segregation often accompanies unemployment and deprivation. Some 13 per cent of Hungarian Roma still live in 'isolated' settlements (telep), some thirty-five years after a national campaign was launched to end such segregation (Szekélyi n.d.). Of equal concern, however, has been the emergence of villages from which all non-Roma have migrated and into which Romany families have congregated. The quality of Romany housing also still tends to be worse than that of non-Roma (Ringold 2000: 13). Nor has land privatization benefited Roma to a significant degree, despite the fact that Roma are twice as likely to live in rural communities as non-Roma. Even where legal provisions exist, as in Romania, most Roma former cooperative farm employees have, under pretext of land shortage, not received the 0.5 hectares of land to which their years of membership entitle them (ibid.).

In terms of educational qualifications, the picture remains almost uniformly gloomy across the region. Whereas 50 per cent of Bulgarians and slightly more Romanians proceed to secondary education, less than 10 per cent of Roma in these countries make it this far (Medina and McDonald 2001). Recent progress in Hungary shows that government initiatives can make a difference. Whereas in 1993 only 3 per cent of Romany children entered schools where it was possible to take the baccalaureate school-leaving exams (Kertesi and Kézdi 1994), by 1998–9 the figure had risen to 16 per cent, while as many as 65 per cent went on to some form of training for skilled work (Kemény 2001: 66).[5] However, 25 per cent of Gypsy children still fail to complete primary school. In several countries the most crippling aspect of educational policy for Romany people is the de facto segregation of their children into 'special needs' classes and schools. In Hungary these are known as 'c' classes, where 'c' is both the third rank and serendipitously stands for 'cigány', i.e. Roma. Romany children remain massively over-represented in schools for the mentally handicapped in Hungary. In the Czech Republic, the government concedes that approximately 75 per cent of Romany children attend 'special schools' (for the retarded), and more than half of all 'special school' students are Roma. This extraordinary disparity has been condemned by a United Nations committee of experts (ERRC 1999). Educational failure has consequences 'down the line', not just for employment possibilities, but for all forms of social integration. Thus, in Hungary, newspapers aimed at the Romany audience have minimal readerships.[6] According to one Hungarian survey of 10,000 'Gypsies', 90 per cent were unable to name a single Romany political party.[7]

Analysis of such postsocialist deprivation patterns is, however, beset with difficulties. For one, it tends to overlook the existence of unemployment, poverty and deprivation in the socialist period (e.g. Clarke 1999, for a Russian example). For another, the terms themselves are often not adequately defined. As János Ladányi has pointed out for Hungary in the 1990s, 'There are no official definitions of poverty and no poverty lines that are accepted by the experts' (2000: 68).[8] He concludes that 'poverty is when somebody cannot live like others do'. An alternative to this relativizing approach is to insist on a definition of poverty that stresses its absolute character. I prefer to define poverty as life below the World Bank line of 'four purchasing power parity dollars per day', the local minimum-standard-of-living 'basket'.[9] This leads me to argue that it is the 'relative deprivation' (Runciman 1966) rather than the 'poverty' of the Roma that has intensified in the past ten years. There is no doubt that the Roma fall deeper below the 'deprivation line' than other groups. Deprivation among Roma also lasts longer, as Hungarian household surveys have clearly shown.[10] While Roma made up only 4 per cent of the total sample, roughly in line with their national presence, they constituted 33 per cent of the long-term deprived (Mészáros and Fóti 2000: 305–7).

Such statistical representations of Romany misery are the stock-in-trade of many reports published on postsocialist 'poverty' and discrimination. They illustrate the extent of inequality between Roma and non-Roma across the region and provide policy-makers with a broadly accurate sense of some of the challenges facing these societies. But what sense can ethnographers, who are supposed to know rather more about life on the ground than the survey producers, make of this kind of brute data? What regional, social and other differences are concealed, and why do these matter? How have the Romany peoples dealt with 'the changes' and how can qualitative ethnographic data alter our sense of the issues that have to be addressed in order to alleviate their problem? How can this in turn help us to conceptualize the reproduction of massive deprivation? To answer these questions I shall first present and critique the influential underclass theory that is increasingly applied to the Romany peoples, before going on to illustrate the gains from an ethnographic approach.

## The history and politics of 'underclass' ideas

According to Iván Szelényi and Rebecca Emigh (2000: 3–4), the Romany people are emerging as a racialized underclass. An 'underclass' is constituted by persons who are likely to remain unemployed and poor for their entire life because of their lack of education and marketable skills, and whose children are likely to be locked into a similar social position, thereby becoming separated from the rest of society as the 'untouchables', the 'undeserving poor', or the 'no-hopers'. Aware of the political uses to which the term 'underclass' has been put, as part of an effort to blame the deprived for their own misfortune and justify 'small state' welfare programmes, the authors reject a behavioural definition. They return instead to the original use of the term by Gunnar Myrdal (1963), who 'used it to designate the unique position of the long-term deprived, who were not benefiting from the post-war economic boom … because they did not have, and could not acquire, the education and skills demanded in a diversified economy' (Szelényi and Emigh 2000: 3). By adopting William Julius Wilson's (1987) racial perspective, they aim to transcend Myrdal's 'economically deterministic understanding' of the underclass. Finally, drawing on Pierre Bourdieu, they analyse both 'the objective problems of structural unemployment' and 'the subjective classificatory struggles of ethnicity'. With this double focus they hope to avoid the pitfalls of American new-right rhetoric attacking the 'welfare dependent', 'the subset of deprived mired in crime' (*ibid.*: 10).

While acknowledging the attractions of the term for authors who wish to engage an American academic audience, for two sets of reasons it seems to me unhelpful to identify an underclass in the Eastern European context.[11] The first set has to do with the inherent imprecision and recurring connotations of the term itself.

Gunnar Myrdal was an experienced commentator on American ways with such impeccable Swedish social-democratic credentials that he could never be imagined as contributing to the discourse of the moralistic 'right'. However, it is in fact questionable whether Myrdal's use is as 'structural' as Szelényi and Emigh (2000) would wish. Far from being a scientific term, it seems Myrdal searched for an English word to fit an existing Swedish folk term, *underklass*, which is 'not really an integrated part of the nation at all but a useless and miserable substratum' (Myrdal 1963: 41). The Swedish term was a derogatory one, used by the prosperous to suggest something uncouth, bad-mannered, lacking in breeding and status. It suggested that the rising working class still lacked cultural capital, and its adoption by Myrdal may reflect his own prosperous farming family background.[12]

In this sense, Myrdal was evoking a tradition of representations that goes back at least to the middle of the nineteenth century. Karl Marx, in *The Class Struggle in France* (1849) had identified a *Lumpenproletariat* as

> heterogeneous clusters of individuals who stand on the margins of the class system because they are not fully integrated into the division of labour, people who live on the crumbs of society, people without a definite trade, vagabonds, people without a hearth or home.
>
> (Marx and Engels 1958: 55)

Three years earlier Friedrich Engels had used this notion to discuss Irish labourers in Britain in derogatory terms (1845). This behavioural sense of a class apart or under (referred to in English using an appropriately imperial metaphor as 'outcaste') was part of middle-class common sense, as illustrated in the journalism of Henry Mayhew (1851).[13] It derived its force in popular and journalistic speech from its suggestion of an alternative to familiar patterns of class differentiation. Whereas other social classes are constituted by their relations with one another, the 'underclass' is formed by its absence of relations

with others. Perhaps the closest English term to it, one which it evokes by association, is 'underworld', with the suggestion of a separate and pathological social
space with its own rules and regulations. Up to a point such remodelling is
valid, if some households are excluded from the forms of interaction and citizenship through which most groups experience a sense of belonging and trust in
society. But as the behaviour described becomes more or less strange to
respectable commentators, so the political implications of designating it as
'underclass' behaviour shift (Bourgeois 1995).

Moving back to the present day, we can illustrate the problem by looking at
a group of migrant Roma in Budapest. According to a recent study (Kováts
2000), a Romanian Romany family lives during the summer months out of
doors in a public park in Budapest while its members beg around the railway
stations. They make a monthly journey to the Hungarian–Romanian border
where they renew their visas, but manage to avoid paying fares on these trains
through complex manoeuvres with the guards and a willingness to take an inor-
dinately long time about their journeys. They live in the park in part in order to
avoid paying for accommodation, but also to get away from unpleasant encounters in the kind of hostel where lodging would be available to them (Vajda and
Prónai 2000: 101–2). If the notion of a class outside or under society character-
izes any individuals, it would surely have to fit this family. Yet all the
ethnographic evidence on Roma who derive a significant income from begging
(e.g. Piasere 1982; Tauber n.d.; Engebrigsten 2000) suggests that such families
also rely upon more 'regular' income streams and in other contexts appear as
'normal,' 'assimilated' Roma. So to describe such people in terms of 'underclass'
is problematic, because it exaggerates the reality of separation and in so doing
reproduces the very ideology by which the exclusion of the 'Gypsies' tends to be
justified (the exclusion which produces the 'problematic' behaviour in the first
place).

There is striking evidence of this process of ideologically constructed exclusion in recent doctoral research by the Norwegian anthropologist Ada
Engebrigsten who, uniquely among ethnographers of Romany peoples, has
carried out research both among Roma and among their peasant neighbours in
western Romania (2000). For the peasants, the 'Gypsies' are always 'people
without' to whom a good *gospodăr* ('householding farmer') may give as an act of
charity. While some Gypsies are truly beholden to their peasant patrons, in
recent years several *ţigani* families in this village have acquired major material
resources which the peasants need. But despite the shift in relationships
between Roma and villagers, everyone – including the Roma – continues to
pretend that it is the *ţigani* who remain the supplicants. In so doing a crucial
Romanian peasant myth is sustained: that because the *ţigani* have no land they
are dependants of the villagers, who in effect 'live off' the peasantry. In a final
twist of the gyre, the peasants treat 'giving work' to the *ţigani* as an act of alms
and in this way legitimize to themselves the fact that they only reciprocate in
goods rather than cash or (as between peasant households) in labour

(Engebrigsten 2000: 340–62).[14] For the peasants the myth of Gypsy dependency ensures the 'voluntary' giving of cheap labour by the Gypsies, while for the Roma it ensures that when their current good fortune passes they can revert to their 'traditional' relationship. But the construction of the *ţigani* as a burden and parasite on the village remains a myth.

The tendency of 'underclass' imagery to exaggerate differentiation has been a feature of the literature since the word 'underclass' leaked out of academic discourse to become part of mediatized 'common sense' in the 1970s. For William Julius Wilson,

> what distinguishes members of the underclass from those of other economically disadvantaged groups is that their neighbourhood or social milieu uniquely reinforces their marginal economic position or weak attachment to the labour force. The dual problem of marginal economic position and social isolation in concentrated deprivation areas is an important distinction that cannot be captured by the standard designation 'lower class'.
>
> (Wilson *et al.* 2000)

This geographical specificity is a major factor in some studies of Roma (e.g. Ladányi 1993) but academics should be wary of hastily adopting popular uses of 'ghetto' imagery, which in most cases tend to exaggerate the degree of residential segregation of minorities (Kusmer 1997: 706). Ladányi's candidate for ghetto status is the eighth district of Budapest, where around 30 per cent of the inhabitants are Roma. Yet this is to concede that two out of three residents are not Romany. Only one in six of Budapest Roma live in this district (Ladányi 1992: 80) and they actually seem to be less poor than those in other areas of Budapest.[15]

The main danger in exaggerating the 'difference' of the most deprived is that it blinds us to the contingent features of their position. Historical evidence suggests that those who have been labelled as belonging to another world beneath the mainstream can emerge from it with remarkable speed. For example, the prospering, propertied classes in London in the late nineteenth century feared an 'outcast' city, in which an irreversible decline in economic standards, degeneration of moral fibre, a self-reproducing descent into criminality and other forms of social exclusion (for instance, from the educational system) would make return to normality and civility for the generation to come all but impossible (Stedman-Jones 1984). But what happened to 'outcast London'? Its major social problems were all but eliminated in the early twentieth century, not through Darwinian selection and physical extermination, as many had expected, but through a transformation of the economic and social environment (Stedman-Jones 1984: 348–9).[16] If Eastern European economies are allowed into an expanded European free trade area, who can assert with confidence that the position of the Roma is bound to remain as it is today?

We should not forget an altogether darker side to underclass ideas. Perhaps the most disturbing formulation came within the German social-medicine tradition which labelled the underclass as '*asozial*', implying people cut off from the civilizing effects of participation in 'normal' social life (Weindling 1989; Peukert 1989: 208–35). For many years at the end of the nineteenth and beginning of the twentieth centuries, such ideas shaped a social policy that was particularly hostile to and repressive of the lowest social layers, as in the 1926 Bavarian Law for the Fight Against Gypsies, Vagrants and the Workshy.[17] Later, of course, the term '*asozial*' became 'Germanized' and transmogrified into the Nazi notion of *Gemeinschaftsfremde*, the sense of which is conveyed by one translator as 'community aliens' (Peukert 1989). The *Zigeuner* were, of course, the prototype of these 'aliens'. Contemporary social scientists should be wary of reviewing such usages in postsocialist Eastern Europe. On 4 August 2000 a right-wing MP in the Slovak parliament declared that 'inadaptable Roma' should be placed in 'reservations' to reduce the crime rate. He went on to say that the state must stop providing social benefits to 'people who harm it', arguing that such payments were 'inhumane to the rest of the population'.[18] In this part of the world, in contrast to most of 'the West', this kind of language, with its overpowering odour of the nineteenth-century bio-social terminology taken over by the Nazis, was never systematically attacked and expunged from the mainstream of public culture in the post-war period.[19]

From Slovakia too comes a telling final example of the way that structural senses of underclass ineluctably mutate. As I write, an article has just been published by a former research partner of Iván Szelényi, who has since parted company with the team. Michal Vašečka now adopts precisely the behavioural sense of underclass rejected by Szelényi, informing an educated public readership that 'expert and professional circles see the Roma becoming an "underclass"' characterized by 'general resignation, low respect for authorities, a low level of social control, and poor labour ethics' (2001: 171). Szelényi cannot be held responsible for the beliefs of his one-time associate, but since academics have so little control over the ways others use our ideas (Gans 1997), it is extremely risky to give any credence at all to a loose and vague term like 'underclass', with all its derogatory connotations.

## 'Underclass' and the 'culture of poverty'

A second set of arguments for rejecting the term 'underclass' is centred on the notion that people living on the margins of society have a distinct culture, which on closer inspection is alleged to be not a 'real culture' at all. Under socialism, terms such as 'poverty' and 'structural inequality' were largely taboo and excluded from social science discourse. This did not, however, prevent the circulation of concepts close to the modern American sense of underclass, most importantly that of the 'culture of poverty', associated above all with the anthropologist Oscar Lewis (1966). The main features of this approach are its implication that the lives of poor people are disorganized, so that their economic position determines their values in a predictive fashion. These were misleading assumptions in the slums of Puerto Rico and Mexico, but in the context of the East European Romany peoples they are positively pernicious.

The idea that Romany peoples and other marginal groups 'lack culture' is the legacy of an unanthropological understanding of public culture predicated on notions of civility. István Kemény has carried out sociological investigations of 'the Gypsy/poverty question' in Hungary since the early 1970s. In a recent popularization of his findings he tells his readers that the number of Hungarian Roma who speak Romany has fallen from around 20 per cent in 1972 to around 4 per cent in 1993 (1999: 10). Such a dramatic 'language swap' would be almost unparalleled and would certainly merit special analysis; but in fact this finding is not supported by evidence from other sources and the simplest explanation of this extraordinary statistic may lie in faults in the data collection. What I find most striking about Kemény's presentation is that he simply hands the data on without comment, because within his 'culture of poverty' model, language is not accorded serious recognition as a source of cultural capital. It is telling that Kemény and his colleagues refer to the *Romungros* (otherwise known as 'Hungarian' or 'musician Gypsies') as 'Hungarian-speaking'. Within specialist publications, particularly those aimed at teachers and others who work with these people, it would be appropriate to recognize that some speak Romani-influenced dialects of Hungarian, others ethnolects in which not only intonation but also lexicon are influenced by earlier Romany elements.[20]

Failure to pay attention to distinctive Romany social patterns shapes the way public institutions confront the Romany minority. In the early 1990s another group of Hungarian sociologists set out to investigate social problems in a remote village and to make recommendations for alleviating them. At the turn of the twentieth century the Romany population of Csenyéte was a small minority, which made its living through a combination of music-making, mud-brick production (for house building) and other services to the peasantry. Seventy years on this village had become a 'Gypsy only village' (*elcigányosodott*). The interventions of the outside intelligentsia led to a whole series of positive changes, ranging from the restoration of a bus service, through the establishment of a nursery and a scheme for low-interest 'small business' loans (Kereszty 1998). The researchers did not, however, attend to cultural resources of the Roma, and when the ethnomusicologist Katalin Kovalcsik enquired about collecting Roma (folk) stories, for use in the local school, she was told by one of the researchers that the folk culture had long ago 'died out', and that she should collect material from other places where the 'Gypsies' had not been 'totally crushed'. Two days after moving into a local Romany household Kovalcsik discovered why the researcher had never heard any stories: they were told during wakes in the small hours of the morning, when the sociologists were asleep. The old stories and songs had not been 'forgotten', and Kovalcsik went on to show that such performances constituted a valuable cultural resource. These Roma were refusing to turn over and die (Kovalcsik and Kubínyi 2000:

5). The inhabitants of villages like Csenyéte face huge challenges constructing a whole village out of a design for living which was developed in the days when they were a service minority living alongside a peasant majority. The social relations sustained through pre-dawn wakes, given the disappearance of so many other opportunities for social interaction associated with employment, may provide them with a network of support and a more promising basis for launching new economic activities than anything available to unskilled ethnic Hungarians.

A second prominent feature of the Culture of Poverty model is the trope of disorganization and collapse of social institutions. It is vividly illustrated by Péter Ambrus's discussion of the impoverished, mixed Hungarian and Romany community at Dzsumbuj in Budapest, where 'the absence of any stability' was 'the most characteristic feature of the life of the poor' (1988: 78). However, one person's disorder can be another's order. Romany people may organize their activities successfully, but in ways differing from those of their more respectable (and fortunate) neighbours. In a study of migration strategies among a number of different Hungarian Roma groups, as well as foreign Roma in Hungary, a persistent question of the researchers concerned the access of these Roma to accurate information on labour markets and openings for them in their target countries. Not one of the research teams reported any reliance on 'reliable' official or press information. Yet, with a few exceptions who fitted the expectation that the migrants would be 'uninformed chancers', the subjects were in fact better versed than their researchers in the issues that concerned them (Kováts 2000). While it may seem disorganized to arrive at Budapest Western railway station with no Hungarian, not much money and a request to be directed to the 'Romanian market', the man who did so found a job and lodgings, and survived to tell his tale to the investigators! (Vajda and Prónai 2000: 104; cf. Hajnal 2000).

At the simplest level, the distinctive pattern of problem-solving among Roma leads families to come up with original solutions to unexpected problems. One of Ivan Szelényi's research team reports on changes in another 'Gypsified' village in northern Hungary, where – to give a sense of the depth of deprivation – the daily menu of the poorest families can read as follows:

> Breakfast: potato in paprika and onion sauce, tea
> Lunch: pasta with potatoes, potato soup
> Dinner: cooked potato with lard or onion
> (Durst n.d.: 55)

In this village, as in many Romany communities, one of the biggest changes since 1989 has been the gradual disappearance of cash from the economy. The only item on the above menu that had to be purchased for cash was the tea. In this context, small welfare payments are crucial. As Durst points out, multi-generational pooling networks have been re-formed. In line with the official spacing of payments through the post office in Hungary, 'in the first week of every month regular social welfare is paid out, as well as unemployment benefits. The second week is for child aid, the third for family supplement and the fourth for pensions' (*ibid*.: 83). As long as one's family network contains several generations, every week of the month brings in some new money to meet essential cash needs. At the present moment, it is true, such family networks do little more than facilitate survival. But it is these same networks that provide the reliable information-flows which the Romany migrants use when judging the most appropriate strategy for moving and remaining abroad. It is only the analysts' models which make these strategies seem like 'social collapse' or 'disorganization'. And the fact that Romany peoples in these circumstances turn 'back' on their families need not be seen as a sign of entropy or involution, but as another expression of their 'cultural capital'. Only in the eyes of a very myopic modernization school can 'kinship' stand opposed to enterprise, business and corporation.

A third problem with the Culture of Poverty model is the notion that there might be a single, coherent way of adapting functionally to long-term deprivation.[21] What actually happens among deprived people is always more complex (cf. Hannerz 1969). Likewise for the Romany peoples in the postsocialist world, one finds a complex patterning of strategies among people who share rather similar social conditions. The research on migration, for instance, provides illustrations of poor Roma who plan to leave Hungary en masse as a form of political protest against intolerable local conditions, as well as of individuals who work abroad in the European Union as illegal employees and of young entrepreneurs who seek to migrate to Canada in search of 'a more favourable tax regime for business' (Kováts 2000).

For all these reasons, rooted in the history of underclass ideas and their various political uses, I prefer the blander term 'social exclusion'. This has the virtue of making it clear that we are talking of an on-going process rather than a fixed state, and it focuses attention on the primarily political struggles that determine who is defined as 'in' and 'out', rather than on 'deviant behaviour' and 'criminality'. As Ignatiev (1995) has shown, for much of the nineteenth century the Irish in America fell into a category similar to that of blacks today, but through the electoral interests and activities of the Democratic Party the structural position of the Irish was altered and they 'became white' without their 'neighbourhood' or 'social milieu' altering significantly. The term 'underclass' suggests that there is something inherent to the group or its situation that makes this kind of process quite incomprehensible.

## A ladder, not a gorge

Might the Roma in Eastern Europe today look forward to a transformation comparable to that of the Irish in nineteenth-century America, or the 'outcasts' of Victorian London? Some are clearly pessimistic about their immediate prospects. The vast majority of the several thousand Hungarian Romany people who have gone to Canada do not in fact believe that they are refugees from political or other persecution (Kováts 2000), but they play the refugee game because it often seems to be the only one in town for Roma who wish to improve their standard of living.[22] However, even less agile performers than these transnational migrants are developing new strategies. Ózd is the urban centre of a region of northern Hungary previously dependent on outdated heavy industry, where the situation of unemployed Romany has long been considered especially dire. In 1980 there were 35,000 jobs in this former steel town; by 1996 a mere 15,000. The proportion of Roma among the unemployed is approximately 50–60 per cent, and among the long-term unemployed this figure rises to over 80 per cent (Artemisszió Foundation 2000). It has been part of the unchallenged common sense of the Budapest intelligentsia that the Roma of Ózd are 'finished', that without qualifications or experience in any industry other than steel, there is 'no way out' of their impasse. But recent research by a non-governmental foundation which plans retraining programmes for Roma, in tandem with the innovative leader of the Romany Self-governing Council, indicates that a significant number have begun to find solutions. Several hundred now commute on a weekly basis to the west of the country, to towns like Székesfehérvár, where they can find cheap accommodation while they work in the booming industry of this region. As yet little more is known about the roots of this network, but it is remarkable that the World Bank reports that, contrary to public belief, unemployed Romany persons are *more* likely to seek work than their non-Romany counterparts (Ringold 2000: 16).

Not all Romany people are well adapted for such juggling and balancing. Leo Howe has shown with respect to Northern Ireland that a group's historical relationship with the state decisively shapes strategies in communities of the long-term unemployed (1990). Frances Pine's ethnographic investigations in Poland have also demonstrated that a certain disrespect for 'authority' is the *sine qua non* for survival as entrepreneurs at the bottom of the social pile (1996: 140–7, 1998: 117). It seems in the Romany context that those who were persecuted for longest as 'nomads' and 'vagrants' are the ones who have maintained the most 'ambitious' stance *vis-à-vis* authorities and the state, who have managed to make the most of the new world order around them (see Stewart 1997; Day *et al.* 1998/9). Yet the Ózd case is all the more remarkable in that the Romany people involved are the *Romungros*, people who attempted to buy into the socialist deal, whereby people had to give up their freedom in order to obtain security, and who benefited considerably by doing so.

In the village where Engebrigsten carried out her research, the economic openings available to the Roma were transformed in two ways after the death of Ceauşescu. First, all official employment, in the collective farm, on the railroads, in the factories, came to an end. Second, however, within two years an annual gift of clothes and other second-hand goods arrived from a Scandinavian country. Intended for 'the needy Gypsies', once these goods had been divided among themselves, they were mostly sold on to or otherwise exchanged with the local peasants, with whom the Roma needed to maintain good relations. Some families have made large amounts of money in this business, through the kind of 'shameful' behaviour which the 'respectable poor' would avoid at all costs, for it is behaviour which is enough to cause members of the dominant societies to be classified as *ţigani*. Again, it must be stressed that the flexibility of the Roma brings more than merely short-term advantages. The trade in foreign second-hand goods is one of the more profitable sectors of the Romanian retail sector and one in which Roma play a significant role. Engebrigsten's villagers are on the bottom rung of a long ladder. In stepping on to this ladder they find, as do others in the postsocialist world, that it helps to work with a radical separation of the social world. As Pine has found elsewhere,

> Trust and morality are implicit at the local level but do not extend to the wider society. Rather, the centre is viewed almost as a field of opportunity, in which gaps can be located to pursue entrepreneurial dealings; these dealings are imbued with little or no sense of moral obligation, and there is little sense of shared identity with the centre.
>
> (1998: 121)

The centre may view the practices of those on the periphery as akin to those of an underclass or mafia, but that is not how matters look from the bottom up.[23]

## Racial regimes, the state and the definition of the 'excluded'

In both the academic literature on Roma and the practical interventions of activists, a Human Rights model offers an alternative to the 'underclass'. While 'underclass' theorists focus on social, educational and welfare policy and practice, the Human Rights perspective suggests that juridical changes and legal challenges to established practice can offer a road to 'liberation'. Like that of the 'underclass', this model has been taken over from the USA, from where many of the dedicated activists come. In an ambitious international comparison of 'racial regimes' in three post-colonial societies with a legacy of black slavery, the political scientist Anthony W. Marx focuses on the role of the state and elites working within it to shape racial relations (1998). He suggests that in the USA and South Africa, after the end of slavery and achievement of independence from the original colonizing power, the state enacted formal rules of domination according to racial distinctions. By contrast, in Brazil neither racialist ideologies nor policies of racial domination emerged to encourage a national unity of 'whites' against 'blacks'. Marx goes on to argue that 'official policies of exclusion according to race have drawn boundaries solidifying subordinated racial identity' (1998: 264). Indeed, US racial patterns cannot be understood without taking account of this legacy, and the very notion of an underclass can be seen as a response to a very particular history, which culminated in the flowering of the civil rights movement.

Three great contrasts emerge when this history is set alongside the experience of Eastern Europe. First, with the partial exception of Romania, where many Gypsies were held in slavery until the middle of the nineteenth century, Romany peoples were nowhere subject to distinct, discriminatory *legislation*, as blacks were in the USA.[23] There were of course all kinds of informal discrimination and negative and damaging stereotypes, which were not codified. However oppressive and objectionable, such unspoken rules as persist in rural communities do so without formal institutional back-up from the state. In short, discrimination is not a legal phenomenon as it was in America and South Africa, and so a strategy which focuses solely on the law is misplaced.

Second, in contrast to the USA Roma have not been defined by a 'one drop rule', according to which even 'one-eighth blacks' were black, or by any rule at all.[24] Rather like Brazil, significant mixed populations have emerged, attitudes to which have varied greatly. Achim (1998: 125) has argued that many ex-slaves were assimilated in the Romanian case. From Hungary, too, there is evidence that the radical opposition of *cigány* and Magyar may be of recent construction. Ladányi and Szelényi (2000) have shown that there have been times in Csenyéte when 'Gypsies' were able to declare themselves publicly as Magyars and were not residentially segregated from other poor village dwellers. The ability to 'pass' as a member of the majority is an important marker of the plasticity of social categories. There are differences from country to country in this respect, depending not only on facts of physiognomy (it is easier for most Roma to pass as Romanians than as Czechs) but also on the racialization of ethnicity in the sense of Szelényi and Emigh (2000). In Budapest, Romany women of the eighth district climb the hill by bus to the exclusive villas in the Buda hills where they are employed as cleaners. Because they dress appropriately and lie about their address, their employers do not know that they come from the 'dreaded, crime-infested' ghetto.[25] This experience contrasts markedly with that of residents of the Chicago ghetto (Wacquant 1993).[26]

Finally, following Anthony Marx's argument, we see that forms of racial conflict differ systematically in Eastern Europe and the US. Lacking the kind of identifiable target provided by a racializing legislature, Roma have been largely unable (as yet) to fight for collective redress. They have also been hindered by the prohibition on ethnic Romany politics under socialism. There are signs that this has begun to change, partly as a result of groups of Roma migrating en masse to places where they can challenge their treatment in the spotlight of international publicity.[27] The kind of reactive racial politics found in the USA has not emerged in Eastern Europe, with the partial exception of the Czech Republic where skinhead attacks take on some of these elements.[28] It is striking that the 'beating' remains the standard way of enforcing ethnic domination in the Romanian villages with which I am familiar. From the village of Barşana in the southern Carpathians, Dumitru Budrala and Csilla Kató (n.d.) report incidents that illuminate current tendencies in inter-ethnic relations. In the local elections of June 2000, for the first time a local Romanian-speaking *Băiesi* stood for mayoral office in a village dominated by shepherds. This was seen as an unprecedented event, and the ethnographers were told that the Romany man would have been lynched if he had won. In fact not more than 16 out of nearly 3,000 voters chose him, and even his own family refused to vote for him because he appeared on the ticket of a party representing 'Roma' – that is, Romany-speaking Roma.

At the same election a rather different conflict revealed other features of Romany–shepherd relations. The mayoral candidate obtained the bulk of the *Băiesi* votes and forced a run-off at the second round with Ion B., the favourite of the shepherds, a man who had been the village baker in the 1980s, when bread was rationed. In those days Ion B. had made the '*ţigani*' queue at the front of his shop for hours to obtain their twice weekly ration, while he served shepherds out of the back door upon demand. During the campaign, the candidate who won the Romany vote had begun a programme of public works in the separate, Romany section of the village, the first time that public money had been dispersed in such a way. According to Budrala's account, on the night of the run-off some 600 young shepherds gathered in the village square and a small group began to shout out insulting rhymes: 'Ion B., you should stand up firm, we won't be governed by scum. He's nothing but a bloody Gypsy who doesn't give a damn!'

Budrala and Kató conclude that, had the shepherds not got the result they wanted, the night could have had a tragic end. For the shepherds of Barşana, the *Băiesi* are simply not *omi* (men). At first blush this sounds like just the sort of racial distinction that characterized white/black relations in the USA. But the ethnographic context makes it clear that the shepherds do not think of the 'Gypsies' as being non-human in the way the Nazis did of their victims, or the way some racists represent blacks as being in some way sub-human. For the shepherds, being a *Băiesi* is more about not being manly, having no idea of shepherding and of what is required to be a proper householder, *gospodăr*. At an earlier election I witnessed in this village, the shepherds had refused to vote for a man acknowledged to be by far the most competent candidate because he came from a poor region of Romania with an unflattering reputation. They did not want to be seen to be governed by a *moldovan*. *Ţigani* are lower on this same scale of humanity, but they are not off the scale altogether as in modern racial distinctions, in which the 'other' carries no worth at all. One of the dangers of importing outside frameworks for understanding local ethnic conflict is precisely that it may unwittingly promote this shift to racism.

A striking Hungarian example of this was the battle over the Rádió Street evictions in the prosperous town of Székesfehérvár in 1999 (Horváth 2000: 11–175). Some poor rent-defaulting Roma were due to be evicted from decaying property sited on newly valuable land in the centre of the town. They were to be moved to former military barrack accommodation in nearby villages. The mayor of one of these villages announced that he did not want Roma moving into his territory. Charges of racism and discrimination filled the air. The mostly foreign Human Rights and civil rights activists urged a general campaign against racism, accusing both the Székesfehérvár council and the village mayor of racial discrimination. János Ladányi and Aladár Horváth, a local Romany politician, argued on the contrary that the whole issue had economic and social roots. They proposed to the village mayor that if he objected to the relocations on the grounds that a rich town should not unload its social problems on to resource-poor rural communities, then the Roma would support him. If, however, he took the 'we want no Gypsies' line, he would be denounced as a racist. The mayor sided with Ladányi and Horváth and so a front was formed against the town council, which was painted as self-ishly seeking to avoid its responsibilities. Through avoiding the language of culture, of ethnicity and even of racism, it was possible to forge a winning alliance and a local majority. A campaigning rhetoric of 'human rights' and 'racial discrimination' would have run the risk of uniting the two local authorities against a minority which has to seek allies where it can find them.

## Conclusion

It is unlikely, given the protectionist labour market politics pursued within the European Union, that the deprived of postsocialism will fare as well as the London poor in an age of expanding industrial employment after World War I. János Ladányi has argued that the crisis of totally 'Gypsified' villages lies above all in the denial to these Roma of the social inspiration they formerly derived from contact with richer and better connected 'others' (2000). The 'musician Gypsies' who advanced furthest in the past benefited from their awareness of possibilities in the world through their close-up observation of their clients. It is hard to see today how residents of peripheral villages like Csenyéte can make good without mass migration to more prosperous regions. But then not all Roma live in such desperate conditions as Csenyéte, and for those with a foothold in the cities examples of how the poor can use opportunities opened by the market may yet prove appropriate. I have argued that the Roma have resources of their own, and do not have to rely totally on the inspiration of outsiders to challenge their fate.

The historiography of 1920s and 1930s London speaks of industrialization as the motor of change, of the rapid increase in factory employment and a rise in real wages. This explanation is in part an artifact of the archive sources available. The resourcefulness of the former 'outcasts', their own ability to make use of the 'good times' (and remember these were hardly boom years) is lost from the record, but these too must have played a role. In our time, if a similar trans-formation of deprivation is to occur in parts of Eastern and South Eastern Europe, it will not be achieved solely by (re-)industrialization, but will have also to come from the service economy and from more flexible forms of economic activity such as have emerged in parts of the advanced capitalist world in recent decades. The nature of the market economy has altered, but the opportunities the world-capitalist market provides for entrepreneurial initiative, the spaces it opens for people to lift themselves without constraint of status or background, have if anything grown broader. I have argued that some of those slated for inclusion in the underclass are already confounding their labellers and proving themselves well suited to the new world. Others will follow.

Finally, since this book deals with those who have survived the application of a form of Marxism, it seems appropriate to recall Richard Evans's (1997) observation that one of the first uses of Marx's rhetoric of *Lumpenproletariat* was by the German Social Democratic party to exclude the non-respectable poor from their purview and mark out a 'desirable' working class. One hundred years later this same notion of *Lumpenproletariat* decisively shaped communist policy towards the Gypsies (Stewart 1997, 2001) in almost wholly negative ways. It would be a shame to extend its shelf life unnecessarily.

## Acknowledgements

The research which led to the writing of this article was generously funded by the Leverhulme Trust, United Kingdom (Grant F/134/C1 *The Persecution of Gypsies*). I would like to take this opportunity of thanking the Trust for its support of a wide-ranging and (inadvertently) prolonged set of investigations. Iván Szelényi and János Ladányi invited me to the original meeting of their Ford Foundation funded research on Racialisation and Feminisation of Poverty in Post Communist Eastern Europe and I would like to thank them both for that and more recent opportunities to sharpen our understandings through intellectual debate. I would also thank Katalin Kovalcsik for pointing me in the direction of a number of crucial references.

## Notes

1   I use the term 'Romany peoples' as a means to bridge various contradictory needs when talking of the people who are called 'Gypsy' in Eastern Europe. The difficulties involved in naming are all but crippling. Only some of the 'Gypsies' speak Romany as a mother tongue. Most of these call themselves *Roma* (or, according to dialect, *Rom*). Many more, however, speak a Romany-influenced dialect of the majority language of their country, and their language use could be said to be diglossic. Most of these *in some contexts* will refer to themselves either as *Roma* or as *cigány*, *ţigani*, *cigan*, etc. Yet others speak no Romany at all, and while in Romania, for example, some of these may refer to themselves as *Băiesi* (*Béás* in Hungary), others will call themselves 'Romanian Gypsies' or *Rudări*. These groups sometimes claim links with other Romany populations, but at other times they may deny them. But this is not the end of the problem, since shared language does not necessarily mean shared identity – not all the Romanian speaking 'Gypsies' in Romania think of themselves as sharing an 'identity'. Thus in Wallachia in southern Romania, some Romanian-speaking *ţigani* insist they are in reality ethnic Dacians (*Dac*) and not *ţigani Român* or *Rudări*. It is not the task of the ethnographer to impose a spurious uniformity on all these people. And yet it would be equally wrong to deny the 'family resemblances' that sociological, historical and ethnographic studies indicate, and in this sense the

attention they have recently been receiving, particularly from non-governmental organizations, is fully warranted.

2  For further analysis of the nature and rhythm of the recession in different countries of the region see Szelényi and Emigh 2000: 23–7.

3  It is difficult to measure Romany unemployment precisely, since the official statistics generally preclude ethnic differentiation. However, Kertesi 2000 presents detailed data for Hungary.

4  For example, current Hungarian child benefit is mostly paid as a tax credit and thus discriminates directly against the unemployed. In general, Hungarian welfare payments seem to benefit the 'slightly' deprived most (Braithwaite *et al.* 1999: 112).

5  Governments have promoted this welcome trend by increasing financial support in the form of educational scholarships.

6  The recent creation of a Radio 'C' (for *cigány*) in Budapest is a rare but inspiring example of an imaginative cultural intervention.

7  See Havas *et al.* (1995: 80). The figure is almost certainly higher today due to the existence of local and national Romany self-governing councils.

8  See also Milanovic (1998) and Jovanovic (1998).

9  See Milanovic (1998: 65–6) for concrete illustrations in 1993.

10  This is one of the most important markers of the nature of deprivation in modern industrial societies. It is striking that for instance in the USA very few of the bottom 19% earners expect to remain in that category (though most of the movement is simply into the next quintile). In Russia 'nearly one half of households that were very poor in summer 1992 were not considered such a year later' (Klugman, 1995).

11  I have the highest respect for Iván Szelényi's work, which has always combined a compelling macro perspective with a genuinely felt humanism about the lives curtly circumscribed in the figures produced by surveys. I have already abused Professor Szelényi's generosity and tolerance by suggesting some of the dangers of his terminology in a volume that he himself edited (Stewart 2000). But a reading of the evidence that has become available since my original foray makes me more, not less, worried.

12  I thank Ulf Hannerz for discussion on this point. Myrdal's interest in the reproduction of poverty through what he termed 'circular causation resulting in a cumulative process' was expressed in 1944 in his very first book, which probably influenced Oscar Lewis's formulation of the 'culture of poverty' in the 1960s (see below).

13  A related, if more structural, notion of a class cut-off cropped up later and in a very different context in Eastern Europe when in the 1930s the sociologist Ferenc Erdei characterized the former serfs as a 'society below society' (1983 [1943]). Cf. Gans 1997 and Kusmer 1997 for histories of 'underclass' in the US literature.

14  This is all part of a more general representation of the 'ţigani' as foreigners in the village, a people without roots in the soil, which radically misrepresents their integration into the local division of labour and the intensity of their interactions with the villagers.

15  Compare this to the 86 per cent of Chicago Blacks who live in the South Side, the most extreme case of US residential segregation on record (Abu-Lughod 1997).

16  Compare the case of contemporary Naples, where Italo Pardo has shown how the *popolino* – people who are typically seen, by journalists, by politicians and social reformers, as a *misera plebs*, 'an underclass – a grasping and backward *lumpenproletariat* that, dragged down by its culture and beliefs, is irredeemably caught into negative reciprocity and resigned to marginality and deprivation' (1996: 2) – have successfully managed to avoid falling into the pit of immorality to which it is repeatedly condemned in official discourse.

17  See Eiber (1993: 43–5) for the text of this law.

18 According to the Radio Free Europe report, Moric said 'placing Roma in reservations would be "completely normal" as "in America there are also reservations for the Indians"'. He said that if Slovakia does not place 'inadaptable Roma' into reservations now, 'they will place us there twenty years from now'. Moric also said it has been 'statistically proven' that most 'retarded people' come from among the Roma and asked, 'What is humane about morons being allowed to give birth to more morons and raise the percentage of morons and crazies in the nation?' (RFE/RFLL Newsline 4(150), part II, 7 August 2000). On 21 September 2000, Moric's parliamentary immunity was lifted to allow him to be prosecuted for incitement to racial and ethnic intolerance.

19 The communist concern with the anti-working class character of Nazism notoriously minimized the anti-Semitic drive of Nazi thought (see e.g. Young 1993: 141).

20 Fieldwork currently being conducted by Livia Jaroka in Budapest suggests that the Romani element of Hungaro-Romani is in fact being intensified and renewed due to the cultural hegemony of the Vlach, Romany-speaking population. See also Matras 1998 for a discussion of para-Romani.

21 Many influential Hungarian writers on the culture of poverty remained trapped within the excessive functionalism suggested by Lewis. See e.g. Solt 1998.

22 Kováts's researchers, who have long-term experience in the field, interviewed a wide range of Roma in Hungary and in Canada.

23 Jews were of course viewed similarly when they became prominent in new lines of business in the nineteenth century. It is interesting to speculate whether the Romany category gaźo, the 'other', to whom Rom have no moral obligation, may yet provide a template for constructing the kind of impersonal dealings necessary for successful entrepreneurship, as the notion of the goyim helped Jews.

24 In Romania it appears that, with possible exceptions in some areas in the last seventy years of the institution, slavery was of the 'household', not 'productive' or 'plantation', sort and seems to have allowed considerable freedoms to its subjects (Achim 1998). Abolition took place relatively tranquilly and there was no reimposition of formal discrimination after the liberation.

25 See Dominguez (1986). It is striking that in Eastern Europe the kinds of discussions which German police forces engaged in over whom to include in the Zigeuner category are largely absent (see Lucassen 1996).

26 Livia Jaroka, personal communication.

27 But see Abu-Lughod (1997) for a cautionary note concerning Wacquant's data.

28 See, for example, RFE/RFLL Newsline 5(47), part II, 8 March 2001.

29 The case of Romania deserves separate discussion, in part because of the war years when roughly 30,000–40,000 Roma were deported by the Antonescu regime, and also because of the flurry of house-burning after Ceauşescu's fall. These might be related back to the historical legacy of slavery, but this line of argument requires further archival investigation.

# References

Abu-Lughod, J. (1997) 'The specificity of the Chicago ghetto: comment on Wacquant's "Three pernicious premises"', International Journal of Urban and Regional Research 20: 357–62.

Achim, V. (1998) Ţiganii în istoria României (The Gypsies in the History of Romania), Bucharest: Editura Enciclopedică.

Ambrus, P. (1988) A Dsumbuj: egy telep élete, Budapest: Magvető, Gyorsuló Idő.

Artemisszió Foundation (2000) 'The Ózd micro-region, a background report,' manuscript in the possession of the author.

Biró, Z.A. and A. Biró (eds) (1997) *Igy élünk: elszegényedési folyamatok a Székelyföldön*, Regionális és Antropológiai Kutatások Központja, Csikszereda: Pro-Prink Könyvkiadó.

Bourgois, P. (1995) *In Search of Respect: Selling Crack in El Barrio*, Cambridge: Cambridge University Press.

Braithwaite, J., Grootaert, C. and Milanovic, B. (1999) *Poverty and Social Assistance in Transition Countries*, New York: St Martin's Press.

Budrala, D. and Cs. Kató (n.d.) 'Mockery and luxury houses: reconsidering Roma (Băiesi) identity in Romania', manuscript in the possession of author.

Clarke, S. (1999) *New Forms of Employment and Household Survival Strategies in Russia*, Coventry: ISITO.

Day, S., E. Papataxiarchis and M. Stewart (1998/9) 'Consider the lilies of the fields', in S. Day, E. Papataxiarchis and M. Stewart (eds) *Lilies of the Field: Marginal People who Live for the Moment*, Boulder: Westview, pp. 1–24.

Dominguez, V. (1986) *White by Definition: Social Classifications in Creole Louisiana*, New Brunswick: Rutgers University Press.

Durst, J. (n.d.) 'The formation of a Romanian rural ghetto', working paper in the Ford Foundation Study on Racialisation and Feminisation of Poverty in Eastern Europe.

Eiber, L. (1993) '*Ich wusste es wird schlimm': Die Verfolgung der Sinti und Roma in München, 1933–45*, Munich: Buchendorfer.

Engebrigsten, A. (2000) 'Exploring Gypsiness: power, exchange and interdependence in a Transylvanian village', PhD thesis, University of Oslo, November.

Engels, F. (1845 [1887]) *Die Lage der arbeitenden Klasse (The Condition of the Working Class in England in 1844)*, translated by Florence Kelley Wischnewetzky, New York: John W. Lovell.

Erdei, F. (1983 [1943]) 'A magyar társadalom a két világháború között (Hungarian society between the two world wars)', in F. Erdei (ed.) *A magyar társadalomról (On Hungarian Society)*, Budapest: Akadémia.

ERRC (1999) *Country Report. A Special Remedy: Roma and Schools for the Mentally Handicapped in the Czech Republic*, Budapest: ERRC.

Evans, R. (1997) *Rethinking German History: from Unification to Re-unification 1800–1996*, London: Routledge.

Gans, H. (1997) 'Uses and misuses of concepts in American social science research: variations on Loic Wacquant's theme of "Three pernicious premises in the study of the American ghetto"', *International Journal of Urban and Regional Research*, 20: 504–7.

Hajnal, L. (2000) 'Budapesti oláh cigányok migrációs stratégiái', *Mozgó Világ* 10: 105–8.

Hannerz, U. (1969) *Soulside: Enquiries into Ghetto Culture and Community*, New York and London: Columbia University Press.

Havas, G., I. Kertesi and I. Kemeny (1995) 'The statistics of deprivation', *New Hungarian Quarterly* 36: 67–80.

Horváth, A. (2000) *Cigánynak születni: tanulmányok, dokumentumok*, Budapest: Új Mandátum.

Howe, L. (1990) *Being Unemployed in Northern Ireland: an Ethnographic Study*, Cambridge: Cambridge University Press.

Ignatiev, N. (1995) *How the Irish Became White*, Durham and London: Duke University Press.

Jovanovic, B. (1998) *Changes in the Perception of the Poverty Line during the Times of Depression: Russia 1993–96*, Washington: World Bank.

Kemény, I. (1999) 'A magyarországi cigányság szerkezete (The structure of the Hungarian Gypsies)', *Régio* 1: 3–15.

——(2001) 'A Romák és az iskola', *Beszélö* 1: 62–8.

Kereszty, Zs. (1998) *Csenyéte Antológia (Csenyéte Anthology)*, Csenyéte: Bárkönyvek.

Kertesi, G. (2000) 'Cigány foglalkoztatás és munkanélküliség a rendszervaltás elött es után', in A. Horváth (ed.) *Cigánynak születni*, Budapest: Új Mandátum.

Kertesi, G. and G. Kézdi (1994) 'Cigány tanulók az általános iskolában', in *Cigányok és iskola, Educatio Füzetek, 1996. 3. szám. KSH munkaerö-felmérés, 1993. évi adattár*, Budapest: KSH.

Klugman, J. (1995) 'Poverty in Russia – an assessment', *Transition Newsletter*, at http://www.worldbank.org/html/prddr/trans/so95/oct-ar2.htm.

Kovalcsik, K. and Zs. Kubínyi (2000) *A Csenyétei daloskert*, Pécs: Gandhi Közalapítvány, Gimnázium és Kollégium.

Kováts, A. (2000) 'Magyarországon élö romák migrációja (The migration of Roma living in Hungary)', *Mozgó Világ* 10: 77–95.

Kusmer, K. (1997) 'Ghettos real and imagined: a historical comment on Loic Wacquant's "Three pernicious premises in the study of the American ghetto"', *International Journal of Urban and Regional Research* 20: 706–11.

Ladányi, János (1992) 'Középsö-Józsefváros északi területére készülö rendezési terv programja (City rehabilitation in Central-Josephstadt in Budapest)', *Tér és Társadalom* 3–4: 89–162.

——(1993) 'Patterns of residential segregation and the Gypsy minority in Budapest', *International Journal of Urban and Regional Research* 17(1): 30–41.

——(2000) 'The Hungarian neoliberal state, ethnic classification and the creation of a Roma underclass', in I. Szelényi and R. Emigh (eds) *Poverty, Ethnicity, and Gender in Eastern Europe during the Market Transition*, Westport, Conn.: Greenwood Press.

Ladányi, János and I. Szelényi (2000) 'Adalékok a ésenyétei cigányság történetéhez', in A. Horváth *et al.* (eds) *Cigánynak születni: tanulmányok, dokumentumok*, Budapest: Új Mandátum.

Lewis, O. (1966) 'The culture of poverty', *Scientific American* 210(October): 10–25.

Lucassen, L. (1996) *Die Zigeuner: Die Geschichte eines polizeilichen Ordnungsbegriffes in Deutschland 1700–1945*, Köln: Böhlau.

Marx, A. (1988) *Making Race and Nation: a Comparison of the United States, South Africa and Brazil*, Cambridge: Cambridge University Press.

Marx, K. and F. Engels (1958) *Selected Works*, vol. 1, Moscow: Progress Publishers.

Matras, Y. (1998) 'Para-Romani revisited', in Y. Matras (ed.) *The Romani Element in Non-Standard Speech*, Wiesbaden: Harrassowitz, pp. 1–27.

Mayhew, H. (1851) *London Labour and the London Poor: a Cyclopaedia of the Condition and Earnings of Those that Will Work, Those that Cannot Work, and Those that Will Not Work*, London: G. Newbold.

Medina, N. and C. McDonald (2001) *Final Report to the Education Sub-Board on Roma Education Research Project*, dated 28 April; to appear on forthcoming OSI/ESB website.

Mészáros, A. and J. Fóti (2000) 'A cigány népesség jellemzöi Magyarországon', in Á Horváth (ed.) *Cigánynak születni: Tanulmányok, dokumentumok*, Budapest: Új Mandátum.

Milanovic, B. (1998) *Income, Inequality and Poverty during the Transition from Planned to Market Economy*, Washington: World Bank and http://www.worldbank.org/research/transition/pdf/BrankoEd3.pdf.

Myrdal, Gunnar (1963) *Challenge to Affluence*, London: Gollancz.

*Newsweek Magazine* 18 September 2000, 'The new face of race' and other articles: 50–66.

Pardo, I. (1996) *Managing Existence in Naples: Morality, Action and Structure*, Cambridge: Cambridge University Press.

Peukert, D. (1989) *Inside Nazi Germany: Conformity, Opposition and Racism in Everyday Life*, Harmondsworth: Penguin.

Piasere, L. (1982) 'Mare Roma: catégories humaines et structure sociale. Une contribution à l'ethnologie Tsigane', thèse pour le doctorat du 3.ème cycle, Universtité de Paris. Published in *Études et documents balkaniques* 6.

Pine, F. (1996) 'Redefining women's work in Poland', in R. Abrahams (ed.) *After Socialism: Land Reform and Social Change in Eastern Europe*, Providence and Oxford: Berghahn, pp. 115–32.

——(1998) 'Dealing with fragmentation: the consequences of privatisation for rural women in central and southern Poland', in S. Bridger and F. Pine (eds) *Surviving Post-Socialism: Local Strategies and Regional Responses in Post-Socialist Eastern Europe and the former Soviet Union*, London: Routledge.

Ringold, D. (2000) http://www.worldbank.org/research/transition/pdf/BrankoEd3.pdf.

Runciman, W.G. (1966) *Relative Deprivation and Social Justice: a Study of Attitudes to Social Inequality in Twentieth-Century England*, London: Routledge and Kegan Paul.

Solt, O. (1998 [1976]) 'A hetvenes Évek Budapesti szegényei', *Profil* (Samizdat 1976), reprinted in *Méltóságot mindenkinék, Összegyütött írások, elsö kötet*. Budapest: Beszélö, pp. 242–88.

Stedman-Jones, G. (1984 [1971]) *Outcast London: a Study in the Relationship between Classes in Victorian Society*, Harmondsworth: Penguin.

Stewart, M. (1990) 'Gypsies, work, and civil society', *Journal of Communist Studies* 6(2): 140–62. Simultaneously published in C. Hann (ed.) *Market Economy and Civil Society in Hungary*, London: Frank Cass.

——(1997) *The Time of the Gypsies*, Boulder: Westview.

——(2000) 'Spectres of the underclass', in I. Szelényi and R. Emigh (eds) *Poverty, Ethnicity, and Gender in Eastern Europe during the Market Transition*, Westport, Greenwood Press.

——(2001) 'The development of communist policy towards Gypsies and Roma, 1945–1989, a case study,' in W. Guy (ed.) *Between Past and Future: the Roma of Central and Eastern Europe*, Hertford: Hertfordshire University Press.

Székelyi, M. (n.d.) 'Ethnic group inclusiveness and success among the Roma in Hungary', paper presented at the Annual Meeting of the AAA, San Francisco, November 2000, Roma in Eastern Europe Panel.

Szelényi, I. and Emigh, R. (eds) (2000) *Poverty, Ethnicity, and Gender in Eastern Europe during the Market Transition*, Westport, Greenwood Press.

Tauber, E. (n.d.) 'Die Andere geht mangel: Zur symbolischen Bedeutung des mangel bei den Sinti Estraixaria'.

Vajda, I. and Prónai, Cs. (2000) 'Románia a romák Magyarországon', *Mozgó Világ* 10: 101–4.

Vašečka, M. (2001) 'Roma', in *Slovakia 2000 – a Global Report on the State of Society*, Bratislava: Institute for Public Affairs.

Wacquant, L.J.D. (1993) 'Urban outcasts: stigma and division in the black American ghetto and the French urban periphery', *International Journal of Urban and Regional Research* 17(3): 366–83.

——(1997) 'Three pernicious premises in the study of the American ghetto', *International Journal of Urban and Regional Research* 20: 341–53.

Weindling, P. (1989) *Health, Race and German Politics between National Unification and Nazism, 1870–1945*, Cambridge: Cambridge University Press.

Wilson, W.J. (1987) *The Truly Disadvantaged: the Inner City, the Underclass and Public Policy*, Chicago: University of Chicago Press.

Wilson, W.J., J.M. McQuane and B.H. Rankin (2000) 'The Underclass', abstract, IEBSS, available at http://www.iebss.com.

Young, J. (1993) *The Texture of Memory: Holocaust Memorials and Meaning*, New Haven: Yale University Press.

Zoon, I. (2001) *On the Margins: Roma and Public Services in Romania, Bulgaria and Macedonia, with a Supplement on Housing in the Czech Republic*, New York: Open Society Institute.

# Part III

# Violent histories and the renewal of identities

---

What new forms of social identity have emerged under postsocialism? What are the long-term legacies of past violence and revolutionary fervour? Can the rediscovery of a repressed history, the retrieval of older forms of religion and ritual, help people to heal the suffering caused by socialism? Why have ethnicity and nationalism been conspicuous in some parts of the postsocialist world (by no means all) and what is the appropriate moral stance for a researcher, when external ideals are contradicted by both historical and contemporary realities?

The increasing international influence of the language of Human Rights, noted by Michael Stewart in the previous chapter, also forms the backcloth to the first contribution in this section. Like Stewart, Robert Hayden is concerned that an external model, in this case one that recommends a form of 'multicultural' democracy for the ex-Yugoslav republic of Bosnia-Herzegovina, is remote from the realities on the ground, which in this case involve extremes of violence. Focusing on sites sacred to more than one faith, Hayden suggests that coexistence in this region in earlier periods was based pragmatically on 'negative tolerance'. The acceptance of group differences in the imperial systems of the past did not alter their 'structural opposition' and the potential of religion to mobilize followers as an ethnic group. When the political context changed, democratic voting showed an overwhelming preference for 'constitutional nationalism'. Instead of indulging in a romantic distortion of past multiculturalism and urging *positive* tolerance where it has never existed, we would do better, argues Hayden, to acknowledge that the aspiration to make polity and nation coincide is precisely the normal basis of sovereignty in the West. The insight may be morally disconcerting but until it is understood there will be no end to the tragicomedy of Western interventions in the Balkans.

Identities of both a collective (ethnic) and a more personal nature are the subject of Piers Vitebsky's analysis of how indigenous inhabitants of the Russian North are struggling to make sense of their postsocialist environment. Socialist policies intended to develop and 'civilize' remote peoples wrought untold damage, especially when they separated children from their parents and men from women, and attempted to cut off the sources of belief that had under-pinned the previous worldview. The old cosmology carried entirely different assumptions about the meaning of property, since animals, land and its products were all considered to have a spiritual as well as a material character. Socialist violence was therefore a 'historical trauma', which devastated these people by forcing 'withdrawal' not only from the land but from familiar kin relations and a whole way of being. It imposed a linear model of 'progressive' time, a cruel irony for people who now see themselves as a helpless, 'dying people'. They have lost the consolation of socialist subsidies and are characterized by high levels of depression, domestic violence and mortality; yet they lack the confidence to seek a future elsewhere. Vitebsky nonetheless concludes positively by showing how some individuals are struggling toward new models of time by rebuilding links to their parents and ancestors, notably through reviving a shamanic heritage.

Finally in this section, Stefan Feuchtwang takes up the theme of time with reference to the persistence of 'superstitions' and critical revolutionary enthu-siasm in the recent history of China. Drawing on the recent theoretical work of Alexander Russo and documenting the impact of violent rupture at the local level, he views the 'cultural revolution' as the apogee of popular fervour. Yet despite the turbulence of the Maoist decades it is also important to recognize continuities, notably in the endemic factionalism of the political system, and in deeply held notions of authority, loyalty and fairness underpinning the 'moral economy'. Following the reforms introduced by Deng, these have been high-lighted again in the radically new circumstances of 'socialist commodity economy', as counters to the new dominance of money and the market. The Party-state has devised new and more indirect methods for maintaining control but it has no solution to the moral dilemmas posed by the use of 'connections' and 'corruption'. Feuchtwang draws particular attention to collectivist counter-currents, notably the survival of popular religious practices, which form the basis for reclaiming 'home' spaces, and also a variety of informally structured religious congregations, some of which are perceived by the Party as a new revo-lutionary threat and repressed accordingly.

# Chapter 8

# Intolerant sovereignties and 'multi-multi' protectorates

## Competition over religious sites and (in)tolerance in the Balkans

*Robert M. Hayden*

One of the more prominent tropes invoked in regard to the Balkans has been (in)tolerance. The 'cultural racism' (Žižek 2000: 4–5; cf. Stolcke 1995) of popular references to supposedly 'age-old conflicts' between 'people who have been killing each other for centuries' has been countered by accounts that show that the recent violence has been created to serve political purposes (see Sells 1996; Donia and Fine 1994; Denitch 1994). According to these latter accounts, far from having traditions of killing each other, peoples such as Serbs, Croats and Bosniaks were living in harmony until their local communities were disrupted by conflicts created by political elites in order to facilitate their accession to or maintenance of power. In this reading, the culture of these peoples has been one of peaceful coexistence, not violent conflict, which is why the destruction of their local communities has been seen as a betrayal of their tradition of tolerance (see e.g. Mahmutćehajić 2000).

In a region in which religion is the primary identifier of modern 'nations' (see Hammel 1993; Bringa 1995: 20–3), the coexistence of structures sacred to different religious communities has been seen as physical evidence of this 'tradition of tolerance'. Thus it is claimed that Bosnia had a 'pluralistic culture' since 'mosques, synagogues, Catholic and Orthodox churches stand side by side' (Sells 1996: 148), and that 'religious rivalry and violence were not part of Bosnia's heritage', because Bosnia's people 'tolerated each other' (Donia and Fine 1994: 11). Such assertions are not unique to the Balkans. The dominant schools of scholarship on 'communal' conflicts in India, for example, have tied the 'construction' or 'emergence' of 'communalism' (respectively, Pandey 1990 and Freitag 1990) to colonialism, or to modernity (Fox 1996; Rudolph and Rudolph 1993). Similarly, there is an assumption that shared religious sites in India, such as those of Sufi saints, represent syncretism and multiculturalism in practice (van der Veer 1994: 200–1). The assumption seems to be that societies such as those of India and Bosnia valued pluralism until modernity spread intolerance.

Under this reading, the task of scholarship is often seen as supporting pluralism, 'to contribute to a critically informed view of the plurality of histories and cultures which make up European identities' (Jones and Graves-Brown

1996: 19), or 'to find ways to argue against the use of the past for racist, sexist and other oppressive purposes' by emphasizing

> the fluidity and changeability of all groups and identities, to insist that all histories – whether written or told by archaeologists, religious organizations or Fourth World groups – must be open to critique, and to expose the interests of the groups responsible for creating and championing them.
>
> (Bernbeck and Pollack 1996: S141–2)

This is a normatively attractive stance, as the effects of mass violence are, without question, terrible for the victims. Yet this comforting task is potentially misleading. Seeing conflict as either eternal or inherent is certainly fallacious – after all, if Serbs, Croats and Bosniaks had been implacable enemies for centuries, they would not have been living intermingled and the question of ethnic cleansing could not have arisen (see Hayden 1996a). Yet the assumption that their intermingling can continue under changed circumstances avoids consideration of under what conditions such coexistence actually is likely, or even possible. This is a curious omission, as it seems to presume that some kinds of sociability are 'natural', thus good, while others are pathological, the kind of naturalistic fallacy usually associated with intolerance.

## Negative and positive tolerance

There is a difference, reflected in dictionary definitions of 'tolerate', between a negative concept of non-interference ('to allow, permit, not interfere with') and a positive one of 'to recognize and respect' while disagreeing with others' beliefs or practices. This difference is reflected in philosophy, where Locke's (1990 [1689]) pragmatic justifications for tolerance as non-interference have been rejected by modern liberals in favor of Mill's (1975 [1859]) and later arguments for the positive benefits of pluralism and diversity (see Mendus 1989). Thus a contemporary read on 'tolerance' requires the affirmative action of recognizing and respecting beliefs or actions with which one disagrees (see Rawls 1971: 205–21).

With this difference in mind, it cannot be presumed that spatial proximity is an indication of a lack of religious rivalry and violence and thus of a tradition of toleration in which the members of the various social groups in contact value each other's differences. Lack of overt conflict may instead indicate only that most people are not willing to risk the damage that might occur were conflict to be open and violent rather than covert and expressed in forms of competition. If conditions change so that the risks of loss are lowered or the chances of gain increase, a 'tradition' of tolerance may quickly transform itself into manifestations of violent conflict, competition carried out by other means.

Pre-war rural Bosnia seems to have reflected such a pragmatism. Lockwood, in his classic study of economy and ethnicity in western Bosnia (1975: 195), found that the Muslims and Christians maintained distinctions in dress, clothing and house type that were 'slightly but significantly different' from each other. Such integration as took place was 'functional', that is, economic, in the marketplace, and thus pragmatic rather than affective. This functional integration of people as members of groups rather than as individuals is also reflected in the institution of *komšiluk* (from Turkish, generally 'neighborhood'), which established clear obligations of reciprocity between people of different 'nations' living in close proximity, but also prohibited intermarriage between members of these religiously defined groups (Bringa 1995: 66–84). Xavier Bougarel (1996: 81–8)[1] has argued that the customs of *komšiluk* defined relations between those whose ties were based on shared space, but that this relationship based on proximity was antithetical to one based on intimacy: marriage. Carrying the distinction further, Bougarel says that while the idea of 'citizen' is abstract, an individual without distinguishing characteristics, *komšija* (neighbor) was always concrete: *this* person with *these* characteristics. Essentially, then, the practices of *komšiluk* happened relations between individuals as representatives of groups who chanced to live in close proximity, while the groups themselves remained in structural opposition, unmixable.

The demise of state socialism in the Balkans provides some opportunities to examine this dynamic of competitive coexistence in a long-term perspective. In this paper, I examine the continuity of competition between religious communities in the Balkans, with particular reference to the construction in close proximity of sites sacred to different communities, and the destruction of such sites. Given the sensitivity of the issues, I wish to make it clear what is *not* being argued. First, I reject the idea that socialism marked a complete break from earlier social and cultural practices (cf. Lampland 1991).[2] I also reject the idea that the socialist period marked a 'time-out from history', the 'forty *lost* years', as Milan Kundera (1995: 226) quotes the phrase while rejecting it (the emphasis is his), since the implication is that after socialism, Balkans societies reverted to their true, and truly violent, selves.

My approach is to investigate the social processes that unfold when the question of the identity of sovereignty – to whom the state belongs – is raised in a multinational polity in which most members of the ethnically defined majority vote to establish a *state* (a territory with a government) in which their group alone comprises the sovereign *nation*, a construction that I have called 'constitutional nationalism' (Hayden 1992, 1999). With this mutual definition of nation (ethnic group) and state (the territory and a government in which the ethnic nation is sovereign), the symbolism of group status inherent in religious sites may lead to the transformation or destruction of monuments identified with non-national Others. These processes are certainly not unique to the Balkans, nor to postsocialism.

## Inconvenient facts and ethical discomfort

The explanations that I pursue in this paper are discomforting, to say the least, to those who take the position that since identities are constructed (which is hard to deny), 'deconstructive thought is necessary for historical and political progress' and thus that the ethical task is to 'problematize the naturalized notions of ethnic conflict' (Campbell 1998: 14–15). From this perspective, violence is unnatural, criminal, the result of the machinations of particular evil politicians. However, this position misses the possibility of what Hannah Arendt (1963) called the 'banality of evil',[3] that committed by utterly ordinary people. Other writers of markedly dissimilar temperament seem to agree on this, at least in regard to civil war. Thus Abraham Lincoln, describing the USA in 1863, may be compared to Clifford Geertz, writing of Indonesia in 1965:

> Actual war coming, blood grows hot, and blood is spilled ... Confidence dies, and universal suspicion reigns. Each man feels an impulse to kill his neighbor, lest he first be killed by him. Revenge and retaliation follow. And all this ... may be among honest men only.
>
> (Lincoln 1989 [1863]: 522–3)

> the actual eruption of violence comes more as a completion, a rounding off, than as a breaking into something new. The oft-remarked end-game quality of the massacres, the readiness and near-ritual calm ... with which the victimized delivered themselves up to those who victimized them, had less to do with cultural attitudes or the power of the army, both of which were more agent than impetus, than with the fact that ten years of ideological polarization had convinced virtually everyone that the only thing remaining to be seen was which way, in the event, the balance would tip.
>
> (Geertz 1995: 7)

The question becomes one of determining what kinds of situations produce this banal evil. In pursuit of this question, the postmodern presumptions of fluidity and malleability are misleading, because even if identities are malleable in *some* circumstances, this does not mean that they are malleable in *all* circumstances, and the limits of malleability cannot be explored from the *a priori* position that there are none.

In taking this approach, I am consciously ignoring a number of moral questions. One is the matter of individual guilt, although I do wish to counter any view of collective guilt (cf. Hayden 1996b). The distinction between the circumstances under which many people are likely to commit atrocities and the actions of those who do, or do not, commit them is basic to the concept of justice; and since not all will victimize others, those who do so cannot find absolution in the similar predispositions of most others (Todorov 1996: 137–8). At the same time, though, failing to try to understand which circumstances are likely to be conducive to atrocities would mean abandoning the chance of trying to structure events so as to prevent or at least limit their occurrence. The morality of failing to point out the kinds of circumstances in which we can be sure that some 'revenge and retaliation will follow, among honest men only', is more than suspect.

My stance is bound to be discomforting, because it counters positions that many would like to believe, on what they regard as the best of moral principles. It is, however, consistent with Max Weber's suggestion (1975 [1919]: 147) that convincing an audience to accept 'inconvenient facts' is a moral achievement. Certainly it is more comfortable, and bound to be more popular, to condemn acts that are abhorred rather than to try to understand how ordinary, banal people could commit them. Yet that stance substitutes comfort for questions and is thus a form of intellectual cowardice. The price of understanding is the discomfort caused by investigating that which most see only as warranting condemnation.

## Competition over religious sites in the Balkans

Just before the start of World War I, F.W. Hasluck (1973 [1929]) carried out monumental studies of the transformation in the Balkans of Christian sites into Islamic ones and the reverse, and of 'ambiguous sanctuaries' claimed by members of both faiths.[4] He interpreted this competition as a long-standing practice in the 'the ancient world' (Hasluck 1973: 564–656):

> A religion carried by a conquering race or by a missionary priesthood to alien lands superimposes itself, by force or persuasion, on an indigenous cult; the process is expressed in mythological terms under the figure of a personal combat between the rival gods or of the 'reception' of the new god by the old. Eventually either one god or the other succumbs and disappears or is relegated to an inferior position; or again, the two may be more or less completely identified and fused ... The 'ambiguous' sanctuary, claimed and frequented by both religions [Christianity and Islam], seems to represent a distinct stage of development – the period of equipoise, as it were – in the transition both from Christianity to Bektashism and, in the rare cases where political and other circumstances were favorable, from Bektashism to Christianity.
>
> (Hasluck 1973: 564–5)

Hasluck's work concentrated on churches that were transformed into mosques; on attempts to transform churches into mosques which failed because of what was considered bad luck, ill omen or witchcraft (e.g. repeated collapse of minarets, fatal falls by muezzins during the call for prayer, hauntings and appari-tions); on the destruction of churches; on the desecration and secularization of churches (turned into baths, storehouses and the like); and on the visitation by Muslims to sites that remained explicitly Christian.

The practice of shared ritual space continued at least until the early 1990s in Kosovo (Duijzings 1993, 2000). Muslim Gypsies were observed by Ger Duijzings as pilgrims at the celebration of Assumption Day at the Serbian Orthodox monastery of Gračanica in 1986, 1990 and 1991. Muslim Albanians and Serbs had long taken part in pilgrimages to the fourteenth-century Zočište monastery and Church of the Healers near Orahovac, but by 1991 increasing displays of hostile nationalism by Serbs led Albanians to boycott the pilgrimage. In September 1999, the Zočište church was blown up, presumably by Albanians, despite the supposed protection of NATO troops (Glas Kosova i Metohije 1999). However, in an apparent echo of the failed transformations reported eighty years earlier by Hasluck, it was reported in February 2001 that the local Albanians of Zočište have decided to rebuild the monastery and church, because four of the Albanian men who had participated in its destruction in 1999 became psychologically ill shortly thereafter, manifesting a curse that had descended on the Albanian people.[5] Duizjings also reports on disturbances at the Ostrog monastery in Montenegro, when Muslims have appeared to worship and the Orthodox priests of the monastery have felt threatened; and mentions (2000: 85, n. 17) the removal in about 1996 of a Roman Catholic altarpiece from a church in Montenegro that had been shared by Orthodox and Catholic worshippers.

It is clear that sharing of sites, saints and even ritual practices was common in the Balkans during the Ottoman period and even afterwards. However, should such sharing be seen as indicating 'tolerance' or as manifestations of competition? Hasluck noted that day-to-day utilization of 'ambiguous' shrines by members of two religious communities was utilitarian: 'Practically any of the religions of Turkey may share the use of a sanctuary administered by another, if this sanctuary has a sufficient reputation for beneficent miracles' (Hasluck 1973: 68–9). Further, he described believers sharing such a site as being among the unlearned, so that 'all sects meet on a common basis of secular superstition' rather than doctrinal Muslim or Christian beliefs (Hasluck 1973: 69). Such sharing could go on without any attempt to assert challenge to control over a site *unless* members of elites, 'in the event of successful aggression, stand to gain both in prestige and materially' (Hasluck 1973: 69), at which point the challenge was likely to be made.

The question of national sovereignty arose in the Balkans in the mid-nineteenth century, and there was a striking rise in the destruction of Muslim religious sites there as Christian populations achieved independence from the Ottoman Empire. For example, independence for Serbia meant the demolition of mosques throughout the country. While guidebooks of Belgrade now note that the oldest building there outside of the old fortress is a small mosque built in 1690, when the Ottomans abandoned that fortress in 1867 there were more than fifteen mosques in the city.[6] The Serbian–Turkish war of 1876–8 caused about a million Christians and a million Muslims to 'change their living space' (Protić 1989: 94). A picture of Niš in about 1880 shows six mosques (Stoianovich 1992: 102, fig. 65); only one of them now remains. But most of the Muslim population had left earlier, since in 1830 the Ottoman government not only agreed to the full autonomy of Serbia, but also to the departure from the principality of all Muslims except for those within the six fortresses directly under Ottoman control (Jelavich 1983: 241). The last major exodus occurred after the creation of Yugoslavia in 1919, although some Turks and Muslims remained in Macedonia, Sandžak and Bosnia (see Banac 1983).

Coexistence of Muslim and Christian shrines seems to have lasted longest in places where national sovereignty was longest delayed. For example, in Bosnia European colonialism succeeded Islamic rule when the Austro-Hungarian Empire took control over Bosnia from the Ottoman Empire in 1878. Both empires excluded popular sovereignty but had somewhat different concerns in regard to competitions among the local populations. Austria saw its role as that of 'a great Occidental Empire, charged with the mission of carrying civilization to Oriental peoples' (Austrian Administrator of Bosnia Benjamin Kallay, quoted in Donia 1981: 14). The Hapsburg policy was aimed at preserving the *status quo* while reducing conflict between ethnic and religious groups (Donia 1981: 22). Bosnian Muslims, however, perceived their status and economic conditions as declining under colonial rule. Their intense opposition to conversion of Muslims to Christianity led to the promulgation in 1891 of an ordinance regulating conversions that, in Donia's words (1981: 59), 'established the government as a referee between the contending religious communities in Bosnia'. In 1890, Muslim leaders petitioned Vienna to rectify their situation, claiming, among other things, that mosques had been turned into churches, and that monasteries had been built on Muslim graveyards (Donia 1981: 140). Clearly, the Muslims felt that their leading, not to say dominant, position in Bosnian society, established under the Ottoman Empire, was diminished by Hapsburg rule.

At the same time that Muslim dominance diminished, Christian claims to higher status arose, literally, in the form of churches. While Ottoman law did not allow for the construction of new churches and required government permission even to repair old ones (Donia and Fine 1994: 39), some Christian churches had been built in Ottoman cities. They were required to be much lower in height and smaller in size than were the mosques in their vicinity, as can still be seen from the old Orthodox churches of Skopje and Sarajevo. Similarly, houses of Muslims were by law higher than those of non-Muslims (Sugar 1977: 76; cf. Stoianovich 1992: 96–9). Ironically, the large churches whose proximity to mosques was cited in the 1990s as proof of Bosnia's 'tradition' of 'tolerance' were built under Hapsburg colonial rule. The even-handedness of the conflict-averse Hapsburg Empire in Bosnia encouraged challenges by those previously subordinated, but limited their ability to destroy the sites erected by the previously ruling people.

A rather different case of long-term competition over territory through the creation of religious structures is provided by Mart Bax (1995) in his analysis of the Marian shrine of Medjugorje, which developed as a major Roman Catholic pilgrimage site following reports of visions of the Virgin Mary in 1981. Bax shows how the strategically important mountain was from the mid-nineteenth century claimed separately by both the Serbs and the Croats of the region. This contest was effectively stalled by conflict-averse states, the rulers of which did not depend on public support: first, the Ottomans, then the Austrians, then the new Yugoslav state (which, unlike Serbia in 1867, had to incorporate all groups) and finally the communist regime after 1945. However, in the period when communism was failing, the Marian visions permitted mass mobilization of local and other Catholics that established the place as definitively Roman Catholic, hence Croat. While Medjugorje is officially in Bosnia, there is very little sign of the Bosnian state there, and many Croats refer to it as part of Croatia.

Of course, it is the abandonment of the pretense of even-handedness that has allowed, even encouraged, the destruction of religious shrines in the regions of the former Yugoslavia, while reconstruction of destroyed religious structures is still a matter of stating claims for status and territory. It is reported that 600 mosques in Bosnia were destroyed by Serb forces in 1992–3.[7] The most noted of these was the sixteenth-century Ferhadija mosque in Banja Luka, which had been under UNESCO protection. Not only was the Ferhadija mosque razed, but even the stones were removed from the site, in July 1993. Demands by the international community that the mosque be rebuilt have been rejected by the government of the Republika Srpska, which is busy rebuilding a large Serbian church in the center of the city that had been destroyed by Croatian forces in 1943. Elsewhere in Republika Srpska, mosques are being reconstructed even though the Muslim population that they are to serve still lives in tents.[8] The value of these mosques as symbols of the Muslim community's return and claim to political authority is clear from the speech of the second-highest Muslim religious figure in Bosnia, on the occasion of the opening of a mosque in the town of Sanski Most in August 2000: that there was a need to build mosques because of all the churches being built in Bosnia and Herzegovina.[9] These recent destructions reveal the importance of borders and the creation of ethnic states. The violence, including the sexual violence, was all about the unmixing of heterogeneous populations (Hayden 1996a, 2000). However, strikingly, there was much less violence in places where borders were not in question (Hayden 2000; Ron 2000). Just as almost all Muslim structures were destroyed during the formation of the Serbian nation-state in the nineteenth century but not once that state, once consolidated, extended its territory over unresisting populations in the 1920s, in the 1990s religious structures were destroyed in places that were suddenly to be consolidated into a new ethnic state, in Bosnia (by Serbs and Croats) and in Kosovo (by Albanians).

## Similar phenomena elsewhere

The use of shrines as symbols of dominance is not limited to the Balkans. Meron Benvenisti has documented the intentional eradication of much of the Muslim character of the Palestinian landscape by the Israeli government after 1948, with a chapter devoted to the destruction, conversion and other transformations of Muslim religious structures and shrines to saints (Benvenisti 2000: 270–306). He includes pictures of a 'Muslim holy tomb incorporated into an [Israeli army] war memorial' after being renamed from the Tomb of Sayadnih Huda to the Tomb of Judah (Benvenisti 2000: plate 21). Another picture is labeled 'Muslim holy place turned into a Jewish synagogue. The Tomb of Imam Ali in Yazur has been converted into a synagogue and a yeshiva' (Benvenisti 2000: plate 22). Benvenisti reports that of about 140 mosques in Palestinian villages 'abandoned' in 1948, 100 were leveled at that time by Israeli forces; and of the rest, twenty are abandoned and in various stages of decay, while

> six are being used as living quarters, sheep-pens or stables, carpentry shops or storehouses; six have been or are at present serving as museums, bars, or tourist sites of some sort; four are being used in whole or in part as synagogues; and two have been partially renovated for Muslim worship, but that use has been prohibited.
>
> (Benvenisti 2000: 289)

Of course, the contestation is still two-way, with Palestinians (re)converting or destroying Jewish shrines that come under their control. Thus in Nablus, following the capture of the town in 1967, Jews began to visit a Muslim shrine which, they claimed, was on the site of the Tomb of Joseph; increasingly frequent visits by Jewish settlers after 1975 led to a prohibition of Muslim worship there and, in 1992, the installation of Torah scrolls and the covering of the prayer niche indicating Mecca (Philps 2001). With Israeli withdrawal from Nablus in 1995, clashes between Palestinians and the Israeli soldiers who were still guarding the tomb and letting Jews but not Muslims worship there, led finally to a battle that forced the military to withdraw. The Palestinians, again in control of the site, removed all signs of its use as a synagogue and uncovered the prayer niche again. There is no other religious symbol in the now restored building. However, 'the Palestinians painted the dome Islamic green, but after Israeli protests it reverted to neutral white' (*ibid.*). A more clear instance of contest, if not exactly tolerance, is hard to find.

Sharing of shrines continues in Palestine, between and among the various Christian denominations and Muslims (Bowman 1993). These sharings may also produce contestations, depending on the configurations of pressures on the groups involved by the Israeli government, on the one hand, and on opportunities afforded by offers of sectarian-based support from outside the region. Crucially, these manifestations of sharing do not manifest a real syncretism of belief, as neither Muslims nor Christians take part in each others' rituals or liturgies if to do so would conflict with Islamic or, conversely, Christian tenets (Bowman 1993: 449). The reasoning here seems pragmatic, and Bowman states that alliance and enmity depend largely on perceptions of interests of the groups concerned (Bowman 1993: 432).

India could also present many similar examples (see e.g. Hayden n.d.; Malhotra *et al.* 1993; Ludden 1996). The Indian literature, however, tends to treat events such as the destruction of the mosque at Ayodhya as aberrations from the promise of secularism of the Indian state and not in terms of competition of groups (Bernbeck and Pollack 1996). What may be different in the case of India is that transformations may be taking longer there, due to the policies of recognition of all religions that are embodied in the Indian constitution and that have led to much effort by the pre-BJP governments of India to accommodate Muslim sentiments. Still, the destruction of shrines in Punjab in 1947 (in India and in Pakistan) when a colonial regime that was able to ignore popular sovereignty was replaced by new states premised on the sovereignty of the majority nation, ethnically defined, seems strikingly congruent with events in the Balkans in the 1990s.

## Multi-multi protectorates and the denial of the consent of the governed

In the soon-to-be-former-Yugoslavia, the political model for which people voted, when finally given the chance to do so after the fall of state socialism, was that of the classic European nation-state, in which the ethno-nation is sovereign in its own state (Woodward 1995; Hayden 1992, 1999). There were several problems with this model, however. In Bosnia, there was no single sovereign Bosnian people because the population of Bosnia and Herzegovina partitioned themselves into Muslims (after 1994, 'Bosniaks'), Serbs, Croats and others; and overwhelmingly, the Bosnian Serbs and Herzegovinian Croats were unwilling to be incorporated into a Bosnian state that the international community may have recognized but they themselves did not.[10] In Croatia, the Serbian regime of Slobodan Milošević aimed propaganda at the Serbs who made up local majorities in some parts of Croatia to convince them that an independent Croatia would be hostile to them; unfortunately, the Croatian regime really *was* hostile to the Serbs (see Mirić 1996, 1999). In Kosovo, the Milošević regime used the fears of the minority Serb population to justify repression of the majority Albanian population (see Vickers 1998; Maliqi 1998; Mertus 1999).

These problems were resolved in different ways. In Croatia, most of the 570,000 Serbs registered there in the April 1991 census were driven out, more than 200,000 in the 'Operation Storm' action by the Croatian army in August 1995.[11] In Kosovo, of course, NATO attacked Serbia in what was supposedly a humanitarian war, an attack which prompted Serbian forces to try to ethnically cleanse much of Kosovo of Albanians. While most of these Albanians returned after NATO drove out the Serb military and police forces, Albanians drove out most of the Serbs and other non-Albanians immediately thereafter. Thus in Croatia and Kosovo, the problem of the largest minorities was resolved by that most successful of twentieth-century central European mechanisms for dealing with such problems, ethnic cleansing (cf. Silesia and the Sudetenland in 1945, or Greece and Turkey in 1922).

Bosnia was both different and the same. There, in order to prevent the Serbs and Croats who rejected inclusion in Bosnia from partitioning it, the international community recognized Bosnia as an independent country despite the very clear position of the Bosnian Serbs and Herzegovinian Croats that they would go to war rather than be included in that state. As then-US Ambassador to Yugoslavia Warren Zimmermann admitted in 1993, the US government's 'hope was that the Serbs would hold off if it was clear that Bosnia had the recognition of Western countries. It turned out we were wrong' (Binder 1993). Ambassador Zimmermann's failure to mention the Bosnian Croats is somewhat odd, as it was already clear by 1993 that Croatia's President Tudjman had agreed with Serbia's President Milošević on the partition of Bosnia in 1991 (Burg and Shoup 1999: 82; Lasić and Rašeta 2001).[12] Thus rather than being granted recognition because a Bosnian nation united to form a Bosnian state, Bosnia was recognized precisely because the Bosnian population divided into separate peoples, in an effort to impose the state on those who rejected it. The wars in Bosnia were aimed at making heterogeneous territories homogenous – this is, after all, what 'ethnic cleansing' is all about – and have largely succeeded (Hayden 1996a). Ever since then, the international community has been confronted with the logical impossibility of building democracy in a place where very large percentages of the population deny their consent to the project.

The result has been a weird parody of democracy, in which the agents of the 'International Community', who control Bosnia, insist on holding elections and then ignore the results, because the parties that have won have been the same nationalist ones that brought the country to civil war in 1992. The international High Representative, who is by definition neither a citizen of Bosnia nor subject to any control by the citizens of Bosnia, has removed elected officials, banned political parties and imposed legislation when the elected parliament has refused to pass it. In one of the more memorable statements in world parliamentary history, the High Representative, in response to the failure of the elected parliament to pass a law he wanted, thereby enacted it 'until the Parliamentary Assembly adopts this law in due form, without amendments and no conditions attached'.[13] In March 1999 the High Representative summarily removed the elected president of the Republika Srpska from office after the man refused to nominate the High Representative's choice for prime minister,[14] while in March 2001 the High Representative removed the elected Croatian member of the Bosnian state presidency even though, or perhaps because, the party the man represents continues to get the largest number of Croat votes in Bosnia.[15]

In all of this, the High Representative has come to act increasingly like the leadership of the League of Communists of Yugoslavia, which also acknowledged nationalism by creating an unworkable constitution and then largely ignoring its provisions. This is not necessarily a bad development – most Bosnians never lived so well or so peacefully as in socialist Yugoslavia, at least after the 1960s – but it does indicate that Bosnia is a protectorate under a government imposed upon the people against the will of many of them, perhaps most. This new protectorate rejects electoral control by the Bosnian peoples over what is supposedly their own government in the name of what is known in Bosnia, with no little sarcasm, as 'multi-multi',[16] slang for the international community's insistence on multi-ethnic, multi-religious, multi-lingual, multi-sexual-identity tolerance. But is this 'multi-multi' construction meaningful to those supposed to live in it?

That Bosnia is actually meant to be meaningless to its putative citizens is shown by the history of the symbols developed to represent it. The Dayton Constitution (Art. I.6) provides that 'Bosnia shall have such symbols as are decided by its Parliamentary Assembly and approved by the Presidency', the primary symbols being a flag and a coat of arms. Unsurprisingly, the Serbs, Croats and Muslims could not agree on common symbols for a state which the leaderships of the first two groups had never had any real interest in joining in the first place. The solution of the High Representative was to create a special commission, which designed a 'neutral flag': a gold triangle on a blue background with a row of white stars, in which 'the triangle represents the three constituent peoples of Bosnia and Herzegovina, the gold color represents the sun, as a symbol of hope; the blue and the stars stand for Europe'.[17] Thus the HR intentionally chose a design that had no emotional connection with anyone in Bosnia and Herzegovina. When the flag was unveiled at a press conference, even the HR's own press spokesmen laughed when a reporter pointed out that the flag 'looks like a cornflakes box'. A similar design was chosen by the High Representative for the

> official seal by which BiH will be represented internationally, on the country's passport, for use on official documents ... and by embassies and consulates: a design that follows the design and themes of the flag ... blue, with a triangle of yellow colour in the top right side corner, and a row of five white stars running parallel to the left side of the triangle.[18]

In fact, the primary consideration driving selection of the flag was the Winter Olympics in Nagano, Japan: the deadline for selecting the flag was set with the Games in mind.[19] The flag was certainly flown in Nagano and flies on the East River and in the foyer of the State Department, but it has been little seen in Bosnia itself except when the HR has insisted that it be flown. There is little indication that practically anyone in Bosnia not in the employ of the international community has any affection for this flag – but then, the consent of the elected representatives of the Bosnian peoples is not very relevant for decision-making there.

Thus the symbols of Bosnian statehood have been chosen by the international community rather than by Bosnians themselves, from designs that have meaning to the international community rather than to Bosnians themselves, according to a schedule determined by the publicity calendar of the international community rather than the desires of Bosnians themselves. Presumably unintentionally, the HR has thus symbolized Bosnian statehood as far more important to the international community than it is to Bosnians themselves, while at the same time showing that the governmental structures created at Dayton will not work if they are left under control of Bosnians themselves. Multi-multi, then, is a condition that is mandated, imposed on those meant to live it since they otherwise reject it.

## Democracy as a Lockean project

I do not mean to reject secularism and passive tolerance, at least as goals, or imply that Serbian destruction of Bosnian mosques, or Kosovo Albanian destruction of Serbian churches, or similar events in Palestine or India, are morally justified. To the contrary, the 'ethnic cleansing' of Bosnia since 1992 and of Kosovo since 1999 alerts us to the potential consequences of rejecting state structures premised on the equality of all citizens for ones premised on the supremacy of the majority ethnic or national group, which claims sovereignty unto itself rather than placing it in the body of equal citizens (see Hayden 1999). At the same time, if efforts to ameliorate conflict are to be realistic, it is necessary to recognize that the link between democratization and nationalist conflict is strong (cf. Snyder 2000).

Simply put, the temptation for political elites to invoke 'the nation' and its putative interests in order to garner at least short-term support is very strong, because it usually succeeds, even in places in which the call of nationalism is widely recognized as sirenical. In Bosnia, for example, in the spring of 1990 the population was overwhelmingly opposed to the legalization of nationalist political parties, yet by the fall of the same year, almost all of these same people voted for separate nationalist parties (Goati 1992), and even after the war that resulted from this vote, all of the leaders who had destroyed the republic were re-elected. It is not coincidental that the countries in Eastern Europe that have been most successful in establishing multiparty democracies have been precisely those that were most homogenized earlier in the twentieth century: Poland, Hungary, the Czech Republic and Slovenia. The point was brought home to me by a Hungarian in Belgrade in 1995 who said that, as a Hungarian patriot, he was glad that Transylvania had been awarded to Romania after World War I, because if it were still part of Hungary, a relatively homogenous Romania would be on the fast track for inclusion in NATO and the EU while Hungary would be kept back because of the problems involved in dealing with its large minority population.

Even in those European countries that are both explicitly bi- or multinational (Belgium and Switzerland) and democratic, this happy coincidence is predicated on the existence of territorial polities (cantons) that are themselves conceived of as mononational (see Fleiner and Fleiner 2000). This coincidence reminds us that modern democracy was conceived along Lockean lines, as a pragmatic instrument for constructing government based on the will of the people as expressed in voting. Far from celebrating differences, American democracy, at least, required ignoring social differences ideologically while excluding non-whites from the sovereign people. Thus John Jay, in *Federalist Paper* no. 2, pretended that the population of the new United States, in 1787, formed 'one united people – a people descended from the same ancestors, speaking the same language, professing the same religion ... very similar in manners and customs' (Madison *et al.* 1987 [1787]: 91). Not surprisingly, 'Negroes of the African race' were excluded not only from voting but overwhelmingly from citizenship by the new constitution that Jay was promoting, a view ratified by the Supreme Court in 1857 in *Dred Scott*.[20] In this putatively homogenous political entity, Lockean principles of pragmatic politics (divisions of power, ambition being made to counter ambition) were deemed applicable. The Millean project of inclusion seems practical only once the Lockean system is institutionalized in territorial polities that are themselves homogenized, and only insofar as the inclusion does not serve to create political configurations in which a concentration of a newly enfranchised group may lead to demands for separation.

It might be suggested that the Lockean institutions themselves should not survive if they cannot ensure the achievement of the liberty espoused by Mill. Yet can any institutions of government impose toleration? There is a potential paradox built into the idea that a limited government based on the consent of the people (the ideal of Locke) can be harnessed to a project as great as imposing tolerance on an unwilling population. In such cases, the Millean mandate is outside the boundaries of democracy unless and until the governed consent to it, especially, as Locke noted, because belief cannot be compelled. It is tempting to try to avoid this problem by proclaiming basic liberties and access to social goods as 'rights', not subject to political negotiation but rather by judicial determination. Yet this begs the most basic issues of democracy: the source of laws, the source of judicial authority, the selection of judges and, ultimately, the very concept of accountability of the rulers to the ruled that Lockean democratic institutions are meant to provide. From this perspective, then, insistence on Millean multi-multi destroys democracy.

Of course, sufficient acceptance of Millean principles would change the dominant political assumptions of a polity to the point at which Lockean tolerance is unneeded. It is hard, however, to argue that what Bosnians need is help to 'learn to live together', since they already had learned to live together over the forty-five years of 'communist dictatorship', informed by the ideology of 'brotherhood and unity'. That ideology worked only as long as it was not necessary for the people(s) of Bosnia to constitute themselves as a nation, which they have not done and continue to show few signs of doing.

## Tolerance, statehood and dictatorships of virtue

As noted at the start of this chapter, the popular image of the Balkans as a land of 'age-old hatreds', in which 'those people have been killing each other for centuries', is wrong. Were it correct, Serbs, Croats, Bosniaks, Albanians, Macedonians *et al.* would not have been living so intermingled (and after 1945, increasingly intermarried) as to have made ethnic cleansing a possibility. On the other hand, that these people have been living intermingled does not mean that they have not been divided, overwhelmingly, into self-identified groups distinguished mainly by religion. In this context, sites sacred to one religiously defined community have been the centers of competition, and occasionally conflict, for generations. In some circumstances, this competition has led to a pragmatic (Lockean) tolerance, in the form of non-interference with the practices of others. In other circumstances, however, this Lockean pragmatism has been overcome by the opportunities suddenly afforded, as nation-states were consolidated, to end the competition by the destruction of the Other's presence, physically (ethnic cleansing) and symbolically (destruction or transformation of religious sites associated with the Other). This intolerance, however, is actually a reflection of popular sovereignty, as a state is created as that of one particular nation, for that particular nation, by that particular nation.

This manifestation of intolerant popular sovereignty is not simply a Balkan phenomenon. This paper has noted parallels in Israel/Palestine and in India/Pakistan, and the examples can be multiplied.

It is not enough to say that times have changed, which actually means that times *should have* changed, and that non-Western Europeans may not construct the kinds of nation-states that were constructed in Western Europe because the process of doing so is so terrible. Of course, religious toleration is easier in those parts of Europe in which churches are being closed than it is where churches are being built; but then the construction of mosques in European cities where the churches are closing could produce the kinds of reactions that have led to the destruction of mosques where churches are being built (Bosnia) or of churches where mosques are being built (Bosnia, Kosovo).[21] Since self-confidently Western countries now impose 'sanctions' on those less human-righteous, one is quickly brought to the morally odd position of denying economic assistance to poorer countries on the grounds that they violate human rights, thus condemning both minorities and majorities to further poverty – an odd human rights stance, one would think.

It may be that Millean positive tolerance is most likely to develop only following the establishment of Lockean democratic institutions, as indeed has been the trajectory in those countries now called 'Western'. Short-circuiting this trajectory seems at the moment to be premised on the superiority of multi-multi protectorates over the intolerant sovereignty of the nation-state. But a dictatorship of virtue is, in the end, still a dictatorship.

## Conclusion

What links the various modern cases referred to in this paper, and the postsocialist Balkans, with earlier instances of the conversion or destruction of religious sites, is the arrival of popular sovereignty in the region. This linkage gives a rather troubling twist to Katherine Verdery's suggestion in the introduction to this volume that postsocialist studies may be informed by and inform postcolonial ones. The specifics of state socialism are less pertinent to events in the former Yugoslavia than the consolidation of nation-states in places in which that classic process of European modernity had been prevented. Similarly, in postcolonial settings, the most devastating conflicts have occurred in places in which the officialized identity of the sovereign nation has excluded a large part of the population (Tambiah 1989). In Europe, this process may be seen as Hegel turning Marx on his head, as leaders of populist movements invoke the historic destiny of their nations as justification for not only independence but also the repression of minorities. It seems that while economically the worker has no nation but labor, politically the workers are mobilized as members of nations, not labor, at least as long as the supposedly threatening minorities are there to be scapegoated. The fact that analysis shows the conditional, fluid nature of such constructions is irrelevant to their success; as Benedict Anderson has quipped, when he said communities were imagined he did not at all imply that they were imaginary (cf. Hayden 1996a). The cultural racism of Balkans stereotypes is thus a fine inversion of the myth of European tolerance. Ironically enough, Yugoslavia ceased to exist when its peoples adopted the classic paradigm of modern European political and social thought, and fought to construct nation-states. Apparently their inability to become postmodern without having gone through modernity renders them non-European, despite their following the socio-political logic most central to central Europe.

Studying all of this is discomforting, to say the least: perhaps I may conclude by adding one more element to Chris Hann's call for investigations of the connections between lofty ideals and social realities in the new democracies of postsocialist Europe. However defined, 'democracy' requires some mechanism by which the will of a collectivity ('the people' defined in some way) is made manifest. It is possible that only some definitions of such a collectivity are durable, despite the fluidity of identity formations under some circumstances, and the seeming variety of criteria that may be used to define 'the people'. Marx clearly had it wrong: the worker *does* have a nation other than labor, even as the interests of workers of different nations *should* be congruent. Even so, the consequences of implementing the logic of nationalism are clearly destructive. Anthropologists may be able to show why a logic of catastrophic practical consequence has such strong political appeal. If the probability of catastrophe is made clear, the pragmatism of Lockean tolerance may be so as well. Or so one may hope.

## Notes

1  While I cite the French original, my own reading comes from the excerpts translated into Croatian and published in *Arkzin* ca. 1997.
2  In South Asian studies, the similar presumption that colonialism marked a disjunction from earlier practices so pronounced as to be, essentially, the starting point for all that followed (which seems a presumption of postcolonial analyses) has been challenged recently by those who see strong continuities between pre-colonial, colonial and post-colonial social and cultural formations (see e.g. Lorenzen 1999).
3  Arendt seems to have cribbed this phrase from a letter to her by Karl Jaspers (quoted in Neier 1998: 222).
4  Actually, his studies were even broader in their details, with, for example, footnote references to sites shared by Muslims and Jews (Hasluck 1973: 69, n. 1).
5  *Politika* (Belgrade), 21 February 2001 (http://www.politika.co.yu/2001/0221/01_14.htm). It should be noted that *Politika*, the major Serbian news daily and one of the pillars of the Milošević regime until 5 October 2000, is not necessarily the most reliable source for information of Kosovo. The *Politika* story is translated and amplified on the JUSTWATCH-L listserv, 21 February 2001 (http://listserv.acsu.buffalo.edu/archives/justwatch-l.html).
6  I am grateful to Andras Riedlmayer of Harvard University for a listing of mosques destroyed in Serbia after 1862, along with sources on them, in an email message to me on 1 March 2001.
7  *Balkan Conflict Report* 167 (August 2000).
8  'First mosque rebuilt in Bosnian Serb entity since the end of war opens', Agence France-Press, 27 August 2000.
9  'Bože, širi Hrvatsku!', *Feral Tribune* 779 (20 August 2000), internet edition. *Feral Tribune* is a long-standing critic of the nationalist parties in Croatia and elsewhere in the former Yugoslavia, and the title of this article ('Lord, expand Croatia') is a pun on a well-known Croatian nationalist phrase, 'Lord, protect Croatia' (*Bože, štiti Hrvatsku*). The article in question is primarily about the speech of a Croatian Catholic priest at the dedication of a church on the Croatian–Montenegrin border, begging Christ and Mary, mother of God, to help change the border in order to enlarge Croatia. Bax (1995) provides a study of religion and violence in this region.
10  I argue this point at very great length in chapters 5–9 of my 1999 book. A comparable interpretation is found in Burg and Shoup (1999) and Woodward (1995). A Muslim/Bosniak counter to this view is Mahmutćehajić (2000).
11  And, of course, most Croats who had been living in areas under Serb control in Croatia, 1991–5 (the 'Republika Srpska Krajina'), were also driven out, with many killed.
12  There was a difference of opinion between the Croats of Herzegovina and those of central Bosnia concerning Bosnian independence, with many of the latter in favor of it while the former were overwhelmingly opposed, wishing instead to annex Herzegovina to Croatia. The Croatian Democratic Union regime of Franjo Tudjman in Zagreb removed pro-Bosnia Croats from the leadership of their party's Bosnia

branches, which dominated Croatian politics in Bosnia, and actively worked to destroy Bosnia.

13 Proclamation of the Law on Citizenship of Bosnia and Herzegovina, Office of the High Representative, Sarajevo, December 1997.

14 http://www.ohr.int/press/p990305a.htm.

15 http://www.ohr.int/roundup/bih010301.htm#2.

16 I can give no source on this; 'multi-multi' is now standard slang in Bosnia.

17 *OHR Bulletin* 65, 6 February 1998.

18 OHR press release, 'Coat of arms of BiH', Sarajevo, 20 May 1998.

19 *Ibid.*

20 *Dred Scott v. Sandford*, 55 US 393 (1856). It was to overcome this decision that the 13th, 14th and 15th amendments to the US constitution were passed after the Civil War.

21 Recent discussions of such tensions are Ewing (2001) and Wikan (2001), although both authors might well reject the analysis in this paper.

# References

Arendt, Hannah (1963) *Eichmann in Jerusalem: a Report on the Banality of Evil*, New York: Viking Press.

Bakić-Hayden, Milica (1995) 'Nesting orientalisms: the case of former Yugoslavia', *Slavic Review* 54: 917–31.

Banac, Ivo (1983) *The National Question in Yugoslavia*, Ithaca: Cornell University Press.

Bax, Mart (1995) *Medjugorje: Religion, Politics and Violence in Rural Bosnia*, Amsterdam: VU University Press.

Benvenisti, Meron (2000) *Sacred Landscape: the Buried History of the Holy Land since 1948*, Berkeley: University of California Press.

Bernbeck, Reinhard and Susan Pollack (1996) 'Ayodhya, archeology and identity', *Current Anthropology* 37 (Supplement): S138–142.

Binder, David (1993) 'U.S. policymakers on Bosnia admit errors in opposing partition in 1992', *New York Times* 29 August: 8.

Bougarel, Xavier (1996) *Bosnie: Anatomie d'un Conflit*, Paris: Editions La Decouverte.

Bowman, Glen (1993) 'Nationalizing the sacred: shrines and shifting identities in the Israeli-occupied regions', *Man* (n.s.) 28: 431–60.

Bringa, Tone (1995) *Being Muslim the Bosnian Way*, Princeton: Princeton University Press.

Burg, Steven and Paul Shoup (1999) *The War in Bosnia – Herzegovina: Ethnic conflict and International Intervention*, Armonk: M.E. Sharpe.

Campbell, David (1998) *National Deconstruction: Violence, Identity and Justice in Bosnia*, Minneapolis: University of Minnesota Press.

Denitch, Bogdan (1994) *Ethnic Nationalism: the Tragic Death of Yugoslavia*, Minneapolis: University of Minnesota Press.

Donia, Robert (1981) *Islam under the Double Eagle: the Muslims of Bosnia and Hercegovina, 1878–1914*, Boulder: East European Monographs.

Donia, Robert and John Fine (1994) *Bosnia and Herzegovina: a Tradition Betrayed*, New York: Columbia University Press.

Duijzings, Ger (1993) 'Pilgrimage, politics and ethnicity: joint pilgrimages of Muslims and Hindus and conflicts over ambiguous sanctuaries in former Yugoslavia and Albania', in Mart Bax and Adrianus Koster (eds) *Power and Prayer: Religious and Political Processes in Present and Past*, Amsterdam: VU University Press, pp. 80–91.

——(2000) *Religion and the Politics of Identity in Kosovo*, New York: Columbia University Press.

Ewing, Katherine Pratt (2001) 'Legislating religious freedom: Muslim challenges to relations between 'church' and 'state' in Germany and France', *Daedalus* 129(4): 31–54.

Fleiner, Lidija Basta and Thomas Fleiner (2000) *Federalism in Multiethnic States: the Case of Switzerland* (2nd edn), Bâle: Helbing and Lichtenhalten.

Fox, Richard (1996) 'Communalism and modernity', in D. Ludden (ed.) *Contesting the Nation: Religion, Community and the Politics of Democracy in India*, Philadelphia: University of Pennsylvania Press.

Freitag, Sandria (1990) *Public Arenas and the Emergence of Communalism in North India*, Delhi: Oxford University Press.

Geertz, Clifford (1995) *After the Fact: Two Countries, Four Decades, One Anthropologist*, Cambridge, MA: Harvard University Press.

Glas Kosova i Metohije (1999) *Crucified Kosovo: Destroyed and Desecrated Serbian Orthodox Churches in Kosovo and Metohije (June–October 1999)*, Prizren: Media and Publishing Center of Raška and Prizren Orthodox Eparchy; updated internet edition: www.decani.yunet.com/destruction.htm.

Goati, Vladimir (1992) 'Politički Život Bosne i Hercegovine, 1989–1992', in Srdan Bogosavljević, Vladimir Goati, Zdravko Grebo, Jasminka Hasanbegović, Dusan Janjić *et al.*, *Bosna i Hercegovina izmedju Rata i Mira*, Beograd: Institut Društvenih Nauka.

Hammel, Eugene (1993) 'Demography and the origins of the Yugoslav civil war', *Anthropology Today* 9(1): 4–9.

Hasluck, Frederick W. (1973 [1929]) *Christianity and Islam under the Sultans*, New York: Octagon Books.

Hayden, Robert (n.d.) 'Antagonistic tolerance: competitive sharing of religious sites in South Asia and the Balkans', ms.

——(1992) 'Constitutional nationalism in the formerly Yugoslav republics', *Slavic Review* 51: 654–73.

——(1996a) 'Imagined communities and real victims: self-determination and ethnic cleansing in Yugoslavia', *American Ethnologist* 23: 783–801.

——(1996b) 'Schindler's fate: genocide, ethnic cleansing and population transfers', *Slavic Review* 55: 727–78.

——(1999) *Blueprints for a House Divided: the Constitutional Logic of the Yugoslav Conflicts*, Ann Arbor: University of Michigan Press.

——(2000) 'Mass rape and rape avoidance in ethno-national conflicts: sexual violence in liminalized states', *American Anthropologist* 102: 27–41.

Jelavich, Barbara (1983) *History of the Balkans, vol. 1*, Cambridge: Cambridge University Press.

Jones, Siân and Paul Graves-Brown (1996) 'Introduction: archaeology and cultural identity in Europe', in P. Graves-Brown, S. Jones and C. Gamble, *Cultural Identity and Archaeology: the Construction of European Communities*, London: Routledge, pp. 1–24.

Kundera, Milan (1995) *Testaments Betrayed*, New York: HarperCollins.

Lampland, Martha (1991) 'Pigs, party secretaries and private lives in Hungary', *American Ethnologist* 18: 459–79.

Lasić, Igor and Boris Rašeta (2001) 'Operacija Bosna: Kratka Povijest Hrvatske Agresije na BiH', *Feral Tribune* 806 (24 February), www edition.

Lincoln, Abraham (1989 [1863]) 'Letter to Charles D. Drake and others', in Abraham Lincoln, *Speeches and Writings, 1859–1865*, New York: Library of America.

Locke, John (1990 [1689]) *A Letter Concerning Toleration*, Amherst: Prometheus.

Lockwood, William (1975) *European Muslims: Economy and Ethnicity in Western Bosnia*, New York: Academic Press.

Lorenzen, David (1999) 'Who invented Hinduism?', *Comparative Studies in Society and History* 41: 630–59.

Ludden, David (ed.) (1996) *Contesting the Nation: Religion, Community and the Politics of Democracy in India*, Philadelphia: University of Pennsylvania Press.

Madison, James, Alexander Hamilton and John Jay (1987 [1787]) *The Federalist Papers*, edited by Isaac Kramnick, London: Penguin.

Mahmutćehajić, Rusmir (2000) *Bosnia the Good: Tolerance and Tradition*, New York: CEU Press.

Malhotra, K.C., Saleem Shah and Robert M. Hayden (1993) 'Association of pomegranate with a shrine in Maharashtra', *Man in India* 73: 395–400.

Maliqi, Shkëlzen (1998) *Kosova: Separate Worlds*, Prishtina: MM.

Mendus, Susan (1989) *Toleration and the Limits of Liberalism*, London: Macmillan.

Mertus, Julie (1999) *Kosovo: How Myths and Truths Started a War*, Berkeley: University of California Press.

Mill, John Stuart (1975 [1859]) *On Liberty*, New York: Norton.

Mirić, Jovan (1996) *Demokracija u Postkomunističkim Društvima*, Zagreb: Prosvjeta.

——(1999) *Demokracija i Ekskomunikacija*, Zagreb: Prosvjeta.

Neier, Aryeh (1998) *War Crimes*, New York: Times Books/Random House.

Pandey, Gyanendra (1992) *The Construction of Communalism in Colonial North India*, Delhi: Oxford University Press.

Philps, Alan (2001) 'The day the dream died', *Telegraph*, 3 February, colour supplement; www edition.

Protić, Milan St (1989) 'Migrations resulting from peasant upheavals in Serbia during the 19th century', in Ivan Ninić (ed.) *Migrations in Balkan History*, Belgrade: SANU.

Rawls, John (1971) *A Theory of Justice*, London: Oxford University Press.

Ron, James (2000) 'Boundaries of violence: repertoires of state action along the Bosnia/Yugoslavia divide', *Theory and Society* 29: 609–49.

Rudolph, Susanne and Lloyd Rudolph (1993) 'Modern hate', *New Republic* 208 (22 March): 12.

Sells, Michael (1996) *The Bridge Betrayed: Religion and Genocide in Bosnia*, Berkeley: University of California Press.

Snyder, Jack (2000) *From Voting to Violence: Democratization and Nationalist Conflict*, New York: W.W. Norton.

Stoianovich, Traian (1992) *Between East and West: the Balkan and Mediterranean Worlds. Vol. 2: Economies and Societies*, New Rochelle: Aristide D. Caratzas.

Stolcke, Verene (1995) 'Talking culture: new boundaries, new rhetorics of exclusion in Europe', *Current Anthropology* 36: 1–24.

Sugar, Peter (1977) *Southeastern Europe under Ottoman Rule, 1354–1804*, Seattle: University of Washington Press.

Tambiah, Stanley J. (1989) 'Ethnic conflict in the world today', *American Ethnologist* 16: 335–49.

Todorov, Tzvetan (1996) *A French Tragedy: Scenes of Civil War, Summer 1994*, Hanover: Dartmouth College/University Press of New England.

van der Veer, Peter (1994) 'Syncretism, multiculturalism and the discourse of tolerance', in C. Stewart and R. Shaw (eds) *Syncretism/Anti-Syncretism: the Politics of Religious Synthesis*, New York: Routledge.

Vickers, Miranda (1998) *Between Serb and Albanian: a History of Kosovo*, New York: Columbia University Press.

Weber, Max (1975 [1919]) 'Science as a vocation', in H. Gerth and C.W. Mills (eds and trans) *From Max Weber: Essays in Sociology*, New York: Oxford University Press, pp. 129–56.

Wikan, Unni (2001) 'Citizenship on trial: Nadia's case', *Daedalus* 129(4): 55–76.

Woodward, Susan (1995) *Balkan Tragedy: Chaos and Dissolution after the Cold War*, Washington: Brookings Institution.

Žižek, Slavoj (2000) *The Fragile Absolute*, London: Verso.

# Chapter 9

# Withdrawing from the land

## Social and spiritual crisis in the indigenous Russian Arctic

*Piers Vitebsky*

## Introduction

If Tolstoy had set Anna Karenina in a modern community of Tungus or Chukchi reindeer herders, he might have opened by saying that all happy communities are alike, whereas each unhappy one is unhappy in its own way.[1] The picture today is one of increasing diversity, with regions and peoples moving further apart, like a galaxy or a universe after a big bang. Yet this diversity has moral implications which are paradoxical and uncomfortable: increasing diversity seems to go hand in hand with increasing unhappiness. This situation justifies the use of 'postsocialism', but the last syllable is more tricky. It works for the past: there was an ism called socialism, but now we need to recognize rather a postsocialist field of inchoate possibilities, out of which may arise many possible forms, feelings, structures and discourses. What makes them 'post' is that it is the previously existing socialism which has defined the range or scope of those possibilities.

The material which I shall draw on is specific to a community of reindeer herders in the far northeastern corner of Siberia. These are a community in the Sakha Republic (Yakutia) of Even (pronounced Evén, Russianized plural Eveny), one of the Tungus-speaking peoples.[2] But my argument applies to most communities among the thirty-odd indigenous peoples of the Russian North and Far East. Their situation represents just one of many localized forms of a problem which is common to the entire postsocialist world: the project of dealing with the past in order to constitute a viable future through complex processes of remembering, forgetting and re-interpreting; and within this, the vital process of transmission between generations.

The 'crisis' is economic, demographic, psychological – indeed, it covers the whole of human experience. In order to emphasize how interlinked all of these are, I have narrowed the selection to 'social' and 'spiritual', terms which are not usually spoken in the same breath. I shall draw together discussions on the one hand of regional budgets, land claims and clan collectives; and on the other hand of shamans, reindeer spirit doubles and psychotherapy. All of these meet in the problem which Caroline Humphrey (1983: 375) summarized many years ago as the problem of 'what it is to live to good purpose' under socialism. She rightly perceived that *Soviet* society's confident certainties about this were really very mysterious and could not be taken for granted at all. Indeed, it was the confidence itself which was the mystery; and while the Soviet mystique has been demystified, the *post-Soviet* mystery has only deepened. Why are people so unhappy now that they are 'free'?

The reason that we are constantly reminded about the problem of 'living well' is that indigenous people themselves (like many citizens of Russia) feel that they are in a state of 'crisis'. There is an apocalyptic vocabulary of despair, inertia and paralysis (cf. Ries 1997). Casual conversation is peppered with words like *raspad* (decline), *polnyy krakh* (total crash) or *konets sveta*, which conveniently means both 'the end of the world' and 'the end of light'. ('Mummy, what did we use for light before we used candles?' 'Electricity, dear.') At the same time, we should recognize that what may seem like a masochistic addiction to problem rather than to solution is a distinctive kind of rhetoric, which can serve at the same time as a cover (*krysha*) for people's own very purposeful activities of *vyzhivanie* ('surviving', or 'making do'). Post-Soviet doom rhetoric contains a paradoxical mixture of historical inevitability on the collective level (so why do anything?) and arbitrariness on the level of personal biography. As Skultans puts it, writing of Latvia, some people 'complain not only of the painfulness of past experiences but also of the incoherence of their life stories. They have failed twice over, both as agents and as authors' (1998: xii). The 'crisis' is one of feeling on some level that you may have a past, but that you cannot see how this leads into a future.

Among indigenous peoples of the North this takes on a special tone: '*my vymyrayuschiy narod* (we are a dying people, a people on the verge of extinction)'. A term which was widely used a hundred years ago by visiting ethnographers has now become internalized as a key defining feature of a community's identity. It is hard to believe in 'sustainable development' (as often advocated by outsiders for the huge, wild landscapes on which these peoples live) if you believe that your language, your 'culture', your family and your very genes will shortly cease to exist. Questions of legal frameworks and land rights are vital for the viability of these communities. Reindeer herding and hunting use huge tracts of land in an extensive way (the community I know best contains 800 people and survives by roaming over one million hectares), and many local leaders struggle heroically today to ensure that their communities remain viable during the process of decollectivization. But I shall suggest that this 'crisis' has other dimensions as well. To live without a vision of the future is also a psychological state, and I shall argue that psychological models can help us to understand this kind of feeling and to place it within its social context.

The self-image of futurelessness is one which has been extensively explored in the field of psychotherapy and related disciplines. Even when scholars like Slezkine (1994) remind us (with subtle irony) that Soviet missionaries were sometimes well-intentioned, my indigenous friends constantly remind me of how the Soviet state systematically undermined or directly attacked their beliefs and family structures. But the state's actions were also often violent, and I shall explore the past and future of indigenous peoples in terms of violation and reparation – specifically, in terms of the long-term impact on indigenous people's personal and family lives. This exploration of postsocialism must include the question: what are the after-effects of violent state policies, and responses to them, such that some people adapt better than others, or in different ways? I cannot deal with this question here on the wider comparative level; but I believe that the same question can be asked on the microcosmic level of each person's own life story, and shall summarize three such lives below.

In most cases, it was people's parents who were the direct victims of this violence. The idea of having or not having a future draws our attention sharply to the dimension of time. Just like the metaphors of socialism, the metaphors of the 'field of postsocialist possibilities' likewise look forward from a worse time to a better time. Terms such as sustainability, self-determination, land claims, participation, identity, environment, knowledge, power, rights, rule of law and cultural revival function both as technical terms of analysis and as inspirational moral metaphors for directed, purposeful change (so it is not surprising that they can merge readily with the global rhetoric of 'development'; see e.g. Vil'chek et al. 1996). As a term within the range of time metaphors, the word 'crisis' implies a perception of a turning point, a moment of 'make or break'. To pass through this moment successfully would require a reconciliation between past and future, a restoration of a healthy link between them. As I shall show, this kind of connection is exactly what psychotherapy dwells on so articulately, through ideas such as those of 'trauma' and 'reparation'. I shall return to psychotherapy later, particularly in the context of people's individual life stories.

## Land and migration

Land is the ground for the lives and experience of northern indigenous peoples. It is both a material base and a base metaphor for much else that matters to people, encompassing landscape, territory and space. In all these senses, it corresponds in part to 'property'. But local interpretations of land introduce a further dimension which does not always feature in discussions of property – one of associations, memories and ideas of kinship. In this context, land becomes a very curious kind of property. It is not only something to be competed for, as in all the talk of the 'clan collective' (rodovaya obschina) and the long wait for a 'law on land' or in disputes between administrative regions over boundaries drawn on a map. For many people, the land has become something to be abandoned or escaped from. On one level, it can be said that young people are simply moving away from a collapsing rural economy. But at the same time, they are turning their backs on certain forms of memories and relationships.

First, let us look at this process of abandonment in a straightforward geographic and demographic sense. There was an earlier process, enforced by the state, of removing indigenous women and children from the land and separating them from the men who remained out there with the herds. This process was mostly carried out in the 1960s and there are thus virtually no adults today below the age of 40 who spent their childhood on the land. In the 1990s, there began a new process of (spontaneous) migration from the land, in which the indigenous peoples need to be understood in the wider context of other ethnic groups, each of which can be called 'unhappy in its own, different way': the disorganized process of decollectivization has left most of them without the infrastructure of the state farms, but with little of the necessary social or economic framework to function as private individuals or groups.

In the first process, the Soviet state aimed to 'civilize' indigenous people and rationalize their economy by removing women from the land, where they were thought to be not usefully employed, and bringing the children into boarding schools in the newly created villages. This is now seen by most people as leading to the destruction of the family and to the brutalization and disorientation of children. The relationship of women both to men and to the land was completely reshaped. Before these reforms, women were at the centre of family camps in which the tent occupied a space of largely female activity set in a wider landscape of largely male activity.

To a considerable extent this sense of concentric gendered space around the tent still holds – except that there are hardly any women at the centre to do the women's job. The tent as centre of its own world has itself become peripheral to a new kind of centre. Women's concept of home has shifted from the isolated tent in the mountains to the log-cabin in the village. If their man is a herder, he is absent from this home almost all the time. Consequently, the far-flung tent now exists in a gender vacuum. Babies are born in the village hospital or even in town. Except during the summer holidays, the hearth of just one tent in the camp is the domain of one woman who is employed by the farm as housekeeper and dinner-lady (*chum-rabotnitsa*). The other tents clustered around are like small bachelor dormitories, while the tent with a woman in it becomes like a canteen.

Some men were kept on the land as their roles as hunters and herders were turned into regulated employment. But for all women except the *chum-rabotnitsa*, this process wiped out any commitment to a way of life on the land. Some of these roles were given back to women within the framework of the newly established villages, but in an institutionalized form. Rather than being basic elements of a full, kin-based social identity, they were reconstituted as paid activities answerable to the state farm (*sovkhoz*) or collective farm (*kolkhoz*) administration. The key women's roles as mother, wife and partner in economic decision-making were nationalized, while for many men the male roles of husband and father were simply abolished, as they had little prospect of ever meeting a woman or getting married. Not surprisingly, relations between the sexes have become deeply problematic; women marry outsiders and suicide among young bachelors is particularly high (Wolfe and Vitebsky 2001).

The entire Soviet enterprise of 'mastery' (*osvoenie*) of the remote North and its economic, social and political integration presupposed that its populations should be served with frequent, cheap aviation. One could say that the Soviet Union reshaped the North exclusively to be plugged in to the wider Soviet polity. In the last few years, the once-familiar biplanes and helicopters have become a rarity, and many people are trapped in remote villages with no cash and no access roads, short of supplies and living a subsistence existence, perhaps unable ever to visit any other place for the rest of their lives. In the great Soviet vision, space and distance were themselves the region's greatest resource. They have now become the region's greatest burden (Vitebsky 2000).[3] Those who can manage to do so are moving out, using whatever transport is available. These flows operate in very different ways for the three basic ethnic identities in this region and I shall characterize these briefly in order to highlight the specific features of the indigenous peoples' position.

First, European immigrants, especially Russians and Ukrainians, work mostly in the domain of mining and engineering. They now tend to migrate out of the North altogether. This amounts to a reversal of the process which brought such Europeans to the region in the first place and seems to signal the end of the distinctive Soviet phase of industrialized 'mastery' of the North (Heleniak 1999). The Sakha Republic (Yakutia) contains a second ethnic stratum: the Sakha (Yakut) are a locally dominant Turkic-speaking people numbering over 300,000 and traditionally occupied in the raising of cattle and horses (Vitebsky 1990; Argounova 2001). Their rural economy is now severely depressed and young Sakha are flowing to the city of Yakutsk. This is not unlike processes which have been seen in much of the world since at least the beginnings of the industrial revolution. But in this region it is a new phenomenon. The Soviet polity held such processes in check through a highly effective system of residence permits which made it almost impossible for anyone to live or seek employment where they were not registered. By combining this with an elaborate system of direct and indirect subsidies which created employment and a total social world for everyone in the place where they were supposed to live, the state made those communities viable.

Minority indigenous peoples such as the reindeer-herding Even are caught up in a third pattern. Whereas Europeans can return from this remote frontier to the centre of their own world in western Russia or Ukraine and rural Sakha (Yakut) can move to Yakutsk, their capital and centre of their own world, the indigenous northern minorities, who live in the remotest settlements of all, suffer from rural frustration without the outlet of migration. Even though their villages are the most depressed of all, their young people do not seem to have the confidence to migrate. The establishment of the village (which is generally coterminous with the state farm) amounted to a contract in which the state offered infrastructure and management in exchange for the production of animals. Now that the state is no longer able to fulfil its own part of the bargain, the indigenous people are left with little support or purpose.

## The soul of property

These radical changes in the relation between humans and land and between men and women mediated through the land, can reasonably be interpreted as changes in concepts and relations of property, impacting on the distribution of social entitlements between people (Hann 1998: 6). However, this is insufficient to understand social relations among indigenous peoples such as the Even. The way in which these relationships are conceived locally requires a consideration of the realm of *soul* or *spirit*. An important change has been brought about in this respect through a *violation* of the reindeer herders' family and inner life by the Soviet state.

Ideas of soul or spirit (expressed respectively by the Even word *ommi* and the borrowed Sakha word *icchi*) imply that the things to which people relate need not be inert or passive objects of people's actions, but can have a will and agency of their own. 'Objects', in particular land and reindeer, may themselves choose the persons with whom they want to form relationships. As later examples will show, these choices can intervene decisively in the lives of humans. In many social relationships between two partners (whether persons or kin groups), there is a third partner in the interaction, namely the spiritual force or intentionality of various things, but especially of the land and of animals. This force articulates and helps to define the relationship between the other two, and may even direct or steer it. I suggest that this does not so much negate our usual understanding of the concept of 'property', but rather enhances it. We could say that objects and things function all the more intensely as mediators of social relationships if they are thought to participate in the dialogue themselves. This kind of thinking is familiar from many other regions such as the Pacific, but we are not so used to recognizing it in socialist and postsocialist worlds.

There is a scale of how much an object may embody *ommi* or *icchi*. This scale corresponds roughly with positions along the spectrum of natural resources from minerals, through plants, to animals. There is also a close correspondence with the ethnic identities which are most closely bound up with the exploitation of these resources. This shows how deeply embedded these ideas are in indigenous views of natural resources as an idiom of entitlement. First, minerals such as coal, tin and gold are mined by 'Russians', meaning Europeans (in fact, mostly Ukrainians). Though I have heard vague reports about 'superstitions' (*sueveriya*), these have no elaboration comparable to the underground guardian spirits of European and Indian folklore or the devils in tin mines in Bolivia (Taussig 1980) or Malaysia (Skeat 1900). Plant produce like berries, jams, vegetable seeds and medicinal herbs is, on the other hand, regarded by all ethnic groups in a way which is deeply Russian in tone. They travel with a biography or pedigree of their previous human owners, going to places and situations which those people will never visit in person but extending their social networks. One could say that plant products serve as an extension of the person, combining images of infinite multiplication and regeneration, along with the benignity of giving pleasure and health to others – social capital in branching vegetable form.[4]

The indigenous understanding of animals goes much further, into a realm where Russian consciousness does not venture, except perhaps in the fairy tale. In the book-keeping culture of the *sovkhoz*, a reindeer has no more soul or ability to function as a medium of social relations than does a lump of coal for a Ukrainian miner. The indigenous *sovkhoz* book-keeper will run her or his private or social life on a very different assumption. The political economy of souls is based on a key notion of the equivalence and mutual substitutability of animal souls and human souls. This equivalence emerges especially clearly at moments of great danger. Many Even people today still keep a *kujjai*, a reindeer which you specially consecrate for your own protection and which acts as a kind of spirit double (Alekseyev 1993).[5] Your *kujjai* is consecrated to the spirits, and when you are threatened it places itself in front of you and dies in your stead. Each time your *kujjai* dies, you know it has saved you from death (even though you may not know what the threat was) and you must then consecrate another deer to maintain the same level of protection. The animal which dies must be closely associated with the person it saves, but is often interpreted as also representing another person with whom it is likewise associated, and who thereby becomes the first person's saviour.

In one example which I witnessed, a young man was stabbed in a fight one winter and it was touch and go whether he would survive. Attempts were made to summon a helicopter by radio in order to airlift him to hospital in the town. But low cloud and persistent snow in the mountains surrounding the isolated settlement meant that day after day, as the boy's life slipped away, no help came. Then came a day of reindeer racing on the frozen lake. One particularly strong deer, which had once belonged to the dying boy but which he had then given to another man, won a race spectacularly, but then suddenly collapsed and died in front of everyone. Immediately people started taking this as a sign that the boy would live after all. And indeed, within a few minutes, despite low cloud and what seemed like zero visibility, a helicopter clattered down over the excited race course and picked up the boy – who did survive.

How can we understand a reindeer as an item of property, which was given by that boy to a friend, was then kept and ridden by that friend, and then turned towards the boy again and gave up its life to save him? A reindeer's soul is a special form of the essence of a thing, of property which articulates a social relationship outside a jural framework and beyond the ken of the *sovkhoz*. It is what makes the reindeer into a special kind of 'commodity', one which is not fully alienated when it is given away or sold. The book-keeper views it as consisting merely of meat, hide and antlers, but its soul is what makes a reindeer into an item of property which is effective at mediating relationships. So when we talk of a withdrawal from the land, for indigenous communities this is more than just the geographic or demographic process of migration which I described earlier. It implies a withdrawal from the kinds of social relationship which are embodied, engaged, validated or negotiated through the idiom of that land, or which can be projected on to it. Animals are moving counters on this vast game board. When they are thought to exercise agency they themselves become players on this vast stage. They are the kind of embodiment which is easiest for us to interpret in terms of 'property' – but the kind of force or essence which they embody also appears in mountain passes, streams, the fire inside each tent, and human graves and burial sites (cf. Vitebsky 1992).

Thus, this withdrawal from the land is not simply a withdrawal from economic hardship and from the collapse of the rural infrastructure. It is also a turning away from a way of creating identity and from a specific social morality. In the terms which I laid out at the beginning, it is a withdrawal from one's past and thus from a certain kind of future as a continuation or development of that past. This may be done willingly or unwillingly, consciously or unconsciously, or more likely in an uncertain mixture of these. But the failure of the Soviet project can be taken as one illustration of what is regarded in psychotherapy as a very powerful truth: one cannot simply cut off one's past. Many people do not want to do so, and one of the most powerful strands in the postsocialist world is the multiplicity of attempts to rediscover or recreate the past by reconstructing narratives of both personal and collective history.

I suggested earlier that socialist and postsocialist sensibilities both view time as a moral dimension, but there is a crucial difference. In the moral time of socialism, it was desirable to sever your present from your past, in order to move forwards unencumbered to a radiant future. In postsocialism, this severing no longer satisfies, and a (necessarily reconstituted) vision of the past now flows into this vacuum. Ironically, the Soviet past has already moved up into at least one of the positions of a golden age – it has become 'traditional'. This is much more complex, because there is no longer a prescribed destination. So 'withdrawal' from the land, from animals and from kinship is related to a complex modification of the threads between past, present and future. This modification is highly paradoxical, as people struggle to withdraw from some aspects of the past and to reconstitute other aspects in accordance with their own reconstructions.

## Violation

Such attempts at reconstruction, and the time dimension within which they are set, bring us to the heart of the rhetoric of despair and to the widespread loss of faith in the future. In the discourse of psychotherapy and related fields, this is interpreted as a characteristic feature of the aftermath of what is called 'trauma'. For example, Terr (1990) shows how children whose school bus was hijacked and who were imprisoned in an underground bunker became unable to envisage themselves at future stages of their lives. This inability to visualize one's own future is now widely documented among victims of many forms of abuse.

Trauma arises from the experience of a terrible event, combined with an inability to process and resolve the disturbing feelings which that event has aroused. There is a loss of future because the past, formerly a healthy template, has become a 'pathogenic' one.

This kind of approach is now widely used in treating refugees and victims of civil wars, earthquakes and other natural and political disasters, and can help us to understand what has happened to indigenous people in the Siberian North. The motives of the Soviet state in its dealings with its indigenous citizens were complex, as was its impact. Slezkine (1994) and others have documented the missionary fervour, the ironies, the cruelties and the achievements. A final moral judgement is doubtless impossible, but I shall focus on certain central acts of violence perpetrated upon its indigenous citizens. I argue that the need to live with this violence, and even to collude with it, left many people in a state of deep moral ambiguity. But the working through of this trauma and of this moral confusion takes more than one generation. Behaviour patterns and moods among the later generation are an outcome of something which was present in the original experience of the parent. This unresolved psychological condition has continued to affect subsequent generations down to the present.

The indigenous peoples of Siberia live with a very high level of depression and of domestic violence. Many of my friends and acquaintances have died by suicide, in fights, or when travelling across this dangerous landscape while intoxicated. The late Alexander Pika (who devoted his life to the cause of indigenous peoples and himself died in a typical local kind of boating accident in Chukotka) estimated that around one-third of the entire indigenous population die violent or unnatural deaths (Pika 1993). Though this is problematic, we need to develop a model to explain which kinds of violence in the past lead to which kinds of social problems, including violence, today. One has only to think of the entire generations of little children taken off to boarding schools to ask what model of parenthood they imbibed and how this has affected their upbringing of their own children.

Direct intensive military or police action against indigenous populations was confined to certain specific actions. However, I suggest that violence should be understood in a broader sense, to include violence as desecration (Parkin 1986: 205–6) and denial of identity and racial value. For indigenous peoples whose territory was controlled by an ideology which was initially alien, this is something additional to the many sufferings which many Russians had to endure under the Soviet regime. For the reindeer-herding Even, from being a community-based way of life in which the landscape was one's home, herding was changed to a form of productive industry which attempted to reduce the landscape to a vast open-air factory floor and the herders to factory workers (Vitebsky 1992: 232–3). This can be seen as a deprivation of voice (Morris 1997). Though there were periodic reversals of policy, the overall thrust of Sovietization amounted to a Russification and the downgrading of ethnic identity. The most important indigenous performative art forms were forbidden and expression allowed only through tightly controlled European formats such as the novel and the oil painting. Controlled re-enactments of shamanic trances were staged in the national theatre in the city, while real shamans were being rounded up outside (Suslov 1931) and exiled, imprisoned or even shot. Of particular importance for the future were the creation and maintenance of conditions which make it difficult or impossible to mourn adequately (Falk 1996). For example, while lists are now available of the numerous shamans known to have been persecuted (the Sakha Republic [Yakutia] in Vasil'eva 1998: 149–65), it is still not possible for their descendants to erect a public memorial to them. The interpretation that such a monument might be politically dangerous seems implausible, considering the memorials set up to other highly politicized categories of victims and the limited political force of shamanism today. One informant suggested that it was the spiritual force of the shamans which was seen as dangerous: people feared that a memorial might act as a focal point for their vengeful souls.

As part of my attempt to understand the trans-generational impact of violence, I am exploring patterns of trauma and reparation in the individual biographies. The following three persons indicate a tentative typology. The first has not even begun a quest for resolution to the dilemma of his past; the second is caught in a complex quest for resolution, which, however, continues to elude him. The third has harnessed traumatic aspects of her past and converted them into a force for her own future. Significantly, in doing this she has become a public figure.

### Vadim

A feature of violence which is well documented in the psychological literature on trauma is that it can lead to an identification with the persecutor. In trans-generational terms, the activity of a powerful outside influence allows or encourages the denial of the parent by providing an anti-parent or revolutionary role model, e.g. young Communists in previous generations.[6] Vadim is typical of many people who grew up under Communism. From a reindeer-herding origin, he became a Communist Party official. He took part in many actions which denigrated and undermined the culture of his people. While pursuing a successful career as a writer on 'traditional' indigenous themes (the trap of the compliant indigenous writer), he was actually very cruel towards members of his own community. Much later, I discovered something which he takes great pains to conceal, even in this enlightened age: that his father had been executed by the Communists. Here is a classic case of denial of the parent combined with an identification with the persecutor. In concealing his father's fate, he denies his father. In order to conceal his own vulnerability, Vadim has joined his father's enemies. Hence he becomes a destructive person to his own people: in psychological terms, he 'kills them off' again and again, because they remind him of his father's weakness and of his own betrayal. For Vadim, even today, there seems to be no resolution, nor even an unconscious search for resolution.

## Ivan

My second example is someone who is groping for a resolution of a difficult ancestral heritage, though not yet finding a way through. Ivan came to his present village as a child with his mother from another region. He has worked all over the state farm's territory as a reindeer herder and a horse herder, feeding the spirit of the fire wherever he goes and acquiring an intimate knowledge of the mountain ranges and streams on the territory of whichever herd he works with. But wherever he goes, the spirits of the land keep reappearing in his dreams and ordering him to move on. Each time he does so, but nonetheless someone close to him gets killed and he interprets this as a substitute for his own death, narrowly averted. The person who dies thus functions in a similar way to the *kujjai*, or consecrated reindeer, described above. The case of Ivan highlights the intense link between land and identity, in which the question of where you belong makes up an important part of who you are. Here, the land does not accept his attention and respect. It communicates with him personally and directly, but only to reject and exclude him. As with Vadim, so Ivan's story contains no feeling of resolution, despite his attempts at living well: the same, bad scenario keeps recurring again and again. This trapped feeling is expressed through the idiom of substitution. Ivan has also lost many reindeer doubles. But his state of irresolution is more deadly than that. He manages to escape dying himself, but only at the price of someone else's life. Each time, Ivan is threatened in a dream and runs away. Someone else is then killed and he is left feeling that they have died in his stead.

## Olga

But not everyone is condemned to non-resolution. Attempts at self-redefinition, for example through nationalism or cultural revival, may sometimes provide fulfilment and resolution. But here too, there are important changes in idiom. My third example is someone who is finding a way forward from a shamanic heritage through a complex reinterpretation of the shaman's role as healer. Olga is middle-aged, the daughter of the great shaman who died many years ago. She suffered from fits as a child, which she interprets as the calling of the spirits, their attempts at giving her a traditional shaman's initiatory sickness. But her father realized how politically dangerous this calling would be for her at that time and instead made her go to the city to train as a doctor. On one occasion when she was still a little girl at school, she was told that her father had died. In a panic she rushed home and found that he had not in fact died, but that he was seriously ill, in some mysterious kind of coma. For many years he had been forbidden by the Soviet authorities to trance, or to practise his shamanism. In fact, he was lucky to avoid persecution and even death. But on this occasion the local representative of Soviet power allowed him to go into a trance in order to recover. People who were standing by were astonished that a man who had been unable to walk or stand up suddenly was able to get up and do a very vigorous trance. Olga says that the reason her father got ill was that he had been prevented for so long from following his calling – we could say that he was suffering from trance deprivation. She herself became a modern urban educated young woman. But in recent years, and long after his death, her father's shamanic robe and drum mysteriously reappeared from where he had hidden them in the forest, and he has now started to communicate with her through a spirit medium. Though she is still frightened of the implications, she considers it possible that he will guide her and instruct her to the point where she may become a full shaman, though of a modern sort adapted to the more cosmopolitan world in which she lives. As with Vadim, there is a symbolic parricide here, only this time it is reversed and repaired. Olga's father appears to die at the hands of the Communists, but he recovers by repeating the shamanic performance which had been forbidden to him. Later, she turns her Communist-approved profession of medical science back towards a modern adaptation of his calling. She takes each of these steps on her father's instruction: the medical training while he is alive, the return to shamanism after his death, guided by him through a spirit medium. Olga has made a decisive move forward which Ivan has not yet managed to do: she has started to resolve the trauma of the Soviet state's repression of a charismatic parent.

## Existential versus historical trauma

I have suggested that some kinds of late socialist and early postsocialist psychological distress and moral confusion arise from the shock of state policy and its inherent violence, which I linked to the psychological term 'trauma'. It may be useful here to make a distinction between *existential trauma* and *historical trauma*. Existential trauma refers to experiences which are shocking or upsetting, but are accepted as part of life, of what one should expect. A typical example might be a shaman's initiation ordeal, or many understandings of death, such as I have worked with in the past (Vitebsky 1993). A historical trauma, by contrast, means something like the advent of Soviet power. These are linked respectively, at least in basic principle, to a cyclical or steady-state view of time, versus a linear view, but one in which one feels trapped rather than optimistic.

I presented Olga's move, from the child of a persecuted shaman to becoming a distinguished doctor, and now maybe on to a revivalist shaman, as a way of transcending the trauma of her father's persecution and the suppression of his power within herself. This is strikingly similar to what she might try to accomplish in some form of psychotherapy. But her development goes beyond the resolution of a merely personal problem. It offers a resolution of a historical trauma. Initially she suffered an existential trauma: the first stages of the initiation tortures of a shaman, which her father had undergone fully and which she began to undergo as a child. But this existential trauma, which contains the seeds of its own resolution through actual initiation and practice, was cut off in mid-stream and supplanted by another kind of trauma which was absolutely historical. A shift was forced on her, from a developmental or cyclical kind of 'change', to an irreversible change. Her response, or healing process, has involved developing some form of accommodation with this shift in which it no longer appears as completely, damagingly, irreversible.

Olga is an unusual person. What she is doing with her own life is something which most people cannot do for themselves. It is for this reason, among others, that she has become a public figure locally, because her experience can be made to stand as a more articulate and fully worked out symbol for many people's experiences and dilemmas. What state socialism has done, through its linear eschatology, is to force a forgetting of the ancestors. This forgetting created a specific kind of trauma, the trauma of a sundering of children from their parents. For many people, the generation gap became a trauma in its own right – or rather, the precipitator of individual traumas, or chains of traumas, in the lives of successive generations (even where this is not acknowledged, as with Vadim). In the postsocialist period, this has left people with the task of re-remembering, without clear guidance about what to remember or where these memories are supposed to lead them. Now that the state no longer frames a vision of the future, it is striking how metaphors of the state as parent seem to have faded as well. A powerful image of collective orphanhood in Russia is the rapidly increasing number of young parents who are losing or giving their children away to children's homes (Lena Rockhill, personal communication). In the first instance, the state targets people as bad parents, but there is little vision of what good parenting should be. In the second case, I interpret this as parents passing on to their children in a literal sense the abandonment that they feel themselves on the symbolic level.

The situation of today's young adults is strangely contradictory. On the one hand, it is now possible in principle to explore their own often disturbed upbringing in terms of the traumas of previous generations (Skultans 1998). At the same time, the explicit and implicit violations of their past are not fully acknowledged or resolved, and people are being pulled away from this past by their growing preoccupation with a cosmopolitan, consumerist outside world which pays no attention to such matters. If these young people are becoming truly cut off from most of these memories, then what kind of break from their parents does this mark? Should this be seen as a kind of liberation, or as denial, storing up new problems for the future? This is the heart of the puzzle: how to work out a relationship between the past and the future which is not toxic but nourishing; to deal with the ambiguity between liberation or release on the one hand, and loss or grief on the other – or in less psychological and more historical-political terms, between revolution, and reaction or restoration.

## Conclusion

I began with Anna Karenina, whose story ends in suicide under a train because she sees no future. Living well or not living at all are two extreme opposite ways of taking control of your own destiny. For most people the challenge is to find a way of living somewhere in between, with a limited and unstable degree of control. People in the Far North do not throw themselves under trains, because in most areas there are no railways, and helicopters have become expensive and very rare. But they do kill themselves at a distressing rate. Like everyone in the postsocialist world, they face a diversity of uncertainties and of possibilities. As well as clan collectives built on local structures, there are also *biznes* opportunities for selling antlers to Korea, or opportunities to get involved with foreign interventions by environmentalists or anthropologists. But access to such possibilities is very uneven, and when a town's factory or mine closes, there is no alternative (cf. Pine, this volume). The *sovkhoz* changed the reindeer people from hunters, who were ever alert to changing opportunities in the behaviour of animals and landscape, into a remote rural proletariat whose younger generation have forgotten how to live on the land. The herding people are in despair now because they are moving from a situation in which they did not need diversity of opportunity into one in which they need it urgently, but are denied access.

Because of their small numbers and inward-turning impulse to self-destruction, the situation of many indigenous peoples is reminiscent of the idea of biodiversity at a big moment of mass extinction. Variety, or biodiversity, is the best guarantee that some life-forms will survive into the future. But the rhetoric of the *vymyrayuschiy narod*, or 'dying people', is the most openly brutal variant of the familiar phrase in development discourse about 'winners and losers'. Every anthropologist, working in settings as different as reindeer collectives and Polish factories (where property does not include reindeer souls but where the problems of past and future are similar), hopes that, as dinosaurs crash to the ground around them, our own friends will be among the small, furry mammals who survive and find a way to flourish.

## Acknowledgements

I am grateful to Otto Habeck, Chris Hann, Frances Pine and Emma Wilson for commenting on an earlier draft.

## Notes

1   Thanks to John Tichotsky for pointing out the relevance of this quotation.
2   The Even are an Asiatic people, speaking a language of the Tungus-Manchurian family. Like the other indigenous peoples of Siberia, they were subject in Soviet times to special development policies as 'Small' (*malye*) peoples, recently euphemized to 'Small-Numbered' (*malochislennye*) peoples of the North (Vakhtin 1992; Vitebsky 1996).

3   For example, the Sakha Republic (Yakutia) contains only one million people but is
    almost the size of India.
4   A kind of idiom which is highly elaborated among shifting cultivators of tropical
    jungles, e.g. Vitebsky 1993: 228–9.
5   My young daughter and I both have one of these.
6   I am struck (and disturbed) by the similarity to the rejection of parents and ances-
    tors, under the influence of evangelical Christianity, among the aboriginal Sora,
    with whom I have worked in India (Vitebsky 1998).

## References

Alekseyev, A.A. (1993) *Zabytyy mir predkov* [Forgotten World of the Ancestors],
    Yakutsk: Sitim.
Argounova, T. (2001) 'Scapegoats of *natsionalizm*: ethnic tensions in Sakha (Yakutia),
    northeastern Russia', PhD thesis, Scott Polar Research Institute, Cambridge.
Falk, A. (1996) *A Psychoanalytic History of the Jews*, Cranbury, F. Dickinson University
    Press.
Hann, C. (ed.) (1998) *Property Relations: Renewing the Anthropological Tradition*,
    Cambridge: Cambridge University Press.
Heleniak, T. (1999) 'Out-migration and depopulation of the Russian North during the
    1990s', *Post-Soviet Geography and Economics* 40(3): 155–205.
Humphrey, C. (1983) *Karl Marx Collective: Economy, Society and Religion in a Siberian
    Collective Farm*, Cambridge: Cambridge University Press.
Morris, D.B. (1997) 'About suffering: voice, genre, and moral community', in A.
    Kleinman, V. Das and M. Lock (eds) *Social Suffering*, Berkeley: University of Cali-
    fornia Press, pp. 25–45.
Parkin, D. (1986) 'Violence and will', in D. Riches (ed.) *The Anthropology of Violence*,
    Oxford: Basil Blackwell, pp. 204–23.
Pika, A. (1993) 'The spatial-temporal dynamic of violent death among the native
    peoples of northern Russia', *Arctic Anthropology* 30(2): 61–76.
Ries, N. (1997) *Russian Talk: Culture and Conversation during Perestroika*, Ithaca, Cornell
    University Press.
Skeat, W.W. (1900) *Malay Magic: Being an Introduction to the Folklore and Popular Religion
    of the Malay Peninsula*, London: Macmillan.
Skultans, V. (1998) *The Testimony of Lives: Narration and Memory in Post-Soviet Latvia*,
    London and New York: Routledge.
Slezkine, Yu (1994) *Arctic Mirrors: Russia and the Small Peoples of the North*, Ithaca and
    London: Cornell University Press.
Suslov, I.M. (1931) 'Shamanstvo i bor'ba s nim' [Shamanism and the struggle with it],
    *Sovetskiy Sever* [The Soviet North] 3–4: 89–152.
Taussig, M. (1980) *The Devil and Commodity Fetishism in South America*, Chapel Hill:
    University of North Carolina Press.
Terr, L. (1990) *Too Scared to Cry: Psychic Trauma in Childhood*, New York: Basic Books.
Vakhtin, N.K. (1992) *Native Peoples of the Russian Far North*, London: Minority Rights
    Group (reprinted in their *Polar Peoples: Self-Determination and Development*, 1994:
    29–80).
Vasil'eva, N. (1998) 'Shamanstvo v Yakutii, 1920–1930 gg', [Shamanism in Yakutia
    1920–1930] unpublished kandidat dissertation, Yakutsk State University.

Vil'chek, G. Ye., L.R. Serebryannyy and A.A. Tishkov (1996) 'A geographic perspective on sustainable development in the Russian Arctic', *Polar Geography* 20(4), 249–66.

Vitebsky, P. (1990) 'Yakut', in G. Smith (ed.) *The Nationalities Question in the Soviet Union*, London and New York: Longman, pp. 304–19.

——(1992) 'Landscape and self-determination among the Eveny: the political environment of Siberian reindeer herders today', in E. Croll and D. Parkin (eds) *Bush Base: Forest Farm – Culture, Environment and Development*, London and New York: Routledge, pp. 223–46.

——(1993) *Dialogues with the Dead: the Discussion of Mortality among the Sora of Eastern India*, Cambridge and New York: Cambridge University Press; Delhi: Foundation Books.

——(1996) 'The northern minorities', in G. Smith (ed.) *The Nationalities Question in the Post-Soviet States*, London and New York: Longman, pp. 94–112.

——(1998) 'A farewell to ancestors? Deforestation and the changing spiritual environment of the Sora', in R.H. Grove, V. Damodaran and S. Sangwan (eds) *Nature and the Orient: the Environmental History of South and Southeast Asia*, Delhi: Oxford University Press.

——(2000) 'Coping with distance: social, economic and environmental change in the Sakha Republic (Yakutia), northeast Siberia', report for Royal Geographical Society and Gilchrist Educational Trust.

Wolfe, S. and P. Vitebsky (2001) 'The separation of the sexes among Siberian reindeer herders', in S. Tremayne and A. Low (eds) *Women as 'Sacred Custodians' of the Earth?*, Oxford: Berg, pp. 81–94.

# Chapter 10

# Remnants of revolution in China

*Stephan Feuchtwang*

## Introduction

In the Soviet bloc socialism was gradually emptied and attenuated, drained by growing dissidence and economic and political stagnation. China experienced an opposite process: saturation. Socialism in China was pickled by the contradictions of state-led egalitarianism and popular power enthralled by an icon. After saturation, reform and economic growth required repudiation of socialism, but the continuity of the Communist Party required its retention. In 1981, its sixtieth year and five years after Mao's death, the Communist Party of China delivered a ceremonial verdict:

> Comrade Mao Zedong was a great Marxist and a great proletarian revolutionary, strategist and theorist. It is true that he made gross mistakes during the 'cultural revolution', but, if we judge his activities as a whole, his contributions to the Chinese revolution far outweigh his mistakes. His merits are primary and his errors are secondary.
>
> (FLP 1981: 56)

By means of a series of Party decisions, particularly the decision in 1992 'to establish a socialist market economy',[1] regulation, licensing and law have replaced the politics of mass mobilization. But, quite unlike the ending of 'actually existing socialism' in Eastern and Central Europe and Russia, the beginning of the end in China was a renewal of popular revolution.

The first questions I want to raise concern *what* failed and the *nature* of that failure. The answers will provide a basis for asking the central question, which is 'Are there socialist remnants in contemporary China?' The idea of remnants is intended to evoke E.B. Tylor's comparative anthropological method of the 1860s and evolutionist idea of survivals, but without his universal evolutionary assumptions behind it. Perhaps some irreversible historical process has occurred that is not a necessary, progressive step in human evolution. In any case, what has been superseded persists. I would add that people live in different histories and senses of time simultaneously. But to the evolutionist, the totalizing modernist and, for that matter, to the postmodernist, socialist remnants would be an inappropriate reality, fossils whose persistence puzzles analysts of the contemporary society. Thus popular religious practices have long been described by Chinese socialists as 'superstition', i.e. beliefs and customs that are false according to the evolutionary schemes propounded by the Party and by social scientists. They are viewed as products of a time from which the best of us have advanced. It is this view and the power by which its agencies insist upon it that is at issue here, as well as the validity of the claim that economic and social relations have transformed and so made something into a past.

Now revolutionary socialism is itself a superstition. The cult of Mao's personality, for instance, is frequently described as 'feudal superstition'. According to one exceptionally critical analyst, it was the 'apogee' of Chinese feudalism:

> in the Mao Cult a perfect symmetry was achieved between politics, ethics, morals, and psychology. If we take Qin Shihuang [who united the warring states and became the first emperor of a unified China in the third century BCE] to be the progenitor of this style of feudal culture, then Mao Zedong is its historical conclusion.
>
> (Li Jie in Barmé 1996: 144)

Let us see what the life of fossils actually turns out to be.

Mao as an icon is a very visible 'superstition' in post-Mao China, hanging as a talisman in cars and revered as a protective deity. In Ten Mile Inn, a village in the former revolutionary base area of Jinjiluyu, it is a part of the wedding ceremony for the new couple to pay obeisance not only to the ancestors of the groom but also to a portrait of Mao on the domestic altar (Hu Zongze 2000). The remnant has a life. We might even say that the Chinese Communist Party is a fossil, whose continuing life is an ever-present reminder of other possibilities. Habits and recollections of collective organization and socialist ideals live on after the exhaustion of revolution. They cast their shadow over the commercialization of exchange and the privatization of formerly collective or state-controlled economic relations. It is not simply that single-party rule remains in place. It is the rule of a Communist Party claiming revolutionary continuity, socialism with Chinese and capitalist characteristics. Could this not invite charges of hypocrisy and corruption of the ideology by which it justifies itself? The persistence of this fossil represents a permanent potential provocation. In following up these suggestions I start with a global historicization of socialist revolution. I will then examine some religious practices and institutions, particularly but not only in rural areas, and argue that these revived fossils also carry habits and ideals of the more recent, socialist and collectivist past.

The Party-state has changed to some degree. The change means that it rules less directly than when it was an engine of planning and mass mobilization. This has made room for an openly ironic if not cynical view of both it and its past, as well as for creating public spaces where a moral authority is asserted that is not that of the Party, but which government agencies seek to control by indirect means. Non-governmental moral authority includes reminders of collective and socialist ideals, as well as older ideas of public good.

## What failed, and how?

The remarkable argument of Alessandro Russo (1998) is that the Chinese Cultural Revolution was the last flourish of revolutionary socialism, the last circulation of political categories that are now historical only in the sense of 'past'. The concepts of revolutionary class and Party, and the revolutionary conception of history itself have lost their transformative character. They had been at once conceptual and programmatic categories, containing a critical potential. A category of this kind is 'civil society', which is still not fossilized, possibly because it is a much milder and more doubted category of the Enlightenment project than those of critical and revolutionary Marxism, which radicalized it. Russo (1998) points out that Mao removed these transformative categories from Stalin's framework of evolutionary inevitability and turned them into an issue of political will. Three times (1957, 1966 and 1967) Mao expressed the worry that capitalism, rightists and revisionists would probably defeat 'us' (all revolutionaries). This idea highlights the uncertainty of history and the importance of subjective factors. The issue of defeat and how to prevent it, whether 'we' have a will to revolution, split workers and all other classes in a struggle for revolutionary virtue. In 1966–8 in China the issue was how to maintain political argument and organization in what was already a state governed by a Party that had ceased to practise revolution. Culture and ideology, press, propaganda, schools and universities were all at stake, since they were so closely linked to repressive apparatuses, and so disciplinary and conservative in their routinized political consequences.

In proclaiming the uncertainty of victory, Mao quoted the popular story of Monkey in the Journey to the West: 'overturn the palace of the king of hell [by which he meant the Ministry of Culture and Propaganda, now owner of TV stations] and set the little devils free'. The little devils were students and workers. Factories were linked with universities and schools as the prime bases for the emergence of new forms of political organization. They were to emancipate themselves from the Ministries and the Party that led them. In the second half of 1966, new political organizations proliferated beyond Party control, self-authorized but always making an iconic reference to the authority of Mao and to 'revolution'. They attacked the establishment with vigour. At the top of the state apparatus, Mao was able to assert sufficient authority to order bureaucrats to enable new revolutionary organizations to acquire paper, printing facilities and so forth. Bureaucratic procedure remained but was ordered to serve revolution from below.[2] Russo sees the fall of the Shanghai local authorities in January 1967 as a turning point. Within a few months a strange phenomenon had spread: the great variety of political organization that had emerged was factionalized in remarkably similar ways in virtually every work unit and brigade. The mixture of real political experimentation from below with opportunism, including opportunities to settle scores and to act on envious ambition to supplant those in desired positions, became a segmented structure of factions linking the most local to the most central levels of command. Political vengeance, 'tit-for-tat struggle' in the words of the time, came to dominate the mixture. Experimentation in education and worker organization, including the Revolutionary Committees set up from 1968 onward, was absorbed back into the Party-state at all levels.

Russo rightly calls this an impasse. It lasted for ten years, until cut through by Deng's policies of inequality and moneymaking as the only strategy capable of preserving the Party-state. His answer to 'what failed?' is: the politics of revolution and its ideal of egalitarian and collective justice, to be won by the politicization of worker–factory organization. As an explanation of how it failed, however, factional saturation leaves many questions begging. What brought about the reduction of revolution to factions? It seems insufficient to blame opportunism and envy since these are in turn the products of a social context to be explained. Another answer might be the mixture of ideological radicalism with the break-up of formal governmental authority, leading to reliance on personal loyalties.[3] Whatever a fuller explanation might be, Russo's answer, despite its inadequacy, is a useful pointer to the postsocialist condition in China. Factionalism preserved what it curtailed and continued into a new era of contained experimentation. Subsequently, as I shall show, further base-level institutions were created outside the Party-state and required a new strategy of indirect control on its part.

From the 1950s to the 1970s, the Party was the sole channel of experimentation with new forms of rural collectives and rural industry. The pattern was always the same: a local initiative by low-level Party cadres was reported and adopted upwards, before being generalized from the top in a mass mobilization campaign. Experimentation with decollectivization in Anhui province in the late 1970s and with village elections in Guangxi province in 1980–1 also began locally, before being adopted upwards and then generalized downwards by the same Party mechanisms, though now without the mass meetings and demonstrations of the Mao era.[4] I shall come to further changes. But it is important first to establish continuity. According to a study by Mobo Gao (1999), the Cultural Revolution was never merely a power struggle between rival factions but involved real issues, which came to the attention of leaders by various routes, before being deployed in attacks on rivals. A key issue both then and now is power-holder corruption and unfairness (*bu gongdao*, a long-standing cause of rebellion in China's history). It typically refers to the use of authority to favour relatives and associates, while those without connections suffer hardship and even physical abuse. A higher authority's pronouncement on an issue of *bu gongdao*, brought to its attention by mediated petition from below, is interpreted on its way back down the hierarchy in various ways, depending on local factional rivalry. A cascade effect carries the pronouncement down through a line of lesser emperors and the centralization of authority is accomplished through informality rather than institutionalization. This is how the system of factions is reproduced.

Another study of factionalism in Chinese Communist politics describes three basic conditions in one-Party organization for factions: channels of communication among political associates are exclusive; factions provide the only outlets for their political interests, and their forces are organized in a command structure (Huang 2000: 7). But around this structure things have changed. So let me turn to the changes.

In Chinese the word for 'faction' (*pai*) refers principally to the taking of sides in ideological contestation. But in describing the petition and cascade mechanism as factional I am referring to a political organization that is made out of dyadic relations of personal loyalty.[5] They are of course affected by ideological side-taking, and during the years of ideological contestation that was indeed the language of factional loyalty. Now ideological lines are less clear and less politicized. The ideological aim is no longer the achievement of Communism by struggle, but rather the nationalist ambition of making China more powerful, keeping it unified and advancing its material standard of living. In addition, codes of law, administrative regulations and the gradual extension of impersonal enforcement have to some extent checked the informality of rule. The need to keep track of expanding and ever more complex economic activity has led to rapid growth of bureaucracy – for instance the doubling of the size of Shulu county administration in the 1980s (Blecher and Shue 1996: 205). The state cadre is better educated and often acts as an entrepreneurial force itself, sometimes – as in Shulu – for public benefit, but in other cases for personal and privatized corporate gain. But informalism remains noteworthy. Although Blecher and Shue found a relatively fair-minded bureaucracy, they were still

> repeatedly struck with the flexibility, and even sometimes the utterly ad hoc manner, with which bureaucratic processes and procedures might be changed, either to conform to changing routines at higher levels of the state apparatus or to accommodate local needs and interests.
>
> (1996: 206)

Tension is evident everywhere, as Bruun observed in a street of private businesses in the western city of Chengdu, Sichuan province. It is a tension 'between the attempt from above to integrate through the rule of law and the strategy from below to build up secluded totalities. Arbitrariness in bureaucratic practice and personal interpretation of regulations fill up the space between them' (1993: 125). The law becomes a relevant reference point only when the unfairness of local bureaucrats becomes an issue and someone is able and willing to refuse their interpretation of it. The norm is to establish communities based on trust, what Bruun calls 'secluded totalities', through personal links and personal interpretation of regulations. According to Bruun, 'The concept of "fair treatment" (*zhengdang*) is in fact far more commonly used than references to the law' (1993: 127).

In sum, the abiding characteristics of the Chinese Communist Party and its state are factions, regulation, bureaucratic procedure and contestation over fairness. Seen in a longer historical perspective, the People's Republic added to pre-republican bases of patronage the huge and centralized apparatuses of the Party-state and its 'systems' (*xitong*). The category of fairness became a hope absorbed into the categories of socialism and revolution. Now it can be grounds for accusing those who avoid regulation. In many villages the hope of fairness, for example when land was redistributed in the early 1980s, was accompanied by the idea that anyone who is better off must have got a better deal because of their connections (Liu Xin 2000: 161–9).

Of course, factions still need to be explained. Starting at the bottom, one basis is the segmental structure of most long-settled and relatively stable villages, subdivided by kinship. Patronage networks are another basis, both in the countryside and in cities. They exacerbate personal and professional rivalry and feed into the brokerage that takes place between governmental and non-governmental agencies. These networks have to be understood in the context of the formalities of administrative regulation and bureaucratic procedure on the one hand, and through a discourse of raising issues and claiming justice on the other. Finally, there is the play of personal association within the command structure of the Party, ministries and armed forces. All this and more must be added to Russo's analysis.

The value of Russo's analysis is not that it provides a rounded view of all the determinants of social and political relations in China, but that it suggests a postsocialism that is at once global and peculiar. For historical reasons, China developed the peculiarity of voluntarism (or informalism) both within and promoted through a great governmental apparatus. Its socialism is the combination of the relatively recent experience of a popular politics of emancipation and revolutionary struggle, saturated and preserved by a great Party-state organization that was both the agent and the principal constraint of that struggle. This agent abandoned direct planning and licensed the rapid expansion of capitalist relations and global connections, while preserving within itself and its pronouncements remnants of a revolutionary socialist past. The contradictory politics of top-down emancipation were replaced by 'money', an abstract and equal measure. According to an observation of the poet Yang Lian, everyone in China is agreed on 'money as the measure of freedom'. In citing this observation, Russo adds that 'the ideological primacy of money could not have been established without its imaginary association with "equality", namely its representation as an alternative to a specific failure of a set of egalitarian politics' (Russo 2000: 2).[6]

At this point I want to introduce some qualifications, which render this 'freedom' less abstract and more peculiarly Chinese.

## 'Freedom' to exploit

One very common Chinese image for the realm of freedom in which money reigns as a measure of success is the ocean. To plunge into the ocean is the action of someone relinquishing a salaried career in a state-run unit to go into business. The ocean is the economy decollectivized and removed from direct state control. It is therefore an economy that has lost its moral dimension. At the same time the Party-state remains a notional space for moral accusation, as Liu Xin (2000: 182–3) showed for the villagers he studied in the far north of China.

After the end of direct administration (through ministerial control, communes and planning negotiations), the whole economy has become a realm of direct exchange. But the complexity of decisions in this realm is reduced by networks of personal connection, which are distinguished from fair, regulated contractual arrangements and purchases, and from sheer bribery. Personal connections are themselves subject to moral criteria. Everyone is able to distinguish between purely instrumental connections and relations that are a mixture of instrumental manipulation and moral obligation, in which longer-term trust is created and within which there is an elaborate reciprocity of gift exchange. The distinction is drawn with the aid of a well-established and rich vocabulary, contributing to an institution of moral accountability for the earning and maintenance of reputation or 'face' (*mianzi*), affection (*ganqing*), reciprocity (*bao*) and human responsiveness (*renqing*). As Yang (1994) has shown, the art of making relations is named and formulated with relish in urban China. Whereas she concentrates on the more instrumental end of the spectrum, the ethical aspects of longer-term relationships have been elaborated in rural studies by Yan (1996) and Kipnis (1997). Of course, strategies and ethics to regulate interpersonal conduct exist in every culture, but the open and explicit formulation of the Chinese codes is nonetheless remarkable.

Personalized loyalties (*lishang wanglai*)[7] did not disappear in the period of collectivization and socialist mass mobilization. On the contrary, they were central to the working out of factions. But the public space within which they worked then was a realm of organized fairness and unfairness, not an ocean of commerce, finance and enterprise. Now they mark out a set of obligations beyond whose seclusion an ocean of fortune, instrumentality and exploitation – regulated or not – is continuously expanding. To adapt the language of the villagers studied by Liu Xin (2000) and Yan Yunxiang (1996), beyond human responsiveness is the realm of gain, which comes either through luck (*fuqi*) or fairness, or through the unfair deployment of personal connections or the amoral skills of instrumental networking. It is an ocean full of money fish to be ruthlessly and opportunistically pursued. Regulation and the investigation of corruption can make the pursuit fairer, but negotiation and mutual back-scratching are the norm. Yet from this amoral economy reserves flow into the moral sphere. From oceanic wealth come contributions to the economy of gifts, reciprocity and donations to public works, such as the building of ancestral halls and temples, which build reputations for beneficence. Use of one's capacity for organization and social networking skills for the construction and provision of non-governmental public goods builds moral authority at home, both in the countryside and in the towns. The scale of this 'home' is small or large according to the scope of the public work and the ambition of the donor or organizer.

In the rest of this chapter I will give examples of this 'home' place of moral authority. It is a space beyond the domestic spaces where expectations not only of reciprocity but also of fairness are maintained. The first set of examples explores the afterlife of two localized collectivities – local temples and ancestral halls, and the brigades of agricultural work that replaced them.

## Territorially defined public institutions

Territorially defined public institutions in the countryside have two pasts, pre-Revolutionary and Revolutionary, created by two discontinuities. The first discontinuity was the result of a series of measures that destroyed the economic base of the previous main collective institutions of the countryside. Various forms of trusts had exercised corporate control over land and other means of production, such as irrigation systems or offshore reaches for the gathering of marine products, and utilized revenues from them for performance of rites to honour ancestors and local guardian gods. In addition, all over China public subscription supported buildings for the honouring of ancestors, for divination, petition and pledge, and for the holding of festivals.

A series of direct campaigns against superstitious practices began with the intellectuals' movement in 1919 for scientific progress and democracy and a worker–student alliance, which spread an urban conception of peasant backwardness that is still prevalent. In the 1930s both Nationalist local governments and reforming warlords mounted attacks on temples and their property. The cultural nexus of local elites that had patronized these public institutions in their homes was increasingly transformed into a predatory urban-based class (Duara 1988: 250–3). Temples became bases either for their bully-militia or for the organization of rebellious militia (Thaxton 1983: 90, 153–6, 192). Campaigns against superstition were steadily intensified during collectivization under the Communist government. Land reform destroyed the economic base of these public institutions, first by confiscating and distributing the land of corporations and trusts, then by collectivizing production and the distribution of income through the work points system so eliminating household subscriptions to support the performance of rites and the maintenance of ritual goods. Revolutionary ardour culminated in mass mobilization to destroy the Four Olds (old ideas, culture, customs and habits) during the Cultural Revolution. It is important, however, to note that settlement patterns were not changed by collectivization. Boundaries of production teams often coincided with hamlets or neighbourhoods previously focused on sub-lineages, or locality-god shrines, or both. Higher levels of administration sometimes brought together quite separate localities, but at base level so-called 'natural' settlements were left intact. Socialist ideals, a Party and its own leading figures were superimposed upon kin groups and loyalties to ancestors and gods.

Campaigns of mass organization to defeat enemy classes intensified in the 1960s. As Richard Madsen has described (1984), city youth volunteered for immersion in the countryside to propagate devotion to Maoist socialism. They competed with each other for hard work in the fields and to be seen as paragons of selflessness. They set up daily study sessions and broadcast several times a day from village loudspeakers to praise instances of good political attitude and work performance, and to criticize laggards. Production improved. Pilfering was reduced and the idea of acting as part of a collective gained in strength and respect. Madsen concludes that

> The Mao Study rituals in effect allowed the peasants to keep some of their old moral traditions – for instance the idea that a good person was one who treated the entire village like his big family – and integrate them into some of Mao's teachings about the goodness of selflessly serving the people as a whole.

> (1984: 149)

An older moral authority was reproduced within a new one. Before long, careerist hypocrisy and disillusion corroded enthusiasm. Mass meetings became a drudge during the saturation years of factional struggle. Nevertheless, two generations had been brought up on mass mobilization campaigns and the routines of their political rituals.[8] They emphasized criteria of equality and service to the collective good, particularly as expectations of leaders. Opportunistic rivalry could conceal these ideals, but as a potential for accusing leaders of corruption or hypocrisy they were always present. Meanwhile the destruction of older bases of moral authority and collective identity was a slow process that in many places was never completed. Even in Ten Mile Inn, where Communist-led campaigns to exterminate old customs and feudal superstitions began in the late 1930s, they were not completed. In 1942 village militia men destroyed the statues in all but one of the village's eight temples, but a militia member saved the statue of the Ninth Dragon Lord, said to have been the most efficacious and responsive embodiment of a god in the village, and hid it in his home. In subsequent campaigns, the Ninth Dragon was moved from home to home, and in the culminating and most thorough campaign during the Cultural Revolution a decoy statue was handed over for destruction, before the real one was discovered and destroyed. The same ruse was used to preserve genealogies, in this case successfully (Hu Zongze 2000).

In Meifa, an inland village in southern Fujian province, an ambitious young man called Chen Zaimou was put in charge of the brigade militia. He was also the leader of one of the two local factions. His rebels attacked the village temple housing the local guardian god Fa Zhu Gong, and tore off its roof. Zaimou himself did not dare to take a direct part in this action, forcing others to do the dirty work. They confiscated the main figure of Fa Zhu Gong. A brave villager stole it back, but it was later discovered and handed over to Zaimou's faction, who chopped it into pieces. Eventually the building itself was saved when Chen cadres suggested that it be turned into an evening school. Meanwhile Li Congmin, leader of the opposing faction and head of the brigade, was a member of a local lineage that the Nationalist government had grafted on to the far larger Chen lineage, an arrangement preserved in the Communist organization of the brigade. Li Congmin forced villagers identified as belonging to enemy classes at gunpoint to burn down the Chen ancestral hall. No one would volunteer, since all were afraid of the spirits of vengeful ancestors. (Feuchtwang and Wang 2001: chapter 4).

These are instances of a pattern that in broad outline can be found all over China. Destruction of the shrines and suppression of the rites of petition to protecting gods and ancestors could only be accomplished by force, because many feared it would bring misfortune. On the other hand the strength of Mao's leadership and the professed rectitude of the Party held such fears in abeyance. For many people, the possibility that their grievances would be settled justly in a new and worldly hierarchy, up to the person of Mao himself, replaced the authority of gods and the old rituals of responsiveness. But after the deaths in the same year (1976) of Premier Zhou Enlai and Chairman Mao Zedong, the hardship, cruelties and political uncertainties of the time, of ideals congealed into factional careerism, could not be deferred to a secular future.

## The displacement of collectivism on to local loyalties

Then the gods and ancestors were absorbed into a collective present. Now the Cultural Revolution is itself a repudiated past, of which everyone who was alive in it claims to be a victim. The primacy of class categories has been replaced by a government-sponsored patriotism. Greatly increased geographical and social mobility and a focus on economic interest and the improvement of life chances undermine local loyalties. Nevertheless, religious buildings have been restored or newly built and many rituals restored, financed by public subscription and large single donations. There has been no restoration of landed trusts, but efforts have been made to reconstruct a 'home' locality in the places that were formerly collectives, while in urban places 'home' sets of interpersonal relations that can be trusted create their own attachments to old and new places. These are more than simply a revival of the former local institutions. They include new spiritual and recreational practices and are, as I shall argue, influenced by the disciplines and standards of the recent socialist past. On the other hand, they are not simply old forms infused by the politics and rule of the Party-state and organized by its cadres. On the contrary, Lü (2000: 184–9) gives several examples of the revival of lineage organization and the compilation of genealogies becoming semi-official and replacing or filling the forms of village government, and I will show the same is true for the rebuilding of local temples.

A good example of the recurrence of a socialist standard and its transformation is the use of the slogan 'Serve the people' (wei renmin fuwu), possibly the most common slogan of the Mao era. It is still repeated, but now with a previously unheard distancing from current political leadership. People say that in the Maoist years 'slogan pushers didn't know the people. We are the people. We serve ourselves and so we serve the country.'[9] Such sentiments are an extension of the trend set by some writers in the 1980s 'to distinguish between "the motherland and the people" (zuguo) and "the government or the state" (guojia)' (Nesbitt-Larking and Chan 1997: 155). The same slogan was used in 1999 by an old cadre involved in planning the reconstruction of a temple for Guan Di in Ten Mile Inn. In earlier times he would have proven his leadership qualities by organizing and participating in the building of irrigation canals and ponds to retain rainwater. Now he did the same by managing the rebuilding of a temple.[10] He still conceived himself to be serving the wishes of fellow villagers, since he viewed the temple as a public good.

Resurgence of fears held in abeyance by the strength of the iconic figure of Mao and faith in Party rectitude can be seen in the rebuilding of temples in Meifa. Two events in 1981 led to a popular revitalization movement. First Chen Zaimou died from unknown causes while still in his early thirties. Then Li Congmin, the man who had been brigade leader and forced people to burn down the ancestral hall, became mentally ill. Some villagers said that the angry gods and ancestors had attacked them. Such stories of gods offended by their homelessness have been recorded in other villages (e.g. Guo Zhichao 1985). Someone, usually an older person, has a dream in which the village deity appears and expresses his resentment over the lack of a respectable dwelling. That person then convinces other older persons, those who can recall the festivals and the temple most vividly, to form a group to gather subscriptions for reconstruction and the holding of festivals. They select a capable person to manage the project. In Meifa, the person so entrusted was renowned for having sacrificed his political career for the sake of the villagers. As a senior cadre in the Commune at the height of the hardship of the famine following the Great Leap Forward in 1961, he had, behind the scenes, led the reconstruction of the Chen ancestral hall. Two years later, through a sworn brotherhood of Chen lineage members, he was implicated in a feud between Meifa and a neighbouring brigade. He was stripped of his Party membership and official positions and, when his protection in the county administration was removed by a rival faction, imprisoned for two years. Through all these vicissitudes, he never lost his enthusiasm for the revolution led by the Party and he insists that all he has ever done is to serve the people. To the villagers, he stood out against the current office-holders as the epitome of a good cadre, and was therefore often called upon to represent them or to mediate in disputes between them and the local Party or state (Feuchtwang and Wang 2001: chapters 4 and 5).

Hu Zongze (2000) has also documented the emergence of non-Party leaders through their donations and engagement in temple activities in Ten Mile Inn. They too are called upon to mediate in disputes. Yet in the same village, Mao is a new figure of reverence on domestic altars. Both here and in Meifa, current Party and village cadres have been involved in building temples and ancestral halls. The old institutions of divination and pledge allow residents to recall an archaic sense of time and of loyalty, a transcendent history into which they can feed personal senses of human responsiveness that have been radically disturbed, both by people like themselves and by forces beyond their control. The authority they establish in these public spaces is a basis for criticizing and demanding justice from the state. This public property is not a trust or a corporation, but depends entirely on voluntary subscription and peer pressure within a common and inherited sense of place.

In sum, the revival of pre-Nationalist and pre-Communist public religious institutions is not a recurrence for two reasons. First, they depend on the earned wealth of households to a much greater extent than before. Second, they now exist in an unavoidable and crucial relation to government. The secluded homelands of trustworthiness that revitalized temples and halls promise, and their leaders embody, are composed in relation to a Party-state that *should* embody it.

## Direct criticism and ironic nostalgia

A moral economy has been created at a new and critical distance from a Party-state that proclaims socialism and a fair market economy. Writing about a movement of villagers to return to their homeland from the settlements to which they had been forcibly relocated, Jing Jun (forthcoming) notes how often their petitions used the concept of sacrifice (*xisheng*). They had been moved in the course of the building of a famous dam on the Yellow River but, because of a technical mistake, the water level planned for the reservoir had to be lowered, so the lands of these villagers were not after all flooded. Instead they were taken over by state and military farms. After the formal end of the Cultural Revolution in 1976 the displaced villagers began returning and forming squatter villages outside the state farms. They sent letters of petition to officials in Beijing. In 1982 they marched to the local administrative city carrying a white banner, the colour of mourning, on which was written in black 'Return to homeland, sacrifice to ancestors'. They had no claims in law, but invoked the moral right to be returned the land in which their ancestors are buried.

Sacrifice (*xisheng*) for gods and ancestors had been transposed in Party slogans to sacrifice for the sake of the Greater Us (*da wo*). The Party also claimed that it expended great sacrifices for the people, and it expected loyalty in return. Now the petitioners transposed the same word back to a local and longer genealogical history and its avatars. They demanded reciprocity from the government of their motherland for the sacrifice they had been forced to make for it. Their appeal did in fact get a response in the form of funds to relieve poverty, but this was considered inadequate. The villagers have continued to demand the return of their ancestral land, and to assert a sense of injustice and sacrifice.

The transition from activist revolutionary self-sacrifice to a similar critical distance is evident in the completely different context of Marxist political dissent.

Young revolutionary enthusiasts began to express dissent soon after the institutionalization and internalization of factions in 1967–8. Four young men pasted a huge wall-poster 'On Socialist democracy and the legal system' on the walls of Beijing Road in the city of Guangzhou in 1974, the culmination of a critique begun years before. One of them, Wang Xizhe, continued this protest in an essay he published in 1979. In it he criticized Mao as a peasant emperor and formulated a refined manifesto for the rule of law and socialist democracy (Chan et al. 1985). Such dissent against Communist bureaucrats extended into the post-Mao era and flowed directly into the 1989 movement for political reform, which can be viewed as continuing some of the ideals of Marxist revolution into a programme for the creation of democratic procedures. The self-sacrifice of some of the most famous student speakers and their strident claims to leadership in 1989 also betrayed continuity with the style of Maoist political rituals, with the added self-consciousness of individual heroism. At the same time there has been a persistent nostalgia for Mao, evident in ironic but fond re-settings of the anthems and images of Maoism to pop beats and fashion accessories (Barmé 1996).

All of these strands of critical distance, the demand for just reciprocation of sacrifice, the push for socialist democracy, the offer of heroic self-sacrifice, use of the past against the present but with irony, and deification of Mao are examples of socialist remnants. The habit of congregational participation with professions of comradeship and mutual support, formerly cultivated in the political rituals of mass mobilization, now starts from the more individuated basis of household income; but connections with collective institutions are strong, not only in local religious practices but also in less firmly located manifestations, where places are occupied ephemerally, without dedicated architectural fixtures.

## Networks of congregations

Devout, quietist meetings of Christians occurred behind closed doors during the Cultural Revolution, when they did their best to avoid getting involved in politics. Refusal to register officially has continued that defiance in many parts of China. Hunter and Chan (1993) provide a number of examples, such as the Apostolic Church members they visited in the mountains of southern Fujian province (pp. 185–218). These Apostolic Christians reject the Chinese church–state hierarchy and maintain a brotherly and sisterly direct democracy and an ethos of mutual support through a network of congregations. Their very existence is a rebuke to the inequalities and autocracy of the post-socialist state but they lack the place-based public authority of church or temple. Rather, the network of congregations is another institutionalization of the secluded totality of reciprocity and fairness or goodness that I have been calling 'home'. It is not just Christian: the notorious Falun'gong (Buddhist Wheel) movement is one of very many networks, whose members gathered in convenient open spaces to exercise *qi* energies. A similar network of congregations was that made up of groups of dancers of *yang'ge*, an originally exorcistic dance that was transformed into a secular mass display of Party policies. It later faded out but has been revived by autonomous groups who perform every evening in Beijing streets and come together for the great annual temple fair on the mountain of Miaofeng, to the west of the capital. [11]

The *yang'ge* dance groups will probably be registered and recognized by the government's Cultural Bureau. *Qi* exercises, similarly organized by autonomous groups, started as a method of indigenous Chinese science, have been promoted and are also registered by government. A government poster in Beijing in the late nineties carried the slogan 'Healthy activities (*huodong*) to establish the deep and lasting development of the spiritual culture of the masses'. As Maria Kett (2000: chapter 8) observes, whether or not sponsored by government, *qi* exercises are undertaken for rounded wellbeing and they carry an explicitly moral content. It is important to add that the word for activities (*huodong*) is a safe change from *yundong*, a term highly charged with references to campaigns of mass movement. The Buddhist Wheel method is likewise a cultivation of wellbeing, not just for the body, mind and spirit of its followers, but also through them for 'society'. As part of what they themselves refer to as a body–mind–spirit practice, followers include peaceful and clarifying protests against misrepresentations of their method in their striving for what they call a consummation of wellbeing for themselves and for the salvation of others.[12] In this case the government declared the movement to be 'unscientific' and, following a protest of silent meditation outside the headquarters of the Chinese Communist Party in central Beijing on 25 April 1999, passed a decree (not a law) classifying it as an illegal 'cult'. This repression carries many features of Mao-era mass-movement campaigns, including meetings in every work unit. Such campaign policing is a tradition established in the 1950s which, after the saturation years of the Cultural Revolution, no longer sparks great enthusiasm (Dutton 2001). Falun'gong followers on their part have demonstrated their willingness to sacrifice themselves to police brutality and to risk death in detention by continuing to protest against the detention of fellow practitioners. They have the same altruism as the student leaders in 1989. They also have the same zeal as the early Cultural Revolutionaries, and the same willingness to swim against the tide that Mao promoted for a time (Gao 1999), beyond the control of those who represent a more sober face of Falun'gong to a global audience.

They seek to purge 'evil' in society, but they do not involve themselves directly in politics and avoid formal organization.

The defiant juxtaposition of a moral space with the agencies of a Party-state is what most of these networks have in common. In the Falun'gong case, followers included a large number of Party, state, military and university staff, who could have served as a method of indirect control. The Party continues to graft government on to local associations and organizations of all descriptions. It does so in several ways: by requiring the association to have an official anchor, a registration, or having it in turn act as a revenue collector (Bruun 1993: 122); it also takes steps to ensure that leaders of non-official organizations are elected or appointed into political positions such as village leaders. But in the case of Falun'gong and other networks of congregations their scale and diffuse structure have been perceived as a potentially destabilizing threat. 'Destabilization' is a negative invocation of the Cultural Revolution.

Return to that Revolutionary upheaval is not possible. Instead, in more or less fleeting occupations of public spaces a non-governmental moral authority is asserted against an amoral economy, and in critical juxtaposition to a state and its justifying ideologies of wellbeing, fairness and Chineseness. Christian congregations, though increasing, are a still a small minority. Looser, Buddhist congregations are more common. But there is no large church that, as in Russia or Poland, maintained a negotiated existence with a Communist state and now provides an autonomous pillar of legitimacy.

Chinese 'home' spaces are seldom sectarian religious groups of the sort expanding in postsocialist Eastern Europe (Richardson 1997). Some networks of congregations resemble New Age religious networks, but they are not inflections of the Judeo-Christian preoccupation with ontology and inner truth.[13] And the firmly rooted local institutions do not fit into the New Age model at all.

A huge variety of 'home' spaces, their contents and forms, have been created where expectations not only of reciprocity but also of fairness are kept alive. Some of them, such as the Apostolic Christians, the *yang'ge* dancers, and the dam protesters reclaiming their sacrifices, repeat or invert ideals that had been those of revolutionary socialism. Others, such as Falun'gong, continue a zeal that traditions of charismatic teaching for moral and physical regeneration have mobilized, one tradition of which is Maoist. Yet others are purely political, such as the dissidence of people like Wang Xizhe. Their networks may include small meetings, but not the occupation of public spaces.

The most common and widespread of all are the public spaces of temples, ancestral halls and their ritual occasions. They rehearse a sense of fairness that preceded and now sometimes includes reminders of the idealism associated with the heroic years of revolutionary leadership by the Chinese Communist Party and the icons of its leadership. But, like fossils, these reminders are absorbed into a different material. It is an amalgam that juxtaposes the ethics of personal loyalties and social strategy, the politics and fortunes of 'socialist market economy', a slowly growing judicial system, and the combination of secular history with lineal regeneration and a transcendental sense of time in which ideals of fortune and fairness are lodged. They are united only in contradistinction to and negotiation with an expanded and self-transforming Party-state.

## Notes

1 Chairman Jiang Zemin's political report to the Fourteenth Party Congress, October 1992.
2 Many thanks to Michael Schoenhals for pointing this out.
3 Lü (2000: 134–5) points to this unintended consequence of the Cultural Revolution.
4 O'Brien and Li (2001: 465–7) make the point that the village election experiment was made first by ex-cadres in this case, an indication of a new basis for initiative outside the Party but soon absorbed into it.
5 This refers to a long-established anthropological concept of factions. See, for instance, Nicholas (1965).
6 Compare Ku's observation in the Pearl River area, where villagers circulated stories supporting a common saying that 'the Communist Party is good at naming ways to make money, but bad at serving the people' (1998: section 6:5).
7 A longer translation of lishang wanglai is 'the principles of reciprocity governing personal relations, vertical and lateral'. Thanks to Chang Xiangqun for her thorough review of the literature and for her field research, allowing me as her supervisor to reflect on this aspect of Chinese social morality before she completes her own, definitive study of lishang wanglai for a PhD at City University, London.
8 By political rituals I mean the dances, postures and slogans learned by schoolchildren, as well as the habits of listening to reports, conducting self-criticism and mutual evaluation under a leader in small groups organized not only in schools but in rural teams and urban work units first studied by Whyte (1974).
9 These were the words of an anonymous young man interviewed for a programme on New China, broadcast on Radio 3 of the British Broadcasting Corporation in November 2000.
10 He was talking to my colleague Wang Mingming on a visit accompanied by Hu Zongze, who was conducting a re-study of the village first studied in the 1940s by the British couple, David and Isabel Crook.
11 Thanks to Florence Graezer for this information, which is from field research for a doctoral dissertation at the Centre Chine, EHESS, Paris.
12 See for instance the website instruction from their master, Li Hongzhi: www.clearwisdom.net/eng/2000/July/21/JingWen072100.html.
13 Buddhist retreats into ascetic calm and disciplines of self-negation or Daoist enhancement of material energies and one-ness with the Way resemble hermetic traditions in other parts of the world, including Christian retreats. There are also Buddhist traditions of preparation for a New Age that resemble Christian salvation for a post-Apocalyptic heaven on earth. But they contain no Creator/Destroyer God. Stress on God inside the Self and the Self of God outside pervades not only these Christian but also a great many of the more world-affirming and 'Eastern' techniques offered by New Religious Movements in North America and Europe for tapping the power of the inner self to remake the world. They have spread into capitalist business seminars (Wilson and Cresswell (eds) 1999, introduction by Bryan Wilson and chapter by Paul Heelas). But, Chinese traditions are more cosmological.

# References

Barmé, Geremie (1996) *Shades of Mao: the Posthumous Cult of Mao*, Armonk: M.E. Sharpe.

Blecher, Marc and Vivienne Shue (1996) *Tethered Dear: Government and Economy in a Chinese County*, Stanford: Stanford University Press.

Bruun, Ole (1993) *Business and Bureaucracy in a Chinese City: an Ethnography of Private Business Households in Contemporary China*, Berkeley: Centre for Chinese Studies Chinese Research Monograph 43.

Chan, Anita, Stanley Rosen and Jonathan Unger (eds) (1985) *On Socialist Democracy and the Chinese Legal System: the Li Yizhe Debates*, Armonk: M.E. Sharpe.

Duara, Prasenjit (1988) *Culture, Power, and the State: Rural North China, 1900–1942*, Stanford: Stanford University Press.

Dutton, Michael (2001) Review of Harold M. Tanner (1999) *Strike Hard! Anti-Crime Campaigns and Chinese Criminal Justice*, *The China Quarterly* 162: 575–7.

Feuchtwang, Stephan and Wang Mingming (2001) *Grassroots Charisma: Four Local Leaders in China*, London: Routledge.

FLP (Foreign Languages Press) (1981) *Resolution on CPC History (1949–81)*, Beijing: FLP.

Gao, Mobo (1999) 'Factional politics in the CPC: a case study of the rise and fall of Li Qinglin', *China Report* 35(1): 41–59.

Guo Zhichao (1985) 'Minnan nongcun yige shgude minjian zongjiao chutan (An inquiry into the folk religion of a community in rural southern Fujian)', in *Renleixue Yanjiu (Anthropology Research)*, Xiamen: Xiamen University.

Hu Zongze (2000) 'Religion and politics in Ten Mile Inn: a historical portrait (1940s to 1990s)', summer research report, Department of Anthropology, Harvard University.

Huang Jing (2000) *Factionalism in Chinese Community Politics*, Cambridge: Cambridge University Press.

Hunter, Alan and Chan Kim-kwong (1993) *Protestantism in Contemporary China*, Cambridge: Cambridge University Press.

Jing Jun (forthcoming) 'Big dams and cold dreams: a return-to-homeland movement in northwest China', in Charles Stafford (ed.) *'Every Banquet Must End': the Separation Constraint in China and Beyond*, London: Athlone Press.

Kett, Maria (2000) '"Accommodating the self": health, wealth and well-being in a suburban Chinese village', unpublished PhD dissertation, University of London.

Kipnis, Andrew B. (1997) *Producing Guanxi: Sentiment, Self, and Subculture in a North China Village*, Durham and London: Duke University Press.

Ku Hok-bun (1998) 'Defining Zeren: cultural politics in a Chinese village', unpublished PhD dissertation, University of London.

Liu Xin (2000) *In One's Own Shadow: an Ethnographic Account of the Condition of Post-Reform Rural China*, Berkeley: University of California Press.

Lü Xiaobo (2000) *Cadres and Corruption: the Organizational Involution of the Chinese Communist Party*, Stanford: Stanford University Press.

Madsen, Richard (1984) *Morality and Power in a Chinese Village*, Berkeley: University of California Press.

Nesbitt-Larking, Paul and Alfred L. Chan (1997) 'Chinese youth and civil society: the emergence of critical citizenship', in Timothy Brook and Michael Frolic (eds) *Civil Society in China*, Armonk: M.E. Sharpe.

Nicholas, Ralph (1965) 'Factions: a comparative analysis', in Michael Banton (ed.) *Political Systems and the Distribution of Power*, London: Tavistock, pp. 21–61.

O'Brien, Kevin and Li Lianjiang (2001) 'Accommodating "democracy" in a one-party state: introducing village elections in China', *China Quarterly* 162: 465–89.

Richardson, James (1997) 'New religions and religious freedom in Eastern and Central Europe: a sociological analysis', in Irena Borowik and Grzegorz Babiński (eds) *New Religious Phenomena in Central and Eastern Europe*, Kraków: Nomos.

Russo, Alessandro (1998) 'The probable defeat: preliminary notes on the Chinese Cultural Revolution', *Positions* 6(1): 179–202.

——(2000) 'Inequalities and "class analysis": the intellectual predicament of the Cultural Revolution', paper delivered at the University of Westminster, Centre for the Study of Democracy, International Conference on New Directions in Contemporary Chinese Cultural Studies, January.

Thaxton, Ralph (1983) *China Turned Rightside Up: Revolutionary Legitimacy in the Peasant World*, New Haven: Yale University Press.

Whyte, Martin King (1974) *Small Groups and Political Rituals in China*, Berkeley: University of California Press.

Wilson, Bryan and Jamie Cresswell (eds) (1999) *New Religious Movements: Challenge and Response*, London and New York: Routledge.

Yan Yunxiang (1996) *The Flow of Gifts; Reciprocity and Social Networks in a Chinese Village*, Stanford: Stanford University Press.

Yang, Mayfair Mei-hui (1994) *Gifts: Favors, and Banquets: the Art of Social Relationships in China*, Ithaca: Cornell University Press.

# Part IV
# Stretching postsocialism

How far does it make sense to view China as postsocialist? Why is it insufficient to approach Central Asian societies with frames of reference drawn from the Islamic Middle East and/or from postcolonialism? If socialism as an ideology has collapsed, what new ideals currently under discussion in the heartlands of Eurasia might form the basis of a new ideology, with powerful resonance in peripheral places? The papers in this section stretch the idea of postsocialism in more ways than one. The ethnography ranges from newspaper production and consumption in southern China (Latham) to the dynamics of decollectivization in Uzbekistan (Kandiyoti) and the 'political imagination' in Kalmykia (Humphrey). All of these chapters take up issues raised in the Introduction concerning the scope and applicability of the term 'postsocialism'.

In Chapter 11 Kevin Latham confronts the problematic character of the Chinese case, already addressed by Feuchtwang in the preceding chapter. The Party has retained control, but Latham is not inclined to link legitimacy (as numerous observers of the political scene in Eastern Europe have in the past) to economic growth rates and rising levels of consumption. Certainly there was a phase of rampant consumerism in the highly commercialized region of his field-work; but even young people have recently tended to put this behind them, and high rates of saving seem to be common today. Without entirely denying the role that consumption can play as a 'palliative', Latham emphasizes that it also tends to widen visible social differentials. He attributes legitimacy not to material performance but rather to the Party's deployment of the 'rhetorics of transition' (which he seems to find more successful than Feuchtwang). As long as people can hold on to the conviction that some further, higher stage lies ahead of them, perhaps just around the corner, they remain complicit and the hegemony of powerholders is undisturbed.

In Chapter 12 Deniz Kandiyoti asks how far the analytical toolkit developed by social scientists working on socialism in Eastern Europe can be transferred to Central Asia. Clearly there are major differences, since the new states of this region were previously integrated into the Soviet imperial system, but Kandiyoti shows that familiar models of 'dependency' and 'postcoloniality' do not work well here. It is even less adequate to suggest that postsocialism has brought a simple 'retraditionalization', marked by the resurfacing of groups grounded in kinship and religion. Following Caroline Humphrey, Kandiyoti emphasizes the importance of ethnographic perspectives for understanding how collective farms really worked under socialism. They were much more than a 'veneer', beneath which traditional practices could continue undisturbed. They left an institutional legacy that continues to shape agrarian developments in Uzbekistan, and they also left a moral legacy; here too, rural women have a strong sense of grievance as a result of the partial decollectivization that has taken place, widening differentials in a context of land hunger.

Humphrey herself takes up a quite different theme in Chapter 13, the changing 'political imagination'. The Soviet Union was characterized by a rigid ideology, supported through pedagogical indoctrination and an elaborate ritual system. This has collapsed, but what is to replace it? One candidate is 'Eurasianism', a set of ideas that may strike Western observers as incoherent, even fantastic, but which in the smaller republics of Central Asia find strong resonances in local traditions, given their long history of asymmetrical relations with Russia. Drawing particularly on the case of Kalmykia, a very poor republic in which the question of legitimation via consumption goods does not arise, Humphrey shows how Eurasianism can blend with authoritarian currents in an unstable political setting. It may seem a preposterous 'hyper imaginary', but Eurasianism offers people principles and values with which they can identify; presently only one influential strand in an ideational flux, it has the potential, according to Humphrey, to develop into a new ideology. The fuzzy jurisdictional boundaries of the Russian republics differ significantly from the state forms evolving in the new Eastern Europe, and raise doubts about the general applicability of the term 'postsocialist'.

# Chapter 11

# Rethinking Chinese consumption

## Social palliatives and the rhetorics of transition in postsocialist China

*Kevin Latham*

## Introduction

The emergence of a wide range of consumer practices alongside the development of markets and capitalism 'with Chinese characteristics' has been one of the most evident markers distinguishing China's post-Mao social landscape from the one that preceded it. The burgeoning literature on post-Mao China has also paid great attention to China's so-called 'consumer revolution' (Davis 2000b; Chao and Myers 1998; Li Conghua 1998; and cf. Latham (forthcoming A). However, more than twenty years into reform, it is clear that one cannot think of either the post-Mao reform period or of its characteristic consumption and consumer practices as unitary and unchanging. In this chapter I argue that it is time to rethink those understandings of China's consumerism which have seen it as a social palliative, enabling the Party to retain control despite the ideological void left by the demise of Maoism.

The question of how to understand 'postsocialism' in the formerly socialist countries of Eastern Europe and the Soviet Union must necessarily be approached differently in China. With the Communist Party still firmly holding on to power, the question I address first is whether or not it is useful to think of China as 'postsocialist' at all. I suggest that an investigation of consumption can reveal some of the ways in which China is usefully thought of as postsocialist. However, it will be important to clarify *how* China is postsocialist.

In her influential volume on the fall of socialism in Eastern Europe and the Soviet Union, Katherine Verdery (1996) has argued that socialism's weakness in Eastern Europe stemmed from a crisis of legitimacy that was crucially related to consumption (Verdery 1996: 25–9, cf. also Gellner 1994). In the Chinese case a similar logic suggests that consumption works as a 'social palliative'. Hence, in the third section of this paper I consider Verdery's argument for Eastern Europe and the relation between consumption and legitimacy as it has been formulated in the Chinese case. Consequently, I argue that twenty years into the post-Mao reform period, consumption does not simply give a positive gloss to reform, but may equally reveal its negative aspects. Once we move away from a simplistic materialist assumption that consumption keeps people politically docile, we can also see consumption practices as potentially divisive and threatening to the legitimacy of Party rule.

Finally, I will argue that we should pay attention to other sources of legitimacy in postsocialist China, and in particular to various forms of representation and understanding that I have called 'rhetorics of transition'. Whereas Verdery argues that it is time to abandon notions of 'transition' for Eastern Europe (Verdery 1996: 227–8), I argue that in China one cannot understand how the Party retains hegemonic legitimacy, and power, without understanding these rhetorics of transition (cf. Latham 2000).

## Postsocialism in China

Since the introduction of Deng Xiaoping's radical economic reforms in 1978 following the death of Chairman Mao in 1976, China has undergone massive social as well as economic changes (Davis and Harrell 1993; Davis and Vogel 1990; Davis et al. 1995, Feuchtwang et al. 1988). Collective farming was abandoned in the early days of reform and private entrepreneurship was encouraged. The government withdrew state subsidies from many areas of social and economic life, scaled back welfare entitlements, removed centralized distribution systems and allowed 'free' markets (ziyou shichang) to spring up all over the country. Hence, twenty years into reform, although the Chinese Communist Party (CCP) is still firmly in power, the question inevitably arises as to whether China is in fact 'postsocialist'.

The answer to this question must depend to a large degree on how one understands the term 'postsocialism'.[1] China is still run by the CCP, which maintains a substantial loyalty to the rhetorics and practices of state socialism formulated in the name of Marx, Lenin, Mao and Deng. The Party places itself, rhetorically at least, in the vanguard of socialist transformation and modernization of the country. Yet one can still identify clear re-distributive tendencies in the Party's handling of the economy. Although reform is proceeding apace, China still has a large, though diminishing, proportion of the economy in state ownership. These factors suggest that China is not yet postsocialist. However, the Chinese case is complex and a notion of postsocialism does have some advantages.

More than a decade ago, Nee and Stark identified a 'hybrid version of socialism that accepts practical compromises and mutually contradictory principles as a given condition of social life' (Nee and Stark 1989: 31). I contest the notion of one 'hybrid version of socialism', not least because, as I will suggest below, there were always significant differences between the Chinese and Eastern European or Soviet cases. However, this notion of coexisting yet mutually contradictory principles and practices is a useful starting point for understanding China's postsocialism.

The 'post' of 'postsocialism' in the Chinese context does not signify a straightforward 'after' in either logical or chronological terms.[2] Rather, it incorporates and is based upon many of the same principles and assumptions of its supposed antecedents. Contemporary China has to be understood not only in terms of the radical economic changes and social transformations that have taken place over the last two decades of reform, but also in terms of what has *not* changed.

A good example is the case of China's state-owned enterprises. On the one hand, they are undergoing continuous changes. They have gone from being the primary organizational structure of production to being simply one among many. In recent years they have had to grapple with hard-hitting reforms aimed at raising productivity and efficiency. On the other hand, China's state-owned enterprises have continued to demonstrate 'mutually contradictory principles' that combine the elements of their socialist past with the new empowerments of the reform period freedoms. Decentralization and marketization within the state plan led to rapid economic growth but left many of the underlying problems of industry unresolved. At the same time, reform gave local managers both the economic incentive and the means to spend their retained surpluses on expansion and consumption (Smith 1993: 83). In the 1980s state-owned enterprises often pursued policies of 'blind expansion' and diverted their profits into welfare-spending in accordance with the old socialist principles of the work unit, not the new formulations of the market economy (Smith 1993: 65–6). It follows that in postsocialist China consumption is not simply a matter of individuals making choices in emerging free markets but also includes expenditure by enterprises and state-owned institutions.

Michael Palmer provides another example of how consumption in China is subject to quite different imperatives from those normally associated with capitalism (Palmer forthcoming). He explains how, with economic reform, the law has come to recognize 'the consumer'. However, although substantial effort has been made to put in place a legal framework for consumer protection, this effort continues to bear the imprint of a strong state interest and to rely heavily on old-style campaigns, administrative controls, criminal law and notions of mediation familiar in the past. For example, the state has been proactive in organizing the China Consumers' Association but it has resisted the notion of consumers forming autonomous unions to lobby for consumer rights. Any such unions would be potentially political in the Chinese context because they assume active participation of citizens in policy formulation. The Chinese government, by contrast, prefers its citizens to be the passive subjects of paternalistic government. Once again we see the coexistence of mutually contradictory principles and practices that bear the marks of the past.[3]

Hence, to understand China in the reform period and the nature of Chinese postsocialism, one needs to pay attention to both the radical breaks and the continuities that exist alongside each other and mutually inform one another. This means that one has to consider the contradictions, tensions and disjunctures that result from such awkward juxtapositions. Even when present practices are radically new, one needs to place them in terms of what came before them and what has persisted from that past. However, as we shall see with the case of consumption, the present bears the marks not only of the past, but also of the projected future.

## Consumption as a social palliative

Verdery argued that consumption under socialism in Eastern Europe and the former Soviet Union became unavoidably political: wearing a pair of blue jeans, for instance, could signify resistance to a system that claimed a monopoly in defining people's needs and how they should be met (Verdery 1996: 27–9).[4] In China, the CCP used to claim and enforce this monopoly with a far greater force and effect than seen in Eastern Europe, symbolized by the clichéd images of Mao suits and bicycles.[5] However, since the 1980s the Chinese population has grown accustomed to meeting most if not all of its everyday needs on the open market. Chinese people have been able to choose whatever clothes they like, subject to availability and expense. However, despite this apparent freedom of choice, China scholars have like their counterparts working on Europe also pursued the political significance of consumption in the reform period (Davis 2000a and b; Davis *et al.* 1995; Croll 1997; Tang 1996).

The starting assumption for many debates about the reform period has been that economic liberalization must at the very least have opened up chances for accompanying political liberalization. It is taken for granted that new economic freedoms opened up new choices and ways of thinking to China's urban populace (e.g. Davis and Harrell 1993: 3; Davis 2000). This thinking has been demonstrated in the 1990s debates surrounding the emergence, or otherwise, in China of a more or less Habermasian 'public sphere'.[6] However, even if some scholars have been reluctant to impose notions formulated for a specifically European situation on to contemporary China (Perry 1995a and b; Wasserstrom and Liu 1995; Sidel 1995; Wakeman 1993; Huang 1993a), this debate has nonetheless assumed that liberalized economic activity (most notably new forms of consumption) necessarily entails specific forms of politics.

For Verdery, the failure to meet consumer aspirations in Eastern Europe and the former Soviet Union was central to the weakening of socialism. In these regimes she identifies a crucial tension: 'between what was necessary to legitimate them – redistributing things to the masses – and what was necessary to their power – accumulating things at the center' (Verdery 1996: 26). This tension led most socialist regimes to neglect individual consumption while favouring production and accumulation or control of the products (cf. Runciman 1985). Verdery argues, drawing on Kornai (1980) that shortage was at the heart of the socialist system both in production and consumption. Power was derived from the ability to please consumers, as in capitalism, but through the accumulation of resources needed by other people. Individual consumption was displaced to the 'second' or 'informal' economy and thus became political (Verdery 1996: 27–8). The socialist state stimulated consumer appetites by insisting that under socialism standards of living would rise and by representing consumption as a right. Yet it frustrated consumption by withholding the goods people needed. Verdery, echoing Borneman (1990), sums up the contrast between consumption under socialism and capitalism: 'Capitalism ... repeatedly renders desire concrete and specific, and offers specific – if ever-changing – goods to satisfy it. Socialism, in contrast, aroused desire *without* focalizing it, and kept it alive by deprivation' (Verdery 1996: 28).

Consumption and legitimacy have been similarly linked in post-Mao China. In short, the argument is that consumption and consumerism have come to fill an ideological void left by the demise of Maoism. Ci Jiwei (1994), for instance, has argued that the hedonism of individualistic and materialistic consumption in the reform period has to be understood in contrast to the utopianism of the Mao period (see also Croll 1994). Ci does not simply see the movement from utopianism to hedonism as a simple transition from one out-dated ideology to a new materialism. Rather, he argues that Mao's utopianism was in fact itself centred around hedonistic assumptions, which, however, deferred rewards to a utopian future. When Mao promoted asceticism it was in order to bring about the satisfaction of material needs in the future. Thus, the hedonism of the reform period should be seen not simply as a rejection of what went before but rather as a twisted *continuation* of it. According to this argument, materialist consumption kept the population satisfied when the previous certainties collapsed in the reform period. Communism and the class struggle, the foundations of political understanding in the People's Republic since 1949, may have been left behind, but the rewards they had always promised were to be found in the present rather than postponed to some never arriving future.

Tang Xiaobing (1996) has identified two related social discourses in contemporary Chinese culture. On the one hand, he suggests, there is an anxious affirmation of ordinary, everyday life in materialist urban consumption habits (Tang 1996: 113). On the other hand, there is a continuous negotiation with the remnants of Maoist utopianism that urged people to reject this 'everyday life'. This is visible in artistic representations of the countryside which are often replete with romanticized images of socialist utopia. Here we see another example of coexisting contradictory principles in post-Mao China. However, at the heart of Tang's argument is the formulation of consumption as a social palliative. Despite the 'hangovers' of past ideologies in everyday life and its representations, post-Mao consumption and materialism is taken to ameliorate the 'anxieties' arising from the demise of utopianism.

Similarly, Liu Kang has identified a gap, dating back to the Mao period, between the realities experienced by people in their everyday lives and the rhetorics and imagery of Mao's utopianism, which could no longer offer ideological security to the populace (Liu 1997: 120). In the post-Mao era, consumption and the culture industries, have taken over where Mao's 'culture of the masses' failed:

In contrast to Mao's culture of the masses, the contemporary culture industry, or the commercial popular culture, succeeds precisely by affirming the social relevance of everyday life ... It seems that the contemporary Chinese culture of the everyday has increasingly become the site of dialogical contention of a variety of forces, among which the culture industry, or the commercial popular culture, and China's local and national forms and styles, including the revolutionary legacy of the culture of the masses, intersect and penetrate ... However, everyday life under such circumstances may reveal the degree to which the human psyche bears the irrationality and contradictions of a crazed 'gold rush with Chinese characteristics' in the age of global capitalism.

(Liu 1997: 121–2)

Although these arguments are not homogeneous, there is nonetheless a recurring theme running through them. Consumption is said to work as a social, or social-psychological, palliative, helping to maintain the legitimacy of the CCP at a time when the certainties upon which its power has been traditionally based have been undermined by reform. Other versions of the argument make similar assumptions.[7]

Hence, in China, as in Eastern Europe and the Soviet Union, we find consumption linked to political legitimacy. However, I shall argue that the relation between consumption and politics is more complex than this basically materialist argument would suggest. We have to look at other practices and rhetorics of the reform period to see how the CCP maintains its 'legitimacy' in times when its own authority may be starting to seem increasingly anachronistic.

## Power and legitimacy in post-Mao China

Power is not a function of consent. In itself it is not a renunciation of freedom, a transference of rights, the power of each and all delegated to a few ... the relationship of power can be the result of a prior or permanent consent, but it is not by nature the manifestation of a consensus.

(Foucault 1982: 219–20)

The argument that consumption functions as a social palliative directs attention to the issue of legitimacy, which has been left unquestioned in the discussion so far. We must be careful not to equate legitimacy with consent. The fact that the Chinese populace has not, on the whole, shown public dissent against the CCP does not mean that it consciously consents to the regime. The events of 1989 make that clear, even if those actively involved in protest were a very small minority in China. It would also be erroneous to suggest that the authority of the CCP rests solely on coercion and violence, or the barely concealed threat of it. Although Chinese people may not feel 'free' to speak out openly against the government in public, most would feel able to do so in private and would probably not consider themselves subject to, or in danger of being subject to, state violence on an everyday basis.[8]

Legitimacy is a complex issue. To keep things simple, I consider legitimacy in this context to be constituted in people's everyday actions, which themselves manifest relations of power (cf. Foucault 1982, 1986). In China, the legitimacy of the regime is not a positively declared mandate given to the Party, but rather the product of billions of everyday actions of 'muddling along' and 'getting on with one's own life'. In this way, the 'legitimacy' of the CCP is not fixed and permanent but requires continual work on the part of the Party ideologues and policy-makers. In fact the CCP, more than anyone else, is fully aware of its need to engage in a continuous manufacturing of its own legitimacy. This awareness and its accompanying sense of vulnerability have been revealed recently, for instance, in the Party's heavy-handed responses to the Falun Gong.

Runciman (1985), in a classic account of state socialism drawn from Polish examples, presented an argument for the general framework of de-legitimation in state socialist regimes. The crux of his argument was that

> Where the contradictions in a particular society reach the point that its institutions are ceasing to function in such a way as to preserve the minimum of consensus and order, then they will be resolved only by a suffi-cient concentration (or reconcentration) of power in whichever dimension of social structure affords the opportunity for doing so.
>
> (1985: 15)

However, the situation in China is fundamentally different to that which Runciman dealt with in Poland. The difference is the extent and nature of economic reform and social change in China, which makes Runciman's static model of political structures unacceptably rigid. As I shall discuss below, the key to CCP legitimacy, but also its vulnerability, is the rapidly changing nature of Chinese society. However, change in contemporary China is more evolutionary than revolutionary even if at times it proceeds at a blinding pace. What we need is a model of legitimacy that accommodates change and transition rather than pathologizes it.

Although I argue that change has been fundamental in supporting the CCP's legitimacy, this is not because all the changes are positively received by the Chinese populace. Nor is it because consumption provides a materialistic pallia-tive for social disorientation. Rather, it is because the hegemony of the Party works discursively through a number of 'rhetorics of transition' (see below), which require the notion of a rapidly changing and developing society. If China were to be perceived to stop changing, these rhetorics of transition would become meaningless, or – worse – they would be seen to be false. In this sense the hegemonic legitimacy of the CCP is fundamentally linked to notions of change. I shall return to this issue in the conclusion of this chapter, but first we need to reconsider consumption in China.

## Rethinking Chinese consumption

The improved standard of living, which most Chinese started to experience in the reform period, won a lot of support for reform from the general populace. This was particularly the case in the 1980s when the contrast with the preceding decade was both stark and fresh in people's minds. Furthermore, it is also true that consumption of one kind or another has often provided the most accessible measurement of these rising standards, both for China scholars (Chao and Myers 1998; Davis 1993: 75; 2000a and b) and Chinese citizens themselves. For example, expenditure on dowry items at weddings has again become an indication of the wealth and status of the bride's family and the brideprice and size of the wedding banquet of that of the groom's (Siu 1993: 180–8; Davis 1993: 65–6).[9] It is also easy to contrast the wedding gifts of bicycles, sewing machines, blankets and furniture, which were highly prestigious items in the early 1980s, with the wide-screen televisions, motorbikes and laser-disc karaoke systems of the 1990s.

On fieldwork trips in the 1990s, it was commonplace to hear Chinese people extolling the great improvements in their lives since economic reform started.[10] They ate better food, they wore better clothes and they enjoyed much more choice when purchasing either. In the cities the number of food outlets has increased several-fold. Chinese homes are now commonly adorned with refrigerators, colour television sets, video-cassette or VCD players, stereo hi-fis and washing machines. These consumer items, along with better housing, increased leisure time and disposable income (Davis 1993, 2000; Wang 1995) have all contributed to a strong sense of improvement in people's lives as well as a largely unquestioned acceptance that life has been easier and more comfortable under reform than it was under Chairman Mao.[11] Thus, the argument that consumption has worked as a social palliative is not to be dismissed out of hand. However, it pays excessive attention to material needs and overlooks the fact that some consumer practices work against legitimation.

Consider, for instance, the realm of media consumption where changes in the reform period have gradually undermined the Party's conception of the role of the media in society (Latham 2000, forthcoming C). The CCP has clung to the basic principle, established under Mao before 1949, that the media should operate as the mouthpiece of the Party (see also Zhao 1998; Li 1991; Huang 1994; Lull 1991; Hussain 1990). Their official task is to promote the socialist modernization of the nation. Media organizations are not allowed to carry any news contrary to the interests of either the Party or national security – loosely defined categories that allow Party officials to intervene across a wide range of issues from human rights to religion.[12]

However, the Party's control of the media in China is not the monolithic dictatorship it is often presented to be in the Western media. The principles of Party-controlled news production in particular are *potentially* draconian, but Party control operates according to a loosely defined system of self-censorship that furnishes senior editors both with the responsibility not to cause political unrest, and with the opportunity to stretch the limits of press freedom, particularly when in search of commercial gain (Latham 2000; Li Zhuren 1998). In this way, through the 1980s and even the 1990s (following the Tiananmen incident of 1989, which set back media liberalization) Chinese journalists have slowly but surely extended the realm of possible reporting. Due to the CCP's firm adherence to the principle of a media 'mouthpiece' and the restriction of political reporting, this has more recently taken the form of populist and sensationalist reporting rather than political adventurousness (Wilson 1997; Li Zhuren 1998). They have been designed to sell media products and advertising, not overthrow the government.

During this period, China has continued to open up to the rest of the world (cf. Wang 1999). More and more foreign tourists and businesspeople visit China each year. More and more Chinese citizens travel abroad to holiday, work and study. The accessibility to Chinese people of foreign media increases every day. Tens, if not hundreds, of millions of Chinese already have mobile phones, pagers and faxes that link up to the outside world.[13] Foreign, including Hong Kong Chinese, newspapers are readily available in tourist shops. Phoenix, the Murdoch-owned satellite television entertainment channel broadcast from Hong Kong, is watched widely throughout the country. Foreign hotels and even some government-owned work units, not to mention the many illegal satellite link-ups, relay foreign satellite television channels such as the BBC and CNN into people's homes (cf. McGregor 2001). In Guangdong province the four Hong Kong terrestrial television channels are officially relayed via cable networks and viewed by millions daily. In addition, despite government fears and attempts at control, the Internet, which enjoys rapidly growing use in China, makes both foreign news-sites and even dissident political sites available to many Chinese with a computer, a modem and a telephone line. With China's entry to the World Trade Organization, China's Hollywood film imports are expected to double in the next few years.

This process of opening up exposes hundreds of millions of Chinese to alternative forms of media production, alternative sources of news and alternative ways of seeing the world. The Chinese population as a whole is not straining at the leash to seek out dissident political views and one should not overstate the political implications of this process. However, this massive proliferation in forms of media consumption renders the Party's understanding of the media as its mouthpiece increasingly anachronistic. The mouthpiece model of media production is based upon the notion of a hermetically sealed populace which consumes only media messages produced under controlled conditions. Yet the open-door policy has gradually weakened the seal until it has become decidedly leaky. In these ways Chinese media consumption can work contrary to Party control as well as in support of it.

As the reform period matured, Chinese consumers matured with it. The novelty of abundant foreign goods, enormous choice and the freedom to consume wore off. This is marked by the changing symbolic significance of China's 'free markets'. *Ziyou shichang* (literally 'free market') was the name given to street markets in the 1980s where private entrepreneurs could set up stalls selling goods. However, although these markets still exist today, the proliferation of private shops and enterprises has diminished the symbolic significance and novelty that these markets had in the early days of reform.

It is important to remember that people in their early twenties or younger, who make up a vast proportion of the overall population, have never personally known anything different. Hence, for them, comparisons with the austere years under Mao tend to carry less weight than they do with older generations. China's consuming population is also incredibly diverse. Even among the Han Chinese, there are vast differences in consumption habits, between peasants, factory workers, urban and rural residents, young and old, men and women and people of different religions. At the same time there are important differences between North and South, between hinterland and coastal provinces, mountainous areas and plains and other ethnic minority groups in China. Proximity to Beijing, Hong Kong, Taiwan and overseas Chinese communities can make a significant difference in the ways in which people think, act and consume. We therefore have to consider how the period of reform and the accompanying rise of consumption and a more consumer-oriented society have themselves contributed to the diversities within Chinese society.

As Gamble (forthcoming) has recently argued for the case of Shanghai, consumption and consumerism can be 'fracturing and divisive'.[14] He highlights the generational gap which has emerged between young Shanghainese and their parents as a result of their attitudes towards and desires for consumer goods. Parents were much more easily satisfied. They were also more likely to consume on behalf of others, not least their children. The younger generation, by contrast, was far more motivated by consumption for themselves. At the same time, conspicuous consumption has come to make visible the great differences in wealth between those who can afford it and those who cannot. Gamble also found that young wealthy Shanghainese associated themselves more closely with the affluent lifestyles of their Chinese counterparts in Taiwan or the United States than with their fellow citizens. Similarly, in her ethnographic survey of consumers and vendors in a Nanjing market, Veeck (2000) has documented the emergence of increasing class differences. Due to economic and structural factors as well as consumer attitudes and expectations, the trend is towards ever less personal and atomized relationships between consumers and vendors. According to Veeck, there is no sign of the emergence of a greater sense of community centred around the market, as has been documented in other societies (Veeck 2000: 122–3).

In my own recent work on newspaper production in the southern city of Guangzhou, which has been at the forefront of reforms since the early 1980s, I have found that the notion of 'the consumer' has increasingly come to play a part in the decision-making and editorial processes of journalists (Latham, forthcoming B). Some newspapers are now targeting particular perceived categories of consumer. Journalists at the paper in which I carried out research, for instance, aimed at young upwardly mobile executives. These target readers were often identified in the newspaper by reference to their consumer lifestyle. Hence, the paper carried articles about Guangzhou's booming restaurant culture, the entertainment sector, car purchasing, designer fashions and mobile phones.

However, this target readership was not simply an abstract notion. It featured practically in the daily practices of journalists and editors. Every afternoon, the duty editor of the paper chaired an editorial meeting to discuss the contents and progress of the next day's paper. This meeting was attended by key journalists and all the desk editors of the paper. At one such meeting that I attended, the team discussed the results of a recent reader survey that the paper had commissioned. The survey suggested that although they were hitting their target audience in several key areas, the overall reader profile was younger than they wanted. It showed that a large proportion of the regular readership consisted of high school and college students. Although the editors were pleased with the popularity of the paper, they were nonetheless concerned that it did not get a reputation for being 'the student paper'. For one thing, this would be bad for advertizing revenues.

As a result of this finding, the journalists and editors made concerted efforts to write pieces that would appeal to the slightly older, more mature and wealthier target audience. News items were selected and worked upon with the target readership specifically in mind. The business and economics section of the paper came under particular scrutiny. The chief editor of the paper paid personal attention to the section and on subsequent days, extra time in the daily meeting was devoted to discussing the relation between articles and the desired readership. The notion of the target reader fundamentally affected decision-making processes, what the newspaper looked like and what the staff of the paper worked on.

Consumption practices in China have thus become an important means of differentiation and division (cf. Wank 2000; Wang 2000). Chinese people have become increasingly aware of differences in spending power, of differences between rural and urban areas and between generations, between men and women, and between the coastal and the hinterland provinces. Consumption and economic reform more generally have brought about increased social division, but consumption also draws attention to these social divisions and makes them apparent to Chinese people in their everyday lives.

In fact, the long-term development of consumption in China has been an urban phenomenon and the application of the social palliative argument to rural areas requires careful consideration of the different circumstances. Although rural per capita spending led the way in the early 1980s, after 1985 it slowed considerably. Meanwhile urban consumption rose steadily in the 1980s and spurted shortly after 1992 (Chao and Myers 1998: 353). This highlights the importance of examining situated contexts of consumption. Hence, even if the social palliative argument may have some force in relation to Chinese cities, its application to rural areas requires careful consideration of the different circumstances.

In the Pearl River Delta in the late 1990s, I found that consumption among the young was also coming to stand as a marker and measure for negative aspects of economic reform. In the course of research into media consumption habits in Guangzhou between 1997 and 1999, I interviewed small groups of young people, some of whom I had known for over ten years.[15] These were principally young, single college graduates in their twenties, although I received similar responses from older and married people also. These interviews revealed a strong awareness among the interviewees of the changed economic circumstances compared to the beginning of the decade and the late 1980s. Many interviewees in the late 1990s expressed the need to be more cautious about expenditure, even though greater spending opportunities were now available to them. Several reported how in the late 1980s they had spent their new 'wealth' freely and with little concern for saving or the future. In the late 1990s, by contrast, they said they felt the need for caution. To some extent, this change of attitude could be explained by the fact that the interviewees were slightly older, more mature and more inclined to think about their futures, including marriage. However, all in fact had greater disposable income in the late 1990s than at the start of the decade.

One young man in his late twenties, for instance, explained how in the late 1980s he had regularly gone out with friends and would think nothing of spending 10 yuan on a late-night meal, a disco or some other form of entertainment. At that time, 10 yuan would have constituted about 5 per cent of his monthly income of around 200 yuan. Yet, he explained, although he still regularly went out with friends he would now think more carefully before spending even 10 yuan, even though his salary was nearer 800 yuan per month and the real value of 10 yuan was much reduced. This change was therefore not simply a matter of changing economic circumstances. When I suggested that perhaps he was simply getting older and 'wiser' with his money, he insisted that this was not the case. In fact, he actually *spent* much more than he used to in real terms, but he felt more cautious about doing so. The difference, he said, was in attitude. He had seen the economy wax and wane. He had seen his business rise and fall and whereas consumption had sometimes been fun 'in itself' ten years before, now it was far more important that one obtained value for money.

With another interviewee, I was discussing a mutual friend who had recently got married and had a baby. The interviewee, another young man in his early thirties, complained that this friend no longer came out to restaurants, went bowling or had fun. I asked if that was not understandable in the circumstances – after all, he had a new family to enjoy and support. The interviewee agreed, but added, 'The thing is, everyone is like that – I have plenty of friends who are not married, don't have children and earn reasonable salaries, but they think about saving now and just watch the television.'

By the end of the 1990s the Chinese government was also concerned about falling levels of consumption. Many Chinese families in the last few years, particularly following the Asian economic crisis, have preferred to put their spare money into savings rather than increased consumption. The government, in response, has tried to promote consumption by various means, including the imposition of a hefty tax on savings interest introduced in the second half of 1999 and measures to make bank loans more easily available to consumers (Roberts et al. 1999).[16] Chinese people now often prefer to put their money into savings either as a safeguard against economic downturn or to prepare for expenditure such as their children's education. This suggests that, rather than looking to short-term material gain as a means to overcoming the 'anxieties of everyday life', Chinese people are increasingly adopting very practical strategies of economic prudence to avoid future anxieties. Savings, rather than consumption, seem to be the new social palliative.

## Conclusion: China's rhetorics of transition

I have argued that the social palliative argument has some force, particularly with regard to the 1980s, but it fails to provide an adequate explanation of Party legitimacy in the post-Mao period. Yet the question of legitimacy is a pressing one. In the European and former Soviet cases that concerned Verdery, the socialist regimes clearly lost it. In China, however, the CCP continues not only to hold on to power as firmly as ever but also to maintain some kind of legitimacy. Yet, paradoxically perhaps, this grip on power comes in times when the Chinese populace probably have less to fear in terms of political intimidation than at any time since the founding of the People's Republic. It is hard to envisage the return to the intense and terrifying widespread intimidation that accompanied political campaigns such as land reform or the Anti-Rightist movement of the 1950s or the Cultural Revolution period between the 1960s and 1970s. The events of 1989 proved that the CCP is still perfectly capable of terrifying political violence and active dissidents still live under constant threats of imprisonment or worse. Yet what preoccupies the vast majority of the population today is not the fear of being the next political target of a mass mobilization campaign, but the economic and social concerns of everyday life.

State violence, or the threat of it, still figures in the equation. Dissident voices are treated with zero tolerance but they are a small minority. This means that we have to look for alternative explanations of the CCP's 'legitimacy' that do not refer to state violence alone. The main problem with the consumption-as-social-palliative argument is that it is founded upon the materialist assumption that meeting the everyday material needs of the masses will produce a politically contented population. Yet even if this was the case early in the reform period when consumption had some novelty, by the end of the 1990s that novelty had largely worn off.

Verdery (1996: 227–8) ended her review of socialism and its aftermath with the suggestion that analyses of postsocialism should avoid the teleology of 'transitology', i.e. approaching the postsocialist period in terms of an assumed transition to Western-style market capitalism. In China, however, this argument is problematic. I do not wish to argue that China is undergoing a straightforward transition to market capitalism and Western democracy, but I hold that the notion of transition *in the local rhetoric* plays an important role in maintaining Party legitimacy.

As Ci Jiwei pointed out (1994) in relation to hedonism and utopianism, China's modernization has been bound up with one or other teleology for decades. However, at the beginning of the new millennium it is not simply that material incentives and rewards have replaced the missing Maoist utopian telos. What we find is that one dominant teleology has been replaced by a whole spectrum of alternative teleologies. I call these 'rhetorics of transition' (cf. also Latham, forthcoming C). For some analysts China is in transition to a market economy through its consumer revolution (Chao and Myers 1998). For others, with its fledgling civil society, it is on the way to open government and liberal democracy, albeit via a rather circuitous route (Davis 1995; 2000a: 12). What I wish to stress is that transition is a key notion in contemporary Chinese discourses. Many students and intellectuals in China voice similar hopes for a transition to democracy, even if the nature of that democracy and the path to reach it via market economic reforms remain obscure. The CCP continues to maintain that China is on track towards socialism, though it has been deferred, once again, into the distant future. Many journalists hope that China is moving, slowly but surely, towards freedom of the press and greater democracy, even if that entails tolerating Party control in the interim (Latham 2000). For many Chinese, on the other hand, the transition means simply a shift to greater prosperity and a better standard of living. These various versions of transition differ widely but they all assume that China and its population are in transition to something.

The Chinese economist Jin Pei, writing about state enterprise reform in the late 1990s, shows how China's transition is utterly ambiguous:

> It is precisely because the programme is not yet clear, that one can only say in general terms that we must 'establish a modern enterprise system' where 'modern enterprise system' is itself a concept awaiting specific content so that different people can define it in different ways: some people think that a modern enterprise system is a company system; some people think that a modern enterprise system is a share-holding system; then there are those who think that a modern enterprise system is not only a company system or

a share-holding system but also includes other enterprise systems of whatever form which have proven successful in recent history; some people even think that a contract system is a modern enterprise system.

(Jin 1997: 10)

We can see that what China's transition is a transition *to* is largely unfathomable, but it is laden with a wide range of hopes for the future. Precisely because the notion of transition has so many different referents, it is a pointless endeavour to try to identify clearly what the telos of transition is. However, one cannot abandon the notion of transition or telos altogether in seeking to understand post-Mao China because it provides one of the key rhetorical mechanisms whereby the CCP sustains legitimacy.[17]

Transition works to maintain a hegemony (cf. Laclau and Mouffe 1985) whereby any discontent with the present is downplayed in order not to endanger the imagined future. This hegemony is not a matter of rigid dominance, but one of constantly shifting complicities. Hence, journalists, for instance, may dislike Party control of the media but they accept it in the present as a necessary route to a more politically and commercially relaxed future (Latham 2000). In fact journalists are in a position of fundamental importance for the maintenance of the hegemony because the combination of their complicity and their hopes for the future perpetuates the public circulation of many of the rhetorics of transition in newspapers, on television or on radio. The nouveau-riche entrepreneurs are similarly complicit because of the important economic weight that they could potentially wield. This complicity, however, is largely conditional upon notions of change and transition. Similarly, consumers may feel confused in the era of post-Mao uncertainties and they may feel unhappy about the anachronistic continuation of one party rule or the evident corruption that has accompanied reform, but they accept all of these, even if grudgingly, in the faith that the future holds something better. It is not so much consumption that works as a social palliative but the notion of transition itself.

The reform period has seen China increasingly divided and differentiated as a society and without Mao's promised utopia the Party has difficulty unifying the Chinese populace behind it in the name of the collective national good (Anagnost 1997). China's postsocialism hinges upon these divisions and the contradictions and disjunctures that accompany them. Our investigation of consumption has also revealed some of the complexities of trying to understand this situation. Consumer practices can be contradictory and divisive. This is not to say that consumerism is bringing about the collapse of the state. It is not. However, it does seriously question the argument that consumption is working as a social palliative. Consumption, in itself, no longer legitimizes the CCP regime, if it ever did. Rather, these rhetorics of transition, for the time being at least, enable the Party to defer utopia, or the new range of utopias, into the future once again.

## Acknowledgements

I am grateful to the Nuffield Foundation for a small research grant for fieldwork in 1996, and to SOAS Research Committee and the Sino-British Fellowship Trust for research funding contributions between 1997 and 1999, without which this paper could not have been written. I would like to thank participants at the Halle conference who made useful comments on my presented paper. I am particularly indebted to Silvia Ferrero and Chris Hann who made detailed comments and suggestions on earlier drafts of this paper.

## Notes

1  I am aware that this is a complex question and a full answer to it is beyond the scope of this paper. Here I present an outline of some of the key issues involved and how I choose to understand China as postsocialist.

2  This is similar to the 'posts' of postmodernism, poststructuralism, postcolonialism or post-Marxism more generally.

3  For further discussion of these issues, see also Dirlik and Zhang 1997. They contend that

> While China disengages from its revolutionary past, as a postrevolutionary and postsocialist society, it still bears the strong traces of that past, which serve as reminders of an earlier challenge to the capitalist world-system. The contradictions are most evident in the anomalous situation of a state that still claims socialism to legitimise itself, but must nevertheless demonstrate that legitimacy by being more successful at capitalism than capitalist societies.
>
> (1997: 8)

4  For further Eastern European comparisons see Gellner 1994, Runciman 1985; see also Hann 1993.

5  Of course, Mao's China was always more complex and less homogeneous than these clichéd images suggest. For the Mao period, as later, one has to consider differences of gender (Whyte 1984; Robinson 1985; Wolf 1985; Croll 1996; Judd 1994; Stacey 1983; Gilmartin et al. 1994; Davin 1988) rural and urban locations (Whyte and Parish 1984; Potter and Potter 1990) and status or class (Watson 1984; Siu 1989).

6  See, for example, Strand 1990; Rowe 1990; Huang 1993b; Zha 1995; Link et al. 1989; Wang et al. 1994; Yang 1994: 287–311; Davis et al. 1995. This debate on the emergence of a public sphere has focused particularly on urban China (see e.g. Davis et al. 1995). It is also true that analysis of Chinese consumption in general has been taken to be an urban phenomenon (see e.g. Davis 2000b; Tang 1996) and extensive analysis on rural consumption remains largely still to be done.

7  Croll, for example, argues that the moral vacuum arising in the post-Mao period and epitomized by flourishing consumerism has been at least in part filled by a revival of Confucianism and guanxi (networking) relationships (Croll 1997; cf. Yang 1994). In this argument it is not only consumption that works as a social palliative but also the revived Confucian morality.

8  We must remember that 'freedom' is itself an historically constituted notion (Bauman 1988).

9  Gillette has also argued that young Hui brides in Xi'an in the late 1990s were under great pressure from their female relatives to wear Western-style wedding dresses and

sport elaborate hair decorations as necessary public markers of family wealth and status (Gillette 2000)

10  I carried out research in regular trips to China between 1992 to 1999. Most of my fieldwork has been based in the southern city of Guangzhou and focused on urban life, although it has included work in rural areas and small towns in the Pearl River Delta and northwestern Guangdong province. It has also included shorter trips to Beijing, Shanghai and Chengdu.

11  Although, in my experience, very few people would want a return to the pre-reform regime and almost all would praise the overall improvements in life since 1978, many urban residents would also point out negative effects of reform such as soaring crime, job insecurity and corruption.

12  Similar regulations have just recently been formulated with regard to news-carrying websites.

13  Cf. Calhoun (1989) on the importance of fax machines during the student demonstrations of 1989.

14  Cf. Li Conghua, who, detailing China's 'consumer revolution', identifies three broad social groupings marked by divergent consumer practices along generational lines:

> China's most dynamic consumers are made up of three separate groups. They are differentiated by age and generation. For all three, the availability of consumer goods and services is a relatively new phenomenon. The s-generation [first generation of single-child policy children] has become accustomed to having newer choices every day; young and middle-aged rural consumers are quickly moving toward modernization; and consumers over the age of 60 now look forward to a rich and rewarding retirement.
>
> (Li 1998: 50)

15  The interviewees were a diverse group earning slightly above average salaries; none were particularly wealthy.

16  See also e.g. *Nanfang Weekend* 6 August 1999: 1, 7; *Guangzhou Daily* 9 August 1999: A6, B6; *Nanfang Metropolitan News* 9 August 1999: 2 for articles encouraging consumption.

17  Others include rhetorics of 'chaos' (cf. Latham 2000) and the size and 'quality' of the population (cf. Anagnost 1997). I have argued that the fear of 'chaos' functions as an 'empty signifier' in Ernesto Laclau's (1996) sense of the term (Latham 2000). A similar argument could be made for rhetorics of transition discussed here.

# References

Anagnost, Ann (1997) *National Past-times: Narrative, Representation, and Power in Modern China*, Durham, Duke University Press.

Bauman, Zygmunt (1988) *Freedom*, Milton Keynes: Open University Press.

Borneman, John (1990) *After the Wall*, New York: Basic Books.

Calhoun, C. (1989) 'Tiananmen, television and the public sphere: internationalization of culture and the Beijing Spring of 1989', *Public Culture* 2(1): 54–71.

Chao, Linda and Ramon H. Myers (1998) 'China's consumer revolution: the 1990s and beyond', *Journal of Contemporary China* 7(18): 351–68.

Ci Jiwei (1994) *Dialectic of the Chinese Revolution: from Utopianism to Hedonism*, Stanford: Stanford University Press.

Croll, Elisabeth (1994) *From Heaven to Earth: Images and Experiences of Development in China*, London: Routledge.

——(1996) *Changing Identities of Chinese Women: Rhetoric, Experience and Self-Perception in Twentieth-Century China*, Hong Kong: Hong Kong University Press and London: Zed Books.

——(1997) 'Desires and destinies: consumption and the spirit of Confucianism', an inaugural lecture, School of Oriental and African Studies, University of London.

Davin, Delia (1988) 'The implications of contract agriculture for the employment and status of Chinese peasant women', in Stephan Feuchtwang, Athar Hussain and Thierry Paircault (eds) *Transforming China's Economy in the Eighties*, London: Zed Books.

Davis, Deborah S. (1993) 'Urban households: supplicants to a socialist state', in D.S. Davis and S. Harrell (eds) *Chinese Families in the Post-Mao Era*, Berkeley: University of California Press.

——(1995) 'Introduction: Urban China', in D.S. Davis, R. Kraus, B. Naughton and E.J. Perry (eds) *Urban Spaces in Contemporary China: the Potential for Autonomy and Community in Post-Mao China*, Woodrow Wilson Center Series, Cambridge: Cambridge University Press.

——(2000a) 'Introduction: a revolution in consumption', in D.S. Davis (ed.) *The Consumer Revolution in Urban China*, Berkeley: University of California Press.

——(ed.) (2000b) *The Consumer Revolution in Urban China*, Berkeley: University of California Press.

Davis, Deborah S. and S. Harrell (eds) (1993) *Chinese Families in the Post-Mao Era*, Berkeley: University of California Press.

Davis, Deborah S. and Ezra Vogel (1990) *Chinese Society on the Eve of Tiananmen: the Impact of Reform*, Cambridge, MA: Harvard University Press.

Davis, Deborah S., Richard Kraus, Barry Naughton and Elizabeth J. Perry (eds) (1995) *Urban Spaces in Contemporary China: the Potential for Autonomy and Community in Post-Mao China*, Woodrow Wilson Center Series, Cambridge: Cambridge University Press.

Dirlik, Arif and Zhang Xudong (1997) 'Introduction: Postmodernism and China', *Boundary 2* 24(3): 1–18.

Feuchtwang, S., Athar Hussain and Thierry Paircault (eds) (1988) *Transforming China's Economy in the Eighties*, London: Zed Books.

Foucault, Michel (1982) 'Afterword: the Subject and Power', in Hubert L. Dreyfus (ed.) *Michel Foucault, Beyond Structuralism and Hermeneutics*, Chicago: University of Chicago Press.

——(1986) 'Two lectures', in M. Foucault, *Power-Knowledge*, Brighton: Harvester Press.

Gamble, Jos (forthcoming) 'Consumerism with Shanghainese characteristics: local perspectives on China's consumer revolution', in Kevin Latham and Stuart Thompson (eds) *Consuming China: Approaches to Cultural Change in Contemporary China*, London: Curzon.

Gellner, Ernest (1994) *Conditions of Liberty: Civil Society and its Rivals*, London: Penguin.

Gillette, Maris (2000) 'What's in a dress? Brides in the Hui quarter of Xi'an', in D.S. Davis (ed.) *The Consumer Revolution in Urban China*, Berkeley: University of California Press.

Gilmartin, C., Gail Hershatter, Lisa Rofel and T. White (eds) (1994) *Engendering China: Women, Culture and the State*, Cambridge, MA: Harvard University Press.

Hann, Chris (ed.) (1993) 'Introduction: social anthropology and socialism' in Hann (ed.) *Socialism: Ideals, Ideologies and Local Practice*, London: Routledge, pp. 1–26.

Huang, Phillip (1993a) ' "Public sphere"/"civil society" in China?: The third realm between state and society', in Phillip Huang (ed.) 'Symposium: "Public sphere"/"civil society" in China. Paradigmatic issues in Chinese studies III', special issue of *Modern China* 19(2): 216–40.

——(ed.) (1993b) 'Symposium: "Public sphere"/"civil society" in China. Paradigmatic issues in Chinese studies III', special issue of *Modern China* 19(2).

Huang Yu (1994) 'Peaceful evolution: the case of television reform in post-Mao China', *Media Culture and Society* 16: 217–41.

Hussain, Athar (1990) *The Chinese Television Industry: the Interaction between Government Policy and Market Force*, London: London School of Economics and Political Science.

Jin Pei (1997) *Where to and Where from: the Current Problems of China's State-Owned Enterprises (Hequ hecong: dangdai zhongguo de guoyou qiye wenti)*, China's Problems Series, Beijing: Jinri zhongguo chubanshe.

Judd, E. (1994) *Gender and Power in Rural North China*, Cambridge: Cambridge University Press.

Kornai, János (1980) *The Economics of Shortage*, Amsterdam: North-Holland Publishing.

Laclau, Ernesto (1996) 'Why do empty signifiers matter to politics?', in E. Laclau, *Emancipations*, London: Verso.

Laclau, Ernesto and Chantal Mouffe (1985) *Hegemony and Socialist Strategy: Towards a Radical Democratic Politics*, London: Verso.

Latham, Kevin (2000) 'Nothing but the truth: media, power and hegemony in south China', *China Quarterly* 163 (September): 633–54.

——(forthcoming A) 'Consuming China: approaches to cultural change in contemporary China', Introduction in Kevin Latham and Stuart Thompson (eds) *Consuming China: Approaches to Cultural Change in Contemporary China*, London: Curzon.

——(forthcoming B) 'Powers of imagination: the role of the consumer in China's silent media revolution', in Kevin Latham and Stuart Thompson (eds) *Consuming China: Approaches to Cultural Change in Contemporary China*, London: Curzon.

——(forthcoming C) 'Between markets and mandarins: journalists and the rhetorics of transition in southern China', in B. Moeran and L. Skov (eds) *Asian Media Worlds*, London: Curzon.

Latham, Kevin and Stuart Thompson (eds) (forthcoming) *Consuming China: Approaches to Cultural Change in Contemporary China*, London: Curzon.

Li Conghua (1998) *China: the Consumer Revolution*, Singapore: John Wiley (Asia).

Li Xiaoping (1991) 'The Chinese television system and television news', *China Quarterly* 126: 340–55.

Li Zhuren (1998) 'Popular journalism with Chinese characteristics: from revolutionary modernity to popular modernity', *International Journal of Cultural Studies* 1(3): 307–28.

Link, P., R. Madsen and P.G. Pickowicz (eds) (1989) *Unofficial China: Popular Culture and Thought in the People's Republic*, Boulder: Westview.

Liu Kang (1997) 'Popular culture and the culture of the masses in contemporary China', *Boundary 2* 24(3): 1–18.

Lull, James (1991) *China Turned On: Television, Reform and Resistance*, London: Routledge.

McGregor, Richard (2001) 'BBC on air with blessing of Beijing', *Financial Times* 10 January.

Nee, Victor and Stark, David (eds) (1989) *Remaking the Economic Institutions of Socialism: China and Eastern Europe*. Stanford: Stanford University Press.

Palmer, M. (forthcoming ) 'Legal protection of the consumer in the PRC', in Kevin Latham and Stuart Thompson (eds) *Consuming China: Approaches to Cultural Change in Contemporary China*, London: Curzon.

Perry, Elizabeth J. (1995a) 'Introduction: Urban associations', in D.S. Davis, R. Kraus, B. Naughton and E.J. Perry (eds) *Urban Spaces in Contemporary China: the Potential for Autonomy and Community in Post-Mao China*, Woodrow Wilson Center Series, Cambridge: Cambridge University Press.

——(1995b) 'Labor's battle for political space: the role of worker associations in contemporary China', in D.S. Davis, R. Kraus, B. Naughton and E.J. Perry (eds) *Urban Spaces in Contemporary China: the Potential for Autonomy and Community in Post-Mao China*, Woodrow Wilson Center Series, Cambridge: Cambridge University Press.

Potter, S.H. and J. Potter (1990) *China's Peasants: the Anthropology of a Revolution*, Cambridge: Cambridge University Press.

Roberts, Dexter, Mark Clifford and Diane Brady (1999) 'Playing the credit card: China is urging consumers to take on debt', *Business Week* 5 July: 20–1.

Robinson, Jean (1985) 'Of women and washing machines: employment, housework and the reproduction of motherhood in socialist China', *China Quarterly* 101: 32–57.

Rowe, W. (1990) 'The public sphere in modern China', *Modern China* 16(3): 309–29.

Runciman, W.G. (1985) 'Contradictions of state socialism: the case of Poland', *Sociological Review* 33(1): 1–20.

Sidel, Mark (1995) 'Dissident and liberal legal scholars and organizations in Beijing and the Chinese state in the 1980s', in D.S. Davis, R. Kraus, B. Naughton and E.J. Perry (eds) *Urban Spaces in Contemporary China: the Potential for Autonomy and Community in Post-Mao China*, Woodrow Wilson Center Series, Cambridge: Cambridge University Press.

Siu, Helen (1989) *Agents and Victims in South China: Accomplices in Rural Revolution*, New Haven: Yale.

—— (1993) 'Reconstituting dowry and brideprice in South China', in Deborah S. Davis and Stevan Harrell (eds) *Chinese Families in the Post-Mao Era*, Berkeley: University of California Press.

Smith, Richard (1993) 'The Chinese road to capitalism', *New Left Review* 199 (May–June): 55–99.

Stacey, J. (1983) *Patriarchy and Socialist Revolution in China*, Berkeley: University of California Press.

Strand, D. (1990) *'Civil Society' and 'Public Sphere' in Modern China: a Perspective on Popular Movements in Beijing, 1919–1989*, Working Papers in Asian/Pacific Studies 90–101, Durham: Duke University Press.

Tang Xiaobing (1996) 'New urban culture and everyday-life anxiety in China', in Tang Xiaobing and Stephen Snyder (eds) *In Pursuit of Contemporary East Asian Culture*, Boulder: Westview.

Veeck, Ann (2000) 'The revitalization of the marketplace: food markets of Nanjing', in D.S. Davis (ed.) *The Consumer Revolution in Urban China*, Berkeley: University of California Press.

Verdery, Katherine (1996) *What was Socialism, and What Comes Next?* Princeton: Princeton University Press.

Wakeman, F. (1993) 'The civil society and public sphere debate: Western reflections on Chinese political culture', in Phillip Huang (ed.) 'Symposium: "Public sphere"/"civil society" in China. Paradigmatic issues in Chinese studies III', special issue of *Modern China* 19(2): 108–38.

Wang Gan (2000) 'Cultivating friendship through bowling in Shenzhen', in D.S. Davis (ed.) *The Consumer Revolution in Urban China*, Berkeley: University of California Press.

Wang, H. and L.O. Lee, with M.J. Fisher (1994) 'Etymologies: is the public sphere unspeakable in Chinese? Can public spaces (*gonggong kongjian*) lead to public spheres?', *Public Culture* 6: 597–605.

Wang, John (1999) 'Signs of opening in telecom', *China Business Review*, May–June: 8–14.

Wang Shaoguang (1995) 'The politics of private time: changing leisure patterns in urban China', in D.S. Davis, R. Kraus, B. Naughton and E.J. Perry (eds) *Urban Spaces in Contemporary China: the Potential for Autonomy and Community in Post-Mao China*, Woodrow Wilson Center Series, Cambridge: Cambridge University Press.

Wank, David L. (2000) 'Cigarettes and domination in Chinese business networks: institutional change during the market transition', in D.S. Davis (ed.) *The Consumer Revolution in Urban China*, Berkeley: University of California Press.

Wasserstrom, Jeffrey N. and Liu Xinyong (1995) 'Student associations and mass movements', in D.S. Davis, R. Kraus, B. Naughton and E.J. Perry (eds) *Urban Spaces in Contemporary China: the Potential for Autonomy and Community in Post-Mao China*, Woodrow Wilson Center Series, Cambridge: Cambridge University Press.

Watson, James L. (ed.) (1984) *Class and Social Stratification in Post-Revolutionary China*, Cambridge: Cambridge University Press.

Whyte, Martin K. (1984) 'Sexual inequality under socialism: the Chinese case in perspective', in James L. Watson (ed.) *Class and Social Stratification in Post-Revolutionary China*, Cambridge: Cambridge University Press.

——(1992) 'Urban China: a civil society in the making?' in Arthur L. Rosenbaum (ed.) *State and Society in China: the Consequences of Reform*, Boulder: Westview.

Whyte, Martin K. and W.L. Parish (1984) *Urban Life in Contemporary China*, Chicago: University of Chicago Press.

Wilson, T. (1997) 'Truth and dare: Chinese weekend paper rakes scandal – and bucks', *Far Eastern Economic Review* 14 August.

Wolf, M. (1985) *Revolution Postponed: Women in Contemporary China*, Stanford: Stanford University Press.

Yang, M. (1994) *Gifts, Favours and Banquets: the Art of Social Relationships in China*, Ithaca: Cornell University Press.

Zha, J. (1995) *China pop: how soap operas, tabloids and bestsellers are transforming a culture*, New York: New Press.

Zhao, Yuezhi (1998) *Media, Market, and Democracy in China: Between the Party Line and the Bottom Line*, Urbana/Chicago: University of Illinois Press.

Chapter 12

# How far do analyses of postsocialism travel?

## The case of Central Asia

*Deniz Kandiyoti*

## Introduction

It is widely accepted among scholars of Eastern Europe that state socialism was a distinctive social formation with its own institutional logic and dynamics of development. Verdery (1996) argued cogently for the 'family resemblances' between socialist countries, coalescing around weaknesses of centralized planning that included plan bargaining, over-investment, soft budget constraints, endemic shortages, paternalistic redistribution and the neglect of consumption. Numerous East European social scientists made sophisticated attempts to identify the distinctive processes by which state socialism was stably (if inefficiently) reproduced (Konrád and Szelényi 1979; Kornai 1980). The logic of these institutional processes was not, Stark and Nee (1989) asserted, derived from capitalist development, either as its polar opposite or its convergent future, but specific to state socialism.

This leads to a series of allied propositions concerning postsocialist transformation processes. Stark argued that differing paths of extrication from state socialism shape the possibilities for transformation in the subsequent stage: 'differences in how the pieces fell apart will have consequences for how political and economic institutions can be reconstructed in the current period' (1992: 20). Burawoy and Verdery (1999) contend that an emphasis on the reconfiguration of existing networks and institutions (or path dependency) fails to take into account the fluidity of the transition process, which is more conjunctural and shaped by complex micro-processes of appropriation and resistance, but they too place some reliance on a model of what went on 'before'. There is widespread consensus that comparisons with an ideal-typical model of the capitalist West are inadequate.

We may agree with Burawoy (1999) that introducing a second ideal type helps us do away with the teleologies and counter-teleologies that follow from insistence on a singular Western model as a yardstick of postsocialist development. However, we need to interrogate this ideal type: what precisely does it consist of and, just as importantly, how far does it travel?

To begin to answer these questions, I find it useful to turn to an earlier usage of the term 'transition'. The term 'crisis of transition' was well established among East European scholars before it came to denote marketization, transformation of property rights and democratization after the demise of socialist states. I will take this meaning of transition as my starting point, since it offers clues about an underlying model of socialist planning. The crisis in question was the long socialist depression of the 1970s and 1980s. The gap between advanced capitalist and state socialist countries, which had appeared to be narrowing in the post-war years, was generally widening by the mid-1970s. There was a growing conviction that state socialism had exhausted its growth potential. Szelényi (1989) points to two versions of this argument: a soft version maintained that state socialism was a reasonably successful strategy of extensive industrialization which had now become redundant, while the hard version claimed that even the task of extensive industrialization had not been adequately achieved. According to the softer version, as the surplus agricultural population was absorbed into the industrial workforce, the strategy of extensive growth had come to an end. The economy could only continue to grow by increasing productivity and developing new technology. By the 1980s virtually all socialist countries were, in Szelenyi's opinion, struggling with this traumatic restructuring of their economies. At this time commentators were still talking about mixed socialist economies and hybrid forms of property (Szelényi and Costello 1996). Nonetheless, these writings provide a useful point of entry for a schematic comparison between East and Central Europe and the Former Soviet Union.

In Eastern and Central Europe the boundaries of the economy and the polity were roughly coextensive and have remained so in most cases. In the Former Soviet Union divisions of labour according to the assumed comparative advantages of different regions, with redistribution from the Moscow centre, meant that some republics were integrated into the Union as primary producers. The surplus from agriculture and primary extraction, though it may have contributed to a comprehensive system of social welfare, was not turned towards extensive industrialization, the hallmark of socialist planning in the Eastern European cases. This is attested to by the weak industrial base of all the Central Asian republics. This division of labour also created significant socio-demographic divergences between republics; whereas the shift of the rural population into non-agricultural occupations became a reality in the 'European' parts of the FSU and birth rates started to decline, in Soviet Central Asia not only were populations overwhelmingly rural but birth rates remained very high, comparable to the neighbouring countries of the South.

These divergences were compounded by ethnic divisions of labour within the Central Asian republics themselves. Members of 'European' nationalities tended to be concentrated in industry and technical services and to be over-represented in urban areas, whereas indigenous nationalities were over-represented in the rural sector of the economy (Lubin 1984). The legacies of the Russian conquest of Central Asia, ranging from settler colonization to military administration, decisively shaped the development of agriculture, commercial cotton cropping in particular, in the territories formerly known as Turkestan. Despite this colonial history, perceptions of Central Asia as an extension of the Turko-Iranian world and of Muslim civilization have encouraged a tendency to view both tsarist and Soviet periods as a mere interruption of much older historical legacies (McChesney 1996). The 'Muslim' periphery was considered so marginal that the dissolution of the Soviet Union gave rise to speculations about a 'new Middle East', on the basis of the presumed cultural affinities and changing geopolitical alignments of the newly independent republics (Eickelman 1993; Menashiri 1998). The recent literature on Central Asia has been dominated by a preoccupation with questions of identity and reassessments of Soviet nationality policies. The socio-cultural effects of Sovietization and Russification have been routinely privileged over any serious engagement with the economic institutions of state socialism and their local manifestations.

The implication is that the central insights gained from analyses of state socialism and postsocialist transformations in Eastern and Central Europe have little or nothing to offer to the study of Central Asian societies. In order to challenge this conclusion, it is first necessary to examine the theoretical frames through which the Central Asian region has been apprehended.

## Between dependency and postcoloniality

Central Asian economies and societies lend themselves readily to two types of theorization. The first is dependency theory, in which parallels are drawn in the Soviet context between the centre–periphery dynamics of unequal exchange between metropolitan centres and underdeveloped peripheries. The second is post-colonial theory, which foregrounds the domination of a hegemonic West (now stretched to include Imperial Russia and the Soviet regime) imposing its version of modernization on subject peoples (Muslims in this case) seen through the prism of Orientalism.

Dependency theory was originally developed to explain the incorporation of the so-called Third World into an expanding world capitalist system, but similar ideas were put forward by authors offering critical perspectives on the encounter between the Soviet state and its Central Asian periphery (Gleason 1991). Nove and Newton (1967) drew attention to the difficulties of conceptualizing Soviet rule as a clear-cut case of colonial domination since it exhibited many contradictory features; despite the centralizing practices of the Soviet state and dominance of the Russians, resources were diverted to less developed areas without any strict economic rationale. A case for treating the Soviet state as an extension of Russian colonization was made by Shahrani (1993), who argued that Soviet policy in Central Asia was a colonial project geared to both economic and ideological control. Economically, the Muslim periphery was exploited for primary commodities, notably petroleum in Azerbaijan and cotton in Central Asia. On the ideological front, the modernization of Central Asian populations required nothing short of a systematic onslaught on existing social institutions, identities and loyalties. This was accomplished through territorial fragmentation, the constitution of artificial ethno-national entities, the severance of links with both the Turko-Persian heritage and the wider Muslim world through the adoption of differently modified forms of the Cyrillic alphabet, and the systematic destruction of Muslim institutions.

Whereas for Shahrani Soviet policies achieved their intended strategic objectives, for Anatoly Khazanov (1995) the key problem of the region remains its underdevelopment. In his view, modernization with only the minimal participation of the native population was largely an illusion:

> The so-called interregional division of labour policy carried out by the Moscow centre clearly contradicted the interests of Central Asia and Kazakhstan, because it condemned the region to the role of a supplier of raw materials which left the region for other parts of the country, mainly in unprocessed form.
>
> (1995: 115)

The subsidies paid by the centre provided inadequate compensation for the profits made from 'unequal exchange', and the problem was accentuated in the last decades of socialism by low per capita investment compared to Union-wide rates and a substantial reduction in capital investment. This limited industrialization did not create an indigenous working class and industrial revenues did not even reach the local budget. Khazanov concludes bleakly that in the post-Soviet period the region is transparently 'another Third World region with unsolved structural problems and minimal potential for rapid economic and sociopolitical development' (*ibid.*: 155).

Missing from all these accounts is a sustained engagement with the actual workings of the Soviet system in Central Asia from an ethnographic perspective. Let us take, for example, the so-called 'cotton scandal' in Uzbekistan (also referred to as the 'Uzbek affair') which occasioned the posthumous disgrace of First Secretary of the UzCP Rashidov and the imprisonment of some 2,600 officials in 1987, following allegations that Uzbeks, at all levels of the republic, had been defrauding the central government through an elaborate system of bribe-taking and padding reports. This showed that there was more to this system of surplus extraction than met the eye. It involved a process of subversion and resistance on the part of republican elites in the face of unrealistic plan targets, but also a process of accommodation on the part of the centre whereby political loyalty was traded for a substantial degree of latitude in internal dealings. The anti-corruption drive and the purges that followed unsettled the compromises that had been struck in the long period under Brezhnev, provoking nationalist stirrings. Many have commented on these events but no one has analysed the various mechanisms at the level of farming enterprises, or of district administrations and central republican bodies that made such accommodation and subversion possible.

The question of ethnic cleavages in occupational structures also shows up the limitations of dependency approaches. Khazanov interprets the scarcity of technical cadres of indigenous nationalities in Central Asia as the result of a process of discrimination and exclusion, particularly since a good command of Russian was a necessary requirement for social advancement and career promotion. However, Lubin (1984) raised the rather provocative question of whether these occupations were ever accorded much prestige by indigenous people, who preferred to remain in trade, services and the second economy. Though lacking in prestige by the official Soviet criteria, such occupations brought higher financial rewards that could be channelled into the reproduction of Uzbek lifestyles and what Koroteyeva and Makarova (1998) called 'native regimes of consumption', including lavish life-cycle ceremonies and the maintenance of clientship networks. Employment statistics reveal very little unless they are complemented by consideration of the ways in which the second economy and petty commodity production inserted themselves into the planned economy of Central Asia.

Unlike Eastern and Central Europe, where local researchers were grappling with the workings of state socialism and producing innovative approaches, the institutional features and micro-workings of the planned economy in Central Asia have by and large remained unexplored. The centre–periphery model also obtained in the production of knowledge, in the sense that Central Asian societies were apprehended through the lenses of Soviet ethnography and sociology on the one hand and Western Sovietology on the other. Soviet ethnography relegated Central Asian societies to the realm of 'traditionalism' by means of a specifically Soviet variant of modernization theory (Kandiyoti 1996). The marriage between the notion of *ethnos* and the commitment to Stalin's evolutionist sequence of socio-economic formations allowed ethnographers to classify local practices as 'survivals of tradition', on the road to the full modernity promised by socialist transformation. The possibility that these practices might be artefacts of the Soviet system never entered the analytical equation. This led to a paradoxical body of writing consisting of both ideologically driven celebrations of the achievements of the Soviet system in transforming Central Asian societies (unveiling women, eradicating illiteracy, creating a socialist workforce and so forth) and another genre of ethnographies bemoaning the apparent limitations of the inroads being made.

If the dependency framework suffers from limitations in the Central Asian context, so in different ways does the concept of postcoloniality. The region was indeed colonized through Russian imperial expansion in the late nineteenth century, before being subjected to new forms of domination by a non-capitalist metropolis after the victory of the Bolsheviks. What adds to the intricacy of this case, however, is the fact that the Bolsheviks evolved their own critique of colonialism as part of their ideological critique of the Russian *ancien régime*. The issue of continuities and discontinuities between the colonial and Soviet periods continues to preoccupy historians and social scientists. The Soviet version of history emphasized that the Central Asian republics participated in the communist project voluntarily and cast local elites as feudal oppressors (Pierce 1960). However, as Brower (1997) notes in his examination of Russian colonial policy in Turkestan, there were numerous areas of continuity and, indeed, of further refinement of colonial policies after the Bolshevik revolution, including the ethnographic project of discovering and mapping ethnic groups. Approaches to postcoloniality in Central Asia may be boiled down to two major variants. The first, best exemplified in works such as Sahni's *Crucifying the Orient* (1997), adopts a 'rape of culture' model which presents the colonial encounter as 'external' to an entirely subjugated people. The second, which finds its most sophisticated expression in Roy's work (1991–2, 1999, 2000), develops the notion of a reverse movement, whereby colonizing institutions are themselves 'colonized' and appropriated by the local societies they seek to shape. Let us consider these in turn.

Sahni presents the Bolsheviks as the direct inheritors of Russian Orientalism, an inheritance that became manifest in the Eurocentricity and racism of their leaders. This Eurocentricity is attributed to the fact that the Russian elite was itself progressively distanced from its cultural roots through the incorporation of European cadres and ideas. Russians were 'mentally colonized' without having become colonial subjects themselves. This implies a perfect homology between the tsarist and Bolshevik projects.

> If the tsarist government sought justification for its colonization in Christianity and Russia's mission on earth as the Third Rome, the saviour of mankind, the socialist government sought refuge in Marxism. There was an uncanny similarity between the two; each projected itself as the sole champion of truth and salvation, with promises of a paradise at the end of the road.
>
> (1997: 110)

According to Sahni, the Soviet project left wholesale destruction in its wake: the destruction of a fragile ecology, the obliteration of local history, the abolition of local scripts and languages and of indigenous cultural forms. The postcolonial moment is therefore one of retrieval of indigenous voices and traditions; in short, very much the stance of postsocialist elites in their search for political legitimacy. An exclusive reliance on textual sources, literary, historiographic and scientific, helps Sahni to reach these schematic conclusions. Reality is described not through empirical explorations of the daily practices of differently positioned groups of people in Central Asia, but through a close reading of texts that are assumed to translate and reflect that reality unproblematically.

In marked contrast, Roy's approach is one of direct engagement with the institutions of the Soviet period and their local effects. He concurs that the creation of the Soviet republics in 1924, to which titular peoples were subsequently attributed, was not meant to create viable independent entities, despite the trappings of statehood. Nonetheless, following Benedict Anderson (1991) Roy suggests that it was the colonial state, in this case the Soviet state, that forged the conceptual instruments (historical, ethnographic, and linguistic) which provided the Muslim republics with the elements of their legitimacy and self-definition. He goes on to claim, *contra* Anderson, that the colonial state was 'sociologically reinhabited by a traditional society' and that there was a 're-appropriation of Soviet frameworks by local elites'. How was this possible? Roy's answer invokes the paradox that the Soviet project of destroying traditional society via 'social engineering' translated into

> a recomposition of solidarity groups within the framework imposed by this system, and also into the creation of a two-level political culture: on the one hand an appearance of conformity with the social project imposed by the authorities; on the other, a subversion of that project by practices of factionalism and clientism.
>
> (2000: 85)

He argues that society in Central Asia restructured itself around the very elements that had been conceived to destroy it. This was achieved through the *kolkhozian*/communitarian system of pre-existing solidarity groups, the recomposition of the world of politics around regional factionalism and the internalization of ethnic identity according to criteria defined by Soviet anthropology.

Roy argues for recomposition rather than simple continuity of traditional society. Collectivization, initiated with the start of the first Five Year Plan (1928–32), involved in his view a systematic territorialization of solidarity groupings to adapt them to the *kolkhoz*. The *awlad* (extended family), the *mahalla* (neighbourhood), and (in the tribal zones) lineage segments were reincarnated as sub-divisions of the *kolkhoz*. Therefore

> What appears as 'retraditionalization' is in fact simply an adaptation to a demand for social organization induced by the state: the solidarity group, whether translated or recomposed, is the individual's entry point into the system; it is the mediator of the relationship to the state and to the rest of society.
>
> (2000: xiii)

It is crucial to note that the recomposition in question is said to have taken place 'within the framework imposed by this system'. However, the system itself is never theorized outside its manifestations in Soviet nationality policies and the ideological project of the Soviet state. Roy's analytic inclinations are revealed instead in the parallels he draws with Atatürk's reforms, which he claims had a greater modernizing influence on Turkey than those of Stalin in Central Asia, which remained more 'traditional' according to criteria such as low degrees of urbanization and high birth rates. Roy implies that these outcomes could be directly attributed to different ideologies and overlooks the fact that changes in rural Turkey had less to do with the ideology of Ataturkism than with the concrete penetration of capitalism into agriculture at a considerably later period. Similarly, we have to entertain the possibility that the concrete institutions of the planned economy and collectivization might have had certain intrinsic properties which furthered the 'recomposition' of traditional society in Central Asia. We also have to investigate whether the process of 'subversion' of formal structures of authority by unofficial networks of clientship and patronage is unique to the Muslim republics, or whether it is merely a local variant of a much broader pattern that occurs in other state socialist contexts. In other words, it is necessary to theorize the economic institutions of state socialism in concrete contexts if we are to make sense of their current transformations. Virtually the only attempt to do this is Caroline Humphrey's ethnography of a Siberian collective farm (1983), which can be instructively compared to Olivier Roy's treatment of the same institution in Central Asia.

## Collective farms compared

Roy argues that the *kolkhoz* in Central Asia is not necessarily doomed to disappear in the course of privatization but provides a frame for collective identities that could form the basis of a civil society. Even when *kolkhozes* are not the simple translation of the local identity groups in the area before Sovietization they have acquired a 'neo-traditional' identity, with their sets of *mahalla* and *awlad*. This, according to Roy, is what differentiates 'European' and Central Asian *kolkhoz*. In the latter case,

> the kolkhoz system is 'traditional' not only as a 'Soviet' system but also as the expression of a Muslim segmented society superficially reshaped along Soviet administrative lines, whose main achievement was to create administrative and political stakes for this segmentation.
>
> (2000: 114)

This line of reasoning makes it singularly hard to integrate Central Asian material into market transition debates, since the command economy is treated as a mere superficial layer, an imported system that has lost out to the 'revenge of traditional culture and society' (2000: 111). This move forecloses a sustained analysis of evolving forms of property, and inadvertently introduces a form of neo-Orientalism. Changes in forms of access to land and property are not evaluated in an institutional framework of evolving property and production relations, but are read back into a cultural model, that of the *kolkhoz* as solidarity group.

Roy considers two mechanisms resorted to by *kolkhoz* leaders to maintain the integrity of the collective in the post-Soviet period while increasing productivity and the autonomy of the extended family: the abolition of the brigade system in favour of family leaseholds, and the adoption of *ijara* or sharecropping. He misinterprets these practices because he abstracts them from the actual day-to-day workings of the collective farm and the vagaries of an ongoing agrarian reform process.

The shift from work brigades to family brigades (*oila pudrati, arenda* in Russian) predates the end of the Soviet system by several years and was the product of the Union-wide reforms adopted during the *perestroika* period. The principal effect of the new system was to reduce the labour force slightly, without a substantial increase in productivity. The family brigade system was modelled on the Chinese household responsibility system but it did not grant farmers the decision-taking freedom that was a key element in China's agrarian success in the 1980s (Pomfret 2000). Uzbekistan's producers remained tied into a state procurement system designed to extract as much cotton for export as possible at low purchasing prices, while subjecting growers to rising input prices. This has left them little marketable surplus beyond what they produce on their household plots and no capital to invest in rural enterprises of the sort which have characterized post-Maoist China. The family brigade system therefore neither is a local initiative nor has it had its intended effects in terms of stimulating productivity or off-farm enterprise.

Roy's assimilation of the *ijara* system to pre-Soviet customs of sharecropping is no less problematic. The term *ijara* refers to leaseholding, which can take several forms. Under all variants the *kolkhoz* retains ownership of the land, giving farmers access to land with leases that vary in detail and length. In the initial stages of agrarian reform, 'independent' farms were created with leases of up to ten years. These were typically allocated marginally productive fields from land reserves. Their contracts with collective farm managers required them to dispose of their produce to the collective at prices which were even lower than state procurement prices. The new farms were therefore very vulnerable, and because they were seen to jeopardize the ability of collective farms to meet quotas of wheat and cotton, the authorities began to curtail their establishment (Mearns 1996). Moreover, as collectives suffered from the general crisis in public finance they started to fall in chronic arrears of payments to farmers, causing a spectacular rate of failure of the 'independents'. The latter were finally separated from collective enterprises by the Parliamentary Decree of 18 March 1997, which granted them juridical status, the right to hold their own bank accounts and to enter into direct transactions with crop marketing boards and suppliers of inputs. These farms are still subject to state procurement quotas and have to enter into contracts with crop processing agencies, but have somewhat more latitude than previously *vis-à-vis* the collectives, and longer leases of up to fifty years.

In such a fluid and complex framework, it is highly misleading to suggest that the *ijara* system is favoured by management in order to preserve the integrity of the *kolkhoz*. Sharecropping is one of a number of leasehold arrangements that currently square the circle of expanding private access to land, in line with the policies promoted by the international donor community, without abandoning the state procurement process for cotton. The continued reliance of the Uzbek economy on cotton as the leading export crop means that (the World Bank notwithstanding) the state cannot contemplate an outright privatization that could disrupt production of this crucial commodity. From the perspective of farm managers, the simultaneous need to provide smallholders with an expanded subsistence base in the form of *tamorka* while at the same time developing and diversifying leasehold arrangements involves a precarious balancing act. In areas of high population density, areas such as the fertile Ferghana valley, if land is leased to farmers on a long-term basis then *tamorka* allocations will have to be cut back, and new families denied any entitlement at all, if the collectives were to retain their own productive capability. This dilemma was freely acknowledged by the farm managers I interviewed. Local managers may indeed be interested in maximizing the autonomy of their enterprises and protecting them from the demands of the state. However, presenting them, as Roy does, as 'neo-notables' who are no longer emissaries of the central bureaucracy overlooks the simple fact that their appointment is still in the hands of provincial governors (*hokims*), themselves appointed by the centre, whose political longevity still depends on meeting plan targets. As with his account of *ijara*, once again Roy's portrayal of the *kolkhoz* fighting to retain its integrity under pressures to privatize 'freezes' a much more complex evolving process of negotiation between the international donor community, the Uzbek state, local managers and other rural groups competing to become the winners of agrarian reform.

Caroline Humphrey's (1983) analysis of the Karl Marx collective in Buryatia superficially resembles Roy's interpretation of the Central Asian *kolkhoz* in that she too highlights the interpenetration of local social organization and Soviet institutions. However, she does so in a very different manner. Humphrey's analysis is grounded in a detailed examination of the economy of the collective farm, where she identifies important sources of internal contradiction. The tight monitoring of production targets and work organization did not prevent the creation of non-legitimate resources in materials and people. In fact, she shows that some unofficial or illegitimate practices were essential to the smooth functioning of collective farms, procuring of inputs and the sale of *kolkhoz* produce. The materials and monies generated outside the plan, including the proceeds of private plots, constituted 'manipulable resources'. These were not investable in a capitalist sense but rather found their way into a system of ritualized exchange which turned individually controlled goods into means of leverage for attaining status. More advantageous positions could be used to increase a variety of personal rights, such as greater freedom to travel, access to goods that were unavailable locally, or access to special shops. The structure of the command economy was not *incidental* to the functioning of the Buryat 'gift economy' but, on the contrary, *constitutive* of the actual forms it took. Buryat concepts of reciprocity were applied to totally new relationships. These mechanisms could not be derived from either official Soviet policies or Buryat social organization, but could only be revealed through a painstaking ethnography of the collective farm itself. This is the crucial ingredient missing from most analyses of Central Asia.

In the second edition of her study (1998) Humphrey has shown the consequences of this deficiency for interpretations of post-Soviet developments. Having already established that the official institutions of the Soviet political economy – the state, the collectives and the households – were always interwoven with multiple unofficial relationships (kinship, patronage and black markets), she proceeds to analyse how the sphere of informal exchanges, previously kept in the background, has moved to centre stage with the collapse of the 'vertical' system of redistribution. This approach calls for careful investigation of the interactions of economic, political and social conditions in the new institutional organization of collective farms. In contrast, for Roy the collapse of the Soviet system has led only to a quasi-reversion to pre-Soviet forms of solidarity and governance which ultimately transcend time and context. The possibility that postsocialist agrarian reform might engender novel forms that cannot be fully grasped through an analysis of pre-Soviet forms or their recomposition under the Soviet system is not seriously entertained. In what follows, drawing on my own fieldwork in Andijan province in Uzbekistan, I attempt to illustrate the fluidity of evolving agrarian relations and the new strains this places on the social contract between collective farm managers and their workforce.[1]

## Shifting entitlements: the view from below

The village of Eski Kishlak, situated in the fertile but populous Ferghana valley, is close to Andijan City and within easy commuting distance to district markets. The main employer is the Eski Kishlak *sovhoz* which was initially restructured in 1992 as an association of *shirkats* (*shirkat uyushmasi*) and finally transformed into a closed joint stock company (JSC) based on the distribution of shares to all members of the collective in 1999.[2] When I visited Eski Kishlak in 1997, *shirkat* land was used for the cultivation of cotton (1,429 ha), wheat (429 ha), rice (10 ha), orchards (8 ha) and various other crops (90 ha). Household labour was mainly allocated to two types of plots: cotton plots cultivated by family leaseholders (*oila pudrati*) for the *shirkat* and *tamorka* land (or personal subsidiary plots)[3] where a local variety of rice, *devzire*, constituted the main domestic cash crop supplemented by vegetables grown in kitchen gardens (*agarot*) (Kandiyoti 1998). The *shirkat* was in chronic arrears of wages and workers were paid only intermittently and in kind. As a result, self-provisioning and sale or barter of produce from personal plots or animals, income from trading and other informal activities, complemented by benefits and entitlements (such as pensions and maternity benefit) constituted the main sources of livelihood. There was little evidence of a leasehold market in land. Instances of individuals leasing additional plots from the *shirkat* were relatively rare and the plots in question were mainly on non-irrigated hilly land (*adir* or *bogara*). However, possibilities for growing additional crops after the wheat harvest on leased *shirkat* land did exist. For instance, Mukarram, a widow living with her two married sons, had leased a piece of land after the wheat harvest in the summer of 1997. She harvested a crop of four tonnes of carrots and gave the *kolkhoz* one tonne in payment for the land. Although she had to pay for tractor hire and for fertilizer (using her earnings from a grocery store she ran out of her home), this was an arrangement that she could honour without a significant outlay of capital.

There have since been significant changes in cropping patterns in Eski Kishlak. The drive for self-sufficiency in grain since independence in 1991 has meant that part of the acreage previously allocated to feed crops and cotton was gradually shifted to wheat. By 2000, the balance in Eski Kishlak had changed in favour of wheat (1,050 ha), with more than a doubling of acreage in the space of three years. It is clearly in the interests of *shirkat* managers to shift out of unprofitable cotton cultivation which binds them into the state delivery system in favour of crops which give them greater flexibility. Although wheat is also subject to delivery quotas, it is possible to plant other crops after the harvest in June (which is impossible with cotton because the crop cycle extends into October). The shift to wheat has stimulated a competitive land lease market. Those who can afford it have started leasing land from the *shirkat* to grow rice after the wheat harvest. There has also been a shift from *devzire*, the local variety, to *ak shali* (white rice), which has much higher yields and fetches a similar price. Whereas previously local variety *devzire* rice was planted in early spring, now a second crop of white rice is planted after the wheat harvest in July and is ready for harvest in September. The fact that the rice harvest coincides with the cotton-picking season does not appear to create significant labour bottlenecks because of the high number of unemployed (*bekarjilar*). There is a visible increase in the supply of casual agricultural labour in Eski Kishlak, as a result both of growing unemployment and of changing cropping patterns, which have produced a substantial increase in labour-intensive operations. In 1997, there were already some signs that unemployed women were forming teams of casual labourers (*mardigor*)[4] offering their services mainly on paddy fields. In 2000, those with access to larger plots and independent farmers were all employing *mardigors*. In 1997 twenty independent farms held with one-year leasehold contracts had the *shirkat*, and three with ten-year contracts. Three years later, there were thirty-two independent farms with ten-year contracts.

It may appear paradoxical that land hunger among rank and file *shirkat* workers has increased at a point in time when, in absolute terms, more land is available for private lease. Population pressure on land is frequently invoked by *shirkat* managers who admit that the allocation of personal subsidiary plots (*tamorka*) and new house plots (*check*) is becoming increasingly problematic.[5] What typically happens is that newly married couples who apply for a separate house plot (*check*) and want to register as a separate household unit, thereby meeting the legal requirement for receiving an additional private subsidiary plot, are denied the possibility of doing so. As a result, multiple family households continue to live together with only one *tamorka* to share among them. Since they technically constitute a single household unit, they are not considered landless. It is quite clear, however, that their household labour resources far outstrip their possibilities of access to land. Furthermore, entitlement to *shirkat* land is now taking place in the context of a new land-lease market. Those who have the means are in a position to lease land for cash, thus enlarging their holdings at the expense of claimants from among rank and file *shirkat* workers. Mukarram, who four years ago was able to plant carrots against a modest share of her produce, and many like her are now squeezed out. This creates deep resentment among *shirkat* workers.

Oyashkhon is the leader of a team of four family leaseholds working on 5 ha of cotton land.[6] She and the other four members on her team, Khatija, Zamira, Roziya and Kizlarkhon, have not been paid their wages although they performed all the manual operations on the cotton crop. Instead, they each received 1 kg of butter, 2 kg of rice, 5 kg of pasta and 100 kg of wheat. When asked whether they were offered a share of the land distributed after the wheat harvest, they all spoke of broken promises and unfair dealings. As Khatija explained, 'They gave us just 10 sotka of land.[7] I planted sunflowers. I had to pay 1,000 sums for a tractor. Irrigation was also up to us. They had also promised to give us machinery, but they did not.' Roziya declared: 'I like being a *dekhkan* [peasant]. If there were land, I would work. They gave the land to those who have money. We are in a poor situation now.' To better grasp the sense of grievance expressed by these women, we must remind ourselves of the terms of the social contract between collective farm managers and their workforce during the Soviet period. Work on cotton plots has long been regarded as a form of *corvee* labour, which hardly pays a living wage, especially since the financial collapse of the collective farming sector. However, *kolkhoz* workers were given various forms of usufruct rights to common land and to personal plots in compensation for their collective labour obligations. There was also an expectation of receiving some assistance with inputs such as tractors and fertilizer for the cultivation of personal plots. Access to formal benefits was complemented by more informal mechanisms of paternalistic responsibility, such as helping workers to defray the costs of life-cycle ceremonies and assisting those stricken by personal tragedy.[8]

Before the expansion of wheat cultivation in Eski Kishlak the amount of common land that could be redistributed for personal use was relatively limited, since the cotton crop cycle does not permit replanting after harvest. Household land resources consisted of house plots, *tamorka* land and sometimes leased non-irrigated land. With increased wheat cultivation, the quantity of common land that can be reallocated to household use has increased. *Shirkat* workers, who receive no remuneration beyond a limited quantity of foodstuffs, feel they are entitled to a share of that land and express bitterness about being fobbed off with tiny parcels of bad-quality land, while wealthier villagers are able to help themselves to choice parcels.

Agrarian reform in Uzbekistan appears to have created new contradictions. On the one hand, it is in the interests of the Tashkent elite to keep up the production of cotton which continues to be the most lucrative export crop and the major earner of foreign currency. On the other hand, pressures to maintain existing cotton deliveries run counter to the interests of local enterprise managers, whose control over land allocation decreases as a direct function of the amount of land allocated to unprofitable cotton production. The managers of Eski Kishlak have clearly succeeded in shifting this balance in their own favour.[9] However, at the enterprise level, the attempt to provide *shirkat* workers with a subsistence base, to which they are legally entitled, while developing leasehold markets, represents an impossible balancing act. Land leased to independent farmers and tenants on a short or longer-term basis reduces the pool out of which allocations can be made to households. The claims of *shirkat* workers to additional plots are marginalized in favour of those who have the means to pay. The fact that this is taking place in a context of contraction of alternative, non-farm employment, which might have created avenues for diversification, fuels intense land hunger and a consequent sense of betrayal.[10]

This state of affairs is at variance with the picture presented by Roy of the *kolkhoz* as a community with unified interests. It is likely to engender further cleavages as agrarian reform policies expand private access to land (even if they stop short of outright privatization). Neither an understanding of pre-Soviet and Soviet institutions nor an analysis of changing legal frameworks can provide us with an adequate apprehension of these evolving realities. These can only be captured through detailed ethnographies that reveal both the intended and unintended effects of these policies, as well as the responses of those who are at the receiving end.

## Pathways of postsocialism in Central Asia

Having argued for the value of an ethnographic approach to post-Soviet transformations in Central Asia, it is pertinent to reflect upon the different directions which scholarship on the region is actually taking. In the earlier sections of this chapter, I tried to identify some of the main discursive elements that have informed scholarship on Soviet Central Asia and show how these departed, in significant ways, from mainstream analyses of state socialism in Eastern Europe. After the break-up of the Soviet Union, the independent republics of Central Asia embarked upon divergent paths of national

consolidation and development conditioned by their differing economic endow-
ments, regional and ethnic cleavages and geopolitical alignments. The growing
literature on the 'successor states' underscores this diversity using analytic
frameworks which privilege processes of state and elite formation or macro-
economic policy formulation (Rubin and Snyder 1998; Bremmer and Taras
1993; Dawisha and Parrott 1997; Gleason 1997; Kaminski 1996; Rumer and
Zhukov 1998). The demise of Sovietology has allowed the 'post-Soviet' field to
be brought within the paradigms of the various social science disciplines, with
political science and economics taking lead roles. The general emphasis on the
macro also reflects the fact that there was no language to talk about the micro-
level and the 'local' in Central Asia except through the idiom of custom,
tradition and ethnicity, a result of the joint legacies of Soviet ethnography and
the assimilation of Central Asia into the broader rubric of 'Muslim societies'.[11]
No region fits better the proverbial blind man's description of an elephant:
Central Asia is perceived as socialist (or postsocialist) from certain angles and
as 'Muslim' from others, our self-imposed blindness prohibiting the integration
of these features into a recognizable, real-life organism.

Two emerging trends in scholarship may offer a way forward. The first
remains centred on the state and elites, but investigates them in a vigorously
comparative way as Stark and Bruszt (1998) have done in their work on East
Central Europe. Jones and Weinthal (2001), for instance, make careful comparisons to explain the divergence in oil and gas development policies in five
Soviet successor states set in the broader context of the politics of oil-producing
states. They conclude that policy choices depend upon domestic constraints,
notably the availability of alternative sources of export revenue and the level of
internal political contestation predisposing state leaders to opt for strategies
that supply them with the resources necessary to sustain the cleavage structure
that forms their political support. Studies such as this illustrate the shift in
analytic frameworks brought about by the demise of the Soviet Union; instead
of a focus on socialist planning, and the reallocative role of the Moscow centre,
we now have analyses of how independent elites manage their national resource
base. The reference point for a country such as Turkmenistan is more likely to
be the *rentier* oil states, with their authoritarian elites and weak civil societies,
rather than other postsocialist countries. Given the additional prominence of
Islamic resurgence, it might seem that the literature on postsocialism is simply
an irrelevance.

Once we avert our gaze from states and elites, however, and engage with
societal transformations that impinge upon daily struggles for survival, we find
that there is much to be learned from ethnographic approaches to postsocialism.
These struggles involve changing forms of livelihood, informal networks, alternative safety nets, new forms of consumerism and the incursions of
international development agencies at the local level. Hence the second
emerging scholarly trend, as yet in its infancy in Central Asia, consists of studies
based on detailed, micro-level analyses informed by ethnographic and sociolog-

ical sensibilities and methodologies. The contributors to Kandiyoti and Mandel (1998) offer multiple examples of how local forms of sociality and association are being put to new uses, how a Soviet *habitus* of consumption is being transformed, and how ethnic and religious identities are mobilized in novel ways.

Paradoxically, *contra* commentators who see the Soviet element of Central Asian identities as a mere veneer, it is at the level of the quotidian that one finds the clearest expression of habits and expectations acquired during the Soviet period, as well as important generational differences in their expression. The elderly woman brigade chief whose life story I recorded in a collective farm in Khorezm presented me with a classic, Soviet-style 'biography', complete with the number of red banners her brigade received for record harvests. She expressed, almost in the same breath, her wish to perform the pilgrimage to Mecca, the *hajj*. She was above all irate about the continual erosion of her pension, a key element of the paternalist social contract of Soviet socialism.[12] Similar juxtapositions are rife, both in the structure of sentiments and in the practices of everyday life. It is commonplace for official gatherings to start with Soviet-style speechifying and multiple toasts involving the consumption of alcohol, and to conclude the occasion with the *fotiha*, the Muslim prayer.[13] The ritual visit paid by newlywed couples to the nearest Lenin memorial lives on in the practice of visiting the statue of Amir Timur, the new national hero. Clearly, there are specifically Uzbek ways of combining Soviet and Muslim identities, which can become politicized in new and unpredictable ways, as local and transnational influences interact. Central Asia is therefore rich in potential lessons for comparative scholars of both postsocialism and Muslim societies. However, for these lessons to be learned the assimilation of the lived realities of Central Asian societies to one or other ideal-type must be resisted.

## Conclusion: what travels? why and why not?

In the opening section of this chapter, I argued that analyses of state socialism in Eastern and Central Europe relied on two implicit assumptions: that of industrialization as the model for socialist planning and that of the nation-state as the unit of political analysis. Such analyses cannot be readily applied to an imperial formation such as the Soviet Union, especially from the perspective of 'peripheral' areas such as the republics of Central Asia.[14] The theoretical lenses trained on Central Asian societies were therefore primarily geared towards analysing their mode of insertion into the Soviet system. A Soviet variant of modernization theory and more critical approaches articulated in the idiom of dependency and postcolonial theory have framed most discussions of the region. A decade after the dissolution of the Soviet Union, we may find that the political economy frameworks that best explain the trajectories of Central Asian states are not those which address state socialism but those attuned to the problems of primary commodity producers. Thus Central Asian scholarship, always an outlier in the discursive analysis of state socialism, may diverge even further from Eastern European patterns as the post-Soviet trajectories of Central Asian societies unfold.

I have argued, however, that the dearth of ethnographies on the local effects of socialist production, property and welfare regimes in Central Asia has significantly impeded our understanding of post-Soviet transformations. Too much new scholarship has merely shifted from analyses of one set of official discourses (Soviet ideology and nationalities policy) to another (policies of national elites and the celebration of 'traditional' collective identities). One of the lessons learned from ethnographies of postsocialism is that processes of transition are fraught with uncertainty. This uncertainty is fuelled by the volatile interactions between macro-level institutions and policies and their reception at the micro-level, where families, workplaces and communities often respond in unintended ways that have a decisive impact on further developments. This proposition, at least, travels extremely well. The various reform packages that are being implemented by Central Asian states are activating new constellations of interest and calling forth contradictory responses and various forms of resistance, including mobilization around symbols of religious and ethnic identity. The phenomena observed on the ground may appear unique in each case, but the *processes* involved are amenable to comparative analysis.

## Notes

1 The first period of fieldwork (1997–9) was supported by an ESCOR (DFID) grant and took place in the provinces of Andijan and Kashkadarya. The second period of fieldwork in the provinces of Khorezm and Andijan (1999–2001) was carried out in the context of a broader UNRISD project on agrarian change, gender and land rights in South Africa, Brazil and Uzbekistan.

2 The aim of restructuring, in line with the decentralization policies implemented since *perestroika*, was the creation of smaller, autonomous units which were to be made more profitable and accountable. The term *shirkat* (enterprise or company in Uzbek) was substituted for *sovkhoz* and *kolkhoz*, tainted by their Soviet associations. The privatization measures adopted more recently consist of defining *kolkhoz* workers as shareholders in joint stock companies. The different sections of the enterprise in Eski Kishlak have once again been brought under a single management. The distribution of shares is based on a calculation of the total assets of the enterprise and the sizes of individual shares are based on length of service and salary level. Property rights over land assets remain unaffected; land cannot be bought, sold, mortgaged or given away and access is mediated through enterprise managers.

3 The *tamorka* is a private subsidiary plot to which all citizens were entitled, with expanded rights since *perestroika*. Since independence, the acreage allocated to households has expanded more than twice compared to 1989. The legal size of private plots was increased from 0.06 ha to 0.25 ha, and eventually 0.35 ha of irrigated land and 0.5 ha of non-irrigated land. The actual size of the plot and its distance from the house depend on local conditions of availability.

4 There is a gendered division of labour among casual workers; teams of men equipped with scythes (*orakchi*) work in teams at the rice harvest, whereas teams of women work at weeding. Men receive 6 kg of rice per sotka harvested (amounting to a minimum of 1,500 sums per day) whereas women receive a daily wage of about 700 sums, which is less than half. This means, in effect, that a family leaseholder may

find it more profitable to let the women of his household get on with the cotton harvest for the *shirkat* while he hires himself out as an *orakchi* at higher rates of pay. This accentuates the feminization of *shirkat* work even further.

5　Although it is difficult to estimate the actual number of households that have no access to land (estimates of as high as 30 per cent were received for the number of landless and unemployed – *yersizler ve ishsizler*), it is widely accepted that their number is growing.

6　Each family leasehold is meant to constitute a separate accounting unit under the new rules of the *shirkat*. They are provided with a chequebook where they record their expenses, which are deducted from their harvest payments when they settle with the *shirkat* management each year. In Eski Kishlak, former brigade chiefs 'manage' the accounts of a group of four to five family leaseholds. However, the new accounting system is poorly understood, and leaseholders complain about not receiving timely and sufficient inputs and then being made to pay for the shortfall in production.

7　A *sotka* is one hundredth of a hectare.

8　Helping by providing produce such as oil, rice and meat that are crucial to wedding, circumcision and funeral ceremonies is quite common. One *shirkat* manager in Khorezm claimed that as many as 600 families were 'indebted' to the collective in this way, and that this accounted for a significant part of his deficit.

9　Compulsory quotas for the distribution of crop acreages are passed down from Tashkent to the provincial, district and farm levels. Farm managers try to bargain within this restrictive framework.

10　The closure of rural industries and the decline in social infrastructure (health and education services in particular) has forced more people in Eski Kishlak to resort to making a living from the land.

11　This tendency is most apparent among authors whose areas of study are the societies of the Middle East and South Asia. For instance, Eickelman's primer on the anthropology of the Middle East (1998) has been expanded to incorporate Central Asia. Although sophisticated in its coverage of Islam, this text displays a more superficial grasp of the Soviet system.

12　The very language used to express such rights, a mixture of Russian and Uzbek (such as *pensiaya chikmak* – to become a pensioner – or *gruppaya chikmak* – to receive invalidity benefit by being allocated to a particular 'group' of disability) indicates their degree of appropriation.

13　This was certainly an eye-opener for a scholar of the Middle East, where both types of events may occur, but never together.

14　The regional disparities to be found within Eastern and Central Europe do not compare in intensity to those found in the Former Soviet Union.

# References

Anderson, B. (1991) *Imagined Communities*, London: Verso, 2nd edition.

Bremmer, I. and R. Taras (eds) (1993) *Nations and Politics in the Soviet Successor States*, Cambridge: Cambridge University Press.

Brower, D.R. (1997) 'Islam and ethnicity: Russian colonial policy in Turkestan', in D.R. Brower and E.J. Lazzerini (eds) *Russia's Orient: Imperial Borderlands and Peoples, 1700–1917*, Bloomington: Indiana University Press, pp. 115–35.

Burawoy, M. (1999) 'Afterword', in M. Burawoy and K. Verdery (eds) *Uncertain Transition: Ethnographies of Change in the Postsocialist World*, Lanham, Rowman and Littlefield, pp. 301–11.

Burawoy, M. and K. Verdery (eds) (1999) *Uncertain Transition: Ethnographies of Change in the Postsocialist World*, Lanham, Rowman and Littlefield.

Dawisha, K. and B. Parrott (eds) (1997) *Conflict, Cleavage and Change in Central Asia and the Caucasus*, Cambridge: Cambridge University Press.

Eickelman, D.F. (ed.) (1993) *Russia's Muslim Frontiers*, Bloomington: Indiana University Press.

——(1998) *The Middle East and Central Asia: an Anthropological Approach*, Upper Saddle River, Prentice-Hall.

Gleason, G. (1991) 'The political economy of dependency under socialism: the Asian republics in the USSR', *Studies in Comparative Communism* 24(4) 335–53.

——(1997) *The Central Asian States: Discovering Independence*, Boulder: Westview.

Humphrey, C. (1983) *Karl Marx Collective: Economy, Society and Religion in a Siberian Collective Farm*, Cambridge: Cambridge University Press.

——(1998) *Marx Went Away but Karl Stayed Behind*, Ann Arbor: University of Michigan Press.

Jones, Luong P. and E. Weinthal (2001) 'Prelude to the resource curse: explaining oil and gas development strategies in the Soviet successor states and beyond', *Comparative Political Studies* 34(1): 367–99.

Kaminski, B. (ed.) (1996) *Economic Transition in Russia and the New States of Eurasia*, New York: M.E. Sharpe.

Kandiyoti, D. (1996) 'Modernization without the market? The case of the "Soviet East" ', *Economy and Society* 25(4): 529–42.

——(1998) 'Rural livelihoods and social networks in Uzbekistan: perspectives from Andijan', *Central Asian Survey* 17(4): 561–78.

Kandiyoti, D. and R. Mandel (1998) Editors' preface, special issue on 'Market reforms, social dislocations and survival in post-Soviet Central Asia', *Central Asian Survey* 17(4): 533–7.

Khazanov, A.M. (1995) *After the USSR*, Madison: University of Wisconsin Press.

Konrád, G. and I. Szelényi (1979) *The Intellectuals on the Road to Class Power*, Brighton: Harvester Press.

Kornai, J. (1980) *Economics of Shortage*, Amsterdam and Oxford: North Holland Publishing.

Koroteyeva, V. and E. Makarova (1998) 'Money and social connections in the Soviet and post-Soviet city', *Central Asian Survey* 17(4): 579–96.

Lubin, N. (1984) *Labour and Nationality in Soviet Central Asia*, London: Macmillan.

McChesney, R.D. (1996) *Central Asia: Foundations of Change*, New Jersey: Darwin Press.

Mearns, R. (1996) *Commons and Collectives: the Lack of Social Capital in Central Asia's Land Reforms*, IDS Working Paper no. 40, Sussex: IDS.

Menashiri, D. (ed.) (1998) *Central Asia Meets the Middle East*, London: Frank Cass.

Nove, A. and Newton, J.A. (1967) *The Soviet Middle East: a Model for Development*, London: George Allen & Unwin.

Pierce, R.A. (1960) *Russian Central Asia 1867–1917*, Berkeley and Los Angeles: University of California Press.

Pomfret, R. (2000) 'Agrarian reform in Uzbekistan: why has the Chinese model failed to deliver?', *Economic Development and Cultural Change* January: 269–84.

Roy, O. (1991–2) 'Ethnies et politiques en Asie Centrale', *Revue du Monde Musulman et de la Mediterranée* 59–60: 17–36.

——(1999) 'Kolkhoz and civil society in the independent states of Central Asia', in M.H. Holt and D.C. Waugh (eds) *Civil Society in Central Asia*, Washington: Center for Civil Society International and University of Washington Press, pp. 108–21.

——(2000) *The New Central Asia: the Creation of Nations*, London: I.B. Tauris.

Rubin, B. and J. Snyder (eds) (1998) *Post-Soviet Political Order: Conflict and State-Building*, London: Routledge.

Rumer, B. and S. Zhukov (eds) (1998) *Central Asia: the Challenge of Independence*, New York: M.E. Sharpe.

Sahni, K. (1997) *Crucifying the Orient*, Bangkok: White Orchid Press.

Shahrani, N. (1993) 'Soviet Central Asia and the challenge of the Soviet legacy', *Central Asian Survey* 12(2): 123–35.

Stark, D. (1992) 'Path dependence and privatization strategies in East Central Europe', *East European Politics and Societies* 6(1): 17–54.

Stark, D. and L. Bruszt (1998) *Postsocialist Pathways: Transforming Politics and Property in East Central Europe*, Cambridge: Cambridge University Press.

Stark, D. and V. Nee (1989) 'Toward an institutional analysis of state socialism', in V. Nee and D. Stark (eds) *The Economic Institutions of Socialism: China and Eastern Europe*, Palo Alto: Stanford University Press.

Szelényi, I. (1989) 'Eastern Europe in an epoch of transition: toward a socialist mixed economy?' in V. Nee and D. Stark (eds) *The Economic Institutions of Socialism: China and Eastern Europe*, Palo Alto: Stanford University Press, pp. 208–32.

Szelényi, I. and E. Costello (1996) 'The market transition debate: toward a synthesis', *American Journal of Sociology* 101N (4 January): 1082–96.

Verdery, K. (1996) *What Was Socialism and What Comes Next?*, New Jersey: Princeton University Press.

## Chapter 13

# 'Eurasia', ideology and the political imagination in provincial Russia

*Caroline Humphrey*

## Introduction

It is well known that over the 1990s the eighty-nine subject territories of the Russian Federation became increasingly independent from Moscow, but anthropologists have so far paid little attention to the various ideologies developed by provincial governments and their links with popular cultures. This chapter discusses 'Eurasianism', a theme of ideology and the political imagination that has become increasingly important in recent times. In April 2001 a 'Eurasian' political movement was officially established in Moscow, led by the political philosopher Alexander Dugin, the advisor to the Speaker of the Duma. The movement is supportive of President Putin and apparently endorsed in a general way by his government (Yasman 2001). I shall be concerned here, however, not so much with this metropolitan movement as with the ways in which the concept of 'Eurasia' has enabled the governing circles of many Asian regions of Russia to create distinctive ideas about the nature of their existence within the Federation. It will be suggested here that the idea, or perhaps more correctly the ideal, of Eurasia is likely to be highly influential, both in conceptualizing federal relations and in shaping the political-cultural character of the constituent regions.

## Ideology, subjectivity and the political imagination

If by 'ideology' we refer to the manipulation of a system of ideas in the service of dominating political interests, then in Soviet times there was only one ideology in Russia, that of the Communist Party.[1] In the last ten years, by contrast, there has been ideological uncertainty at the centre and a burgeoning of new ideologies in the provinces. While the Moscow government has been searching for a new 'idea' for Russia,[2] many regional leaderships have boldly propounded their own ideologies, including political values, policies, educational programmes, rituals and festivals, and so forth. It is not only the governments of Republics with specific ethnic profiles that have been active, such as Tatarstan, but also those of Russian provinces (*oblast*) where leaders want to establish a particular character and policy for their region.[3] What differentiates these new ideologies from the Soviet one is that they are not hegemonic even in their own areas (or perhaps, more cautiously, one should say that they are not yet hegemonic). They are designed to appeal to varied constituencies of voters and business interests in contexts where alternatives exist. At the same time, and this is what distinguishes them from the ideologies of independent countries, they are also addressed 'upwards' to a single centre, that is, to Moscow. The central government retains enormous financial power over the provinces, especially those which are in debt to it, including most of the Asian regions discussed in this chapter. Such resource-poor provinces simply cannot balance their budgets without substantial annual transfers from Moscow. This situation is inevitably unstable: the impulse towards independence and consolidation of local interests is countered by the periodic need to appear in the guise of loyal subjects (regional leaders personally travel to Moscow to negotiate loans and transfers with ministers). At the same time, the political messages from Moscow have varied wildly over the years, from Yeltsin's injunction to the provinces in the early 1990s to 'Take all the power you can' to Putin's attempt to establish direct administrative control. Meanwhile, powerful and wealthy 'oligarchs' can suddenly transform the face of local politics by concluding some major deal in that territory, or indeed by presenting themselves as local election candidates.[4] The ideologies expounded in the provinces are conditioned by these volatile circumstances, which are not hidden and 'naturalized' agendas, as in the classic formulation of ideology, but are in some sense 'known' by everyone via the media, gossip and rumour.

This is why ideology as a category is inadequate on its own to explain the ideational aspect of Russian politics today. While the explicit and relatively stable discourses of regional leaders intent on retaining positions of power can indeed be characterized as ideology, in the actual practice of politics they exist amid the swirling diversity of other, more open, multi-sited and creative opinions and ideas produced by all sorts of people. It is these that I call the 'political imagination'. This term allows us to write about the ways political life is being thought, without presupposing that all such representations are attached to the hidden motives or economic interests of powerful social groups. We need to take account of the political ideas of the impoverished, those who have made fortunes and lost them, the struggling and dispossessed and those who live from day to day, the obstinately different, and the seemingly wayward people, who all together, when one thinks about it, make up the great majority of the electorate (and from among whom, in fact, many current leaders have emerged). The notion of ideology only restricts our understanding and belittles the diverse wealth of ideas, emotions and compulsions that face us here. This chapter suggests that the political imagination does not just interact with ideologies, it subsumes them, i.e. it creates a greater arena within which ideologies exist. Ideologies are thus particular and limited formations of the political imagination. The idea of the political imagination enables us to identify the cultural sources out of which particular new ideologies arise.

Both ideologies and the political imagination are manifest in speeches, declarations, tracts, rituals, and so forth. Thus, the political imagination has a history, and this is important in considering even such a short period as the 1990s. A particular manifestation of a national ideology, for example the initiatory political moment of the presidential speech inaugurating the Khalmg Tangch (Kalmyk Republic) in 1994, had a different purpose and resonance from the trajectory of these same ideas in later years. Not only can this particular moment never be repeated, but it seems that other practices of the political imagination also 'have their time', as it were. There is a period when they have currency and are widely popular, while later they may become somewhat stale, or suspected of trickery; later still they can become the subject of jokes, and finally they may be replaced by other ideas. There are wider, more stable, cultural resources, notably religious ideas, which have nourished the regional conceptions of 'Eurasia' through processes of emptying out and replenishment at particular periods in the last decade.

At the same time, an *ideal* projected in the political imagination, such as that of the 'new Kalmyk person who has nothing in common with the old Soviet subject' (Nuskhaev 1996: 123) can only make sense and become effective in the context of disciplines and practices. While the political imagination is constitutive in the effects of a regional 'sovereign state', the daily practices of governing and appearing to govern, and of welcoming, ignoring or resisting such practices, sustain – or do not sustain – the currency of the ideas. The idea of the 'Kalmyk person' has to impose itself in education and ritual, such that some people at least experience themselves as this new kind of person. In effect, this is to argue for the central importance of the dimension of subjectivity. As Veyne has written, the individual is not opposed to society, nor even to the state, for 'the individual is affected to the heart by public power in so far as he is affected in his image of himself, in the relation he has to himself, when he obeys the State or society' (1987: 7).

Taking a different approach, Mark Urban argues that any particular ideological configuration in 1990s Russia, such as the synthesis of communism and patriotism, is immediately confronted by competitors in mirror-like refractions that litter the 'verbal battlefield in contradictory nonsense' (1998: 979). For example, the democrats' espousal of 'all-human values' is said by Russian nationalists to be a treacherous imposition of false and corrupting categories, because only nations and civilizations can create values. Yet there are some nationalists who claim that what distinguishes the Russian nation above all others is the fact that its values are valid for all humanity (1998: 979). Thus Urban suggests that neither personal authenticity nor logical consistency play much of a role in this exercise of the political imagination. 'What we meet again and again is bombast, strong but shallow representations of the world that recall the concept of auto-communication' (1998: 978). These narratives are performative, but non-practical. They are performative because leaders call into existence certain entities that play a pivotal role in their discourse, such as 'the people', 'the occupation regime in the Kremlin', and so forth. But,

> leadership thus constituted falls victim to its own creations, it finds itself trapped without an opening towards practice, because the entities the discourse has conjured are themselves invested with an agency of another order than that attributed to actual individuals. They exist 'above' the plane of mundane matters.
>
> (Urban 1998: 978)

This is essentially an argument for the separation of the political imagination, existing in a sealed-off sphere of mythicized, binary confrontations, from practical life, not in the abstract but in the particular case of present-day Russia. I would agree with Urban (and regional writers such as Guchinova 1997a) that the 'mythic plane' exists, but suggest that a *theoretical* argument, whereby the political imagination may also be manifested in historically located actions and capable of creating particular subjectivities, deserves ethnographic investigation. In particular, a certain kind of leadership, which I call 'exemplary autocracy', can provide the inter-subjective space for the political imagination to be actualized in society. 'Eurasia' may thus exist mythically in Moscow, where it is constantly challenged and even mocked, but it has a different kind of existence in the regions where subjectivities attach themselves to it.

## 'Eurasia' and the Asian peoples of Russia

The idea that Russia embodies a Eurasian, as distinct from a purely Slavic, civilization has been central to debates about Russian identity for many decades.[5] Yet these were discussions among Russian intellectuals and, with a few exceptions, the idea seemed unacceptable to Asian peoples. What has happened recently is the widespread appropriation of this idea by Asian writers and policy-makers, who have drawn on it for their own purposes. In doing so they project regional visions of the nature of the federal union. At the same time they are creating and sustaining ideas about the nature of their own presence and cultural identity. I shall focus on the 'Inner Asian' regions, that is the Kalmyk, Buryat, Tuva, Sakha-Yakut and Altai Republics. It will be shown that what is emerging is a common vocabulary, rather than a single vision. The ideas of the Moscow movement are only loosely related to the images produced in the provinces, for each region has its own perspective, related to its geographical-strategic position, type of leadership, electoral balance, and ethnic history during and before the Soviet period.

The crucial questions are not about current types of government, for all these regions are characterized by 'presidential' rather than parliamentarian forms of power (Afanas'yev 1998). They concern the exceptional value (and the reasons for that value) to be accorded to small peripheral peoples within the imagined whole of the Russian Federation. This is a scenario that differs significantly from that of European colonial regimes, in which, as Cooper and Stoller have argued, the basic tension was 'how a grammar of difference was continuously and vigilantly crafted as people in colonies refashioned and contested European claims to superiority' (1997: 3–4). In contemporary Russia, on the other hand, the provincial Eurasianists often carefully ignore previous regimes of difference and even downplay historical episodes of terror and repression. What is presented instead is a civilizational commonality between the remote part and the whole, and this is projected in the idea that the Eurasian continent is fated to be a great empire whether it is run by Tatar khans, Russian Tsars or Bolsheviks. This move opens up an ideational space for the phantasmatic rhetorical representation of the given regional culture as injecting its own values and practices into the project of 'Eurasia' as a whole.

The idea of 'Eurasia' is also providing an arena for new political relations to be formed between the provinces. During the Soviet period, the Inner Asian peoples of Russia had relatively few links with one another, since the predominant structure in politics, economics and culture was the centripetal relation through the hierarchy to Moscow. Indeed, the independent creation of lateral relations of a political kind would have been regarded as a violation of the central decision-making role of the Party. It is therefore significant that the 1990s saw the emergence of horizontal inter-republic relations, at least in politics and culture, if not in economics. Although President Putin is attempting to restore a strong vertical structure, not dissimilar to that of the Soviet state, the consolidation of local power regimes will not be easy to undermine. It is from these relatively secure local bases that Inner Asian leaders are making links with one another. For example, in 1998, the President of Kalmykia, Kirsan Ilyumzhinov, intervened to back the main Buryat candidate in the presidential elections in Buryatia. On the cultural front, representatives from the various regions regularly visit one another to attend religious rituals, conferences, youth congresses, etc.

What is the imagined basis for such Inner Asian new ties? A plausible historical template might seem to be the Mongol Empire of the thirteenth and fourteenth centuries, which was itself, of course, also a multi-ethnic state comprised of peoples speaking Mongol, Turkic and Tungusic languages, including the ancestors of all the peoples I am discussing. However, the Chinggisid heritage, that is the notion of the relevance today of specifically Mongol forms of government, is *not* one that has been developed as an ideology, although it exists in the political imaginary of these regions of Russia. Some intellectuals have argued for revival of a Mongol-centred world-view,[6] but for the leaders of the Kalmyks, Altaians and Buryats, although a positive image of the Mongol Empire does not seem to be an impossible idea to swallow, they cannot *identify publicly* with it. For the contemporary state of Mongolia is seen as economically weak. Furthermore, memories are still vivid of harsh repression of anyone accused of 'Pan-Mongolian' sympathies and 'Pan-Mongolism', which is still regarded as 'dangerous' today (Kuz'min and Svinin 1997).[7] In effect, with Chechnya in the forefront of people's minds, it seems that too open an invocation of Mongolian political precedents is still associated with peril, the danger of disloyalty to the Russian state. Such ducking and weaving to avoid direct recognition of a Mongol precedent for 'Eurasia' is evidence of the political nature of the contemporary concept.

Little is clear about what 'Eurasia' actually comprises. In part this is due to the misty and mystical character of the writings of the chief popularizer of the idea in recent times, the historian Lev Gumilev. He extols the glamour and vigour of 'unions' between the Slavs and the steppe peoples, the formative effect of vaguely delineated 'environments', the decisive effect of 'passionate' leaders in creating spiritually powerful states, and simultaneously (paradoxically) the inexorable 'scientific' or 'natural' basis of the success or failure of ethnic communities. In the last decade Gumilev's books have achieved extraordinary popularity among all classes of Russians and non-Russian peoples of the Federation. As Shnirel'man and Panarin argue (2001), Gumilev's disregard of responsible historical scholarship gave free rein to the sway of free-floating suppositions and dangerous ethnic prejudices while lending them pseudo-academic legitimacy. Yet very recently, in autumn 2000, President Putin on a visit to Kazakhstan laid a wreath on a monument to Gumilev and declared Eurasianism to be the ideology of the new Russia. He thus endorsed, and perhaps not only for Kazakh audiences, a vision of Russia's history as determined by emotional and value-laden interpretations of specifically *ethnic* glories, failures, victories and deceptions. Discussions of current social and political organization (e.g. forms of government and taxation) are virtually absent, cloudily effaced by transcendent notions such as the 'civilization of the steppes' or 'national destiny'. The ideational field of 'Eurasia' has generated mythicized binary categories, which have compelled the political imagination in Inner Asian regions towards the exaltation of their own 'spiritual values'. But *contra* Urban (1998), I see this as more than just rhetoric. This ideational field has given a particular direction to actual political initiatives that, charged with fantasy as they may be, have the capacity to change society.

## 'Eurasia' in political context

'Eurasia' has always been an idea directed against the influence of 'the West' in Russia, since it proposes that Russia is not in essence a European country but a unique civilization, created by the union of the Slavic and the Turko-Mongol steppe peoples. The idea re-emerged in metropolitan circles in the 1990s in response to the perceived failure of 'Western' models of democracy and capitalism in Russia. In contemporary versions, the key is the importance of 'the state'. For example, A.S. Panarin writes that what distinguishes Russian history from that of Europe is that, in Russia, progress, and indeed all important initiatory action, derives from the state and not from civil society, i.e. 'it comes down from above' (Panarin 1994). The ideal state is not the exploiter but the protector of the poor and weak (Panarin 1995).[8] Another key theme is the unity and equality of all the peoples in a common Eurasian 'super-nation', which distinguish it from the European colonial empires (Lyr'ye 1994). A further quality of 'Eurasia' is its messianic function. Quoting Toynbee's idea that to achieve an aim you have to go not for it but for *something higher*, Panarin writes that this is true above all of Russia, with its religious, Manichaean radicalism. Russians will not take action for everyday reasons; they need a great idea. Eurasia as a morally pure civilization is such an idea. 'Has the world really finished with the cosmogonic process of creating new civilizational models?' he asks. If the answer is 'yes', countries all over the world have a cruel choice: either join up with the West or remain on the barbarian periphery and probably die out (1994: 86).

Such ideas give rise to unresolved arguments about the delimitation of Eurasia. If 'ecology' and the rejection of modernization and development are taken as key spiritual values, then the geography shifts towards the east. But if Orthodox piety and asceticism are seen as the vital historical source of spirituality, then Armenia and Greece appear as relatively 'close', while a whole string of Catholic Slav countries are ruled out (Poland, Lithuania, etc.). Even more fraught is the question of Islamic territories. Some argue that such lands cannot be part of Eurasia as they belong to a radically different civilization, and furthermore one that stretches far beyond the sacred frontier of Russia. Others advocate including Kyrgyzstan and Kazakhstan, but not Uzbekistan, on the grounds that the former are only lightly Islamicized and are 'really' steppe cultures, while the latter, with its long-settled, urban development of Islam, is essentially alien. Yet other Eurasianists argue that all the Islamic countries of the former USSR should be included in 'Eurasia'. The reason is that, however foreign it may be, Islam has bravely made a principled stand against the corruption and power of the West (for a summary of these positions see Malashenko 1996). This is the argument 'My enemy's enemy is my friend'. In short, we see that 'Eurasia' is not a clearly delimited geopolitical space, but is, to repeat, a deeply political idea.

Certain reactions from the non-Russian regions are wary, and even directly hostile, to Eurasianism. From Buryatia, Urkhanova writes (1995) that for all the talk of admiration of eastern cultures, Eurasianism is nonetheless built on Russian great power statehood. For this reason, the imprecise inclusiveness of Eurasia is dangerous, a cloak for renewed Russian 'imperialism', threatening the precarious sovereignty of the regional republics. Urkhanova concludes that Buryats nevertheless cannot refuse Eurasia, because it has happened to them already. Its apogee was the Soviet Union, which irrevocably tied together the history of Buryats and Russians, bequeathing to both the tragic legacy of terror and the camps. Tatar writers such as Khakim, on the other hand, reject Eurasianism absolutely. For them it represents a 'deified state' with no room for the individual or even any other opinion. The Achilles' heel of Eurasianism, he writes, is that modern Tatars, and all Russian citizens, *are already* free and educated individuals, who are bound to reject its atavistic holism and collectivism (Khakim 1998: 54–5).

Yet the idea of Eurasia re-surfaces among both *nomenklatura*-type Soviet leaders who have reinvented themselves in the new Russia and new generation leaders in the Inner Asian regions and the Central Asian states.[9] The move is far from naive. Rather, these leaders see 'Eurasia' as offering opportunities, though these vary according to geopolitical position. In the case of the Inner Asian regions, Eurasia offers above all an escape from their peripherality, obscurity and insignificance. It does so by creating a confrontation between the rational, materialistic, technologically advanced, individualistic 'West' and the spirituality, irrationality, mysticism and collectivism of the 'East'. The overwhelming tendency among Eurasianists is to elevate Russia's 'third way', which combines the two 'principles', to a metaphysical plane higher than either.[10] The Russian 'spirit' (*dukha*) is said to be supreme, and indeed stands for all humanity, because it combines within itself several mystical antitheses. For example, 'The essence of the [third] antimony of the Russian spirit is yet another mixture of contradictory opposites – an endless freedom of spirit and slavish servility' (Yugai, paraphrasing Berdyaev, 1998: 31). The effect of this kind of vision of Russian civilization, strengthened by widely popular vitalistic ideas like Gumilev's *passionarnost'* in ethnic history,[11] is to attribute priority to the spiritual element. 'Before the Russian soul there open the far distances and there is no bounded horizon lying before her spiritual gaze' (Yugai 1998: 31). It is this space of 'far distances' that provides the opening for the Inner Asian peoples. Not only can they declare that they themselves represent the spiritual superiority of 'the East', but they can also claim that it is precisely this 'input' into Russia which invigorates that country with its essential quality of *dukhovnost'* (spirituality).

Thus, for the Inner Asian indigenous leaders the *answer* to their anxieties over real historical problems, namely that their peoples have been perceived as peripheral nonentities in the Tsarist and Soviet empires, mere appendages providing raw materials to the centre (Guchinova 1997a), lies in proclaiming and publicizing the new eminence that the notion of the Eurasian civilization potentially confers on them. Indeed, a further move is to shift the notional centre of 'Eurasia' away from Moscow to the east. Both Tuva and the Altai are now conceptualizing themselves as the geographic centres of Eurasian space.[12] A consequence of this shift is that it is now Moscow that appears as materialistic, individualistic and corrupted by 'Western values'. In both provinces, books, maps and monuments celebrate this vision. Interestingly, in these regions the basis for spiritual superiority is said to lie in 'nature', notably the sacred mountains of the Altai. In Buryatia, the pure and holy Lake Baikal plays the same role. Famous Eurasianists are quoted to lend weight to such quasi-religious claims. For example, the orientalist mystic N. Roerich is cited in support of the idea that the mountain Uch Sumbur in the Altai has a direct link with the cosmos and that the entire country surrounding it is the land of Shambala, the sacred land of righteousness of the northern Buddhists (*Problemy* 1992: 58). What this does is to lend a sense of inevitability and inviolability to the claims: one might meet some Altaian people and query their spiritual superiority, but it is difficult to criticize a sacred mountain. At the same time, it exploits post-Soviet anxieties about ecological pollution ('we may be poor here, but unlike those corrupted by materialism, we know the secret of pure living').

In this image of the sacred mountain we can see how the issue of mythicization, raised by Mark Urban, can work out in practice. Uch Sumbur, in countless epics, prayers, wise sayings, and so forth, is said to have three peaks, because in the mythic vocabulary three is the proper number for a sacred mountain. In fact, anyone who goes to worship at Uch Sumber can see that it has two peaks.[13] Yet it would be incorrect to argue that this reveals merely a contradiction between 'myth' and 'practical life', for in real life Altaians do conduct rituals of worship of this mountain, *because* it is sacred and therefore has three peaks.

## Political configuration: the example of Kalmykia

There is an important difference between the regions of Buryatia and the Altai on the one hand and Tuva, Sakha-Yakutia and Kalmykia on the other. In the former, the indigenous people are in an electoral minority and political control is in the hands of Soviet-style, ex-Communist Russians. Consequently, proclamations about national destiny and so forth are muted for fear of arousing the wrath of the powers that be. In Tuva, Sakha and Kalmykia, on the other hand, political leadership is largely indigenous. In Tuva, there is a substantial indigenous majority party as a consequence of many Russians fleeing the republic in the early 1990s, having encountered Tuvan hostility. The authoritarian, yet non-charismatic, Tuvan President is so firmly in control, we may suppose, that extravagant flights of nationalist fantasy appear unnecessary.

In Kalmykia, on the other hand, there is quite another, much more politically intense, situation. The Kalmyks are in the majority over Russians and other nationalities, but only just. They elected in 1993 a young President, Kirsan Ilyumzhinov, a millionaire businessman. Ilyumzhinov is handsome and enormously charismatic, and he also 'designs himself' in such a mould, encouraging the notion that he is the reincarnation of Janggar (hero of the famous Kalmyk epic) or the seventeenth-century Ayuki Khan re-born. He flaunts his wealth, rightly seeing that for many ordinary people his wealth is brilliant evidence of his luck and blessedness (Guchinova 1997b). At the same time, Ilyumzhinov is determined to publicize Kalmykia and put it on the world map. He engineered his election as President of FIDA, the international chess organization, and one of his numerous extravagant acts was the construction of a luxurious 'Chess City' in his capital, in which to hold the Chess Olympiad.

Ilyumzhinov supports the idea of Eurasia and he calls the Republic of Kalmykia 'the land of spirit, the temple of the spirit, the planet of the spirit' (Ilyumzhinov 1997: 8). In reality, this is one of the poorest regions of the Federation, and during the 1990s the statistics have only got worse (Katushov 1998; Humphrey 2000). Vast sheep flocks created an ecological disaster in the pastures in the 1980s and now the herds have been drastically cut down, leaving rural people reduced to bare subsistence levels. There are hardly any other natural resources. Afflicted by the first AIDS epidemic in Russia, bordering on the war zone of the North Caucasus, the Kalmyks could be expected to look out on the world, from their dusty land and grim poverty, with timid apprehensiveness. Yet it is here that the political imagination has gone into overdrive.

The very day he got into power in 1993, Ilyumzhinov began setting up one of the most autocratic regimes in the whole of Russia. He abolished the Soviets and appointed his own people as ministers and 'Presidential Representatives' (i.e. the district governors). Local self-government is entirely absent in Kalmykia. In effect, all decisions of any importance are taken personally by the President (Guchinova 1997a: 22). A year later, Ilyumzhinov allowed general elections for a parliament (it is small, only twenty-seven members), and this body has little real power. Soon he wrote a new constitution, called the 'Steppe Code', based on a seventeenth-century Kalmyk precedent, and set up a Council of Elders, consisting of various respected grey-beards put forward by factories, collective farms, etc. He reintroduced the union of religion (Buddhism) and the state. Re-elected in 1995, Ilyumzhinov took the opportunity to change the constitution and extend the period of presidential office. He then initiated various prestige projects, all of which are incomplete: the building of a vast Buddhist temple, the construction of an international airport, the biggest leather factory in Russia, and a new seaport (Volgin 1999: 28). Ilyumzhinov flies to meet the Pope, the Dalai Lama and Saddam Hussein. He tries to attract international capital to Kalmykia by declaring it an 'off-shore' tax-haven.

On the one hand, this is a bold, innovative exercise of power characteristic of the exemplary autocrat (see Humphrey 2000). At least at first, the power relations established by Ilyumzhinov were enthusiastically supported by the electors (Guchinova 1997b).[14] All over Inner Asia ordinary people during the mid-1990s were saying, 'If only we had a leader like that! If only we had a Kirsan!' It is not a secret that Ilyumzhinov's millions have a dubious origin and that he and his close kin have been involved in one financial scandal after another. But perhaps people feel the need for a magical and absolute leader, one who can absorb the black wickedness of power, with the craftiness of a chess-master, and yet present to the world a shining, somehow admirable, surface.

On the other hand, Ilyumzhinov's constitution, the 'Steppe Code', embodies the fated quality of Kalmykia's relation with Russia. The original 'Steppe Code' (1640) is said to have been the expression of the only period of Kalmyk 'state-hood'. Between 1640 and 1771 a Kalmyk khanate existed within the wider polity of the Russian Tsars (Guchinova 1997a: 57–9). Why should a contemporary leader wish to resurrect this precedent? We should remember that the Kalmyks have a deeply tragic history. They experienced massive loss of life when, in 1771, the Torgut elite and their followers fled from Russian incursions back to their original homeland in Mongolia (resulting in the abolition of the khanate), later during the Civil War, around 1920, and again in 1943, when the entire population was deported to Siberia, Central Asia and Sakhalin. The khanate is now seen as a golden age, before any of these tragedies. Its adherence to Russia is imagined as a 'voluntary union', personified in a meeting between Ayuki Khan and Peter the Great.[15] This echoes the standard Soviet account as well as the Eurasian vision of mythic harmony of the metropolis with the steppe. More significant is how aspects of Mongolian political culture surface undeclared in the new 'Steppe Code'. Political relations are imagined in similarly 'kingly' terms to those of the mediaeval Mongol chronicles – in which individual leaders stand for peoples and oaths of loyalty are what count.

The 1990s 'Steppe Code' does not include a statute about separation from the Russian Federation. Ilyumzhinov was in fact criticized by a quasi-opposition (there is no constitutional opposition) on this point. 'Why did you not demand the same sovereignty other regions have taken?' he was asked. But this was mere rhetoric, in the mythic style Urban describes, for the very same 'oppositionists', who were Communists, hotly demanded that central state order be imposed by military force in nearby Chechnya. Guchinova, a Kalmyk political observer, points out how the entire, sporadic opposition to Ilyumzhinov is couched in the old Soviet vocabulary (1997a: 26). It has no positive alternative economic programme, but rests on stale accusations of 'treachery' (*izmena*), and 'debt' (*dolg*) before the people. It is fairly clear that Ilyumzhinov used his 'loyalty' to Russia (i.e. not insisting on the separation clause) as a bargaining chip in negotiations over the budget transfers from Moscow, the life-blood of his economy. But we can perhaps see a deeper meaning to this situation, for the Soviet deportations were seen by many ordinary Kalmyks as a fated punishment for their own sins in neglecting Buddhism (Guchinova 1997a: 61). Although the thirteen years of exile may now be spoken of as unjust, for decades after their return to Kalmykia people were ashamed and frightened to mention it – to the extent that most of the younger generation only heard about it in the 1990s and then often from public sources. Another example of this attitude concerned a Russian from Moscow, who was appointed Prime Minister in Ilyumzhinov's government. He was forced to resign after he had rashly mentioned the word 'resettlement'; even though this was in a quite different context, it was widely held that his outspokenness offended local norms of decency, of silence, of preserving a soft, smiling 'Asian' face over internal disagreements and humiliations (Volgin 1999). Guilt, shame and anger are unresolved, and in this situation the Russian state appears in reified form as the *inevitably present*, quasi-sacred instrument of punishment (perhaps still seen by some as the instrument of retribution for sins).

Ilyumzhinov combines extreme local autocracy with a rather close 'princely' relation to Moscow, cemented by marriage links (unfortunately for him, with Luzhkov, the Mayor of Moscow, rather than the new forces of Putin). He calls the Russian Federation 'Eurasia', and he is the supreme example of the strategy of claiming to represent the spiritual wealth of Asia. In the Kalmyk case, this claim cannot rest on cosmic mountains or sacred seas. Instead, Ilyumzhinov's ideology proclaims its promotion of world religions, first of all Buddhism, but also Orthodoxy and Catholicism. When he was elected President, Ilyumzhinov wanted to grant land to the Dalai Lama, to provide him with a permanent home in Kalmykia. This idea withered in the face of Chinese protests and warnings of its inadvisability from the security services, but along with numerous Buddhist temples built by the laity, the President did erect a large marble statue of the Buddha in the centre of his capital, Elista. When it was realised that the statue of Lenin (whose part-Kalmyk ancestry is not forgotten) faced the other way, the pedestal of the Bolshevik leader's monument was turned round so the two could appear face to face (Guchinova 2001). Ilyumzhinov built a large and beautiful Orthodox cathedral, and even, after his visit to the Pope, a Catholic church. In placards and portraits the President regularly appears flanked by one or another world religious leader. However, Ilyumzhinov also claims a more indigenous source of inspiration, the 'wisdom of the ancestors' (*mudrost' predkov*). His political vision is to produce new generations of young Kalmyks, transformed by this ancestral wisdom (both religious and secular, but always 'spiritual'), who will flood into Russia–Eurasia to inspire and re-invigorate that land. He has appointed a Minister of Ideology and set up a school programme, with a new pedagogical methodology, to produce these young people. They are called *Lichnosti*, with a capital L ('Persons' or 'Personalities'). They are to achieve moral harmony, personal independence of judgement and youthful super-talent and energy. This is to be done through learning and practising the ancestral wisdom. For example, the Kalmyk version of chess has been made obligatory in all schools, as it is said to inculcate a specifically 'Asian' ability to reason and take bold decisions. Just as importantly, wisdom is to be achieved through following the exemplar of the President himself. Teachers and delegates have been sent from Kalmykia throughout Inner Asia to propagate these ideas.

Meanwhile, we can observe that such visions, which are crafted by intellectuals close to the President as well as Ilyumzhinov himself, interact with popular culture and also have a history. The epic Janggar is genuinely admired by many Kalmyks, and in the early 1990s they responded to the idea of Ilyumzhinov's identity with the hero. People declared him to have been 'given by God', and clan leaders prayed to their deities to protect him (Guchinova 1997b). By the end of the decade the deification of the President, the idea that he is actually the reincarnation of a mythic hero, was little heard.[16] Another telling example of such historical waxing and waning was described to me from the Altai. In 1998 there was a public ritual at a holy site, where three retired women teachers were 'possessed' by spirits. A Kalmyk delegate attended this event, and she observed, 'You Altaians are three years behind Kalmykia. We had old women receiving that kind of message from the cosmos a few years back, but now we don't pay them so much attention.'[17]

Such waxing and waning of particular ideas does not mean that the 'Eurasian' political imagination is dying out. Rather, it seems to be transmuting into more everyday, yet fundamental, assumptions that form part of subjectivities. One example is the discourse of the ethnic 'gene-fund', which we now find appearing throughout Russia as the dominant way of conceiving identity. In the case of Inner Asian people the 'gene-fund' idea can be mapped on to (and through) an imagined history of statehood. Altaians, for example, are saying that Russia is the *genetic successor* of the Eurasian Turko-Mongol states of the seventh to twelfth centuries, just as the Altaian people are the genetic descendants of those who made up the Dzhungarian khanate. 'Statehood is like a dress you wear,' said one Altaian. 'It changes all the time, for a hundred years you live in this state, for three hundred years in that. Your name may change. But we remain the same, genetically and by our spirit. We are we.'[18] The gene-fund idea is related to the new discourse of clanship and the aristocratic 'white bone', ideas that had been completely illegitimate in Soviet times. Ordinary Kalmyks today might say, for example, that a certain person is suited to rule *because he is a Torgut*.[19]

Another field for the political imagination is the idea of 'ethno-pedagogy', whereby particular local cultural 'traditions' can be inculcated in the young generation. In Tuva and the Altai, for example, schoolchildren are taken to holy sites (springs, mountains, sacred trees, etc.) and given classes in how to participate in the rites. In Kalmykia, ethno-pedagogy has been actualized in the form of spiritual education intended to train the 'descendants' of the ancestors. It includes

> traditions of thought and life, the philosophy of Buddhism, heroism, love of peace, and wisdom, customs and rituals, dances, songs, love of work, the cultivation of health and the body, respect for the ancestors and the elders, and love for the young, all of which comprises the Spirit and Will of the Kalmyks.
>
> (Nuskhaev 1996: 92)

In Kalmykia, the gene-fund idea and ethno-pedagogy combine, for the generations of young 'Persons' are conceived as 'our gene-fund, which we will pour into and gift to Russia–Eurasia' (Nuskhaev 1996: 117).

Ideas like the reincarnation of historical heroes, the spiritual significance of landscape or the cyclical re-transmission of ancestral spirituality from deceased grandparents to newborn children, are absolutely current among ordinary people. These ideas, and the images produced by political leaders, feed on one another, linking together the 'modern', 'scientific' genetic discourse with the emphasis on inherent Asian spirituality. Scattered evidence suggests that the interaction between the specific ideology produced by Ilyumzhinov's government and the wider field of the political imagination does produce some subjective effect – that is, it appears in the self-related actions and speech of subjects who emotionally either uphold the ideology or revolt against it. For example, it seems that Ilyumzhinov received a stream of letters from people saying that they disagreed so strongly about his new policies that there were family 'schisms' (raskol), husbands and wives got divorced and children left the family home (Ilyumzhinov 1996: 15–16). Of course, subjectivity works in an authoritarian political context in various ways, through various possible types of identification (Salecl 1994: 50). But to go so far as to get divorced 'because of you', as people wrote to Ilyumzhinov, is evidence that the new ideologies are not simply imposed by state structure and state force; they are also deeply felt by people as part of their lives, one way or another. This appears not simply in conflicts between, for example, the atheism of an older generation and the new beliefs, but engages a far wider and more complex range of disjunctive ideas. The concept of 'Eurasia' creates a new field in which images of the body, physical beauty, and kin relations can be realigned. As Guchinova argues (2001), young Kalmyks, who accept the fact of a fundamental 'Asian phenotype', nevertheless seek to re-imagine themselves in relation to specifically European images of beauty and sexual attractiveness. Responding to alternative geographical delineations of where 'Europe' begins and 'Asia' ends (see Bassin 1991), they claim that they are the 'only Buddhists in Europe' (Guchinova 2001).

## Conclusion

I have argued that 'Eurasia' provides an arena of the political imagination in which the Inner Asian peoples can claim a dignified place. The logic of the counterposition of 'West' to 'East', with the superiority of Russia over both, resting on its civilizational harmonic spirituality, pushes the small Inner Asian peoples in the only direction they can take, to proclaim their value as a super-spiritual one. I have been told that many ordinary Kalmyks already regard such statements as ideological hyperbole, as the 'over-the-top' pronouncements of someone who belonged to the early stage of Kalmyk statehood. Yet the structural position of Nuskhaev's great ideas in the realm of the political imaginary, such as the concept of the Personalities destined to flow into Russia, is not dissimilar to the more 'traditional' notion of the three peaks of the sacred mountain of the Altai. These ideas have been subject to a process of ideologization, yet they emerge from a distinctive and particular location in the post-Soviet world. As Ram has argued in an interesting article on the Kazakh writer Suleimenov (2001: 310), Eurasianism is more than just an ideological preference. It involves a poetic reflection on the taken-for-grantedness of central categories, such as language and history in the case of Suleimenov, or kinship and individuality in the case of the Kalmyks. Indeed, we find in Kalmykia an extraordinary *hyper imaginary*.[20]

What has all this got to do with real politics? It is true that 'Eurasia' has no economic content, and the only attempt to propose it as a contemporary political structure in the mid-1990s, by President Nazarbaev of Kazakhstan, fell on largely deaf ears (Prazauskas 1995). Yet the Eurasia Movement has recently become rather prominent in Moscow. It has attracted a number of important religious leaders – Orthodox, Islamic, Jewish and Buddhist – to its rallies. Furthermore, its values are an important element in the broad stream of Russian nationalism and it shares a vocabulary with a large variety of political forces, from the Communists to the National Socialists (Malashenko 1996: 105). Seemingly esoteric terms and the debate on the nature of 'mentality' (*razum*) are part of the general intellectual currency. It should not be forgotten that both Yeltsin and Putin have stated publicly that contemporary Russia needs its own distinctive ideology in order to re-invigorate its people for the new millennium. It is not a large step from this to the spiritual revolution (*perevorot*) called for by Eurasianists like A.S. Panarin (1994: 90). For internal consumption, Putin has laid his cards on the table. His first major speech as President called for a new version of 'the Russian Idea', which has the following four components: belief in the greatness of Russia; statism; community-mindedness; and patriotism. His acclamation of the Eurasian idea in Kazakhstan shows that he is fully aware of the currency of the notion in the Asian regions. In such a context, one can see the attraction of 'Eurasia' for non-Russian peoples. They know it is in a sense fantasy. But it is a chimera that relates them to a powerful discourse, and its very fantastic nature is what offers the possibility of heroically throwing off past humiliations. Like the three peaks of the sacred mountain, it is a super-reality that nevertheless guides people to act in certain ways.

There are many self-declared polities in the world today, particularly in post-Soviet space, which have an uncertain political status within larger entities. They are internationally unrecognized, usually dependent economically; no one in them knows their rights, and no one outside them cares. Such places raise issues of how anthropologists should think about 'the state' (cf. Trouillot 2001). No simple structural delineation is adequate, for there are differently weighted sites within the political space of 'the state', from which imaginaries of empowered existence take form. These visions posit a homology between cultural identity and statehood, something that is always imaginatively possible but seems to be most conspicuously manifested in present-day Russia in those regions where an autocratic exemplary leader is able to force them into existence. The notion of 'Eurasia' has its dangers – perhaps particularly in its Russian nationalist versions, which have hardly been touched on here – for it distracts attention away from institutions, rights and responsibilities, and entirely ignores the poverty and corruption that are so endemic in Russia. But paradoxically it is impelled by a generous vision from the Inner Asian peoples, one in which different cultural–political entities contribute to one another rather than seeking harm and conflict. The interesting questions are to what extent 'the state' of Russia will continue to nourish itself on such phantas-magoric 'ideas', whether 'Eurasia' will cease to be a field of discussion and crystallize into an ideology, and if so, whether it will be confined to the sphere of internal politics, as at present, or spill over on to the international scene.

## Notes

1   For a study of how this ideology was disseminated through the Soviet ritual system, see Lane 1981.
2   In 1996, Yeltsin set up a commission to produce an ideology for Russia, with no conclusive results (Urban 1998: 969). Virtually the first act of Vladimir Putin, when he became Acting President, was to issue a statement of his version of 'the Russian idea'; yet it was still impossible for agreement to be reached on the words of the national anthem (Suny 1999: 140).
3   Examples are Kemerovo Oblast under the leadership of Aman Tuleev (Luk'yanova 1999) and Saratov Oblast under the leadership of Dmitrii Ayatskov (Malyakin 1998).
4   For example, the wealthy Moscow singer Josif Kobzon, rumoured to be closely linked to criminal circles, presented himself for election in the Aga Buryat National Okrug in 1997. He was elected by an enormous majority (Namsaraeva 1997). Eurasian ideas were revived only in the late 1980s.
5   Discussions of the Eurasian character of Russia culminated in the 1920s in a move-ment among Russian emigrés that elaborated Russia's special mission in world history. Among the most prominent of these writers was N.S. Trubetskoi, who proposed that out of two formational streams, the Aryan Slavic and the Turanian (Turkic, Mongolian and Finno-Ugrian) cultures, Russia formed its own original third messianic civilization. P.N. Savitskii emphasized the unification of settled and steppe-nomadic peoples and the importance of the 'Tatar yoke' in the political tradi-tions of Russia (Sokolov 1999). See also Bassin 1991 and articles in *Anthropology and Archaeology of Eurasia* 36(4) (1998) and 37(1) (1998).
6   Galina Manzanova, personal communication.
7   Kuz'min and Svinin write that a revival of Pan-Mongolism would result in the domi-nation of the Halh-Mongols and thus disadvantage Turkic peoples like the Tuvinians and Kazakhs. They conclude: 'Other paths must be found to integrate the peoples on an ethnic basis, but avoiding this dangerous field which would re-draw historical given state boundaries' (1997: 9).
8   Panarin is a conservative, anti-Western Moscow philosopher who combines admira-tion for Eurasianism with Russian Orthodoxy.
9   President Nazarbaev of Kazakhstan was so taken with the idea that he suggested in 1994 the creation of a 'Eurasian Union' (EAS), as an alternative to the Commonwealth of Independent States. This was to be a primarily security-focused union of equal states, with its own elected parliament, executive organs and a common economic and defence policy. The proposal was seriously considered only by Russia and Kazakhstan, however. Russia was interested in advancing its geostrategic position, while Kazakhstan had an interest in an ideology that would link its two main populations, Russians and Kazakhs (Prazauskas 1995: 173–8).
10  The world is eternally divided into two parts – the East and the West. This is not only a geographical division, but also the order of things, founded on the very nature of intelligent being; these are two principles, corresponding to two dynamic forces of nature, two ideas, embracing the whole living structure of the human race.

(P.Ya. Chaadaev, *Sochineniya*, 1989, Moscow, 145–6, quoted in Yugai 1998: 104)

11 *Passionarnost'* is the extraordinary capacity of certain small groups, infused with patriotism and prepared to violate all social norms, to strive passionately to create new ethnic unities and make them flourish 'biologically' and politically (Shnirel'man and Panarin 2001: 20–7).

12 For example, an account from the Altai reads:

> At the forum there was a map of Eurasia. And there on the map was the Mountain Altai, delimited by a square. It is extremely interesting and significant that this point is equidistant from all four oceans (the Atlantic, the Pacific, the Polar Sea and the Indian Ocean). Seemingly, it is not by accident that the ancient Indian sutras and the Altaian *Sudur-Bichik* both count this point of the Eurasian continent as the belly-button of the earth, in Altaian, *d'erdig kindigi*.
>
> (*Problemy* 1992: 58)

13 I am grateful to Agnieszka Halemba for this information.

14 According to opinion polls carried out in 1997–8, just over half the population 'do not trust' the Kalmyk government (Katushov 1998: 327). It is not clear, however, if this attitude also applies to Ilyumzhinov personally.

15 In the words of the President, this was an agreement 'sealed by the Wise Behest (*Zavet*) of Ayuki Khan and Peter the Great about the close union between two peoples' (Ilyumzhinov 1997: 13).

16 Agnieszka Halemba, personal communication.

17 Agnieszka Halemba, personal communication.

18 Agnieszka Halemba, personal communication.

19 El'za-Bair Guchinova, personal communication. In recent years, people are proudly renaming villages, trading firms and shops by the name of their clan.

20 Another example is the book published by Nuskhaev, the Minister of Propaganda, which contains diagrams locating the 'mental life (*razumnaya zhizn'*) of Russia' within hierarchical cosmologies containing such entities as the 'All-spirit of Russia', the 'Noosphere' and the 'Planetary passionate Spirit of the Earthling' (1996: 142–3). The Eurasian (*yevraziets*), writes Nuskhaev, 'is pan-ethnos, all-ethnos, or All-spirit. And All-spirit means unifying and absorbing in itself all the spirits: Russian, Kalmyk, Tatar, Bashkir, Buryat, and so forth' (1996: 125).

# References

Afanas'yev, M. (1998) 'Ot volnykh ord do khanskoi stavki', *Pro et Contra* 3(3): 5–20.

Bassin, Mark (1991) 'Russia between Europe and Asia: the ideological construction of geographical space', *Slavic Review* 50(1): 1–17.

Cooper, Frederick and Anne Stoller (1997) *Tensions of Empire: Colonial Cultures in a Bourgeois World*, Berkeley, Los Angeles, London: University of California Press.

Guchinova, El'za-Bair (1997a) *Respublika Kalmykiya: Model' Etnopoliticheskogo Monitoringa*, Moscow: RAN.

——(1997b) 'Power relationships in an ethnocultural context: the perception of the president among the Kalmyks', *Études Mongoles et Sibériennes* 27: 299–304.

——(2001) 'Metamorfozy kalmytskoi etnichnosti v period transformatsii', unpublished ms.

Humphrey, Caroline (2000) 'Leadership, innovation, and the political imagination in postsocialist Kalmykia,' unpublished ms.

Ilyumzhinov, Kirsan (1996) 'Materialy konstitutsionnogo sobraniya Respublika Kalmykii, 1994', in E.-B. Guchinova (ed.) *Kalmykiya: Etnopoliticheskaya Panorama. Ocherki, Dokumenty, Materialy*, tom 11, Moscow: RAN.

——(1997) *Kalmykiya – Zemlya Dukha: Natsional'naya Ideya*, Elista: KKI.

Katushov, K. (1998) Kalmykiya v geoprostranstve Rossii, Elista: Kalmytskii Institut Gumanitarnykh i Prikladnykh Issledovanii.

Khakim, Rafael' (1998) 'Russia and Tatarstan', Anthropology and Archaeology of Eurasia 37(1): 30–71.

Kuz'min, Yu. V. and V.V. Svinin (1997) '"Panmongolizm" v XX veke', Materials for Parliamentary Hearings October 1997, Irkutsk: Irkutsk State University.

Lane, Christel (1981) The Rites of Rulers: Ritual in Industrial Society – the Soviet Case, Cambridge: Cambridge University Press.

Luk'yanova, Inna (1999) 'Aman vo spaseniye', Profil' 25(147): 59–62.

Lur'ye, S.V. (1994) 'Rossiiskaya imperiya kak etnokul'turnyi fenomen', in B. Yerasou (ed.) Tsivilizatsii I Kul'tury, vol. 1, Moscow.

Malashenko, Aleksei (1996) 'Russkii natsionalizm i islam', Acta Eurasica 'Vestnik Evrazii 2(3), Moscow: RAN, pp. 116–52.

Malyakin, I. (1998) 'Saratovskaya regional'naya ideologiya: poisk v mifologicheskom pole', in I. Alksnis (ed.) Perestroika is Posle: Obshchestvo i Gosudarstvo v SSSR, Rossii I novykh nezavisimykh gosudarstvakh, 1988–1998, Moscow: IGPI, pp. 37–40.

Namsaraeva, Sayana (1997) 'Deputat Buryat', Kommersant-Vlast' 34(240).

Nuskhaev, Aleksei (1996) Konservativnaya Kalmykiya v konservativnoi Rossii, Elista: Kalmytske Knizhnoe Izdatel'stvo.

Panarin, A.S. (1994) 'Zablyudivshchiyesya zapadniki i probudivshchiyesya evraziitsy', in B. Yerasou (ed.) Tsivilizatsii i Kul'tury, vol. 1, Moscow: RAN, pp. 82–94.

——(1995) 'Vybor Rossii: mezhdu atlantizmom i yevarziistvom', in B. Yerasou (ed.) Tsivilizatsii I Kul'tury, vol. 2, Moscow: RAN, pp. 31–49.

Prazauskas, A. (1995) 'Evraziiskoe prostranstvo: integratsionnyi potentsial I ego realizatsiya', Acta Eurasia-Vestnik Evrazii 1: 173–8.

Problemy formirovaniya i razvitiya ekologo-ekonomicheskoi zony 'Gornyi Altai' (1992) Materialy Mezhdunarodnogo Simpoziuma, Pravitel'stvo Respubliki Altai, Gorno-Altaisk.

Ram, Harsha (2001) 'Imagining Eurasia: the poetics and ideology of Olzhas Suleimenov's AZ i IA', Slavic Review 60(2): 289–311.

Salecl, Renata (1994) The Spoils of Freedom: Psychoanalysis and Feminism after the Fall of Socialism, Routledge: London.

Shnirel'man, V. and S.A. Panarin (2001) 'Lev Gumilev: his pretensions as a founder of ethnology and his Eurasian theories', Inner Asia 3(1): 1–18.

Sokolov, S.M. (1999) 'Yevraziiskaya kontseptsiya etnicheskoi istorii Rossii', in T.D. Skrynnikova (ed.) Gumanitarnyye Issledovaniya Molodykh Uchenykh Buryatii, vyp 2, Ulan-Ude: Izdatel'stvo BNTs So RAN, pp. 93–5.

Suny, Ronald Grigor (1999) 'Provisional stabilities: the politics of identity in post-Soviet Eurasia,' International Security 24(3): 139–78.

Trouillot, Michel-Rolph (2001) 'The anthropology of the state in the age of globalization: close encounters of the deceptive kind', Current Anthropology 43(1): 125–38.

Urban, Michael (1998) 'Remythologising the Russian state', Europe-Asia Studies 50(6): 969–92.

Urkhanova, Rimma (1995) 'Evraziitsy i Vostok: pragmatika lyubvi?', Acta Eurasia-Vestnik Evrazii, no. 1, Moscow.

Veyne, Paul (1987) 'L'individu atteint au coeur par la Puissance publique', in P. Veyne (ed.) au colloque de Royaumont Sur l'Individu, Paris: Seuil.

Volgin, V. (1999) 'Konflikt v sisteme vlasti', *Byulleten'*, no. 23, Set' etnologicheskogo monitoringa i rannego preduprezhdeniya konfliktov, Institut Etnologii i antropologii RAN, pp. 27–31.

Yasman, Victor (2001) 'The rise of the Eurasians', *RFL/RL Security Watch* 2(17).

Yugai, G.A. (1998) *Srednii Put' Rossii: konvergentnoe obshchestvo*, Moscow: Moskovskii Obshchestvennyi Nauchnyi Fond.

# Part V

# Democracy export and global civil society

Previous sections have highlighted the widespread search for new values, new moral foundations to replace the ideology of socialism. There has been no shortage of alternative slogans. The final section concentrates on one of the most popular on offer from the West and systematically propagated in the major programmes of aid and development. The ideal is known programmatically as civil society. But what does this mean in reality? Does it, from the point of view of the majority of citizens, produce anything more than a new ideology, one perhaps even more remote from their needs than that of socialism? How is it linked to accelerating globalization, and to new patterns of competition between the core capitalist regions?

In Chapter 14 Ruth Mandel explores the mechanisms of foreign intervention in Central Asia, particularly Kazakhstan, in the 1990s. Major donors have been committed to the support of non-government organizations. Mandel shows that these seeds have not fallen on fertile soil; they have generated DONGOS and GONGOS, rather than the approved model of Western NGO. The most enduring effect of the aid effort so far has been the formation of a new local elite of 'development professionals'. The trouble is that the value produced by these people takes the form of project 'deliverables' that are unlikely to have any bearing on the deteriorating living conditions of the mass of the population. Meanwhile the young professionals imbibe a set of Western values and earn Western salaries. They become unemployable in their local societies. Some may end up providing financial support for large extended families, but others seek work abroad and sever local ties. Efforts to bring interventions more in tune with local institutions have not borne fruit and Mandel also points to the potentially conflictual consequences of aid programmes for inter-ethnic relations. In sum, nothing remotely resembling the normative objective of Western civil society is achieved.

Mandel considers the resemblances between development professionals in Central Asia resemble and their equivalents elsewhere in the developing world. The ideals of good governance and civil society, the postulated links between democracy, rule of law and market efficiency, are the same as those advocated elsewhere; but she finds that political circumstances in the aftermath of the Cold War exposed Central Asia to an exceptionally strong, 'missionizing' variant of the global ideology of Western donors. Local development elites here could mount no alternative; as in the history of cargo cults, repeated failures to deliver the goods does not lead them to lose faith, one reason being that they are able to further their own interests quite successfully.

In the following chapter Steven Sampson draws on comparable materials from many years of personal involvement in civil society programmes in south-eastern Europe. He analyses a constellation of new elites, whose emergence is evidence that the initial phase of postsocialism has now come to an end. In this new era, which he calls 'post-postsocialism' or PPS, the shock of the new has given way to new forms of subordination to global forces. These produce different processes of integration and fragmentation for the four new elite groupings identified by Sampson: the class of professional politicians and officials, the *comprador* bourgeoisie, the domestic business elite and the mafia warlords. The chapter concentrates on the Euro-elites, a sub-section of the *comprador* bourgeoisie, whose members are employed primarily in short-lived projects funded by Western donors. These new elites mediate global resources and exert power downwards, but they are also embedded in new hierarchies of obligation, including obligations to project organizations and to more abstract principles. As in Central Asia, the Euro-elites of the Balkans have to balance these new obligations with their private projects.

Don Kalb did not present a paper at the Halle meeting but his contributions at the time made him the ideal person to approach for an 'Afterword'. He came up with something rather more: a substantive chapter, which looks back over the previous chapters and sets postsocialism in the wider context of a 'globalist narrative' that is undergoing major changes as core capitalist powers engage in new forms of competition. Kalb recapitulates the reasons for rejecting standard models of 'transitology' and a hollow, ethnocentric model of civil society. Exploring the micro dynamics of 'path-dependency' offer a partial corrective, but close attention to historical institutional change is insufficient. It is also crucial to investigate how both economic performance and power relations are shaped by 'spatial linkages'. Kalb argues that strategic location provides a key to understanding the relative 'transition successes' increasingly claimed in some parts of Central Europe. Even here, he reminds us, development has been highly selective and large social groups have been rendered increasingly marginal. The basic dilemmas of the postsocialist societies, he suggests, are no different from those of their Western European neighbours. As the European Union half-heartedly pursues its programme of expansion, Kalb offers an original and optimistic vision of the role the anthropologist might play in 'tracking phase two'.

# Chapter 14

# Seeding civil society

*Ruth Mandel*

Observers of postsocialism have a penchant for metaphors of transportation when describing the challenges these societies have faced over the past decade. Gerard Roland has stated that '[T]he transition from communism to a free-market economy is like changing the engine on an airplane while it is still flying' (2001). Moving from the aeronautic to the oceanic, Elster *et al.* (1998) sub-titled their book *Rebuilding the Ship at Sea*. But whatever the metaphorical vehicle, there now is a wide recognition of formidable, even intractable problems. Despite critiques of the attempted wholesale exportation of Western market democracies to the postsocialist world, and the underlying assumptions of 'transitology', 'transition' itself has became a 'mytho-poetic concept' and it remains 'a near orthodoxy' (Holmes 2001: 32). However, a whole host of unexpected obstacles have presented themselves to disrupt the anticipated unilinear trajectory of change. Subsequent to the widespread privatization of state-owned businesses and the introduction of new markets, these 'transitional' countries were beset by economic recession, so that the increased efficiency expected from free markets never materialized. One decade after the emergence of the Commonwealth of Independent States, it is fitting to take stock of what went wrong and why, and to question the initial assumptions of transition itself. Abramson asks anthropologists to consider 'whether the concept of "transition" is anything other than a discursive tool for recasting Cold War dichotomies such as "First World" and "Third World" or "developed" and "developing" worlds into new molds of civil and uncivil societies' (2001: 8).[1]

It is also time to consider unintended sociological consequences. In this chapter I focus on an unexpected by-product of Western 'transition aid' over the past decade: the indigenous development professionals, an aspiring elite, who are part of the human fallout of international development aid. Before looking at the new native development professionals in detail, it will be useful to outline the context in which they have emerged. First, I will discuss briefly the idea and role of *civil society* in relation to international development aid. This leads to a consideration of the role of donors and non-governmental organizations, or NGOs. Finally, I shall analyse the indigenous group that emerges as a consequence of these processes. Most but not all of the material presented is based on observations from Kazakhstan, and drawn from experiences with the major international donor in the region, the United States Agency for International Development (USAID). Other aid agencies have somewhat different agendas, missions and practices.

## Civil society and development agendas

Civil society has been understood uncritically by development agencies as a necessary moral 'good': the ultimate goal in the quest to bring the former Soviet bloc countries in line with Western expectations and values. However, the seeding of civil society has run into numerous stumbling blocks. Impoverished populations hanker after the 'good old days' of the USSR, which in retrospect were for many a golden era marked by stability, an acceptable 'equality of poverty', guaranteed employment, generous social services, universal education and health care, and an absence of street-crime. Corroboration for this nostalgic tendency is provided by a USAID-sponsored opinion poll from August 1999 about the wish to return to communist economic systems. The canvassed citizens of four Central Asian countries showed more than 60 per cent of Kazakhstanis preferring the former system (USAID 2000: 11).[2] These results question not only the design of USAID's policies but also the success of their impact and implementation.[3] These populations are not particularly receptive to Western liberal bourgeois notions of civil societies, given that the 'transition' has brought them sharp social and economic cleavages, massive unemployment, unsafe streets and ubiquitous corruption. Yet the agendas of all private and public development aid agencies have been dominated by the push for civil societies.[4]

It is important to state that this push is *not* unique to development assistance in the postsocialist world, but has been part of the 'good governance' agenda and political conditionality of aid in many parts of the world. The 'good governance' agenda has been advocated in particular by the World Bank. After an acknowledgement that its structural adjustment policies had failed, the Bank shifted its approach. It recognized that one of the problems leading to the failures had been the often intractable combination of pervasive corruption, lack of transparency, and profound inefficiencies in the governments of the countries in which it was giving loans and setting conditions. It was this set of issues that brought about this change in strategy, the 'roll back the state' rhetoric, and support for programmes such as judicial reform, anti-corruption training, and the like.[5]

To contextualize this shift, it may be useful to note that in orthodox, traditional development thinking, democracy has been understood as an outcome of development. In contrast, what Leftwich has called the 'new orthodoxy', departing from tired models derived from 1960s modernization theory, is 'the proposition that democracy is a necessary prior or parallel condition of development, not an outcome of it' (1993: 605). This has turned 'on its head earlier claims of modernization theory that stable democracy presupposed prior economic and social development, as had been the case in much ... of the now developed world, where advancing industrialization normally preceded democratization' (*ibid.*).

The Central Asian context presents a challenge both to modernization theory and to Leftwich's 'new orthodoxy', as it is a region with a Soviet legacy of industrialization, yet has been experiencing deindustrialization for the past decade. Still, the mission statement of USAID announces that it 'promotes decentralization and good governance in pilot cities and oblasts through policy dialogue with the central government, parliament, and other interested parties. USAID encourages public outreach and citizen participation by introducing new practices such as public hearings' (USAID 2000). The specificity of the aid to the postsocialist states has been the *ex nihilo* creation of civil society, not the good governance programmes *per se*. The particular model of civil society imposed on the postsocialist world was reified and under-conceptualized. Most often an associational model (in the tradition of de Tocqueville 1969) of civil society was implied, rather than the more complex models of contemporary civil society theorists (e.g. Cohen and Arato 1995). Many of the civil society projects assumed the form of public sector provisioning, offering an alternative to the collapsed and ineffectual state sector. For example, NGOs such as Save the Children and MercyCorps have moved in where the state services had retreated.

It soon became clear that without the requisite legal regulatory frameworks to support new policies, the manichean trajectory of transition to a market economy lacked any hope of succeeding. However, these legal regulatory frameworks are predicated on adherence to 'rule-of-law', which in turn depends upon this notoriously reified civil society.

It has been assumed that a successful market transition would necessarily generate the conditions for this civil society. A new middle class of property owners and small entrepreneurs would arise and, as 'stakeholders', demand and create a stable and secure democracy. The economists designing the programmes believed that these changes would be straightforward, and they sometimes justified this optimistic assumption with reference to high levels of human capital in the former Soviet Union. Development planners presumed that all that was needed was a measure of sophisticated technical assistance to re-orient an already well-educated population in the desired direction. For them, the critical element needed was imported 'know-how'. British development aid to the postsocialist states was channelled through a new agency, set up under Thatcher, that was actually called the Know How Fund.[6] This meant that the development advisors were not the builders of wells and bridges, but instead the assistance followed in the line of recent trends brought about by policies of structural adjustment. Thus finance experts from Wall Street and the City were brought in to set up stock exchanges and local financial markets; representatives of the big six accounting firms advised on banking procedures; legal experts in privatization and property drafted new legislation in fields such as bankruptcy and condominium law. The development agendas of the major donors have included economic restructuring linked to democratization (civil society), rule-of-law and governance (institutional capacity building). This approach differed sharply from previous notions and practices of development in the traditional recipient countries of the South, and formed part of the sea change in development thinking that has taken hold since the practices of structural adjustment have been disseminated throughout the developing world.

In the case of the postsocialist world, Cold War ideologies have demanded that the economic and political be inextricably linked, in order to promote the explicitly Western-based values of multi-party democracy, pluralism and market economies (Leftwich 1993: 609). This was the motivating mission of the European Bank for Reconstruction and Development, a body established in the image of the World Bank specifically to assist in the restructuring of the economies of the former Eastern Bloc countries. Likewise, the US Government's so-called 'Silk Road Strategy' emphasizes that

> the overarching goal of U.S. foreign policy for the five Republics is stable, democratic, market-oriented development to prevent conflict and the expansion of global threats, and to ensure Western access to the region's substantial oil, gas and mineral resources.
>
> (Pressley 2000)[7]

Clearly, the development assistance for democracy and civil society cannot be decoupled from economic interests and market reform.

The fundamental belief animating the civil society projects, as mentioned above, is that a postsocialist civil society needs to be constructed from scratch, since in the Soviet landscape this social or political space simply did not exist. Any seemingly analogous process or grouping was controlled by the state in the name of the Communist Party, which organized society on behalf of the people. The idea of civil society is to occupy a critical space *outside* the realm of the state, but this was impossible under the old regime since that space was precisely what was unavailable. As Janine Wedel summed up:

> Because the lack of civil society was part of the very essence of the all-pervasive communist state, creating such a society and supporting organizations independent of the state – or NGOs – has been seen by donors as the connective tissue of democratic political culture – an intrinsically positive objective.
>
> (1994: 323, cited in Hann and Dunn 1996: 1)

Echoing this, Donald Pressley of USAID observed in a statement to the US Congress, that 'Central Asia is starting from a weak base: these states are not only undergoing a transformation from the Soviet system, but are "new" nations and lack many of the basic attributes necessary to support democracy and broad economic growth' (2000).

After observing this fundamental difference in social organization, *civil society* assistance proceeded on the assumption that without it democratic values and free market processes cannot flourish. For the most part, the model was taken from the USA and Western Europe, with their proliferation of grass-roots groups and clubs, environmental activists and an unregulated media. The crucial building blocks of civil society, it was decided, were the NGOs, and so foreign donors have been providing support for their creation. Among the stated goals of USAID is support for 'the empowerment of non-governmental organizations (NGO) in targeted areas, including the legal and environmental sectors, in order to promote advocacy and help citizens organize grassroots efforts to implement positive change in local communities' (USAID 2000).

However, the process of creating civil society is overburdened and the expectations, as one critical USAID development worker commented to me, are 'ludicrously high'. Civil society formation through the proliferation of NGOs does not in fact offer a *via regia* to the development of Western market-oriented democracies.

An example of a country struggling with the expectations of Western democracies is Kazakhstan, whose president, Nursultan Nazarbaev, has made it very clear that he wishes his country to be accepted in the community of Western nations. Though Kazakhstan is a member of the OSCE, the president has been unwilling to pay the price of the ticket; in other words, he is reluctant to grant the civic liberties, protection to ethnic minorities, or support for multi-party political systems demanded by international observers and critics.

International monitoring organs such as OSCE regularly criticize Kazakhstan for not adhering to promised electoral reforms and not abiding by agreed-to guidelines.[8] In fact, due to widespread violations the OSCE refused even to send observers to monitor the January 1999 presidential elections. This 'was a severe blow to Nazarbaev's bid to obtain the international approval of the elections' (Dave 2000: 25) and he accused the OSCE of failing to understand the nature of 'Asian democracy'. The government's capricious practices regarding opposition politicians have come to a head in the case of former Prime Minister Kazhegeldin, seen as the only serious threat to the hegemony of Nazarbaev. Having been forcibly retired and charged with numerous crimes, Kazhegeldin has been living in exile for several years. In 2001, he was tried and convicted *in absentia*. Despite this, and continued intimidation and cooptation of the opposition, the government 'has so far exercised restraint in dealing with prominent activists and independent critics' (*ibid.*). Most of the latter have extensive connections with Western NGOs, foundations (e.g. Soros), and other international bodies. In this way the very presence of international development NGOs has forced the civil society hand of the government, ever fearful of bad press in the West. This has not prevented Kazakhstan and other Central Asian governments from indulging in a whole host of activities not usually seen as consistent with the functioning of civil societies, or the observance of human rights. These include jamming and censoring independent radio and television; closing down independent newspapers and magazines; bugging telephones; clandestine monitoring of private email accounts; committing arson in offices of organizations they see as politically threatening; arrest, imprisonment and torture of oppositional activists (particularly in Uzbekistan: see HRW: 2000a, b).

Mindful of these threats to civil and human rights, Evgeny Zhovtis, a high-profile, internationally connected activist, argues passionately that the foreign organizations have a critical role to play in civil society reform in Kazakhstan (1999). The founder of the country's International Bureau for Human Rights, he argues that the only way out of the country's current quasi-totalitarian quagmire is by training a new cadre of elites in the West. Particularly in the field of human rights, he asserts that 'it is necessary to educate a new generation of lawmakers at home and abroad, individuals well-versed in international law who can then gradually reform the legislative foundations of society' (1999: 67).

## Non-governmental organizations: exogenous agendas and professional personnel

Post-Soviet Central Asia exemplifies William Fisher's observation that NGOs have 'become the "favored child" of official development agencies ... imagined as a "magic bullet" which will mysteriously but effectively find its target' (1997: 442). Recipients of massive support by development agencies, they are regarded as instruments of choice for purposes of jump-starting participatory democracy in the best small-town tradition of town meetings, parent–teacher associations and lay boards of directors. Thanks to millions of dollars of development assistance, thousands of NGOs have been founded throughout Central Asia, primarily in Kazakhstan, Kyrgyzstan and Uzbekistan. They represent a wide range of interests, including veterans, ecology, women, artists, refugees and the disabled.[9]

A major problem in the life of an NGO is, in development-speak, 'sustainability', meaning the viability of the project after assistance ceases: will there be a life after outside funding? Development projects are normally subject to evaluation by outside evaluators, and aid-oriented NGOs need to be mindful of this. In practice, aid projects are often short-lived, at the mercy of a host of exogenous forces, including skill at writing proposals and the finesse of their consulting firms or organizational headquarters, located in Brussels, Geneva, or inside the Washington beltway. Sometimes in the case of USAID-funded projects the ideological convictions of the US Congress are decisive, especially in sensitive areas of funding, such as women's reproductive health.[10]

NGOs need to recruit local staff and an important group has emerged of people who maintain a foot in two camps: while hanging on to their poorly paid but prestigious government jobs, they simultaneously work for new 'independent' NGOs. In Central Asia the USAID NGO support project Counterparts

Consortium adopted the position that local NGOs should be entirely autochthonous and develop 'naturally'. However, most development project staff felt this was naive and, moreover, unhelpful. The rules of the US government prevent USAID from funding anything or anyone in the local governments, but what if there are no non-governmental groups to serve as their local counterparts? In these circumstances, some USAID contractors have taken to identifying relevant potential counterparts – all in state jobs – who would be useful for carrying out their projects, and arranging for them to form NGOs.[11] USAID funds NGO training programmes, in which participants are trained in the techniques of proposal-writing, grant-writing, budgets, etc. In this way, state employees assume parallel roles as directors of NGOs and become eligible for development aid funding to further the agendas of the sponsoring development projects. This provides an *entrée* for these individuals into the local development networks, and allows them to receive personal benefits, such as coveted study tours abroad (with attendant *per diems*), or additional professional training. Thus many of the local NGOs are run by elites and professionals already groomed in Soviet times. For example, a hospital-based gynaecologist in Uzbekistan became interested in women's reproductive health, but found her clinic could not receive direct aid for the project they wanted to carry out, as it was a state hospital. She was identified by an international women's health NGO as an ideal counterpart, and they helped her to form an NGO. She still has her hospital position, but as the director of an NGO she qualifies as a recipient of aid. What I term 'developer-assisted NGO development' proved critical in this case.

Thus in many cases 'NGO' is a misnomer, since the organization is controlled by and dependent on USAID money, which is a congressional appropriation and hardly non-governmental. This sort of NGO has been termed a 'DONGO', or 'donor-organized NGO' (Fisher 1997: 448). It is technically distinct from any national government, but it is in reality subservient to other forces in both donor and recipient states, in a legal and regulatory sense. One USAID contractor used the label 'donor artifacts' to describe the local development professionals who are dependent on Western donors for their existence. The same individuals appear repeatedly, since the local NGOs that win funding are the ones run by people who have already been funded by other donors. They have mastered NGO-speak, and the simple fact that they have already received money from other Western donors serves as a recommendation to other potential donors.

One year I served on the board of the USAID-funded project Counterparts Consortium, referred to above, whose entire *raison d'être* has been to fund local NGOs and train potential NGO workers in the requisite techniques for forming them. Not surprisingly, the NGOs successful in their funding applications have acquired the ability to respond to the priorities established by external aid agencies. These include, for example, women's issues, refugee issues, environmental and other advocacy groups for underprivileged and under-represented segments of society, pensioners, the disabled, victims of nuclear and ecological disasters, health-care related groups – all were among the recipients. Proposals that remained unfunded were those to which the Western funders could not relate. They were, in a sense, 'too' local. Some might have had religious inflections, others appeared ethnically irredentist; some had no identifiable purpose at all. If a group applying for funding sounded promising but was not yet up to the standards required, its organizers might be offered training to ensure success in the next round.

A further type of NGO has come to be known as GONGO, which stands for 'government-organized NGO'; like DONGO, on the face of it a contradiction in terms. Central Asian governments generally see NGOs as a threat to their hegemony. At the same time they are desperately interested in attaining the legitimacy that can only be granted by Western governments, and they know that unless they are seen to be supporting the things that matter to the US and the EU countries, they will not gain what they seek (access to credit, World Bank loans, and international and domestic prestige). Furthermore, as some NGOs do the business of government, functioning as deliverers of formerly public services, the governments look the other way. In some instances, the governments have therefore taken to setting up their own NGOs, with deputy ministers and other senior officials as their heads. At international meetings, sometimes only such GONGOs are permitted to represent the country. In authoritarian regimes, obtaining an exit visa is a privilege rather than a right (although this visa, like much else, can usually be acquired with informal payments).

An emerging, critical literature on NGOs in the former Soviet Union tends to highlight problems that are well known to those working in the field. Holt Ruffin and Waugh (1999: 12) draw a distinction between the 'traditional, US-type' NGOs and the new, often foreign grant-dependent NGOs typical of Central Asia. Zhovtis directs our attention to the farcical nature of Kazakhstan's regulatory mechanisms controlling NGOs, and the 'frivolous' (1999: 64) interpretation of the role of the justice department in the obstruction and surveillance of independent associations. He questions the constitutionality of requiring NGOs to register, and to pay often prohibitively high fees for the privilege of doing so; why, he asks, should associations pay for their constitutional rights of assembly? Zhovtis shows clearly how, over the past decade, the early promises of democratic reform have become increasingly stymied legally, to the point where the state 'singles out the members of public associations as some dangerous category of citizens' (ibid.: 65).

Many of the more successful NGOs, if we measure success simply in terms of survival, owe their success to their leadership. The leaders of many new NGOs constitute a new cadre of local development professionals who have been cultivated by the foreign development elites. Whatever the longevity of particular projects, a sustainable by-product has been produced in the form of this new stratum. These are local people whose new value systems are shaped by development agendas. The value system inculcated into the new local development cadre derives in many cases from USAID. The Regional USAID Mission in Central Asia, the dominant development player in the area, arrived with a trinity, united by the formula of 'Transition'. This was based on three offices:

- the Office of Market Transition (OMT);
- the Office of Social Transition (OST);
- the Office of Democratic Transition (ODT).

Typical projects for OMT have been mass privatization, followed later by more specific small-scale projects, and also the creation of a commercial code of law. The OST projects included the areas of housing reform, pension reform and health reform. Finally, ODT has focused on NGO formation and support. The primary task of the Democracy Worker at ODT was to support new NGOs in the region; their relationship to democracy was taken to be self-evident.

All development aid in USAID-Central Asia falls into one of the three rubrics, and the local hires, as they are often called, learn to parse the world around them accordingly. Rather than a *sui generis* class of local development workers, they represent the local stratum of the larger class of international development professionals. Their social capital includes a battery of skills, including fundraising, political know-how and lobbying They are trained to service projects and produce the 'deliverables'. These cannot be assessed using the standard quantifiable measurements of economists; their productivity is therefore measured through public relations and information dissemination. The value which they produce does not consist in goods but in service to international organizations, such as conferences, training seminars, briefings and study tours.

During the present period of abundant aid these new development professionals have circulated and learned how to function in any generic development project. They can adjust quickly to represent the interests of whatever project they happen to be working for, to the relevant branches and ministries of their own government. In the process of learning and executing these essential skills a number of transformations occur. One result of this is that the local people trained in the servicing of the aid industry have been rendered unsuitable to work for their own governments. First, there are the pay differences: depending on one's position, the difference ranges from three-fold to twenty-fold. But in addition, this new cadre has been socialized into a Western-style, non-hierarchical organizational structure, one that prizes openness and often offers easy access to the highest levels of power within their international organizations, and also as the liaisons to their own governments. The style of work is quite different. In the Soviet system workers at all levels were largely ignored and often penalized for any display of initiative and independence. In contrast, the development aid industry tends to encourage and expect personal initiative and creativity. Consequently, many 'local hires' I have interviewed have explained that they would find it intolerable ever to work again in their own governments. Many also experienced an additional transformation in their family roles through becoming the backbone of a large extended kin network. An enterprising, English-speaking 28-year-old would earn four to ten times the national average and provide critical support for the unemployed and unemployable in his or her family.

## Case studies

Between 1994 and 2000, I spent two and a half years in Kazakhstan, carrying out research. The following are condensations of some of the complex situations I encountered during my time there. The names and situations have been altered to protect the privacy of these individuals.

A 20-year-old university student majoring in English, Bota presented herself to a USAID office as able to work in Russian, English and Kazakh. Having already visited the US as a foreign exchange student, her English was charmingly colloquial. She had a friendly, outgoing manner, and was hired as a part-time receptionist. She soon began to help out with translations and interpreting, putting in more hours, as required by her family's circumstances. Her parents, a doctor and a civil servant, together earned approximately $200 per month. Bota's part-time work brought in an additional $300, which helped the family of five, plus two cousins from the provinces who were living with them while they attended university, to make ends meet. After she graduated she moved to a more lucrative job in the private sector, doing PR for the local Coca-Cola office. As a bright, outgoing and confident Kazakh-, Russian- and English-speaking ethnic Kazakh, she was then approached to work for the President's transition team for the move to the new capital, Astana.[12] The position would have catapulted her into the very top echelons of influence and power, but the pay was only half of her current salary at Coca-Cola. When she decided to turn down the offer, she explained, 'In some ways it's very exciting, and I'm flattered, but even if the pay were not so low, I'm not sure I would want to work in that type of organization – I wouldn't have the freedom I have in my job now.'

Sergei taught economics at the main university in Almaty. As a non-ethnic Kazakh he was repeatedly warned that he should look for new employment, and eventually he was made to leave. After a couple of desperate years in the early 1990s, a friend of his with contacts with a foreign firm set him up for an interpreting job. His keen intelligence far surpassed his command of spoken English, and, with nearly no control over grammar, he managed to perform well enough to get a second, then a third job interpreting. He was also a skilled fixer, loyally negotiating the Byzantine politics of early post-Soviet bureaucracy for his employers. Eventually he obtained a full-time job with a new USAID-funded project on insurance reform. Initially hired as an interpreter, he soon became the invaluable man-Friday to the Chief of Party.[13] During this time, he became

quite fluent in the intricacies of the field of insurance and pensions. He participated in numerous World Bank missions and project evaluations. The project
director felt Sergei was wasting his talents, and encouraged him to apply to go
abroad for more training. He helped him write his application, and Sergei won a
coveted scholarship in the USA for a two-year master's degree in economics.
After completing his degree, a contact at the World Bank arranged for a
summer internship. This grew into a series of full-time consultancies at the
Bank, where he now works.

Gulbanu had studied English at university in Almaty. Through a friend, she
was recommended to work as an interpreter for Sharon, a visiting consultant
working on a women's health project. They hit it off, and she was hired on
repeated consultancy trips. When a new USAID project on birth control was
opening its offices Sharon recommended Gulbanu, as someone with local
knowledge who knew both Russian and Kazakh. She duly became the office
manager and married a British consultant she had met on a World Bank
mission. Though no longer married, she was able to remain in the UK where
she is completing a postgraduate degree. She refuses even to entertain the possibility of returning permanently to Kazakhstan to work; instead, she has her eye
on future employment in the international development community.

Marina had studied English in Moscow at the most prestigious institute in
the Soviet Union. Returning to Almaty in the early 1990s with her near-native
fluency she found her way into the city's top circle of freelance interpreters.
Eventually she was offered a full-time interpreting job in the Almaty office of a
New York based law firm. They saw potential in her and trained her to be a
paralegal. She excelled, and was soon offered financial support through law
school in the US if she consented to work for the firm after graduating. She
recently graduated from a law school in the US.

Anatoly had been a nuclear physicist, but after independence the funding for
his lab dried up. He was unemployed for two years before a friend brought him
to his place of employment, a health reform development aid project that
needed high-level computer programmers. Anatoly had no trouble adapting his
computing skills to the specific tasks of the project. He worked there for several
years, during which time his employers recognized his abilities and sent him for
additional training in the US. Through contacts he made, he has been able to
work as a freelance consultant on international development aid projects,
alongside Western consultants. Hoping eventually to settle with his family
permanently in the West, he is currently getting specialized training in the UK.
Former British employers from Almaty have helped him with visas and university admissions, and have arranged consultancies so he can support himself.

Whereas all the above persons were in their twenties when socialism
collapsed, Dina was approaching 50. She was a successful, well-known professor
of history, but it was not possible to survive on an academic salary in the early
1990s. After a couple years of near destitution, she found employment in the
offices of an international foundation which opened in Almaty in 1994. She

ran many of the cultural programmes. Her English was minimal, so her employers sent her on an intensive summer language course in the US. However, when a new American director took over, she lost her job. An American friend in the expat development community, impressed with her dynamism and intelligence, then recommended her to a new aid project that was seeking an office manager who knew English and Russian. She got the job and stayed with it until the project's funding ran out, acquiring the general skills needed to negotiate with USAID bureaucrats, to manage large budgets and to produce the requisite reports and memos. After a period of unemployment, she was hired as office manager by a floundering USAID project. She quickly reorganized the office, fired a number of incompetent local employees and helped open a new office in the new capital. She commanded a high salary – about $20,000, astonishingly high in the local context – which permitted her to send her daughter abroad to study, and to buy a car. Living alone in the new capital, Dina claims this is the first time in her life she has ever felt truly independent and happy. She has managed to master the complexities of the politics in the ministry in which she works, where she functions as an advisor paid by USAID. She has the respect of everyone from the minister on down. However, she complains of being fed up with the corruption she has to deal with on a daily basis, and would like to leave. She hopes to get a job in the international development community outside Central Asia. She has bought her second car in two years – this time an Audi. In the meantime, her inter-ministerial expertise has served her well, as she recently took a new job as the local representative of one of the largest international donors in the country.

## The *mahalla*, indigenization and nationalism

When the first wave of development projects did not bring the hoped-for results, the second round (beginning in the latter half of the 1990s) sometimes took a different tack. It has become 'politically correct' to uncover indigenous social forms, to allay the anxiety that one is not imposing Western models in inappropriate places. Uzbekistan has such a ready-made model, the *mahalla*. USAID has identified *mahallas* in their civil society activities, partnering them with community projects and small business development, including job training and placement (Pressley 2000). This proves ideal for some development projects, but it is problematic for others. The *mahallas* are local organizations, often neighbourhood-based, that take responsibility for the well-being of their constituents. For example they exercise social control over single women and children in 'problem' families, ensure that all families are financially able to provide the requisite hospitality for a circumcision or a wedding celebration, and that no one goes hungry. The *mahalla* organization meets these goals by requiring charitable contributions. This adds to its Islamic inflection, which combines with its patriarchal character. Abramson compares the Uzbeks who participate in them to 'those who operated in both official and black economies under state socialism's attempt to control the distribution of goods and services ... [and] are using social networks as strategies to protect themselves against the uncertainties of economic transition today' (2001: 8).

These characteristics can be problematic for some Western organizations since they are committed to secularism, feminism and democracy. They can also be troubling to local elites, particularly women. Some of the local female elites, socialized as part of a modernizing Soviet project, feel that working through these *mahalla* structures is a retrogressive move. They fear the ascendancy of the *aksakals* (literally 'white beard'), the elderly males who are usually in charge. The *mahallas* survived the Soviet period, but incorporation into the system of local Soviet governance transformed them, e.g. through the addition of women's committees and the like. Now, as part of a region-wide indigenization trend, they are undergoing yet another redefinition.

An even more sensitive issue concerns the new nationalisms prevalent in the region. In Kazakhstan, a major concern is the disproportionate number of non-ethnic Kazakhs in the NGO world, which contrasts with a disproportionate number of ethnic Kazakhs in the government. This is both a result of and an aggravating factor in inter-ethnic tensions. Increasing indigenization brings a mounting consolidation of power in the hands of representatives of the titular national groups in the government and civil service. It thus remains for the fledgling private, development aid and NGO sectors to provide employment to the recently excluded minorities (though in Kazakhstan the Russian population until recently exceeded that of the Kazakh). Some of these unwanted ethnics are the most highly skilled and motivated citizens of their respective countries. Many foreigners in the NGO world, in Kazakhstan in particular, see the non-titular ethnics as the new elite, and justify this privately in terms of their limited opportunities in the state sector. At the same time, they are aware of the indigenization agenda and, since the aid projects depend on the goodwill of government ministries and agencies, some have been quick to practise ethnic hiring. They might make a point of using a Kazakh, rather than a Russian, interpreter at high-level meetings with government officials, believing this will further their cause. Thus Western agencies become complicit in the nationalist project. They cannot press for ethnicity-blind meritocratic hiring, given the tremendous pressures from the home offices or agency clients to produce the requisite deliverables by often unreasonable deadlines. With these instrumentalist practices, they end up being coopted into the nationalist projects of the very governments to which they are working so hard to establish alternatives.[14]

## Conclusions

Foreign aid processes in Central Asia have led to a 'civil society' that operates more as a para-civil service. It functions as a non-state structure parallel to the state, but one less rigidly organized. In some guises, it serves the needs of the state and those of the mass of citizens, particularly where state services have collapsed. But all too often the beneficiaries are the local staffs or those of the donor country or organization, fulfilling exogenous political agendas. The local states tend to view the new development professionals suspiciously, as agents of an unwanted but perhaps essential foreign intervention. At best this new class is tolerated, particularly when connected to organizations such as the OSCE, since suppression would prove too embarrassing to the governments.

The final trajectory of these tolerated, indigenous development professionals is not yet decided, but the situation presented here does not support the analysis of Zhovtis (1999), who calls for the integration of these professionals into mainstream political and governmental work. Perhaps at some future point they will have such a role, but for now many have opted for what they see as an attractive escape hatch: emigration. These people do indeed possess social capital, but its deployment takes the form of writing grant proposals to study abroad, and knowing how to speak convincingly in interviews with the vetting consular officials; this promotes only their own eventual deracinated cosmopolitanism. Western development aid personnel facilitate the dissolution of this precarious, indigenous professional class, by encouraging them on the road to self-improvement, and in many cases, exit from the region.

It is worth considering whether this new social grouping is analogous to local development elites and professionals in South America and Africa, or whether there is something unique about the postsocialist variety. One difference is the missionizing and cargo-cult-like expectations in the early years. These were societies largely closed to Western ideas, values and priorities, and the new local elites played a critical role in the process of transnational, even transcultural percolation of a highly specified set of ideas and values. The developers and their acolytes share a faith that they are moving *out* of bad thinking and *into* enlightened thinking. This enlightened perspective requires that everything which went before should be discredited, and so there has been a wholesale discounting of the entire socialist value system. Unlike their compatriots in their governments, these people have been given a pre-packaged replacement. Elsewhere in developing countries local development professionals have sometimes been able to adopt critical postures towards some of the ideas and messages of the developers, whereas in Central Asia much more is taken as gospel.

The consequence is that, a decade down the road of transition, things look rather bleak. The European Bank for Reconstruction and Development admitted in its recent ten-year report (1999) that the initial approach was far too instrumentalist, that not enough attention was paid to fundamental institutional reform and too much to piecemeal projects. The Bank recognized that new laws in and of themselves do not suffice, but methods of implementation and enforcement are crucial if the Holy Grail of civil society is to be achieved. These conclusions are consistent with the World Bank's shift in its strategy. USAID as well has recognized some of the errors of its initial ways.

Patricia Carley (1995) has stated that the absence of civil society processes in Central Asia is a continuation of the pre-Soviet period when both transhumant and settled peoples lived under various jurisdictions: local, customary law, which remained uncodified until the nineteenth century; Islamic law; regional emirates with absolutist rulers; and finally Russian Imperial administration. During the Soviet period, 'socialist legality' was subject to 'capricious' Communist Party interpretation and the upshot is that 'Central Asians have had little or no experience of a system in which a written, codified law truly functions as an objective arbiter of legality to which all in society are held, even the rulers' (1995: 303). In her view, civil society advocacy groups, as in most Western definitions, must be self-organizing. In the Central Asian Republics, and the former Soviet Union in general, this has not been the case. Those who succeed in getting funded are the new class of people who have achieved a degree of fluency in the culture of Western NGOs. The local development workers have become proselytes of the international development missionaries, and the rhetoric of civil society, privatization and democratization is their catechism. The creation of these local professionals trained to function and operate in an international development culture, is one of the few examples of a durable legacy of the development aid process. Yet, their integration has not been accomplished and their activities have come to form a parallel structure to those of the state – often perceived as rival, rather than complementary. The postsocialist ship, having been rebuilt at sea, is carrying a transformed cargo from the one initially loaded, as it sails on into uncharted waters.

## Acknowledgements

I am indebted to Deniz Kandiyoti, Scott Newton and Michael Borowitz for their intellectual contributions and suggestions. Many of the ideas presented in this essay draw directly from discussions we have had on the topic. I am grateful also to Chris Hann for his superb editorial hand.

## Notes

1 For considered discussions of some of the problems implied by the term, see Hann and Dunn 1996; Berdahl et al. 2000; Abramson 2001; Burawoy and Verdery 1999; for a trenchant critique of the US government policy towards the transition, see Cohen 2000.
2 The other countries were somewhat less: Uzbekistan about 27 per cent; Tajikistan and Kyrgyzstan about 50 per cent.
3 In an official USAID report, referring to the initial enthusiasm for privatization, the Central Asian

Mission staff noted that some policy development has been successful, but policy implementation has been disappointing ... [T]he actual utility of ... privatization in Kazakhstan has been questioned by some as to its success in contributing to economic growth – cynics might argue that it has only transformed the nature of corruption.

(USAID 2000: 118)

4 Moreover, while public agencies have dominated in the postsocialist countries, civil society and democratization programmes also play prominent roles in the NGOs funded by private corporations, such as BP-funded NGOs in South America. (I thank C. Briggs for bringing the South American case to my attention.)

5 In Central Asia, USAID practice is to work 'with the Parliament to adopt procedures and legislative oversight, which improve accountability. This includes encouraging transparent positive dialogue with NGOs and other interest groups, and public seminars or hearings on pending legislation' (USAID 2000).

6 It was run by civil servants from both the Foreign and Commonwealth Office (FCO) and the Overseas Development Administration (ODA); under the current Labour government, ODA was upgraded to the level of ministry and is now the Department for International Development (DFID). The Know How Fund still exists in the regions as a brand name, though it has been phased out in London. For a study of a Know How Fund project in Kazakhstan, an educational television soap opera, see Mandel (in press).

7 At the time of this speech, Pressley was the Assistant Administrator, Bureau for Europe and Eurasia, US Agency for International Development.

8 In its post-election statement after the second round held on 24 October, the ODIHR election observation mission stated that the elections, while constituting a tentative step towards international standards, fell short of the OSCE commitments formulated in the 1990 Copenhagen Document. The electoral process was severely marred by widespread, pervasive and illegal interference by executive authorities in the electoral process and a lack of transparency (OSCE/ODIHR 1999).

9 Jay Cooper estimates that 1,000 NGOs have been registered in Kyrgyzstan alone. For an analysis and exhaustive list of these and other Central Asian NGOs, see Cooper 1999.

10 The US Congress has forbidden the funding of projects that support abortion, directly or indirectly. This has been problematic for regional USAID support of many local women's NGOs, for whom reproductive health is often high on the agenda.

11 'Contractors' are the people and companies hired by USAID to carry out the USAID-designed projects. New projects are put out to a complex process of competitive bidding.

12 Due to seventy years of intense Sovietization and Russification, many Kazakhs, particularly the better educated among the population, are monolingual Russian speakers. Since independence, language policy has privileged Kazakh-speakers, who comprise approximately half the population. See Dave 1996; Fierman 1997.

13 The directors of USAID contracted projects are known as 'Chiefs of Party'.

14 This is less the case in Uzbekistan and Kyrgyzstan whose demographics differ significantly from Kazakhstan, where until recently there were more ethnic Russians than Kazakhs.

## Bibliography

Abramson, David (2001) 'Putting Central Asia on the anthropological map', Anthropology News May: 8.

Berdahl, Daphne, Martha Lampland and Matti Bunzl (eds) (2000) *Altering States: Ethnographies of Transition in Eastern Europe and the Former Soviet Union*, Ann Arbor: University of Michigan Press.

Burawoy, M., and K. Verdery (eds) (1999) *Uncertain Transition: Ethnographies of Change in the Postsocialist World*, Oxford: Rowman and Littlefield.

Carley, Patricia (1995) 'Soviet legacy in Central Asia', in Vladimir Tismaneanu (ed.) *Political Culture and Civil Society in Russia and the New States of Eurasia*, London: M.E. Sharpe.

Cohen, Jean and Andrew Arato (1995) *Civil Society and Political Theory*, Cambridge, MA.: MIT Press.

Cohen, Stephen (2000) *Failed Crusade: America and the Tragedy of Post-communist Russia*, USA: Norton.

Cooper, Jay (1999) 'The real work: sustaining NGO growth in Central Asia', in M. Holt Ruffin, Daniel Waugh and S. Frederick Starr (eds) *Civil Society in Central Asia*, Seattle: University of Washington Press, pp. 214–31.

Dave, Bhavna (1996) 'Language revival in Kazakhstan: language shift and identity change', *Post-Soviet Affairs* 12(1): 51–72.

——(2000) 'Democracy activism in Kazakhstan: patronage, opposition, and international linkages', unpublished ms.

Elster, Jon, Claus Offe and Ulrich Preuss (1998) *Institutional Design in Post-Communist Societies*, Cambridge: Cambridge University Press.

European Bank for Reconstruction and Development (EBRD) (1999) *Transition Report 1999: Ten Years of Transition*, London: EBRD.

Fierman, William (1997) 'Language, identity, and conflict in Central Asia and the Southern Caucasus', *Perspectives on Central Asia* vol. ll, no. 5 (August), Center for Political and Strategic Studies.

Fisher, William F. (1997) 'Doing good: the politics and antipolitics of NGO practices', *Annual Review of Anthropology* 26: 439–64.

Hann, Chris and Elizabeth Dunn (eds) (1996) *Civil Society: Challenging Western Models*, London: Routledge

Holmes, Stephen (2001) 'Transitology', *London Review of Books* 19 April: 32.

Holt Ruffin, M. and Daniel C. Waugh (eds) (1999) *Civil Society in Central Asia*, Seattle and London: Center for Civil Society International, University of Washington Press.

HRW (Human Rights Watch) (2000a) *Leaving No Witnesses: Uzbekistan's Campaign against Rights Defenders*, 12(4), New York: HRW.

——(2000b) *'And It Was Hell All Over Again': Torture in Uzbekistan* 12(12), New York: HRW.

Leftwich, Adrian (1993) 'Governance, democracy and development in the Third World', *Third World Quarterly* 14(3): 605–24.

Mandel, Ruth (in press) 'A Marshall Plan for the mind: the political economy of a Kazakh soap opera', in Lila Abu-Lughod, Faye Ginsburg and Brian Larkin (eds) *The Social Practice of Media*, Berkeley: University of California Press.

OSCE/ODIHR (1999) *Semi-Annual Report, Autumn 1999, Election Observation*, available at www.osce.org/odihr/docs/sar1299.htm.

Pressley, Donald L. (2000), 'Democracy in the Central Asian Republics', hearing at Subcommittee on Asia and the Pacific and Subcommittee on International Operations and Human Rights of the Committee on International Relations, United States

House of Representatives, April 12, distributed by the Office of International Information Programs, US Department of State. Website: http://usinfo.state.gov.

Roland, Gerard (2001) *International Herald Tribune* 30 March: 14.

Tocqueville, Alexis de (1969) *Democracy in America*, ed. J.P. Mayer, New Jersey: Anchor Books.

USAID United States Agency for International Development, (2000) *USAID's Assistance Strategy for Central Asia 2001–2005*, www.usaid.gov/regions/europe_eurasia/car/PDABS400.pdf.

Wedel, Janine (1994) 'US aid to Central and Eastern Europe, 1990–1994: an analysis of aid models and responses, in East-Central European Economies in Transition', study papers submitted to Joint Economic Committee, Congress of the United States, Washington: US Government Printing Office, pp. 299–335.

Zhovtis, Evgeny (1999) 'Freedom of association and the question of its realization in Kazakhstan', in M. Holt Ruffin and Daniel C. Waugh (eds) *Civil Society in Central Asia*, Seattle and London: Center for Civil Society International, University of Washington Press.

# Chapter 15

# Beyond transition

## Rethinking elite configurations in the Balkans

*Steven Sampson*

## Introduction: a new era

The study of Eastern European societies has been plagued by our adherence to concepts. Before 1989, we studied 'socialist societies'. After 1989 these became 'transition' or 'postsocialist' societies (Hann 1994). Postsocialist societies became a general variant of 'transitology', in which the transition to democracy familiar to us from Latin America and Southern Europe was now linked to transition from a state-planned to a market economy. As the label for an entire epoch, 'postsocialism' has been helpful for several reasons. It serves to remind us that the socialist past is very much a part of the after-socialist present. It was also a convenient label, since its vagueness allowed us to escape the task of periodizing. Concepts such as 'postsocialism' and 'transition' have trickled down from transitological theorizing to everyday parlance. For our informants, these terms signify some kind of journey to a better life, and have been used by them as emic labels in trying to comprehend their own realities.

Like so many shorthand terms for the era, 'postsocialism' (or 'postcommunism') and 'transition' came to take on a life of their own. Some used 'postsocialism' as a theoretical concept, others simply as an explanation for all their troubles, while still others found it a convenient rubric to use on a research grant or conference application. What cannot be denied, however, is that postsocialism and transition have had a profound effect on people's lives – both the discourses and the processes. Anthropological research throughout the 1990s has documented 'the shock of the new'. Postsocialist anthropology described how Western influence penetrated daily life in the East, in the guise of global tastes of consumption, mass culture, new social classes, new ways of calculating wealth, new discourses of democracy and new understandings of identity. It was a period which Katherine Verdery (1996) called 'agency over structure', as the very limits of how people perceived and acted on the world collapsed. We saw how people tried to cope with new and unclear standards for finding their place in the world, establishing new criteria for good taste, and demarcating themselves vis-à-vis others as ethnic groups, citizens, or classes.[1] Most importantly, we saw new cosmologies: people recasting their social worlds, their most basic sense of time and space. Transition was truly a new horizon, where 'all was possible, nothing was certain' (Sampson 1994b).

This period of transition, what we call 'postsocialism', is over. We are now in a post-transition stage, what I call 'post-postsocialism' (PPS). It is a period where the shock of the new has worn off and where the larger structures of the new global order have become embedded in people's consciousness. When I say that the shock has worn off, I mean that people in Central Europe, the Balkans or the former USSR now act as if they have some kind of understanding of the frameworks in which they live. People in the PPS world are not as confused as they once were. They are becoming consumers, or they are becoming politicized as nationalists. They are angry and depressed, or just plain tired. Where 'the West', to take the most typical discourse, was once something 'over there', Eastern Europeans now understand that the West is also a place that poses demands. They know that in capitalism you not only make money, you can also lose money as well as jobs. They now know that they have to value their time, that they are more dependent on themselves for achieving security and meaning in their lives, and that blaming the regime or system (or the Jews or the Gypsies) is no longer sufficient. PPS is a new way of life, profoundly different from the 'transition' period. If the postsocialist interim was 'agency over structure', in post-postsocialism structure is emphatically back.

## PPS and the new elites

Acknowledging that we are in a post-transition or PPS era has immediate implications for those groups whom we identify as elites and for how we study them. In the immediate postsocialist period, we observed the emergence of two types of 'new elites': technocratic and cultural. In the first group were the former party leaders, managers and technocrats who took over leadership of the emerging political organizations and ownership of economic enterprises in what Stark (1992) called 'from plan to clan'. This take-over may have been more violent or ruthless in some places, more sophisticated and legalistic in others, but it was basically a continuity of former cadres who seemed to break free of Marxist ideological shackles. They were skilled political operators whose ideologies changed as they became market reformers or successful businessmen.

The second group of transition elites were those whose legitimacy was moral and cultural. They were the intellectuals formerly affiliated with dissident movements, people of moral or intellectual standing: literary critics, sociologists, university rectors, human rights activists, musicologists and historians who became ministers or even presidents, and whose primary slogan was 'return to Europe'.

Whereas the first group of elites tried to appropriate resources from the former state, the second tried to maintain contacts with sources of cultural capital in the West. Over the past decade, both these projects have succeeded, and in this sense these elites have outlived their usefulness. Privatization has occurred; states are being streamlined. Integration with Europe is now a reality if we judge integration by the number of projects or visiting IMF delegations, or by the EU/NATO commitment to stability in south-east Europe. The West is not just a place 'out there'; it is 'here' among us. It is not just a representation any more. It is also a reality with which people have to cope, be it government officials trying to fulfil EU regulations or ordinary workers suffering yet another plant closing and retraining scheme. This irrevocable integration into global frameworks is the hallmark of post-postsocialism, and it also means the emergence of a new constellation of four kinds of elites: first, a local political class; second, a *comprador* bourgeoisie; third, a domestic business elite; and fourth – in regions of conflict – the warlords and mafia chieftains. In the remainder of this paper, I will argue that these elites differ from their predecessors in the nature of their integration into global networks, in the discourses they can employ and in the resources they can mobilize. Let us first describe these four types.

The political class, a French notion that is also often heard in Romania and not necessarily in a derogatory fashion, connotes a class whose primary activity is to set and implement policy. In this sense, they differ from the former communist leaders and managers who were trying to appropriate or hang on to power, and from intellectual and cultural figures who were ostensibly pushed into politics by a moral imperative and give lip service to retreating once things are settled down. The PPS political class have politics as a vocation. They consist of policy-making cadres trained at major national schools of law or administration and have supplemented their training with study, work or training abroad. (Unlike the transition elites, for example, the PPS political class speak English.) In Eastern Europe, the emergence of a professional political class is tied to Western demands for integration into European institutions and to conditions for aid. Hence the continual training courses provided to all leading cadres of PPS societies cover techniques of modern management and public administration, not to mention press relations. This comprehensive training applies to ministers of health, to human resource managers in the central government, to low-level bureaucrats, and even to military and police officials. The political class is also marked by its own local project, in which it attempts to carve out small local empires, often disguised as political parties. Hence, PPS societies are full of new parties created among parliamentarians, break-out factions and consolidated alliances, an extraordinarily large number of whom have received or will receive training from American or German political foundations.

The idea of *comprador* bourgeoisie originated with dependency theory in Latin America. It connotes a local elite who are both inside and outside at the same time. The *comprador* bourgeoisie is a pliable, effective local elite which not only carries out orders from the centre but whose ultimate allegiance and frame of reference also lies with the centre. Today's *comprador* elites are agents of the Western metropoles in their countries; some may become consultants for or even move to the centre, temporarily leaving their home countries. As I use the term here, the *comprador* bourgeoisie includes all those who work in foreign-dominated private firms or organizations. It includes both local businesspeople and the staff working on aid projects, who are often highly paid professionals with the affiliated cosmopolitan attitudes, consumption patterns and lifestyles. I thus extend the definition to reflect the new environment in PPS Eastern Europe, and especially the Balkans, where much of the legitimate business activity is in fact the aid business. Put another way, the local manager of Coca-Cola and the programme director of the Soros Foundation have so much in common as cosmopolitan, *comprador* elites, often articulating the same modernizing 'mission', that they deserve to be conceptualized as a single category.

The third type of PPS elites are the domestic business leaders. They are the legalized manager–owners of the state-owned companies, banks and import-export companies, as well as the local luminaries whose business largely depends on local patronage. They are the newspaper publishers, celebrities and financial operators who are often involved in scandals and who may flee the country once discovered. It is this class who continue to operate with prominent consumption displays, building ever larger mansions, and who are now starting to retreat from the public world of restaurants and luxury cars to a more private existence in secluded mansion estates, private clubs, or the second home on Cyprus. They are the PPS Berlusconis, who seek a stable domestic political climate for their activities, but who, unlike the *comprador* bourgeoisie, do not see their personal careers tied to global networks. Not surprisingly, some of these domestic businesspeople become candidates for 'law and order' political parties.

Finally, the fourth type of PPS elites are the violent entrepreneurs. They are the mafia chieftains and warlords who are clearly more prevalent in those parts of the former socialist world which have undergone state fragmentation and ethnic conflict: the Caucasus, parts of Central Asia, Eastern Bosnia and the zones within and around Albania and Kosovo. Such groups tend to combine illicit trade, cross-border transit of key resources (people, arms, drugs, contraband, cash) and some kind of nationalist/regionalist political agenda. This is especially visible in cases where the central government is weak, as it allows forms of banditry and guerrilla warfare to overlap with these violent entrepreneurial activities. That this group is not simply transitional is signified by their increasing sophistication and the international importance given to 'combating organized crime' or 'anti-corruption'.[2]

As the PPS societies have shaped up in the wake of state collapse and shock therapy, these four elite groupings have consolidated themselves. This new configuration differs from the potpourri of holdovers or former dissidents that could be observed in the mid-1990s. Many of this initial group have left the scene, some pensioned off, others retreating into local business or failing in business, others returning to the world of culture from whence they came. Those who remain find themselves in a new regime in which their contacts or competencies as former party member are no longer useful, or in which credentials as a former dissident are irrelevant to one's current career possibilities as head of a publishing company or director of a local NGO. Rather, it is this new set of elites – interacting and competing – which signifies the post-transition era.

## PPS elites and global forces

What is most new about these PPS elites is the means by which they can deal with 'global forces'. Behind the metaphors of globalization as 'forces' or 'flows', we tend to forget that cultural practices and representations do not just 'travel': they are pushed, pulled, mediated, refused, bounced back and assimilated. PPS elites confront global forces with group interests and strategic practices; they are not just reactive but proactive. This is what makes them elites.

In the immediate postsocialist period, the different states of the region had different reform trajectories. But as a general tendency, the main result of the immediate transition and the effect of global forces has been to reduce the function of the state by transferring its economic functions to private enterprises and its welfare functions to the market or the emerging civil society. The process came about via reforms from within, demands from Western donors, and the demise (or plunder) of state resources carried out under the guise of privatization. Like states elsewhere, the states in the former Second World are just not that important any more. Upper-level state functionaries, for example, have significantly lower living standards than the four elite groups, since they find it harder to supplement salaries with privileges. Major foreign policy and economic decisions are now out of state hands and carried out by intergovernmental or international institutions. It makes more sense to approach Eastern Europe, and the PPS world generally, in terms of regions or formations each with their particular sets of economic, social and elite characteristics. We may, for example, distinguish those states in the 'first wave' of EU-entering countries from those in the 'second wave' or subsequent waves. The relevant unit of analysis may not be states but rather 'waves'. And the declining political resources from the state available to elites make for changes in their composition and strategic practices, not to mention everyday consumption patterns.

Given the declining function of the state and the role of global forces and pressures, the new elites' practice is concentrated largely in how they can exploit or hinder the way in which global forces operate in the local PPS landscape. Unlike socialist elites, who were provincial, and unlike the postsocialist elites, who were busy consolidating their positions at home by plundering the state or simply trying to cope with the new world, the PPS elites are more sophisticated. They are conscious of their transnational aspects, of being at once both within and without; they may live in a country but are not of it. They may speak the local language but they often act within a completely different code, either cosmopolitan or in terms of illegal international trade. They are conscious mediators for global forces and have become skilled at gatekeeping global resources.

Generally speaking, global forces operate in two ways: they bring about both fragmentation and integration. Fragmentation – along class, ethnic, regional or social lines – tends to occur in areas outside zones of capital accumulation and political decision-making. Downwardly mobile social groups and forgotten regions in the core European countries as well as regions of ethnic tension in the Balkans are prone to such fragmentation. Integration occurs in those zones or among those groups who have been brought into the circles of accumulation and central decision-making. The urban areas of Central Europe are in this zone, as are those areas where there has been considerable Western investment in new enterprises or humanitarian aid. The integrated areas are those where the telephones work, where an internet café is close by, where the roads are well-paved, where young people have not all emigrated.

We find fragmentation and integration processes in the metropole, as well as in the postsocialist and Third Worlds. Fragmentation in the metropole is marked by competing citizen visions of a future, a search for new personal identities, anti-EU, anti-immigrant or anti-globalization movements and increasing regional autonomy. In Western Europe, this tendency reflects the fate of large segments of the former industrial workforce feeling that they have lost control and that their elites do not speak for them. Fragmentation in the former Second World and in the Third World has largely taken the form of ethnic or class polarization, often linked to regional secession movements, and is invariably associated with local corruption as either precipitant cause or result. Polities have become smaller, peripheral areas less controllable, and mafia formations emerge to control border traffic between the more integrated and less integrated border areas and between these areas and the EU. Ethnic conflicts are intermixed with conflicts between central authorities and border-crossing warlord groups, who invariably mobilize ethnic ties. This mixture of economic difference, weak central authority and ethnic border zones creates the foundation for the kind of ethnic discontent, crime and paramilitary banditry we see in the western Balkans along the borders of Albania, Macedonia, Kosovo and Serbia, as well as in the Caucasus.

Fragmentation processes are by no means new to postsocialism or post-postsocialism. Socialist societies were also fragmented, but that fragmentation was long term. There was a clearly demarcated caste-like differentiation between the party elite and the masses. People found culturally creative ways to cope with this situation, in terms of dissidence, informal networks, second economy, retreat into the private sphere, jokes, rumours, etc. (Sampson 1986; Wedel 1986, 1992). Fragmentation in the immediate postsocialist period was marked by unclear lines: the fissures, if you will, had not been formed; the 'us' and 'them' were fluid. Today, in the PPS phase, the fissures are more visible. People know where they stand, and even if they are discontent with their position, they also have a clearer idea of who the 'they' are. 'They' can be corrupt politicians, the local NGO activists and their cosmopolitan ways, the 'foreign rulers' represented by the various offices of the High Commissioner (Bosnia/Kosovo) or IMF officials, or the criminal elements who are corrupting our youth and 'ruining our chances' for integration into Europe.

Fragmentation is itself a metaphor for accelerating social differences and contradictory political practices. Despite the prevalence of this metaphor, societies, we must remember, are not 'wholes' which can be split into pieces. To talk about fragmenting of a social world or a political order is really another way of talking about different types of conflicts, of diverse ways by which people gain access to resources, and of fundamental differences in how people pursue their life projects. Here I would conceptualize fragmentation processes into a further set of metaphors to highlight these differences: 'lift-off', in which elites abandon their societies, seeking instead to affiliate with higher-level centres; 'truncation', in which sections of society simply abandon the national project, seceding or dropping out; 'slicing', in which new social lines of demarcation are formed which cross-cut existing class or ethnic lines; and 'burrowing in', in which elites form a new power base by taking over a certain sphere of political or economic activity (legal or illegal) in the form, say, of corrupt local regimes, illegal entrepreneurship, extreme nationalism or use of paramilitary forces. To say that a society is undergoing fragmentation is to describe these kinds of decentralization processes.

Contrasting with fragmentation, integration is the process by which these kinds of fissures are ameliorated or eliminated, and where people are drawn into ever larger units. Integration in this sense is not necessarily synonymous with centralization; rather, it may be understood as wider adherence to some kind of common behavioural norms, cultural or political project, e.g. transparency in government, human rights, market reform, etc. In this sense, new forms of decentralized/privatized public management are not the same as fragmentation or disintegration. Examples of integration processes include outside efforts to undermine local elites by demanding reforms (or by bringing them to The Hague for trial), attempts at modernizing society from above, rebuilding from below (via civil society), and restructuring from within (institutional development). The metaphor here is of constructing or reconstructing society like a building, an edifice (and in this sense, 'institution building' bears an uncanny resemblance to Stalin's notion of 'building socialism'). The work of integration is not carried out solely at the level of the local society. Integration and development are now directed by international actors who bring their own resources, interests, discourses and projects to bear. In the early 1990s, for example, there was 'shock therapy' and 'market reform' in Central Europe. Today there is 'strengthening state institutions', 'building the rule of law' or 'creating a society of tolerance' in the Balkans.

These international actors cannot pursue their goals without relying on local institutions and actors. This fosters the rise of a new, more professional and pliable political class, as well as a new *comprador* bourgeoisie. The latter are a kind of Euro-elite; they do not formulate the EU integration project, but they certainly carry it out. Seen from the top-down, integration perspective, PPS societies are a landscape for carrying out integration projects. Integration rewards those groups who can establish relations with representatives of Western capital, be it financial, political or cultural. For those groups unable to articulate with the West – the non-computer-literate, non-Anglophone, traditional working/peasant populations in the provinces – the choices seem more limited: wait for the state to provide welfare benefits, affiliate with a local leader's party, or join a band of violent entrepreneurs selling commodities any way they can.

The post-postsocialist societies thus experience a variety of fragmentation and integration processes. These, in turn, are linked to different kinds of elites and different elite practices. In broad terms, integration is carried out with the assent of the political class and with the active support of the *comprador* bourgeoisie, who in the current conjuncture function as cosmopolitan Euro-elites, 'lifting off' from their societies. These Euro-elites compete with some elements of the political class and with the warlords, whose political practices often contribute to fragmentation processes. The domestic business elite and other sections of the political class are under pressure from both integration and fragmentation processes. Shielding themselves from threats to their own power, they seek to 'burrow in' so as to establish their own power bases. The unclear legal system in PPS societies means that distinctions of legality/illegality assume importance only to the foreign actors, but less so on the local 'stage'.

If we view the PPS landscape as stretching from the Baltic states to the post-conflict Balkan areas and across to the clientelistic Central Asian societies and the fragmented, war-torn Caucasus region, we find variations in integration and fragmentation processes, and therefore in the nature of the elite configurations. All four categories are present: the political class, the *comprador* bourgeoisie, the domestic business elites and the various Mafiosi and warlords. Like elites everywhere, the four groups are in competition with each other for followers and personal access to resources. Yet because of the fragmentation processes involved, these elites may also be in complementary, competing, or simply different 'worlds'. Elites can lift off and assume cosmopolitan orientation; they can burrow into the political system and create their own power bases in a truncation process; they can retreat from the public sphere and cultivate privatized, even secretive consumption; and they can proceed to take the criminal route, or trade it off for nationalist politics. Elites are elites precisely because they *can* make choices about their actions or set these processes in motion: they can enter politics, retreat back into culture, commute back and forth between politics and business, from illegitimate to legitimate business, or as businessmen or *comprador* bourgeoisie, they can start their own populist movement.

Elite practices thus reflect *processes* of integration and fragmentation, as well as the corresponding *discourses* about how integration and fragmentation are perceived. Here we have ideas of 'a pathway toward Europe' and of being part of a 'first' or 'second wave', and more pessimistically, discourses of 'being stalled', in stagnation, decline or 'falling behind' in the inevitable comparisons between aspiring countries for EU membership, and discourses of 'betrayal by the West'. Thus, an understanding of integration and fragmentation processes, together with analysis of elite discourses and actual practices, can provide the keys to understanding why the post-postsocialist period is indeed a new era. It is beyond transition.

Study of some of the major master narratives and their associated practices can be used to reveal how these new configurations of elites operate. 'Democracy promotion' is one such master narrative, and includes the export of human rights norms and institutions, rule of law, civil society development, transparency in civil administration, and free elections. Other such master narratives are 'market reform and privatization', 'European integration', 'combating social exclusion', 'promoting security', and, finally, 'anti-corruption and fighting organized crime'.

In the remainder of this chapter, I will describe how these processes of lift-off, truncation, slicing and burrowing in operate in one particular integration process – the promotion of democracy – and within one particular group of elites – the *comprador* bourgeoisie operating as project staff. Democracy promotion, invariably involving the export of Western models, involves efforts to foster rule of law, better governance, civil society organizations, respect for human rights, and public administration reform. While democracy promotion may serve to integrate some aspects of these societies with Western institutions, it also has a fragmentary effect, often pitting elites and their followers against each other. We see the formation of new elites in some cases and the isolation or disappearance of other elites in others. I myself am part of this democracy export field, having participated as an external consultant in various civil society support projects in Albania, Bosnia, Romania and Kosovo (see Sampson 1996). These projects have long become a 'way of life', a routinized system for moving resources, people, money, knowledge and practices between East and West. Since East–West relations are not equal, some of these resources move only in one direction. The Western project of democracy promotion is thus mediated by a host of middlemen operating between the central agency in, say, Brussels, and the target community or group somewhere in eastern Moldova. Project life is a global flow of power, a flow in which various local elites have strategic or mediating roles.

## Project life in the Balkans

The Balkans may be a world of kinship, clan and ethnicity, of peasant families trying to make a living, of folklore, migration and violence; but the Balkans are also a world of projects. By 'project' I mean a special kind of activity: short-term activities with a specific goal and output, a schedule and a budget controlled by donors, their contractors, aimed at a target group and taking account of the various stakeholders involved. Projects always end, evolving into policy, or being replaced by new projects. Project society entails a unique set of structures and activities: the project identification mission, the implementing partner, the project unit, the board, the staff, monitoring and evaluation, and, of course, the magic giver, the Donor. Project life entails a special kind of language, almost like the wooden language of Stalinism. Learning something is called 'training of trainers'. Getting better at something is called 'capacity building'. Giving control to someone else is called 'empowerment'. Articulating the project goal is a 'mission statement'. Communicating information is called 'transparency'. Trying to find out what's going on is called 'networking'. Finding the money is called 'fund raising'. Surviving after the money runs out is called 'sustainability'. Taking your money somewhere else is an 'exit strategy'. And when donors are unable to utilize their money, one gets what a Danish report termed 'donor constipation'.

Project society and project jargon reflect project ideology. This is a linear set of ideas about social engineering, often beginning with a 'problem tree'. From the problem tree, project consultants construct a set of goals, activities, inputs and outputs using techniques such as the Logical Framework Approach. Project life requires understanding the key words or concepts, and specifically which words and concepts can generate money: from 'empowerment' one year, to 'good governance', followed by 'income generation', 'institution building', 'network development', 'anti-corruption', and, of course, the ubiquitous 'part-nership'. As part of the transition, social practices and ideas become grant categories. The notion of 'civil society', for example, is understood as the social organization of people to solve problems. But 'civil society' is also a funding category. Project life is a world with a premium on abstract knowledge, by which power accrues to those best able to manipulate the key symbols and concepts. Since these symbols and concepts come from outside, those *comprador* bourgeoisie attached to foreign project organizations – let us call them 'Euro-elites' – occupy a key role in this scheme, competing with the local political class in terms of political influence with key foreign actors and in terms of living standards. Whether these Euro-elites should be called a 'class' can be debated. They certainly have lifestyles, political views and private aspirations that distin-guish them from many ordinary citizens and groups of elites. Moreover, they have the ability to maximize these. They are a social group with a specific lifestyle marked by an attentiveness to what is new in the West, with an under-standable desire to ensure communication with the donor, and insecurity about what will happen when the donors leave. And donors do leave, though often to be replaced by other donors with different agendas.

This world of projects, now exported to the Balkans, provides benefits for some and provokes others. Like all such worlds, it is based on representations or even myths about our own societies. There is the idea that we can export sectors of our own society – here democratic institutions and civil society – as if they were independent of other aspects of social life (such as effective government, functioning markets, rule of law, a stable middle class). There is the assumption that our *models* actually reflect the *realities* of democracy in our own societies. There is the idea of the single 'international community', which is neither international nor communal. There is the idea that Western NGOs and international organizations cooperate effortlessly with each other and with the state; that professional Western NGOs operate on the basis of voluntarism and altruism; that our activities are actually the result of the kind of strategic thinking characterized by the Logical Framework Approach, rather than by the improvisation that occurs when new grant categories suddenly appear and the proposal is adapted to the donor. There is the idea that the only 'capacities' that need 'building' are those in the target countries, and not our own. And there is the idea that a large number of foreign-funded NGO organizations is some kind of index of democracy. Given such representations, it is hardly surprising that we find disillusionment in the Balkans about Western hypocrisy, or that many citizens view NGO activity not as social commitment but as an alternative enrichment channel for intellectuals who will not do other kinds of work. Such attitudes and the conflicts they generate in turn lead to a disillusionment among donors, who tend to blame the locals for their inability to cooperate or who suddenly contract that well-known disease 'donor fatigue'.

One may envision the structure of project life in two ways: first, as a traffic in resources, people and knowledge, and second, as a set of concentric circles of power. As a flow of traffic, the relationship between donors and recipients in the world of projects is one where some resources go from West to East/South and others go in the opposite direction. From the West comes money, transmitted in complicated 'tranches' and often by circuitous routes in countries where banking systems remain primitive. Along with money comes traffic in people: expatriate consultants, foreign project managers, and short-term evaluators and trainers. These individuals often go from country to country, and much of their job is spent talking with other donors, an activity called 'donor coordination', or negotiating with government officials to start up project units. Government officials, not being donors, are useful for smoothing the administration of the programme, and increasingly as co-partners in applying for EU, World Bank or UNDP funds. Promising officials may then be coopted as project managers, either on government salary or, much more attractively, as local staff of the organization/firm implementing the project.

The West–East traffic in money and experts is partially balanced by a traffic in the reverse direction: promising local project managers are invited to conferences, meetings, internships and training in the West. From Eastern Europe, thousands of NGO activists, journalists and officials have been on shorter or longer trips abroad for training and to see with their own eyes how democracy works. In Denmark, for example, the government-funded Democracy Foundation has spent about $100 million over ten years to bring 70,000 foreign NGO activists, local government officials, parliamentarians, teachers, and social and health workers to Denmark on brief study tours. Other programmes run by Western governments have concentrated on NGO leaders, journalists and government officials. The socialization of local NGO activists into the world of projects proceeds with their acquisition of the discourse of global civil society as they go about attending training courses, meeting donor representatives, applying for money and managing projects.

It would be insufficient to view project life solely as a flow of resources, for this hides the power dimension of the system. Project life is also a system of hierarchical concentric circles. At the centre of the circle are the donor organizations in the West and their funding policies (these policies being generated by knowledge producers who help define 'strategic objectives'). This inner circle generates the most abstract type of knowledge. At the other end, there is concrete, local knowledge of real people with everyday problems. This is where we send out appraisal missions to assess 'needs' and to locate 'target groups', including the most 'vulnerable groups' such as refugee women, unemployed families in closed mining areas, handicapped persons or unschooled Roma children.

Visits and field operators are needed at the periphery to gather key information, locate new target groups or issues, or monitor and evaluate ongoing projects. Kosovo, an international protectorate where more than 300 international organizations are operating, is rife with donors coordinating projects and sounding each other out. In practice, this means an enormous number of meetings and follow-up memoranda, as well as interaction with all categories of PPS elites: with the local political leaders for collaboration, with domestic businessmen for procurement, with promising local project staff who will work on implementation, and with other donors to discuss 'security' against bandits and organized crime.

Viewing projects as a hierarchy of concentric circles helps to highlight the power dimension of global project life. Resources, people and ideas do not simply 'flow'; they are sent, channelled, manipulated, rejected and transformed on their journey eastward by the myriad of middlemen at the source, on the way and in the local context. Local elites compete for control over resources, be they money, people, knowledge or ideas:

> *Control over money* involves who is allowed to apply, who is allowed to spend, and who must do the accounting.
>
> *Control over project personnel* is carried out by the Western consultants and project directors, some of whom fly in, while others are resident. Such control requires the recruitment and management of additional foreign specialists and hiring of local managers and support staff. The Western donor representative 'networks with' various other donors, diplomatic missions and local government officials in order to ensure 'transparency'.
>
> *Control over knowledge* involves deciding whom to tell about what; in the world of projects, knowledge involves deadlines, budget lines, key words on applications, the major conferences being held, and coordinating time schedules with others. At the local level, knowledge control involves

knowing which donor is about to give out funds. Since most Western donor consultants are pressed for time, there is a continual monitoring of the next bid, project or upcoming trip. The hierarchical relations of the project system are best expressed in the way the time of foreign consultants is allocated, and the invariable waiting time for those who want to speak with them. Meetings must be scheduled and rescheduled, with donors and foreign organizations taking precedence over meetings with locals or supplicant NGOs. With more information, the number of meetings increases, which means more rescheduling and more waiting. Logistical problems – local traffic, bad weather, phones that don't work, lost messages, power blackouts, delayed flights, unexpected application deadlines necessitating couriers – create a pressure-cooker atmosphere in which the foreign consultants are constantly moving and the hapless target group is endlessly waiting.

*Control over concepts* is the final type of control in the project system. Project ideas are sent, received and manipulated, and resources are always attached to them. Projects are all about attaching ideas to activity, and activity requires money. It involves an understanding of donors and the identification of a target group and an implementing partner. Establishing such partnerships between a donor and implementing partner organization is not difficult if there already exists a local partner with which to implement a project. This partner might be an established network, an NGO or a government office. The idea might be about, say, establishing crisis centres for battered women, a legal aid office or an anti-corruption bureau. The problem for the donor comes when these potential implementing partners do not exist. In that case, they must be created.

Creating such NGOs or implementing organs may be called 'institutional development', 'capacity building' or, at times, 'cloning'. In some cases, the international donor or NGO simply uses its local secretariat to create a local NGO. Cloning of NGOs ensures a role for the parent organization, facilitates continuity of funding for the newly created local NGO, and solves some of the post-partum sustainability problems after donors go elsewhere.

With the fly-in, fly-out missions, the strange vocabulary and the hunt for funds, one might conclude that project life is simply some kind of façade, a vehicle for opportunists to achieve their private strategies. In cases where projects fail or where there is corruption, this is certainly true: private goals undermine any kind of common activity, organizations cease or fracture, and donors become disillusioned. The presence of thousands of such façade NGOs throughout the PPS world is certainly evidence of this phenomenon. However, we have innumerable cases where projects do make a difference and where significant results have been achieved. The Balkans are filled with successful projects where local NGOs deliver key services which ameliorate the damaging effects of uncontrolled markets or which supplement the government social programmes. Hence, civic education or refugee NGOs help to publicize new laws so that citizens and returnees know their rights; human rights NGOs conduct training of law-enforcement personnel in international human rights provisions. Environmental and health NGOs carry out surveys or hold hearings on specific local problems. Educational NGOs help procure textbooks or lobby for school improvements, while youth and women's NGOs sponsor counselling or provide shelter.

Insofar as local NGOs are supported by foreign donors and their projects, there is a linkage between transnational project society and the creation of new elites. Project society is thus a field in which there is a contestation over scarce resources. People compete for money, influence, access and knowledge; they distribute these resources among their own networks and try to prevent others from obtaining access. The successful actors in this competition become the project elites. These elites are intimately tied to Western ideas and funding, not to mention knowledge of English and the skills known as 'project management'. This Euro-elite is not only paid well, but occupies a special position with close access to the donor community. Most of its members are younger, all are anglophone. As trusted project staff earning at the lower levels of the international scale, they tend to earn more money than most of their neighbours, more than even high government officials. They tend to move from one project to another, to find their friends and spouses within project society, and to have similar aspirations to study in the West and to send their children there. By many criteria, we could define this group as a class. However, this class has no resources of its own: they are wage earners working for foreign projects. Their entire world is externally focused, and for many, the ultimate strategy is emigration or at least intense participation in global civil society networks. In this way a potential national elite goes missing. This is the 'decapitation' process, a lift-off of the elites that seems to go hand in hand with the integration brought about by global forces.

Even if they do not physically emigrate, the livelihood of this group of elites is crucially dependent on continued foreign inputs. This tends to give them a more cosmopolitan orientation and leads to a conflictual relationship with the more locally oriented political class. Ultimately, too much lift-off makes some project elites so isolated from their local situations that they become useless to the Western donors. The typical project staff, familiar to foreign consultants, donors or anthropologists working in the NGO sector, tend to be overqualified for some aspects of the job, underutilized in others. By virtue of their positions and access, they are often overburdened by working on several projects or having to help friends and colleagues obtain employment. All are well acquainted with members of the political class, but unlike such individuals in Western Europe, who see politics as a possible career move, these local project elites are trying to maintain their niche.

To understand the pressures under which these elites operate, it may help if I describe one particular slice of project society in which conflicts are especially transparent. Romania, Bulgaria, Albania and Kosovo all have civil society development projects in which a local foundation is created, which then, as a donor, awards grants and training to local NGOs. The funds for these foundations come from a foreign donor such as the USAID, the EU, individual European governments, or from private foundations. These civil society foundations establish a board and a staff which take applications from local NGOs, provide training in how to run organizations, distribute information about the sector to the public and potential donors, decide strategic priorities for civil society development, and monitor the evolution of the NGO sector generally. The foreign consultants' task (in which I participated) is to help in the legal establishment of these foundations, coordinate their activities with the work of other donors, locate and train competent board members who have experience and vision for civil society, advise the board on future strategy and activity, and recruit and train the staff. In all these countries, the foundations have been evaluated positively by several independent evaluators and have obtained respect from many international donor organizations. One explanation for their positive reception is clearly their empowerment aspect: instead of supplicants for funds, which is the position of most local NGOs, this project actually creates donors. As is the case with all donors (even governments), they have responsibilities to *their* donors, to be sure, but they are donors nevertheless.

Although locally established, the heads of these civil society foundations also attend donor meetings together with other foreign donors assisting the NGO sector. As donors and as recipients, they straddle both worlds, reaping both the benefits and the accompanying pressures that this entails. These projects therefore create a specific type of local elite. The elite consist of the local board members who achieve respect and power, and the project staff who obtain good salaries and a special status. The board members and staff of these foundations are respected by foreign donors for their 'competence' and 'professionalism', but they are an object of attention or jealousy by the locals by virtue of their access to foreign resources (money, knowledge, contacts). The conflicts faced by these local elites are articulated as conflicts of loyalty. They must balance the loyalty to the foundation and principles of sound project management with the loyalties to friends and family who desire their resources. Hence, local project managers have talked of cases where one of their friends or colleagues has solicited a job, or applied for a project, where they were nevertheless unable to assist them on meritocratic grounds and accused of disloyalty. Since so many project management procedures are complicated to the outsider or based on abstract judgements, this leads to accusations of favouritism. Why did X receive funds to go to his conference but not Y? Why did A's NGO receive project support money but not B's? Since so much of project life is indeed abstract, the role of elites is to turn abstract concepts into concrete decisions, to channel resources. This channelling represents a combination of abstract decisions (based on principles) and concrete knowledge (whereby the board members know the applicant personally).

It might be thought that a successful project is one where the local project elite subordinates these private obligations to the needs of the project organization. In fact, exaggerated elite loyalty to the organization is more likely to result in lift-off in which the local elite becomes so cosmopolitan so as to become alienated from the local community. Such individuals eventually become the object of derision in the local communities, ultimately losing the local knowledge and contacts for which donors had sought them out in the first place. The elites who are most loyal to their foreign patrons are not necessarily the most capable. It is not because people have *subordinated* their personal goals to the project that makes for successful outcomes, but rather that these project and personal strategies have been skilfully *combined*. Project staff, for example, achieve good incomes, high status and connections to valued Western donors. These can be used to recommend good friends for jobs when a Western donor sets up shop. The question for donors is not whether informal contacts are used, but whether the recommended friend is in fact qualified. Being an elite in the Balkans, as elsewhere, is about who can make recommendations for whom.

This process of utilizing one's position to achieve both organizational goals and private obligations is not without its conflicts. In one project, the project director recommended a very good friend as information officer, someone who came from a well-known intellectual and dissident family. It turned out that the friend, despite his talents, had a drinking problem and was mentally unstable, and had to be discharged; in another case, a friend hired to do accounting started to embezzle small amounts from the travel fund and was promptly fired by his colleague. And in yet another, a board member of a local foundation thought that he was qualified enough to borrow money from the project fund, for which he was asked to resign. Project society, then, is not just about maximizing the ability to exploit project resources to maximize personal goals. It is also about the creation of new loyalties; loyalties to the organization, to 'the project', to abstract meritocratic principles such as 'transparency', which the elites must balance with their social and personal obligations. A typical case was the NGO project director in Kosovo who had to choose between going to the funeral of an uncle and meeting an important donor in Geneva. The individual chose Geneva, incurring the disappointment of family and personal guilt feelings.

Understanding the role of elites necessitates understanding new transnational hierarchies and new combinations of powers and obligations. The pattern varies for the different groups. For the political class, the new obligations are to the European institutions imposing demands on the regime for integration. For the domestic businessmen, there are new obligations to local politicians and perhaps export partners. For the mafia chieftains and warlords, there are similar new obligations among international collaborators or corrupt politicians. Finally, among the *comprador* bourgeoisie and the Euro-elites, as I have shown, we find new obligations to donors and to the project. Being an elite is therefore inherently a middleman situation. The four categories of elites can maximize their private projects and reduce the conflicts by horizontal contacts within or across elite categories. The formation of an ever-increasing number of private elite clubs is one indication that such processes are working. Yet this also creates an even wider set of social obligations. Accusations of corruption, essentially illegitimate flows of resources between elites, are an example of what happens when such obligations get out of hand.

## Project society, elites and the PPS state

This account of project society in PPS societies might at first appear to be a typical case of globalization undermining the state. The tensions between state officials and the NGO sector are illustrative. The intimate relations between NGOs and Western donors are an object of jealousy in some of the poorly paid, poorly equipped government offices. Ministers and state functionaries complain that 'there are too many NGOs', that 'they' are getting money intended for 'us' (the government). Isolated cases of NGO overspending, abuse of funds or inefficiency are used to smear the entire sector. Government officials complain that NGOs tend to have better office equipment than government offices, while salaries for NGO staff tend to exceed those of even the highest officials in local or central government.

Jealous of the resources flowing into the NGO sector, some state officials devise strategies to tap into project resources, ranging from cooptation to sabotage. The most widespread method is for state organs to clone their own NGOs, called GOs and quasi-NGOs or QUANGOs.[3] Throughout Eastern Europe it is common to find independent organizations competing with government-sponsored youth, sport, environment and women's groups, some of which may be politically affiliated. In socialist times, such organizations would have been called 'fronts'. 'Promoting civil society' and 'supporting human rights' are now means by which non-Western countries can procure Western aid. Invariably, much of the money goes informally to the government officials who sit on the boards of these foundations, while other funds are diverted into foreign trips or political campaigns. In this way, international funds inadvertently help to build a local political class, while the scandals about 'NGO mafia' or 'Soros mafia' launched by jealous competitors undermine the credibility of the *comprador* bourgeoisie among the public.

A second strategy by which state actors attempt to tap into the resources of project society is for government officials to sit on the boards of various NGOs as an indication of state–civil society 'partnership'. This practice is hardly objectionable in itself, since public officials may be genuinely interested in the project and can become a lobby for the organization's mission within the government. For example, an NGO helping handicapped youth can benefit from having a board member who works in the Ministry of Health. More often, however, state officials' participation in the NGO sector serves to provide government with knowledge about donor priorities and the means by which to channel eventual donor funds away from civil society organizations and directly to government itself. Throughout Eastern Europe, one is therefore witness to the emergence of government offices for 'civil society partnership' or 'NGO coordination'. These offices or secretariats are now the object of intense donor interest.[4]

Finally, governments may actively seek to undermine the activities of NGOs by imposing barriers to NGO cooperation with foreign donors, limiting financial independence of NGOs or other kinds of legal, fiscal or informal harassment. Some social assistance and humanitarian aid organizations can operate unhindered, since they are viewed as a supplement to state activities. Other NGOs, particularly in human rights, law, media, environment and anti-corruption, may be regarded as adversaries of state agencies, who see them as part of the political opposition. This conflict is exacerbated as NGOs become more influential in their lobbying and 'advocacy' activities, in effect becoming political, though not party-political.

Project society, a set of practices with its associated sets of resources, social groups and ideological constructs, is thus both a threat and a resource for states. One may even differentiate between 'weak' and 'strong' states in terms of their ability to adapt to or coopt project society. Strong states have strong but well-demarcated NGO sectors; there are many interest organizations, and policy-makers find themselves compelled or at least willing to listen to them. Weak states tend either to be actively opposed to project society, or they try overtly to subvert it by the creation of quasi-NGOs and amorphous partnership arrangements with vague responsibility. With unclear boundaries, state and project society have a tendency to undermine each other. Instead of partnership there is conflict, lack of accountability, and tensions between the various elite groups. The push by the West to promote democracy and civil society creates new groups (the NGO staff elites) and fosters competition between them and the political class.

## Conclusion

From the transnational arms smugglers caught on the mountain road between Kosovo and Macedonia, to the cosmopolitan NGO elites zipping off to Geneva, we can see that the elite configurations in the PPS world exhibit a range of variations. This chapter has argued that post-1989 societies have undergone a fundamental transformation. New periods are marked by the emergence of new social groupings with new projects of their own, and this demands a new kind of anthropological understanding of elite worlds. The Euro-elites tied to foreign projects are one example of the kind of new elites that now exist in this post-postsocialist era. Global processes of integration and fragmentation will ensure that they will remain with us for a long time to come. Such groups exemplify the social forces which on the one hand integrate the new societies into larger Western projects, but which on the other hand fragment these societies by 'decapitating' them of promising elites drawn up into cosmopolitan lifestyles and by stimulating competition among elite groups. This competition becomes especially acute because PPS elites are both power wielders and subordinate to the power of others higher up in the global system.

The Euro-elites of project society can be considered part of an emerging *bourgeoisie* of *comprador* type. As part of an international political class, they compete with the local political class in state administration, the domestic business elite and the warlords/Mafiosi. As rival elite groups, some go local, others go transnational. The domestic business elite competes for local influence with the political class, while local warlords/Mafiosi cooperate in both local and transnational networks. A full mapping of local elite formations would thus provide us with valuable insights into post-postsocialism.

It is not enough to describe PPS by invoking the rhetoric of 'global forces' or asserting that the state is being 'weakened'. These forces must be understood in terms of the concrete practices which contribute to elite 'lift-off' from society, or other processes which may have a fragmentary or integrative character. Weak states weaken old elites, but they also create new ones. The new PPS elites are embedded in new hierarchies of subordination. Focusing on these groups can help us understand how and why the transition has been concluded, and why the PPS era is likely to be more resilient, and its elites more tenacious, than most commentators have so far realized.

## Acknowledgements

I wish to thank the participants at the Halle conference and especially Barbara Cellarius and Chris Hann for constructive comments and criticisms of earlier versions of this paper.

## Notes

1   See Sampson 1994a; Verdery 1996; see also innumerable issues of *Anthropology of East European Review* and the *Anthropological Journal on European Cultures*.
2   A typical example reported in May 2001 indicates the extent of these activities and their transnational character:

> NATO Seizes Weapons in Kosova
>
> Italian KFOR troops arrested seven people and seized 'a large truck full of weapons' near Peja on 10 May, AP reported. KFOR Spokesman Roy Brown said in Prishtina the next day: 'This is one of the biggest seizures in the time we have been here.' He added that the haul included '52 rocket launchers, a couple of dozen antitank weapons, five antiaircraft SAM 7 missiles, [an unspecified quantity of] mortars, an 82 millimeter cannon, various rifles and a significant quantity of ammunition.' The truck had Bosnian license plates.
>
> (*RFE/RL Newsline*, 16 May 2001)

3   This term was popularized in Thatcher's Britain in the context of privatization.
4   Curiously, no such offices exist in Western Europe where the association sector is too large and too diverse to be the object of any kind of coordination beyond very specific sectors like 'women', 'youth', 'development' or 'environment'.

## References

Hann, C.M. (1994) 'After Communism: reflections on East European anthropology and the transition', *Social Anthropology* 2: 229–49.

Sampson, Steven (1986) 'The informal sector in Eastern Europe', *Telos* 66: 44–66.

——(1994a) 'Money without culture, culture without money: Eastern Europe's nouveaux riches', *Anthropological Journal of European Cultures* 3: 72–99.

——(1994b) 'All is possible, nothing is certain: horizons of transition in a Romanian village', in D. Kideckel (ed.) *East European Communities: the Struggle for Balance in Turbulent Times*, Boulder: Westview, pp. 159–78.

——(1996) 'The social life of projects: exporting civil society to Albania', in Elizabeth Dunn and Chris Hann (eds) *Civil Society: Challenging Western Models*, London: Routledge.

Stark, David (1992) 'Privatization in Hungary: from plan to market or from plan to clan', *East European Politics and Societies* 4: 351–92

Verdery, Katherine (1996) *What Was Socialism and What Comes Next?*, Princeton: Princeton University Press.

Wedel, Janine (1986) *The Private Poland. An Anthropologist's Look at Everyday Life*, New York: Facts on File.

—— (ed.) (1992) *The Unplanned Society: Poland during and after Communism*, New York: Columbia University.

# Chapter 16

# Afterword

## Globalism and postsocialist prospects

*Don Kalb*

> In an age when all life depends on a lumpy, indivisible infrastructure, the strategies of political collectivities are more vital than the economic decisions of individuals.
>
> (Ernest Gellner 1993: xiii)

## Introduction

Valeru Galit is a police detective in Chisinau, Moldavia. In 2000 he traced a network of kidney-dealers who brought some hundred young Moldavians, mainly young men in their twenties, to Istanbul where, in a defunct textile factory that had been converted into a clinic, they were deprived of one kidney. Their kidneys were implanted in children flown in from the West, whose kidneys did not function well and whose parents were wealthy enough to circumvent the waiting lists of European public hospitals and pay $15,000 to save their children's lives. The young Moldavian boys received $3,000 in cash, the equivalent of more than ten years' back-breaking work in local agriculture. Some weeks prior to the Moldavian elections, in which the ex-communists won a majority of seats in the parliament, Galit tells the journalist of the Dutch daily which published this story: 'Our babies are sold to Western parents, our girls work in your brothels, our boys sell their kidneys. That is the free market. We are meat' (*NRC Handelsblad*, 9 April 2001). The same newspaper reports a survey in Russia in which 20 per cent of adult female respondents stated that they would seriously consider offering their bodies for commercial sex services if they were asked to do so.

The current wave of globalization has three overwhelming properties. First, it erodes the cohesion and coherence of national states, except a few core ones; second, it is characterized by sharply increasing levels of inequality and disparities of power between the cores and the peripheries, between national states but also within each of them; and third, it generally comes to receiving territories in a highly uneven bundle of components (capital, goods, information and people). Whatever this means precisely for any particular location, national hierarchies are replaced by imaginary global ones, and illusions travel faster and further than the supportive hardware that alone can transform them into empowering realities. With public goods in systematic undersupply, individual ambitions become the illusions of which collective delusions are made.[1] The goose-flesh producing power of the Moldavian anecdote lies in its reminder that institutional entropy combined with drastic reductions in the provision of public goods degrades would-be citizens into defenceless victims.

## Portable civil society

Apart from the further evaporation of communist parties and socialist party-states, what possible futures for postsocialist societies could we realistically have expected in 1989 and 1992? In retrospect we know that 'civil society', under conditions of global monetarism, would not enhance the active social participation of former socialist worker-subjects, as was proclaimed. On the contrary, while the new social forms brought great advantages for the well educated (above all those who were between 30 and 40 years old in the early 1990s) and for existing elites, they have disinherited the poor, the unskilled, women, children, minorities and all those whose lives happened to be situated in the periphery rather than the new postsocialist hubs of the emerging global system.[2] Current discussions about the relative 'shallowness' of poverty (e.g. Milanovic 1996) in postsocialist nations as compared to other middle-income countries, or about local poverty lines in Central and Eastern Europe being inflated by an older socialist moral economy, are beside the point. The delusion is primarily about power, social relationships and the redistribution of risks, resources and opportunities implied by the particular direction of social change taken by post-socialist countries, presided over by a close alliance of local elites and transnational actors.

Civil society was the rallying cry of the East European 'refolutions'.[3] It is still the only ideological legacy that this late twentieth-century prime time of nations, the so-called Third Wave of democratization, has conferred upon us. Through ever more active transnational institutions and consultancy channels, it has been systematically implanted in all postsocialist countries, including those new nations that had not developed it on their own. The idea was not new, and it was entirely Western in origin. Many of the emergent political and intellectual elites in the 1990s, not just in Eastern Europe but globally, have been in thrall to this idea.[4] Civil society, an enlightenment notion derived from Immanuel Kant and Alexis de Tocqueville, was a crucial symbolic tool for inverting global post-World War II scepticism concerning the propertied bourgeoisie into a positive nostalgia for its supposed economic independence and enlightened cultural and moral role. 'Civil society's' gradual rise in the 1980s expressed the fatigue of socialist and social democratic imaginations after the various postwar 'modernism in one country' projects had petered out. The fall of the Berlin Wall in 1989 gave an enormous boost to new transnational coalitions, linking East European to other Eurasian elites. This idea helped to shape the entire institutional design of postsocialist countries, from the new constitutions to the privatized economy and frameworks of social policy (Elster *et al.* 1998; Kalb and Kovács, forthcoming). Indeed, it has helped to guide the liberation of a significant part of humanity from humiliating authoritarian regimes that had fallen prey to self-doubt. Who would not applaud that?

Yet the application of an overtly Western definition of civil society, as prescribed medicine and ultimate destiny, on postsocialist landscapes has subsequently led to an unmistakably heightened level of incivility. Civil society, indeed, was the battle cry and self-understanding of the rising urban bourgeoisie *vis-à-vis* autocratic rulers in eighteenth- and nineteenth-century Europe. The condition of late twentieth-century postsocialist citizens, with the possible exception of the intelligentsia, hardly resembled the situation of the historical European urban bourgeoisie. Blue-collar factory workers in mono-industrial peripheral regions, single mothers in provincial towns or ex-collective farm workers can hardly be compared with the classical burgher family in Koenigsberg after Napoleon's invasion, so it is little wonder that the experiment did not turn out entirely well for everybody. Nor did huge geographic tracts on the Eurasian plains enmeshed in centrally administered continental divisions of labour resemble the social constitution of dense urban networks in West and Central Europe, with their long-established practices of local rule and civic autonomy.[5] Civil society in Siberia and Central Asia could only become an item for luxury consumption. It has enabled local networks of well-educated citizens in the main urban centres to form NGOs and do 'good work', e.g. in the professionalization of social policy or economic consultancy, even helping the state to open up for civic engagement and expand democratic competence. But among the rural population, amid small town industrial workers, the less-educated, women and children, it has done much less than it has promised. It has consciously taken away some of the tools and public goods previously taken for granted, as the basis for life projects. It has also done much less than governing elites and global institutions have been willing to concede: while the powerful were gathering for a celebratory banquet, the civil society programmes have stolen the weapons of the weak.[6]

The saddest instance of this immense social divide that I have encountered is the person of Adam Michnik, who in a speech commemorating the fall of the Wall contrasted his own post-Round Table experiences as a successful newspaper publisher and global civil society intellectual with the current misery of industrial workers in Poland.[7] He explained the impoverishment of those rank and file participants in the social movement that made his own victory possible by arguing that they had only been trained to manufacture statues of V.I. Lenin, which nobody wanted to buy any more after 1989. A metaphor, of course, but an intensely humiliating metaphor, and one that retrospectively represses any alternative path out of the economic impasse of the late-socialist 1980s by radically disqualifying the capacities of labour for the new capitalist economy and civil society. Sadly, Michnik is here providing an example of Edward Thompson's (1963) 'enormous condescension of posterity'.

Even within its more specific field of enhancing civic participation and self-responsibility of citizens, the record of civil society is meagre. As Mandel and Sampson show in the preceding chapters (see also Wedel 1999) civil society and the transnational philanthropic and political networks in which it has become enmeshed have often led to a brain-drain of highly qualified personnel, the formation of a 'comprador bourgeoisie', parallel policy structures, the foreign-imposed strengthening of one cluster of political actors over another, not to mention outright corruption. It has not mitigated the general vengeful defamation of blue-collar labour in postsocialist countries (Kideckel, this volume).[8] In the countryside it has been utterly unable to substitute for the destruction of social networks, social capital and hope among village inhabitants after liberalization and privatization (Creed, Giordano and Kostova, this volume). Bulgaria between 1995 and 2000 'lost' an alarming 10 per cent of its population, including perhaps 50 per cent of the better educated among the cohorts between 20 and 40 years old.[9] So much for active participation: the various modes of 'exit' have thoroughly prevailed over 'voice' (see Greskovits 1998, following Hirschman).

Was it a question of the unjustified application of a Western concept on non-Western populations and regions, as Hann suggests? Closer inspection of its record and social function in Central and Eastern Europe has shown that its revitalization in the 1980s was not an arbitrary imposition by the West, but that it had strong local roots, at least in Central Europe. At the same time, it was clear to most observers that civil society as a notion in central European discourse was wedded even more firmly to monetarism than was the case in the West (Szacki 1995). The East European refolutions were perceived as alliances of markets and civil societies against the state. Civil society in the 1990s became ever more associated with capacities to internalize and adapt to market pressures, as an index of self-responsibility. Markets were consciously imposed by local elites on subject populations as a way to teach them 'civilization', to help them unlearn the corrupted ways of socialism, to 'turn fish-soup into an aquarium', in Lech Wałęsa's phrase and above all to reaffirm the virtues of private property rights. Why did the new postsocialist elites put so much emphasis on property rights?[10] Has the twentieth century not shown that the greatest economic gains depended on the creation of oligopoly, integrated and synchronized hierarchies, and public policy to prevent bottlenecks and dilemmas of collective action? As Gil Eyal has suggested (2000), the reason for stressing private property was almost eschatological. It was about moral purification and post-hoc punishment as much as about efficiency. In a workshop in Vienna I once heard Leszek Balcerowicz, Polish Minister of Finance, argue that 'states cannot but crowd-out conscience'.[11] This collapse of civil society themes into monetarist vocabulary shows that the idea was not just imposed by the

West: some 'natives' talked back loudly and received a lot of applause for doing so.

Local elites evidently preferred to listen to monetarists and property rights advocates, but might more interest on the part of global policy-makers and global policy intellectuals for the findings of anthropologists and area-specialists have helped to attune the civil society programme to the peculiarities of the peoples concerned? The answer is crucial for the future of both anthropology and public policy, and lies hidden in the ambitious list of programmatic tasks for anthropologists of postsocialism that Katherine Verdery develops (this volume). My own short version is this: the fall of the Berlin Wall in the name of civil society has given ruling monetarists in the West, trained on combating stagflation and social democracy since the mid-1970s, a chance to develop a new hegemonic Grand Narrative for world history, the narrative of globalism (Kalb 2000). The melting away of opposing global forces and hard territorial boundaries after the Cold War has fostered a triumphant neo-liberalism as the single source for any agenda for social change and development, now vacuously dubbed as 'reform'. This agenda trumpets the triplet of liberalization, stabilization and privatization, and sells this policy package in the name of civil society and development (the 'Washington consensus').[12] Area studies and anthropology, as the messengers of social and cultural complexity and the preachers of respect for difference, have suffered hugely from this monetarist programme for post-national hegemony. No one wants to hear cumbersome, particularistic warnings when others promise unrestrained cognitive and instrumental access to landscapes and people everywhere in the world, a portable toolkit for elite intervention which reduces all relevant forces to just a few factors, largely independent of history and place. The new mantra asserts that the interrelationships and causalities between these factors have a universal sequence, as long as they are not perturbed by the dark forces of local history and culture.

Although several variants can be discovered depending on where we look, the five crucial propositions of the globalist grand narrative are as follows: (1) if commodities are freely exchanged between places and groups, (2) people would learn individual self-interest and abandon their collective passions, (3) which would help them form into civic communities of independent middle-class citizens, (4) who would demand further civil rights from their states and vote against inefficiencies, (5) which would facilitate more trade, prosperity, freedom and growth. Hegemonic globalism, in short, has substituted for the complexities of ethnography a simple self-reinforcing spiral of historical causation and moral teleology from markets to individualism to civil society to democracy to prosperity. This programme is believed to be an accurate representation of the history of the West and an explanation of its global supremacy. Globalism is monetarism writ large, wedded to a narrow notion of civil society of which Central and Eastern Europe was both sender and recipient. Why bother to read anthropology if cultural peculiarities are there to be erased rather than respected, and if there is a portable toolkit available for doing so?

## Vision and method in the anthropology of postsocialism

Anthropologists of postsocialism have found that their subject matter has been even more directly exposed to the forces and paradoxes of this global programme than other regions of the world, while being even less prepared. This is why the anthropology of postsocialism is so rich and has so much to offer in building up a new global and comparative anthropology. The central concepts of this volume (trust, social capital, civil society, etc.) have no long anthropological pedigree. Anthropologists of postsocialism have had to learn to interrogate the critical 'concrete abstractions' that global institutions, global consultants, spin doctors and local elites have placed on the agenda, while closely studying their non-abstracted consequences on the ground. Thus social capital becomes a tool to explain success after privatization (Lampland), the dynamics of Gypsy networks become an invitation to structurize the assumptions of the notion of underclass (Stewart), the cultural revolution becomes important for understanding the resurgence of popular religion in postsocialist China (Feuchtwang), and the topic of Balkan churches leads into an exploration of democracy and the role of the international community (Hayden). In these and other ways anthropologists of postsocialism are learning to talk to global and local policy-makers as well as concerned academic publics. This, it seems to me, is certainly the way anthropologists have to go in the context of the new portable global engineering. More generally, 'area studies' must transform its preoccupation with 'culture-internal' logics of social and personal life and turn its ethnographic eye to the interaction of local and global histories. This is never just a meeting of cultural billiard-balls, but always intricately structured socially and intensely experienced personally.

This leads me to suggest that anthropologists of postsocialism must become even more ambitious, and Verdery's visions of a post-cold war anthropology point the way. The idea of an anthropology of postsocialism is still defensive and retrospective. It suggests that transformation outcomes cannot be directly explained by transition programmes but have unintended outcomes shaped by prior (socialist) conditions, expectations and divisions of assets. This is what I call 'a retrospective cultural area argument'. The political message says: caution, history is present here. Societies are just as much defined by what they were as by what current elites dream they can turn them into. This is a salutary move in response to those neo-liberal economists who imagine that pasts can simply be sent into oblivion by a determined and well-dosed shock-therapy. One methodological catchword here has been path-dependency.[13] The anthropology of postsocialism in this respect joins an ever more important critical countercurrent among institutional and evolutionary economists and historical sociologists who argue for the path-dependence of all transformation outcomes (see Lampland, this volume). Institutional economists, for example, have claimed that the global package of rapid liberalization, stabilization and privatization tends to destroy the capacity of existing institutions to gather information and hinders informed adaptation to change (North 1997; Poznański 1996; Stiglitz 1995, 2000). The transitional crises in postsocialist countries, they contend, were therefore unnecessarily painful, deep and long, and partly (Russia, Ukraine) simply misguided. They argue that this has severely mortgaged future outcomes by devaluing the stock of productive capital, depleting private reserves and demoralizing the public. China, for them, with gradualism reigning, is a more positive case. Here institutional capacities remain intact, economic growth sustains its upward curve and incomes rise more impressively than even the most successful showcases of transition in Central Europe.[14]

Anthropologists of postsocialism take the notion of path-dependency a crucial step further, showing that praxis is necessarily over-determined by the 'unfolding uncertainties of macro-institutions' (Burawoy and Verdery 1999: 7) and their multiple consequences for everyday life. Path-dependent causation, thus, is not just retrospective. Prior conditions, expectations and earlier divisions of assets shape tools for improvisation in contemporary daily practice, in the here and now of an unmapped and insecure terrain that joins pasts with possible futures. This is the strength of ethnography. It can show how everyday practices and social relationships are embedded in the peculiarities of local paths of social change, and in trajectories of possible becomings. Uncertainty is an overriding fact under conditions of global monetarism in all but the core capitalist societies, and it can lead actors to resist the very forces of marketization and state-formation/state-retrenchment that their elites want them to embrace. As Karl Polanyi predicted, the fate of households cannot be entirely entrusted to markets; effective agriculture, for instance, depends more on social and public organization than it does on private property, as Giordano/ Kostova and Lampland emphasize. Compared to more formal institutionalists, then, anthropologists, by offering a close-up view on the capricious micro foundations for action in postsocialism, can offer a realist view of dynamic path-dependencies. Dynamic path-dependency helps to explain how and why memories, knowledge and networks from the past are reconfigured in the present to serve as tools for survival or advantage in situated social practices under new conditions. It thus helps us to understand why so many people in postsocialist countries have not become transition enthusiasts and have instead, by intense trial and error, worked out their own deeply ambivalent strategies and self-understandings. The work in this volume provides excellent illustrations.

However, dynamic path-dependency methods have been unduly restricted to paths in time, to the analytical neglect of paths through space. A more ambitious framework for an anthropology that wants to command public attention is one in which paths through time are systematically linked with 'junctions' in space: that is, with a systematic study of the spatial inter-linkages and social relationships that define territories and communities. This is a call for studying upward and outward, to set intensely local experiences and local outcomes in their wider contexts of commonalties and divergences. These outcomes derive from path-dependencies, but also from the often perverse logics of determinate linkages. What we have called path-dependency would be better seen as a series of 'punctuations' delivered by the wider networks of coercion and exchange in which territories and communities are embedded. The work of Eric Wolf is the outstanding example of this method in anthropology, and his notion of hidden histories captures the interplay between local and global histories as they produce both 'universalizing' and 'localizing' and differentiating outcomes.[15] Part of the strength of the anthropology of postsocialism is that from the very start its subject matter has forced us to take such spatial linkages into account, whether we are studying withdrawal into the household by women in Poland (Pine) or, at the opposite end of the landmass, consumption in the Pearl River Delta (Latham). But has the mapping of the spatial webs been systematic or analytic enough? Has their interrogation through more localized relationships been pertinent? Have we left the anthropological fallacy of localized causation behind? Has fieldwork been adequately combined with methods from research journalism, policy analysis, archival and library research? This is how I would supplement Verdery's call for a post-Cold War anthropology in methodological terms. She employs this notion first to critique the strong 'othering' tendency in Western culture in general and anthropology in particular, which is an important objection. Then she makes a seminal move by saying that in fact the Cold War is not over at all. What the West is prescribing as medicine and destiny for other parts of the world is a wholesale transfer of Western institutions. In other words, the Cold War has shifted gear, has left the obsession with borders and demarcation lines behind and is now engaged in a more sophisticated work of institutional re-engineering. Indeed, this is what the grand narrative of globalism, as well as its subsection on transition, is supposed to facilitate. It is not only about capital flows, even though their acceleration over the last decade may well have driven the process. Nor is it only about the diffusion of Western cultural imagery. It is, as Susan Strange (1996) and Saskia Sassen (2000) have argued, also very much about the diffusion of institutions and administrative standards to crisis-ridden places that are predisposed to buy into the elusive prospects offered by the West.

Anthropology has to take this momentous and manifold process seriously. With its grounded knowledge of places and actors, this discipline is equipped to start the systematic study of how territories and local actors, depending on their specific modes of linkage with the global arena, perceive, link up with, and respond to these pressures. This requires 'encompassing' comparison (Tilly 1984: 125–44) within one broad programme of multiple cases, not just within postsocialism but world-wide: reflecting, subverting and, perhaps, reshaping the globalist programme.

## Tracking phase two

There is firm evidence that we are entering a new phase. After a full decade of post-Wall globalism, uncertainty and even open disagreements about the role of the IMF, the World Bank and the EBRD suggest that the global regime consensus is eroding, even though no alternative can as yet be envisioned (Wade and Veneroso 1998; Wade 2001). This is not necessarily to be welcomed: a coherent global regime seems more necessary than ever. But anthropology may stand to gain as 'economism' loses prestige. The civil society programmes sponsored by the global institutions may at last become 'broadened, relativized and adapted to local conditions', as Hann demands. If anthropologists succeed in linking their local insights to research strategies that explore the critical junctions that connect local process to intensifying institutional dilemmas on higher levels, then they will command more public interest than they have managed up to now.

Phase two is likely to be marked by deep disagreements about the actual public and territorial policy frameworks of transnational markets (Arrighi 1994; Brenner 1998; Gowan 1999; Kalb et al. 2000; Sassen 2000). The cores of capital accumulation of the US, Japan and the EU, poised in stepped-up competition as well as mutual interdependence, have an objective interest in organizing wider spaces for the operation of their capital and labour markets. Capital export from these territorial containers of wealth and power, in the form of foreign direct investment, portfolio investment and currency speculation, has accelerated enormously over the last two decades, as has investment in technology and mergers. But the ostensibly global framework of multilateral institutions that has enabled them to do so has been crucially shaped by the 'Dollar–Wall Street regime' (Gowan 1999). This has made much of the world economy de facto dependent on the dollar, the FED and the recycling operations of the New York stock exchange. We have been witnessing the formation of a new US-based 'world empire', but this has been partially countered by the expansion of the EU and the extension of Japanese networks and policy initiatives into the East Asian mainland. The 'two systems, one country' policy of China and the incorporation of the Chinese capitalist diaspora into the dynamics of the mainland have been further important countercurrents. What seems beyond doubt is that regional frameworks for expanded capital accumulation and social development are usurping some of the facilitating functions of the global infrastructure, and that disputes over the form and content of these regional systems are intensifying. The future of postsocialist countries will very largely depend on the outcomes of these conflicts.

Take, for example, the expansion of the EU: what will happen to the landscapes of eastern Poland, Slovakia and Hungary when funds for the EU's Common Agricultural Policy are severely reduced? Looking a little further ahead, what will happen in the Romanian periphery if Poland is only willing to accept Romania's accession to the EU on the condition that the Poles can continue to claim their 'fair share' of EU means? For how many years will local inhabitants be prevented from seeking work in the old EU? Where will the new borders be drawn, and for how long? Conflicts of interest and contrasting visions of development also characterize the EBRD (Andor and Summers 1998). Under the current French leadership of the bank, earlier French foreign policy plans for Eastern Europe have been revived, but the US representatives, the biggest stakeholders in the bank, are opposed. Whether or not the bank will in the near future invest in anti-poverty programmes, health policies and urban infrastructures, as suggested by French Prime Minister Laurent Fabius, will make a huge difference to East European populations.[16]

Ultimately, at stake here is the issue whether markets and 'openness' are capable of bringing about 'civil society'. Are markets sufficient for creating the broadly spread welfare without which civil society must remain a phantom? The experiment of US-led globalist transition was predicated on the assumption that transnational capital flows are the primary engine of growth and development. By now we have learned that this is an overstatement of what transnational markets can actually do, more a gigantic cargo cult than a well-founded insight. Transnational capital has not moved to Eastern Europe on the scale expected, and local landscapes have been transformed only in narrow zones close to the present EU border. The manufacturing corridor along the highway between Vienna and Budapest remains the largest, and Hungary, by virtue of its early opening to the West, has remained by far the biggest recipient of such flows (on a *per capita* basis). Even here, investment in manufacturing had largely dried up by 2000. New flows in the banking, insurance and telecom sectors are bringing jobs and incomes for well-educated young people in the capital cities, but they will not be sufficient to sustain economic growth rates if, as seems to be happening, growth declines in the West.[17]

Far from large-scale capital transfer leading to an export-led industrial renaissance, the actual experience of Central Europe has been large-scale deindustrialization. Available streams of capital have barely sufficed to save a fraction of the industrial infrastructure from devastation as a consequence of high interest rates, the severing of contacts with eastern neighbours, and oligopolistic competition from the West.[18] The real engine of growth in Central Europe seems, rather, to have been the booming of small services in retail, repair and maintenance, leisure, tourism, health, consultancy and real estate, together with the repatriation of incomes from migrant labour in the West. This is understandable given the notorious underdevelopment of the services sector under socialism, but it is not likely to continue at the same pace after the catch-up phase is completed. All in all, it is not an exaggeration to say that Central and Eastern Europe has partly returned to a preindustrial social structure, with very few areas enjoying access to solid export-based earnings. As a result, all these economies have become thin and vulnerable. Even the new American-type malls around Central European cities, with huge investments from the West and generating direly needed employment for young local workers, are entirely dependent on a projected growth of incomes that may in the end not be realistic (this is clear to anyone who has observed the four or five basic items that most people buy after having spent half a Sunday enjoying the sheer propinquity of the cornucopia).

After ten years of transformation it is common to distinguish three clusters of countries (EBRD 1999). Cluster one consists of the 'successful' Central European countries, whose GDP had by 1999 recovered from the 'transitional recession' to equal (Czech Republic, Hungary, Slovakia) or even surpass (Poland, Slovenia) the level of 1989. Group two, consisting of southeastern Europe plus the Baltic countries, had arrived at somewhere between 60 per cent and 75 per cent of pre-transition levels. Group three, the Commonwealth of Independent States, was the most uneven and averaged only about 50 per cent of the GDP scores it had enjoyed in the last years of socialism. Some countries within that group, however, were decidedly better off than others: the authoritarian states of Uzbekistan and Belarus reached 90 per cent and 78 per cent respectively, while the economies of Ukraine, Georgia and Moldova had disintegrated to levels below 35 per cent. Poverty and inequality counts have risen so drastically that anyone who speaks about 'the success of transition in Central and Eastern Europe' is either a cynic or unable to look beyond macro issues of institutional design.[19]

There is evidently a sharp divide between Central Europe and the CIS. Russia and Ukraine have not only experienced a drastic reduction in their official GDP levels, they have also reached Latin American measures of poverty and inequality (EBRD 1999: 18). Behind these figures there is a crucial institutional contrast (also noted by Michael Stewart in chapter 7). Central Europe has shed large numbers of industrial workers via unemployment and pensions, and has subsequently raised both industrial productivity and wages. This indicates that capitalism has started to operate on the ground. It has also simultaneously increased full-time employment in the tertiary sector. Industrial employers in Russia and the CIS, in contrast, have resorted to the old socialist technique of 'hoarding' labour, keeping wage rises far below inflation, accepting wage arrears rather than dismissals, and failing to raise productivity. Factory communities have not been shaken up to the extent they have in Central Europe; rather, they have stagnated, while poverty and continued dependence on industrial employers have prevented the rise of a more formal and professional service sector. Neo-liberals would explain this contrast in institutional outcomes and key class relationships by giving Central Europe, Poland in particular, a high grade for applying policies of stabilization, liberalization and privatization, and finding the Russian government at fault in a whole series of policy failures (e.g. Åslund 1995; Boycko et al. 1995). Researchers of path-dependency, be they anthropologists, sociologists or institutional economists, dig deeper and point to crucial differences in the capacities of central governments and the nature of the respective postsocialist economies. Institutional economists, for example, argue that the ex-Soviet economy was more monopolistic than the more fragmented Central European economies, which turned price liberalization into an invitation for self-enrichment on the part of producers (Stiglitz 1995). Others would point to the disintegration of trade and exchange networks as a consequence of declining liquidity, caused by high interest rates and the ensuing credit-crunch, and the consequent upsurge of barter, associated with the rise of territorial power-brokers (Burawoy 1994; Burawoy and Krotov 1993; Clarke et al. 1993; Humphrey 2001). In Central Europe they would point to the long history of attempts to decentralize economies in Poland and Hungary, rendering these economies better prepared to respond to market signals and competitive pressures. Some would emphasize the relative power of an organized civil society in preventing perverse outcomes (Minev et al. 2001).

The neo-liberals seem to be withdrawing from the debate and contenting themselves with the routines of their consultancy work (which, of course, continues as if nothing had happened). The richness of anthropological, socio-logical and institutional accounts makes them far more persuasive. However, neither strand makes much analytical sense of space and the spatial linkages involved in postsocialist social change. In accounting for the different outcomes in Russia and Central Europe, it is crucial to note that Bohemia, Silesia and West-Danubia are zones on the doorstep of the capitalist heartlands of the EU. If Russia had bordered on Germany, Russian monopolistic practices would have been interrupted by the subsidized exports of German firms, which would have subverted the barter networks, reduced the space for local power-brokers, and slowed down the administrative disintegration. Russian failure was a failure of the Yeltsin administration as well as of Western advice and aid. Path-dependence theorists are right to advocate gradualism and institution-building in place of 'shock therapy'. But more than anything else, it might have been a failure of space.

Even within Central Europe we gain analytical edge if we combine dynamic path-dependency with spatial linkages. The biggest economic success in Central Europe is Slovenia, which by 1999 had a GDP per capita almost twice as high as the next highest in Central Europe, the Czech Republic. It attained this success without adopting anything from the shock-therapy cookbook, nor did it follow the Hungarian road of FDI-led renewal. In fact, the EBRD has been consistently critical of Slovenian gradualism. The explanation for its competitiveness lies in its early openness towards the European economies, combined with the advantages brought by spatial linkages.

Finally, we must not forget the political linkages that both liberal/globalist and path-dependency explanations tend to obliterate. Polish success vis-à-vis Russia has much to do with the geopolitical interests of the West, concertedly acting to make Poland a showcase of transition even before the disintegration of the Soviet Union. Thus the foreign debt was reduced by half in 1988, a move for which the world's poorest nations have been begging for years, with little response. It is quite possible that the Federal Republic of Yugoslavia would have had a different fate if Prime Minister Markovic, conferring with the IMF in 1990, had been rescued in similar fashion. Belgrade, in the global scenario, did not count ('We have no dogs in this fight', said Secretary of State James Baker later when everything was falling apart). Yugoslavia had to revert to draconic cut-backs on federal spending immediately after the talks, after which the whole deadly sequence of scapegoating, nationalist secession, war and genocide got irreversibly under way.

## Conclusion

Postsocialist citizens were not offered a Marshall Plan after 1989/92. Instead, phase one of their 'transition' brought them globalism, 'technical assistance' by the Harvard Institute for International Development and the Big Six accountancy firms, and an impoverished model of civil society. Phase two is already bringing more intense dilemmas about public policy frameworks at all institutional levels. Depending upon their outcomes, there may be new opportunities for regions and countries to carve out development paths and state/society/market mixes that suit local needs better than the one-size-fits-all suit they have been obliged to wear so far. Whether these dilemmas will be resolved in an environment of democratic choice, technocratic governance or authoritarian coercion will be highly dependent on place and civic action. Tracking phase two for anthropologists of postsocialism will primarily mean studying the ways in which persons, families, localities, communities and regions mobilize for, and respond to, the openings that the 'movers and doers' on higher levels can create or fail to create.

The global upsurge of nationalism and religion and the return of authoritarianism in much of Eurasia must be seen not as the re-enactment of local cultural tradition against cosmopolitanism, but as intense efforts to stall the tide of demoralization and corruption after a long epoch of market-driven transformation. Reactionary movements to prevent the erasure of national status hierarchies, to control the shift in gender relations, and to compensate for the leakages of social and public power, seldom operate in the most enlightened and equitable ways; they do not achieve the efficient and democratic provision of public goods that most Western intellectuals would like to see. Nationalism, religion and authoritarianism can, however, open up autonomous capacities for local social action by channelling collective desires. But here again we really are all in the same ship. Western Europeans, too, hark back to their earlier social democratic and socialist legacies. Surveys show a consistent strong preference for the maintenance of welfare state arrangements within the emergent EU, combined with a continuing allegiance to the national state for its democratic guarantees and potential for autonomous public choice. We are all busy trying to do the necessary repair work on our basic institutions of state and civil society.

## Notes

1  See Appadurai 1996; Hannerz 1996; Kalb 2000; Mittelman 2000. Most of the literature on cultural globalization is in my eyes deficient in describing the particular conjunction with 'financialization' (see Arrighi 1994), monetarism and the associated erosion of public policy. The three properties I am highlighting stress precisely this context.

2  The pattern is not dissimilar from the West, apart from the strong association between poverty and the rural periphery. The actual levels, of course, are far worse. For detailed discussions of the creation and transformation of social policy and poverty in Hungary, Poland and the Czech Republic see Kalb and Kovacs (forthcoming). See also the wealth of case studies on social policy in CEE conducted under the framework of the SOCO programme (SOCO Project Papers), Institute for Human Sciences (IWM), Vienna (http://www.univie.ac.at/iwm/main-e.htm).

3  This term comes from Ash 1989. Civil society as a concept and a political vision was especially prominent in Central Europe. It played a much more limited role in the Balkans and the countries of the former Soviet Union, where nationalism was the most explicit force. However, it was fed back to these emergent nations subsequently as a consequence of their interaction with Western donors and other actors in the interstate system. For the burgeoning literature on civil society see, among others: Cohen and Arato 1995; Hall 1995; Hann and Dunn 1996; Putnam 1993; Shafir 1998. For a broad treatment that combines visions of civil society with a discussion of political economy traditions see Janoski 1998; very useful also is Katznelson 1996.

4  For example the political elites of Third Way social democracy. See Giddens 1998, 2000.

5  See Tilly 1997; this spatial insight also shapes my effort to determine the dynamics of class conflict and cooperation in Western Europe *vis-à-vis* Eurasia and the US; see Kalb 2002.

6  Although from the mid-1990s on the World Development Reports and Human Development Reports have become more sensitive towards poverty issues, they fail to reconcile social policy, education and health objectives with 'structural adjustment' requirements, which are as a rule perverse. For an insightful discussion of the perversity of 'structural adjustment' see Epstein 2001.

7  See Michnik 1999. The speech was given in Vienna at a conference of the Institute for Human Sciences (IWM) and printed in *Dissent*, Fall 1999: 14–16.

8  The eminent Polish sociologist Jerzy Szacki, during a seminar at the IWM in Vienna, Fall 1998, explicitly refused to include labour unions as a part of civil society, because of their 'claiming attitude'. Civil society, in his vision, was primarily about 'self-responsibility'.

9  Personal communication from Dr Diana Mishkova, September 2000.

10  See Grabher and Stark 1997; Stark 1997; Stark and Brust 1998; see also Hann 1998. For sustained, but one-sided, arguments that strong property rights can serve in the interests of the poor (sic) see Soto 2000.

11  Speech at IWM, May 1998.

12  The idea of the Washington Consensus stems from the economist John Williamson (1990). For a good discussion rooted in East European experience see Kolodko 2000.

13  See Aminzade 1992; a classical text is Tilly 1981; see also Stark and Bruszt 1998. The term has become a celebrated concept in research on public policy, see for example Esping-Andersen 1999.

14  See Grabher and Stark 1997; see also Stark 1997; Stark and Bruszt 1998.

15  See Schneider and Rapp 1995. Burawoy *et al.* 2000 provides a very good methodological introduction on fieldwork as a tool for 'studying up and outward'. For some interesting parallels with the earlier methodological development of the anthropology of Europe, compare Boissevain 1975 with Hann 1993: 16–20.

16 (Financial Times, 24 April 2001.) The point is that, unless the EU can offer this form of compensation for the Stability Pact prohibition of budget deficits, then eventual accession is likely to prove a perverse and paradoxical experience not unlike the experience of 'transition' in the last decade (Kalb and Kovács forthcoming).

17 This is not to say that foreign direct investment (FDI) was unimportant, only to emphasize that it is highly selective and, in this region, most areas east of the line Budapest–Warsaw have been de facto excluded (Zysman and Schwartz 1998). A similar story can be told for subcontracting arrangements between Western textile and footwear firms and entrepreneurs in Romania, Croatia or Poland. Such arrangements have been important ways for these firms to acquire export opportunities and marketing skills, but they have materialized only in very specific networks of space and time. Left to itself, capital works by the selection of place rather than by the lifting up of space.

18 The area around Wrocław, Lower Silesia, the restructuring and privatization of which I have been studying closely in recent years, is a good example of such a 'successful' region.

19 Using the low UNDP poverty line for middle-income countries of US$4 per day per household, group one saw an increase of households below that line from 1.4 per cent in the mid-1980s to 12 per cent in the mid-1990s, with the Czech republic and Slovakia scoring less than 1 per cent and Poland over 20 per cent (EBRD 1999: 16). Superficially, these distributions come close to nominal West European poverty scores. Gini coefficients in these countries, used for measuring inequality, resemble the West European equations too. However, while the shape of the curves may be comparable, the absolute levels of course are not. With largely similar price levels, the UNDP poverty line amounts at best to one quarter of the actual poverty lines used by West European governments, such as the Netherlands or Germany. Median incomes in Central Europe do not exceed some 25 per cent of median incomes in Western Europe. Therefore, local measures for the social minimum applied by Central European governments, based on a basket of necessary purchases per household per month and thus taking into account actual price levels, give a more realistic picture of experienced material deprivation. In Poland in 1989 some 14.8 per cent of households fell below that line; in 1997 it was 47 per cent (Tarkowska 2000). The Polish social minimum stood at circa DM 700. Measures for group two are even lower: Bulgaria in 1997, after the introduction of the currency board, peaked to 80 per cent of households falling below a local social minimum of DM 111 per month (Mitev 1998); measures for inequality in Romania were steeper than anywhere else in Europe, except in the CIS.

# References

Aminzade, Ronald (1992) 'Historical sociology and time', Sociological Methods and Research 20(4): 456–80.

Andor, László and Martin Summers (1998) Market Failure: Eastern Europe's 'Economic Miracle', London: Pluto Press.

Appadurai, Arjun (1996) Modernity at Large, Minneapolis: University of Minnesota Press.

Arrighi, Giovanni (1994) The Long Twentieth Century: Money, Power, and the Origins of Our Times, London: Verso.

Ash, Timothy Garton (1989) 'Refolution in Hungary and Poland', New York Review of Books 36: 9–15.

Äslund, Anders (1995) How Russia Became a Market Economy, Washington: The Brookings Institution.

Boissevain, Jeremy (1975) 'Introduction: towards a social anthropology of Europe', in Jeremy Boissevain and J. Friedl (eds) *Beyond the Community: Social Process in Europe*, The Hague: Department of Education.

Boycko, Maxim, Andrei Schleifer and Robert Vishny (1995) *Privatizing Russia*, Cambridge, MA: MIT Press.

Brenner, Robert (1998) 'The economics of global turbulence: a special report on the world economy, 1950–1998', *New Left Review* 229: 1–264.

Burawoy, Michael (1994) 'Why coupon socialism never stood a chance in Russia: the political conditions of economic transition', *Politics and Society* 22(4): 585–94.

Burawoy, Michael and Pavel Krotov (1993) 'The economic basis of Russia's political crisis', *New Left Review* 198: 49–70.

Burawoy, Michael and Katherine Verdery (eds) (1999) *Uncertain Transition, Ethnographies of Change in the Postsocialist World*, Boulder and London: Rowman and Littlefield.

Burawoy, Michael, Joseph A. Blum, Sheba George, Zsuzsa Gille, Teresa Gowan, Lynne Haney, Maren Klawiter, Steven H. Lopez, Sean O. Riain and Millie Thayer (2000) *Global Ethnography: Forces, Connections, and Imaginations in a Postmodern World*, Berkeley: University of California Press.

Clarke, Simon, Peter Fairbrother, Michael Burawoy and Pavel Krotov (1993) *What About the Workers? Workers and the Transition to Capitalism in Russia*, London: Verso.

Cohen, Jean and Andrew Arato (1995) *Civil Society and Political Theory*, Cambridge, MA: MIT Press.

Elster, Jon, Claus Offe and Ulrich Preuss (1998) *Institutional Desing in Post-Communist Societies*, Cambridge: Cambridge University Press.

Epstein, Helen (2001) 'The global health collapse', *New York Review of Books* 6: 33–40.

Esping-Andersen, Gosta (1999) *Social Foundations of Postindustrial Economies*, Oxford: Oxford University Press.

European Bank for Reconstruction and Development (EBRD) (1999) *Transition Report 1999, Ten Years of Transition*, London: EBRD.

Eyal, Gil (2000) 'Anti-politics and the spirit of capitalism: dissidents, monetarists, and the Czech transition to capitalism', *Theory and Society* 29(2): 49–92.

Gellner, Ernest (1994) *Civil Society and Its Rivals*, London: Hamish Hamilton.

Giddens, Anthony (1998) *The Third Way*, Cambridge: Polity Press.

——(2000) *The Third Way and its Critics*, Cambridge: Polity Press.

Gowan, Peter (1999) *The Global Gamble: Washington's Faustian Bid for World Dominance*, London: Verso.

Grabher, Gernot and David Stark (1997) 'Organizing diversity: evolutionary theory, network analysis, and post-socialism', in Gernot Grabher and David Stark (eds) *Restructuring Networks in Post-Socialism: Legacies, Linkages, and Localities*, Cambridge: Cambridge University Press.

Greskovits, Béla (1998) *The Political Economy of Protest and Patience: East European and Latin American Transformations Compared*, Budapest: Central European University Press.

Hall, John A. (ed.) (1995) *Civil Society: Theory, History, Comparison*, Cambridge: Polity Press.

Hann, C.M. (ed.) (1993) 'Introduction: social anthropology and socialism', in C.M. Hann (ed.) *Socialism, Ideals, Ideologies, and Local Practice*, London: Routledge, pp. 1–26.

——(ed.) (1998) *Property Relations: Renewing the Anthropological Tradition*, Cambridge: Cambridge University Press.

Hann, C.M. and Elizabeth Dunn (eds) (1996) *Civil Society: Challenging Western Models*, London: Routledge.

Hannerz, Ulf (1996) *Transnational Connections: Culture, People, Places*, London: Routledge.

Humphrey, Caroline (2001) *The Unmaking of Soviet Life: Everyday Economies in Russia and Mongolia*, Ithaca: Cornell University Press.

Janoski, Thomas (1998) *Citizenship and Civil Society: a Framework of Rights and Obligations in Liberal, Traditional and Social Democratic Regimes*, Cambridge: Cambridge University Press.

Kalb, Don (2000) 'Localizing flows: power, paths, institutions and networks, in D. Kalb, Marco van der Land, Richard Staring, Bart van Steenbergen and Nico Wilterdink (eds) *The Ends of Globalization: Bringing Society Back In*, Boulder and London: Rowman and Littlefield, pp. 1–29.

——(2002) 'Social class and social change in postwar Europe', in Rosemary Wakeman (ed.) *Themes in European History. Vol. 4, Postwar Europe*, London: Routledge.

Kalb, Don and János Kovács (eds) (forthcoming) *Americanization or Europeanization? Social Policy Formation in the Czech Republic, Hungary and Poland*.

Kalb, Don, Marco van der Land, Richard Staring, Bart van Steenbergen and Nico Wilterdink (eds) (2000) *The Ends of Globalization: Bringing Society Back In*, Boulder and London: Rowman and Littlefield.

Katznelson, Ira (1996) *Liberalism's Crooked Circle: Letters to Adam Michnik*, Princeton: Princeton University Press.

Kolodko, Grzegorz (2000) *From Shock to Therapy. The Political Economy of Postsocialist Transformation*, Oxford: Oxford University Press.

Michnik, Adam (1999) 'Ten years after 1989', *Dissent* Fall: 14–16.

Milanovic, Branko (1996) 'Income, inequalities and poverty during the transition: a survey of the evidence', in Stanislawa Golinowska (ed.) *Social Policy Towards Poverty: A Comparative Approach*, Warsaw: IpiSS (in Polish).

Minev, Douhomir *et al.* (2001) *Strategic Objectives and Equity in Policies of Transition: Bulgarian and Polish Cases*, SOCO Project Paper no. 91, Vienna: IWM.

Mitev, Petar-Emil (1998) *Bulgarian Country-Report*, Sofia (later published in Rebecca Emigh and Ivan Szelenyi (eds) (2000) *Poverty, Ethnicity and Gender in Eastern Europe during the Market Transition*, New York: Praeger).

Mittelman, James (2000) *The Globalization Syndrome*, Princeton: Princeton University Press.

North, Douglass (1997) 'Understanding economic change', in Joan M. Nelson, Charles Tilly and Lee Walker (eds) *Transforming Post-Communist Political Economies*, Washington, National Research Council.

Poznański, Kazimierz (1996) *Poland's Protracted Transition: Institutional Change and Economic Growth*, Cambridge: Cambridge University Press.

Putnam, Robert D. (1993) *Making Democracy Work: Civic Traditions in Modern Italy*, Princeton: Princeton University Press.

Sassen, Saskia (2000) 'The state and the new geography of power', in D. Kalb, Marco van der Land, Richard Staring, Bart van Steenbergen and Nico Wilterdink (eds) *The Ends of Globalization: Bringing Society Back In*, Boulder and London: Rowman and Littlefield, pp. 49–65.

Schneider, Jane and Rayna Rapp (eds) (1995) *Articulating Hidden Histories: Exploring the Influence of Eric R. Wolf*, Berkeley: University of California Press.

Shafir, Gerson (ed.) (1998) *The Citizenship Debates: a Reader*, Minneapolis, London: University of Minnesota Press.

Soto, Hernando de (2000) *The Mystery of Capital: Why Capitalism Succeeds in the West and Fails Everywhere Else*, New York: Bantam Press.

Stark, David (1997) 'Recombinant property in East European capitalism', in G. Grabher and David Stark (eds) *Restructuring Networks in Post-socialism: Legacies, Linkages and Localities*, Cambridge: Cambridge University Press.

Stark, David and László Brust (1998) *Postsocialist Pathways: Transforming Politics and Property in East Central Europe*, Cambridge: Cambridge University Press.

Stiglitz, Joseph (1995) *Whither Socialism?* Cambridge, MA: MIT Press.

——(2000) 'What I learned from the world economic crisis', *New Republic* 17 (April), available at http://www.tnr.com/041700/stiglitz041700.html.

Strange, Susan (1996) *The Retreat of the State: The Diffusion of Power in the World Economy*, Cambridge: Cambridge University Press.

Szacki, Jerzy (1995) *Liberalism after Communism*, Budapest: Central European University Press.

Tarkowska, Elzbieta (2000) 'An underclass without ethnicity: the poverty of Polish women and agricultural laborers', in Rebecca Emigh and Iván Szelényi (eds) *Poverty, Ethnicity and Gender in Eastern Europe during the Market Transition*, Westport: Praeger.

Thompson, Edward (1963) *The Making of the English Working Class*, New York: Vintage.

Tilly, Charles (1981) *As Sociology Meets History*, New York: Academic Press.

——(1984) *Big Structures, Large Processes, Huge Comparisons*, New York: Russell Sage Foundation.

——(1997) 'Democracy, social change, and economies in transition', in Joan Nelson, Charles Tilly and Lee Walker (eds) *Transforming Post-Communist Political Economies*, Washington, National Academy Press.

Wade, Robert (2001) 'Showdown at the World Bank', *New Left Review* 7: 124–38.

Wade, Robert and Frank Veneroso (1998) 'The East Asian crash and the Wall Street–IMF Complex, *New Left Review* 228: 3–24.

Wedel, Janine R. (1998) *Collision and Collusion: The Strange Case of Western Aid to Eastern Europe*, New York: St Martin's Press.

Williamson, John (ed.) (1990) *Latin American Adjustment: How Much Has Happened?*, Washington, Institute for International Economics.

Zysman, John and Andrew Schwartz (eds) (1998) *Enlarging Europe: the Industrial Foundations of a New Political Reality*, Berkeley: University of California Press.

# Index

Page references for notes are followed by n

Abrahams, Ray 3
Abramson, David 279, 291
accounting practices 38–9
Achim, V. 148
Afanas'yev, M. 261
agriculture 3, 109; gender 93, 99, 102–3,
    107–8; Hungary 41–50; Turkestan
    239–40, see also collectivization;
    decollectivization
aid see development assistance
akuli 87–8
Alekseyev, A.A. 186
Altai 261, 265–6, 270, 271
Ambrus, Péter 144
Anagnost, Ann 7, 231
Anderson, Benedict 174, 244
Anderson, David G. 3, 9
Andor, László 326
Andor, Mihály 43, 45
animals 186–7
annihilation of the past 77–8
anthropology 1–2, 7–11; postsocialism
    2–7, 322–5
Apostolic Church 208–9, 210
Arandarenko, Mihail 126
Arato, Andrew 281
arendatori 30, 82–6, 87, 88
Arendt, Hannah 162
Argounova, T. 184
Arrighi, Giovanni 325
Ashwin, Sarah 126
Aslund, Anders 32, 327
asozial 142
Atwood, L. 99
Austria 165
authoritarianism 329
Ayuki-Khan 266, 268

Baban, A. 97
Bacon, Walter M. Jr 121
Badone, Ellen 57
Bahro, Rudolph 12, 20, 118
Baker, James 329
Balcerowicz, Leszek 108, 320
Balkans: ethnicity 6; Euro-elites 278;
    fragmentation 302; projects 305–13;
    religious sites 159–60, 163–6, see also
    Bulgaria; Moldova; Romania;
    Yugoslavia
Balzer, Marjorie Mandelstam 7
Banac, Ivo 165
Banja Luka 166
Banmé, Geremie 208
Bârgau, Valeriu 118
Barmé, Geremie 197
Barşana 146–7
Bassin, Mark 271
Bax, Mart 6, 166
begging 138
Beijing 4
Belarus 327
belief 58
Bell, John D. 80, 89
Bellér-Hann, Ildikó 7
Benovska-Sabkova 68
Benvenisti, Meron 167
Berdahl, Daphne 2–3, 62–3, 115
Bernbeck, Reinhard 160, 168
Bigenho, Michelle 66
Binder, David 169
Binns, Christopher A.P. 57
Birtalan, Laura 121
black market 121, 126
Blanchard, Olivier Jean 115
Blecher, Marc 200

Bobek, Martin 117
Boissevain, Jeremy 57
Bolivia 66
Borneman, John 5, 221
Böröcz, József 34
Bosnia 157; multi-multi protectorate
    168–71; nationalism 171; religious sites
    165, 166, 173; ritual 61–2; tolerance
    159, 160–1
Bougarel, Xavier 161
Bourdieu, Pierre 29, 35–6, 37, 40–1, 46,
    60, 137
Bowman, Glen 167, 168
Boycko, Maxim 327
Brada, Josef 32
Brandtstädter, Susanne 6
Braudel, Fernand 77
Brazil 145
Brehoi, Gheorghe 122
Bremmer, I. 252
Brenner, Robert 325
Bridger, Sue 4, 7, 97, 99
Bringa, Tone 6, 61–2, 67, 159, 161
Brook, Timothy 9
Brower, D.R. 243
Bruno, Marta 4
Bruszt, L. 62, 252
Bruun, Ole 62, 200–1, 210
*bu gongdao* 199
Buchanan, Donna 59, 65, 67, 69
Budapest 139, 142, 146
Buddhism 266, 267, 268, 269, 271
Buddhist Wheel 209–10
Budrala, Gh. 146
Bulag, Uradyn 6
Bulgaria 3, 134, 320; land reform 79–88,
    89; mistrust 75; ritual 57–71
Bunce, Valerie 16
Burawoy, Michael 7, 13, 238, 323, 328
bureaucracy 200
Burg, Steven 169
burial customs 6, 68
burrowing in 303, 305
Buryatia 3, 70, 266; collective farms
    247–8; Eurasianism 261, 262, 264, 265;
    politics 12–13
Bush, Larry 122

Cahalen, Deborah 6
Campbell, David 162
Câmpeanu, Pavel 20
Candau, Joël 80

capitalism 12, 115, 327; and consumption
    221, *see also* neo-capitalism
Carley, Patricia 293
carnival 66–7
Cartwright, A.L. 3
Castellan, Georges 76
Castells, Manuel 119
Cellarius, Barbara 9
Central Asia 3, 239–40, 253–4, 277–8;
    collective farms 245–7; dependency
    and postcoloniality 240–5;
    development assistance 281, 282–8,
    292–3; postsocialist pathways 251–3,
    *see also* Kazakhstan; Kyrgystan;
    Uzbekistan
Chan, Alfred L. 206
Chan, Anita 3, 208
Chan Kim-kwong 208
Chao, Linda 217, 224, 228, 230
chemical workers 94, 116, 117, 120
Chen Zaimou 204–5, 206
children 102; abandonment 97–8, 192
China 3, 5, 6, 158, 196–201, 323, 325;
    consumption 215, 217, 224–9;
    criticism 207–8; economy 202–3;
    embeddedness 10; household
    responsibility system 246; networks of
    congregations 208–11; postsocialism
    217, 218–20; power and legitimacy
    222–4; property relations 3–4; public
    religious institutions 203–7; ritual 57,
    58; transition 229–31; women 4
Chinese Communist Party (CCP) *see*
    Communist Party (China)
Cholpecki, J. 107
christenings 59, 60
Christians: Balkans 160–1, 163–6; China
    208–9, 210; Palestine 167–8
Ci Jiwei 221, 230
*cigány see* Roma
civil society 9, 66, 318–22, 326, 330n;
    Central Asia 293; China 198; and
    development 277, 280–4, 292, 306,
    310–11
clan organization 6
Clarke, Simon 136, 328
class 30, 93; *see* working class
coal miners 116–17, 118, 120, 122–3,
    124–5, 126, 127
Cockerham, William C. 128
cognitive capital 89
Cohen, Jean 281

Cold War 17, 18, 20, 324
Coleman, James 35
collectivization 3, 31–2; Bulgaria 86–7;
    Central Asia 245–7; Hungary 41–50;
    Siberia 245, 247–8; Uzbekistan
    248–51, see also decollectivization
colonialism 18, 19, 159
Comisso, Ellen 34, 41
Commonwealth of Independent States
    327, see also Soviet Union
communist parties 13
Communist Party (China) 196, 197–8,
    218; characteristics 198–201;
    legitimacy 222–4, 229, 231; media
    224–6; and networks of congregations
    209–10; and superstitions 197, 206–8
competition 277, 278
comprador bourgeoisie 278, 299–300,
    303–4, 305, 315, 320; Euro-elites
    303–13, 314, see also development
    professionals
consolidation 74–5
constitutional nationalism 157, 161
consumption 4, 10, 215, 217–18, 242, 327;
    China 219, 220–2, 224–30, 231
Cooper, Frederick 262
cooperative farms see collectivization
Corrin, C. 99
corruption 158, 199
Costigliola, Frank 18
cotton scandal 241–2
Cowan, Jane 6
Cozma, Miron 123
Crampton, Richard J. 76
Creed, Gerald W. 3, 4, 33, 59, 61, 62, 66,
    69, 87
Croatia 166, 168, 169
Croll, Elisabeth 4, 220
Crowley, Stephen 124
Csenyéte 141, 146, 148
cultural capital 29, 34, 41, 141
cultural racism 8, 21n, 159, 174
Cultural Revolution 198–9, 204–5, 207,
    208
culture 7–9, 70
culture of poverty 94, 140–3
Czakó, Ágnes 34
Czech Republic 134, 135, 146, 171, 327
Czechoslovakia 81, see also Slovakia
Czegledy, André 4

Dalai Lama 269

Danforth, Loring 68
Dave, Bhavna 283
Davin, Delia 4
Davis, Deborah S. 217, 218, 220, 224, 230
Dawisha, K. 252
Day, S. 144
De Soto, Hermine 2, 9
death rituals 6, 68
decollectivization 3–4, 22n, 33–4; Bulgaria
    30, 75, 79–90; China 199; Hungary
    41–50; Roma 135; Siberia 181
deindustrialization 326–7; Poland 95, 107;
    Romania 94, 116–18
democracy 6, 174, 305; China 230;
    consolidation 74–5; and development
    280–1, 306–7; as Lockean project
    171–3; masculinist 102–3; and social
    capital 66
democratization 20, 67
Deng Xiaoping 158, 199, 218
Denitch, Bogdan 159
dependency theory 216, 253; Central Asia
    240–2; comprador bourgeoisie 299–300
development assistance 4, 30, 277, 279;
    Balkans 305–13; Central Asia 9,
    280–91; and civil society 9, 292
development professionals 300; Central
    Asia 277–8, 279, 286–90, 291, 292,
    293; Euro-elite 303–13
diversity 160, 180
divorce 125, 126
Dobrudzha 76–7, 78, 81–8, 89
domestic business elite 299, 300, 304, 312,
    315
domestic domain 103, 104, 107, 108, 109,
    110n
domination 17
DONGOS (donor-organized NGOs) 277,
    285–6
Donia, Robert 159, 165
Duara, Prasenjit 203
Dubisch, Jill 57
Dudwick, Nora 2
Dugin, Alexander 258
Duijzings, Ger 6, 164
Dunn, Elizabeth 4, 9, 66
Durst, J. 142
Dutton, Michael 209
Dzsumbuj 142

East Germany 5, 62–3
Eberhardt, Piotr 81

economy 34, 239, 327–8; China 158,
    202–3; embeddedness 9–10; formal and
    informal structures 34; and ritual
    58–66, 70
education 134, 135
Eickelman, D.F. 240
Einhorn, B. 97, 99, 102
elections 30
Elias, Norbert 77
elites 34, 298–305, 314–15, *see also*
    development professionals
Elster, Jon 74, 279, 319
embeddedness 9–10
Emigh, Rebecca 136–7, 146
Engebrigsten, Ada 138–9, 144–5
Engels, Friedrich 137
entrepreneurs: *arendatori* 30, 82–6, 87, 88;
    Roma 124
ERRC 135
Eshi Kishlak 248–51
ethnic cleansing 6, 169, 171, 173
ethnicity 5–6, 30; Central Asia 239, 242;
    Even 185; racialization 146; and ritual
    67–8; Romania 119, *see also*
    Eurasianism; Roma
ethno-pedagogy 270
ethnography 2, 7, 252–3, 254, 323;
    Central Asia 241–2
euphemization 40–1, 46, 47
Eurasianism 14–15, 216, 258, 260, 261–3,
    271–3; Kalmykia 266–71; political
    context 263–6
Euro-elites 278, 303–13, 314
Eurocentricity 243
European Bank for Reconstruction and
    Development (EBRD) 282, 292–3,
    325, 326, 327, 328
European Union 325–6
Evans, Richard 149
Even 180–93, 193n
evolutionary economics 36
existential trauma 191–2
experience 34
Eyal, Gil 320

Fabius, Laurent 326
factionalism 199–200, 201
factory workers 4
Fagaras 116, 117, 125–7
fairness 200–1
Falk, A. 189
Falun Gong 209–10, 223

families 101, 103, 107–8, 109, 125–6,
    142–3; rituals 60–1, 64
farming *see* agriculture
Ferree, E.M. 97
Feuchtwang, Stephan 5, 6, 205, 207, 218
Fine, John 159, 165
Firlik, E. 107
Fisher, William F. 284, 285
flags 170–1
Fleiner, Lidija Basta 172
Fleiner, Thomas 172
foreign aid *see* development assistance
formal domain 35, 36–40
Fóti, J. 136
Foucault, Michel 10, 222, 223
Fox, Richard 159
fragmentation 302–3, 304–5
Freitag, Sandria 159
Frolic, Michael 9
Froot, Kenneth A. 115
funeral rites 6, 68
futurelessness 181, 187–8

Gábor, István 37
Gal, Susan 4, 99, 102
Galit, Valeru 317
Gambetta, Diego 75
Gamble, Jos 226
Gans, H. 140
Gao, Mobo 199, 209
Geertz, Clifford 162
Gellner, Ernest 9
*Gemeinschaftsfremde* 140
gender 96–9, 107–8
gender bias 93–4
gene-fund 270
Georgia 327
ghettoes 139
gift economy 59–60, 248
Gilmore, David D. 57
Giordano, Christian 76, 77, 80, 86
Gleason, G. 252
globalism 277, 317–18, 321–2, 325, 329;
    and elites 301–5
Goati, Vladimir 171
GONGOS (government-organized
    NGOs) 277, 286
good governance 280
Gowan, Peter 325
Grabher, Gernot 34
Grant, Bruce 3
Graves-Brown, Paul 159–60

Greece 68
Green Barons (Hungary) 41
Greskovits, Béla 320
Guangzhou 227, 228
Guchinova, El'za-Bair 261, 265, 266, 267, 268, 269, 271
guilt 162–3
Gumilev, Lev 263, 265
Guo Zhichao 206
Gypsy *see* Roma

*habitus* 36, 41
Hajnal, L. 142
Hall, John A. 9
Halpern, Joel M. 6
Hammel, Eugene 159
Haney, L. 97
Hankiss, Elemér 37
Hann, Chris 3, 4, 9, 33, 38, 66, 185, 297
Hannerz, Ulf 77, 143
Harrell, S. 218, 220
Hasluck, F.W. 163, 164
Haukanes, H. 97
Havel, Vaclav 10
Hayden, Robert 160, 161, 162, 166, 168, 169, 171, 174
health 127–8
hedonism 221, 230
Heleniak, T. 184
Hettlage, Robert 86
hidden histories 324
Hirschhausen, Béatrice von 3
historical trauma 191–2
history 7, 32, 89, 198; actualized 77–9; hidden 324; reversible 79–81
Hivon, Myriam 3, 99, 100
Hoffman, Oscar 118
Holmes, Stephen 279
Holt Ruffin, M. 286
Holy, Ladislav 4
Horváth, A. 147, 148
Howe, Leo 144
Hu Zongze 197, 204, 207
Huang Jing 200
Huang, Philip 220
Huang Yu 224
human rights 145–8, 284
Human Rights Watch 133, 284
Humphrey, Caroline 3, 4, 5, 7, 57, 100, 180–1, 267, 328; collective farms 245, 247–8
Hungary 327; collectivization 3, 31;
economy 134, 328; homogeneity 171–2; land redistribution 41–2; post-collective farms 43–50; Roma 135, 136, 138, 139, 141–3, 144, 147–8; transnational capital 326; urbanization 81
Hunter, Alan 208
Hussain, Athar 224

*icchi* 185
identity: constructed 162; ethnicity 5–6; national 6
ideology 7, 258–61
Ignatiev, N. 143
*ijara* 246–7
Ilyumzhinov, Kirsan 262, 266–9, 271
India 159, 168
indigenous people: Central Asia 242; Siberia 180–93, 193n, *see also* Eurasianism
industrialization 148
inequalities 4, 40, 93, 317, 327
informal domain 35, 36–40
informal economy 29, 31, 37–8, 46, 62, 108, 118, 119, 220
integration 302, 303–5
intellectual property 19, 22n
Islam *see* Muslims
Israel 167–8
Ivanova, Radost 60

Janggar 266, 269
Jay, John 172
Jelavich, Barbara 165
Jews, Palestine 167
Jin Pci 230–1
Jing Jun 3, 7, 207
Jiu Valley 116–17, 120, 121, 125
Jones, Luong P. 252
Jones, Siân 159–60
Jowitt, Ken 34
Judd, Ellen R. 4

Kalb, Don 319, 321, 325
Kaleta, A. 109
Kallay, Benjamin 165
Kalmykia 216, 260, 261, 266–71
Kaminski, B. 252
Kandiyoti, Deniz 3, 4, 242, 248, 253
Kaneff, Deema 3, 7, 86
Kant, Immanuel 318
Kató, Cs. 146

Katushov, K. 267
Kay, R. 97, 99
Kazakhstan 263, 264, 280, 283–4;
development 291; development
professionals 288–90; NGOs 284
Kazhegeldin, Prime Minister 283
Kemény, István 135, 141
Kenedi, János 38
Kereszty, Zs. 141
Kertesi, G. 134, 135
Kett, Maria 209
Kezdi, G. 135
Khakim, Rafael 264–5
Khalmg Tangch 216, 260, 261, 266–71
Khazanov, Anatoly 6, 241, 242
Kideckel, David A. 3, 6, 33, 57, 64, 116,
118, 122
kidney dealers 317
kinship see families
Kipnis, Andrew B. 10, 202
Kisban, Eszter 68
Kligman, Gail 4, 9, 57, 59, 68, 69, 99, 102,
103
knowledge 17, 34, 308–9
kolkhozes 244, 245–7, 251, 254
komsiluk 161
Konrád, György (George) 20, 118, 238
Konstantinov, Yulian 4
Kornai, János 20, 49, 118, 220, 238
Koroteyeva, V. 242
Koselleck, Reinhart 89
Kosovo 168–9, 308; religious sites 164,
166, 173
Kostova, Dobrinka 76, 80, 86
Kovács, János 319
Kovács, Katalin 33, 43, 44
Kovalcsik, Katalin 141
Kováts, A. 138, 142, 143, 144
Krementsov, Nikolai 33
Krotov, Pavel 328
Kubik, Jan 6
Kubinyi, Zs. 141
Kuczi, Tibor 34, 43, 47
kujjai 186, 190
kukeri 57–8, 65
Kundera, Milan 161
Kuroń, Jacek 100
Kürti, László 6
Kusmer, K. 139
Kuz'min, Yu. V. 263
Kyrgyztan 12, 264, 284

labor unions 114, 119, 122–3, 124
Laclau, Ernesto 231
Ladányi, János 133, 136, 139, 146, 148
Lampland, Martha 3, 33, 38, 49, 64, 127,
161
land, Siberia 182–3
land reform 203; see also decollectivization
Lane, Christel 57
Langman, Juliet 6
language 141
Lasic, Igor 169
Lass, Andrew 68
Latham, Kevin 217, 224, 225, 227, 230,
231
law 5
Ledeneva, Alena V. 89, 103
Leftwich, Adrian 280–1, 282
legacies problem 34
legality 88–9
legitimacy 10, 30, 88–9; China 222–4,
229; and consumption 217–18, 221–2
Lehmann, Rosa 7
Lemon, Alaina 7
Lent 57
Lewis, Oscar 94, 140
Li Conghua 217
Li Congmin 205, 206
Li Jie 197
Li Xiaoping 224
Li Zhuren 225
life expectancy 127–8
lift-off 303, 304, 305, 310, 315
Lincoln, Abraham 162
Linz, Juan J. 74
Liu Kang 221–2
Liu Xin 3, 201, 202
Liu Xinyong 220
Locke, John 160, 172
Lockwood, William 160–1
Łódź 95, 100–2, 107
Long, K. 107
Lü Xiaobo 206
Lubin, N. 239, 242
Ludden, David 168
Lull, James 224
lumpenproletariat 137, 149
Lur'ye, S.V. 264
Luzov, I. 80

McChesney, R.D. 240
McDonald, C. 135
McDonalds 4

Macedonia 59, 165
McGregor, Richard 225
Mach, Zdzisław 57
Madison, James 172
Madsen, Richard 204
mafia chieftains 299, 304, 312, 315
*mahallas* 290–1
Mahmutcehajic, Rusmir 159
Makarova, E. 242
Malashenko, Aleksei 264, 272
Malek-Lewy, M. 97
Malhotra, K.C. 168
Maliqi, Shkëlzen 168
Mandel, Ruth 3, 253
Mao Zedong 196, 197, 198, 205, 206, 207, 208, 209, 221
markets 4, 20, 325–6
Marmot, Michael 117
Marx, Anthony W. 145, 146
Marx, Karl 137, 174
Matvejevic, Predrag 78
Maurer, William 19
Mauss, Marcel 60
Mayhew, Henry 137
Mearns, R. 246
media, China 224–6, 227, 231
Medina, N. 135
Medjugorje 6, 166
men: agriculture 101, 105; Siberia 183
Menashiri, D. 240
Mendus, Susan 160
Mertus, Julie 168
Mészáros, A. 136
Michnik, Adam 319–20
migration: Bulgaria 61; Roma 143, 144, 146; Siberia 182–4
Milanovic, Branko 133–4, 318
Mill, John Stuart 160, 172
Minev, Douhomir 328
Minkov, Mihail 80
Minnich, Robert 64
Miric, Jovan 168
mistrust 75–6, 89–90
modernity 20, 98, 99–100, 159
modernization theory 280–1
Moldova 317, 327
Mollov, Jordan 80
monetarism 320–1
Mongol Empire 262–3
Mongolia 6, 13, 262–3
moral authority 202–3, 204
moral economy 158, 207

moral vacuum 10–11
Morris, D.B. 188
motherhood 101–2
Mouffe, Chantal 231
Müller, Birgit 4
multi-multi 170
Murrell, Peter 36
Muslims: Balkans 160–1, 163–6; Central Asia 240, 241, 253; Eurasianism 264; Palestine 167–8
Myers, Ramon H. 217, 224, 228, 230
Myrdal, Gunnar 136, 137

nation 161
national identities 17
national ideology 7, 260
national sovereignty *see* sovereignty
nationalism 6, 30, 124, 174–5, 291, 329; Bosnia 171; and Eurasianism 272; Poland 106, 108; and ritual 68, *see also* constitutional nationalism
Nazarbaev, Nursultan 272, 273n, 283
Nee, Victor 218, 238
negative tolerance 157
neo-capitalism 94, 114–18; sub-alternity of labor 118–20
neo-institutional economics 36–7
neo-liberalism 36, 327
neo-serfdom 94, 115
Nesbitt-Larking, Paul 206
Newton, J.A. 240
Nie, Lili 3
Niedermüller, Peter 7
non-governmental organizations (NGOs) 9, 281, 283, 284–8, 307–10, 313–14
non-interference 160, 173
North, Douglass C. 36–7, 323
nostalgia 94, 106–7, 108, 111n, 124, 208
Nove, A. 240
Nuskhaev, Aleksei 260, 270, 271

Ockenga, Edzard 122
Offe, Claus 74, 115
Oi, Jean C. 4, 5
*ommi* 185
Oprea, Ion 118
Orientalism 240, 243
OSCE 283

Palestine 167–8
Palmer, Michael 219
Panarin, A.S. 263–4, 272

Pandey, Gyanendra 159
Parkin, D. 188
Parrott, B. 252
Pasti, Vladimir 115
path-dependency 29, 238, 278, 322–4,
　327–8
Pawlik, W. 107
paysannerie pensée 81, 88
paysannerie vécue 88
Perry, Elizabeth J. 220
Péteri, György 33
Peukert, D. 140
Philps, Alan 167
Piasere, L. 138
Pierce, R.A. 243
Pika, Alexander 188
Pilkington, Hilary 97, 99–100
Pine, Frances 3, 4, 7, 66, 97, 100, 101,
　103, 144, 145
Pinnick, K. 97
Pittaway, Mark 33
pluralism 159–60
Pluskota, A. 109
Pol, Louis G. 121
Poland 326; economy 134, 327, 328–9;
　gendered domains 95–110;
　homogeneity 171; regional identity 6;
　religion 7; rituals 66; urbanization 81
Polanyi, Karl 9, 37, 323
political class 299, 303, 304, 312, 315
political imagination 259–60
politics, and ritual 66–70
Pollack, Susan 160, 168
Pollert, Anna 101, 124
Pomfret, R. 246
Popescu, A. 122
popular sovereignty 173, 174
pornography 97
Portes, Alejandro 35, 48
Pospai, Mircea 118
post-postsocialism 278, 298, 315; elites
　and global forces 301–5; and new elites
　298–301; project society and elites
　313–14
postcoloniality 15–18, 20, 174, 216, 253;
　Central Asia 240, 242–5
postsocialism 12–21, 21n, 115, 297–8;
　anthropology 1–11, 322–5; Central
　Asia 251–3; China 217, 218–20;
　gender bias 93–4; and postcolonialism
　174
Potter, Jack M. 3, 6

Potter, Sulamith Heins 3, 6
poverty 4, 136, 140–3, 327
power relations 278, 317
Poznański, Kazimierz 323
Prazauskas, A. 272
Pressley, Donald L. 282–3, 290
private domain 93, 103, 104, 108, 110n
privatization 20, 43–4, see also
　decollectivization
production 19
projects 313–14
Prónai, Cs. 138, 142
property 3–4, 5, 19, 34, 320; Siberia
　185–7, see also collectivization;
　decollectivization
Protic, Milan St 165
Przeworski, Adam 36
public domain 103, 104, 108, 220
Putin, President 258, 259, 262, 263, 272
Putnam, Robert 35, 66

qi exercises 209
qualitative data 2

racial discrimination 145–8
Rai, S. 99
Rainbow Farming 88
Ram, Harsha 271
Raseta, Boris 169
Rawls, John 160
Reading, A. 107
regional identity 6
reindeer 186
religion 6–7, 159, 329; Balkans 163–8,
　173; China 203, 204–5, 206–7, 208–10
reparation 189
representation 17
Republika Srpska 166
restitutive justice 79
retirement parties 60
retraditionalization 216
retributive justice 5
Rév, István 20, 31, 64
reversible history 76, 77–81
Rheubottom, D.B. 59
Richardson, James 210
Ries, Nancy 4, 181
Ringold, D. 134, 135, 144
risk 49
ritual 6, 57–8, 70–1; and economy 58–66;
　and politics 66–70
Roberts, Dexter 229

Rockhill, Lena 192
Rodina, Vladimir 122
Roerich, N. 265–6
Roland, Gerard 279
Roma 5, 67, 94, 133–6, 142–3, 148, 149n; culture of poverty 141–3; prospects 143–5; racial discrimination 146–8; as underclass 136, 138–40
Romania 3, 94; economy 134; EU accession 326; political class 299; rituals 66, 68; Roma 138–9, 144–5, 146–7; urbanization 81; weddings 59; working class 114, 116–28
Ron, James 166
Róna-Tas, Ákos 34, 37
Rose Valley 57
Roth, Klaus 57
Roy, O. 243–7, 248, 251
Rubin, B. 252
Rudolph, Lloyd 159
Rudolph, Susanne 159
Ruf, Gregory A. 3
Rumer, B. 252
Runciman, W.G. 136, 220, 223
rural studies 2–3
Russian Federation 2, 99–100, 258, 327, 328; economy 134; Eurasianism 14, 216, 261–6, 271–3; ideology 258–61, see also Kalmykia; Siberia
Russo, Alessandro 158, 198–9, 201

Sahlins, Marshall 37
Sahni, K. 243
Sakha 180, 184, 261, 266
Sampson, Steven 4, 9, 118, 298, 302, 305
Sanders, Irwin 60
Sapolsky, Robert M. 128
Sassen, Saskia 324, 325
Schrader, Heiko 5
Scott, James C. 89
Seabright, Paul 5
second economy 29, 31, 37–8, 46, 62, 108, 118, 119, 220
secret histories 7
Sells, Michael 159
Serbia 164–5
Shabad, Goldie 115
Shahrani, N. 240, 241
shamanism 6–7, 189, 190–1
Shanghai 226
Shanin, Teodor 82
sharecropping 246–7

sharks 87–8
shirkats 248–51, 254
Shnirel'man, V. 7, 263
Shoup, Paul 169
Shreeves, R. 97
shrines 163–8, 173
Shue, Vivienne 200
Siberia 3, 157–8, 180, 193; collective farms 245, 247–8; land and migration 182–4; soul of property 185–7; violence 187–91, see also Buryatia; Sakha
Sidel, Mark 220
Sik, Endre 34
Silverman, Carol 67
Siu, Helen F. 3, 5, 6, 224
Skeat, W.W. 185
Skultans, Vieda 7, 181, 192
Slezkine, Yu 181, 188
slicing 303, 305
Slomczynski, Kazimierz 115
Slovakia 140, 327
Slovenia 64, 171, 327, 328
Smallholders' Party (Hungary) 41
Smith, Richard 219
Sneath, David 3, 5
Snyder, Jack 171, 252
Snyder, Tim 115
social capital 29, 30, 34, 35–6, 46, 48, 62–4, 71n; Bourdieu 40–1; and democracy 66; development professionals 292; gift economy 60; and ritual 64–5, 66; workers 118–19
social exclusion 143
social justice 34
social networks 48–9, 63; and ritual 64–5; Romania 125–8
socialism 6, 9–10, 12, 18; China 196–8; and consumption 220–1; domestic domain 107, 109; family resemblances 238; fragmentation 302; and history 78; inequalities 93; nostalgia for 94, 106–7, 108, 111n, 124; political economies 18–19; politics 12–13; and ritual 57, 68, 69, 70; sub-alternity of labor 118–20; women 103; work 104; working class 114
sociology 5, 7
soldier sendoffs 59, 69
soul 185–6
South Africa 145
sovereignty 161, 164–5, 171; popular 173, 174

Soviet Union 3; ethnicity 6; imperialism 15, 16; indigenous people 181–2, 183–4, 188–9; shamanism 6–7, *see also* Commonwealth of Independent States
Srpska 166
Staddon, Caedmon 9
Stamboliiski, Alaxandar 79, 80
Staniszkis, Jadwiga 20, 34
Stark, David 34, 36, 37, 38, 39, 62, 218, 238, 252, 298
state 161, 263–4, 272, 313–4
Stedman-Jones, G. 139
Stepan, Alfred 74
Steppe Code 267–8
Stewart, Michael 5, 135, 144, 149
Stiglitz, Joseph 323, 328
Stoianovich, Traian 165
Stolcke, Verene 159
Stoller, Anne 262
Stone, Richard 117, 128
Strange, Susan 324
Strathern, Marilyn 12
Straussner, Shulamith 128
stress 128
sub-alternity 118–20, 124, 125
subjectivity 260
Sugar, Peter 165
Summers, Martin 326
superstition 158, 183, 197, 203
Suslov, I.M. 189
Svinin, V.V. 263
Swain, Nigel 31, 33, 41, 42, 43
Swedenberg, Ted 68
symbolic manipulation 122–5
symbols, Bosnia 170–1, Romania 126–7, Ukraine 6
Synovitz, Ron 122
Szacki, Jerzy 320
Szalai, Erzsébet 34
Székelyi, M. 135
Székesfehérvár 147–8
Szelényi, Iván 20, 118, 136–7, 140, 146, 238, 239

Tambiah, Stanley J. 174
Tang Xiaobing 220, 221
Taras, R. 252
Tatars 264–5
Tauber, E. 138
Taussig, M. 185
temples 203, 204–5, 206–7, 208–10
Terr, L. 187

Thaxton, Raplh 203
Third World 17, 18, 240
Thompson, Edward 320
Thompson, Stuart 217
Thurnwald, Richard 9
Tilly, Charles 75, 116, 324
time 187
Tishkov, Valery 6
Tocqueville, Alexis de 281, 318
Todorov, Tzvetan 162
tolerance 159, 160–1, 172, 173
Tolstoy, Leo 180
Tonev, Velko 76
totalitarianism 9, 17
trade unions 114, 119, 122–3, 124
tradition 98, 100, 187, 242
transition 32–3, 74, 115, 238–9, 279, 297–8; China 218, 223, 229–31; and civil society 281–2; formal and informal domains 34, 36–40; social capital and experience 34, 35–6
transitology 1, 74, 278, 279, 297
transnational capital 325–6
trauma 187–8, 189–91; existential and historical 191–2
Trouillot, Michel-Rolph 272
truncation 303, 305
trust 29, 34, 48, 75, 108
Tsiaras, Alexander 68
Tudor, Coreliu Vadim 125
Turkestan 239–40
Turkey 245
Turlichene 57–8
Turner, Victor 88
Tuva 261, 265, 266, 270
Tylor, E.B. 196

Uch Sumbur 265–6
Ukraine 6, 327
underclass 5, 94, 133, 136–40, 145–6; culture of poverty 140–3
underworld 138
unemployment 95–6, 97, 100–2, 105; Roma 134, 144; Romania 120, 121, 126
unfairness 199
unions 114, 119, 122–3, 124
United States 145, 146, 282, 325
United States Agency for International Development (USAID) 280, 281, 283, 293; *mahallas* 290; NGOs 284–5, 287
Urban, Mark 260–1, 263, 266, 268

urbanization 81
Urkhanova, Rimma 264
USSR *see* Soviet Union
utopianism 221, 230
Uzbekistan 216, 241–2, 253, 284, 327;
    collective farms 245–7, 248–51;
    Eurasianism 264; *mahallas* 290–1;
    NGOs 284, 285

Vachudova, Milada 115
Vajda, I. 138, 142
van der Veer, Peter 159
Vasecka, Michal 140
Vasil'eva, N. 189
Veeck, Ann 226
Veneroso, Frank 325
Verdery, Katherine 5, 13, 16, 17, 34, 119;
    agency over structure 297;
    consumption and legitimacy 217,
    220–1; family resemblances 238;
    history 7; path-dependency 323;
    property rights 3; ritual 6, 57, 68;
    transition 8–9, 218, 230
Vermeer, Eduard B. 3, 5
Veyne, Paul 260
Vickers, Miranda 168
vigilantism 6
Vil'chek, G. Ye. 182
violence: Bosnia 19, 160, 166, 173; India
    168; Palestine 167; Siberia 187–91
violent entrepreneurs 299, 300, 304, 312,
    315
Vitebsky, P. 183, 184, 187, 188, 191
Vogel, Ezra 218
Volgin, V. 267, 268

Wacquant, L.J.D. 146
Wade, Robert 325
Wakeman, F. 220
Walder, Andrew 4
Walesa, Lech 320
Wang Gan 227
Wang Mingming 5, 205, 207
Wang Shaoguang 224
Wang Xizhe 208, 210
Wank, David L. 227
Wanner, Catherine 6
warlords 299, 304, 312, 315
Wasserstrom, Jeffrey N. 220
Watson, Peggy 97, 102, 117, 121, 128
Watson, Rubie S. 7
Waugh, Daniel C. 286
Weber, Max 10, 75, 82, 88–9, 163

weddings 59, 60, 61–2, 65, 69, 224
Wedel, Janine R. 4, 9, 10, 34, 37, 66, 103,
    282, 302, 320
Weidner, Gerdi 128
Weindling, P. 140
Weinthal, E. 252
Williams, Raymond 40
Wilson, T. 225
Wilson, William Julius 137, 139
Wolchik, S. 97
Wolf, Eric 324
Wolfe, S. 183
Wolfe, Thomas 8
women 4; agriculture 52n, 93, 105–6;
    domestic burdens 93; exclusion and
    privation 96–7, 109; and *mahallas* 291;
    motherhood 101–2; public and private
    domain 103; rights 99; Romania 121,
    126; Siberia 183; unemployment 95–6,
    100–2; Uzbekistan 216
Woodward, Susan 168
working class 128; criticism of 114–15;
    neo-capitalism 116; Romania 120–8;
    sub-alternity 118–20
workplace: feminisation 101; sexualization
    97
World Bank 10, 144, 280, 293, 325

Yahutsk 184
Yakutia 180, 184, 261, 266
Yan Yunxiang 4, 10, 202
Yang Lian 201
Yang, Mayfair Mei-hui 10, 57, 58, 202
*yang'ge* 209, 210
Yasmann, Victor 258
Yeltsin, President 259, 272
Yugai, G.A. 265
Yugoslavia 18, 165, 166, 174, 329, *see also*
    Bosnia; Croatia; Kosovo; Macedonia;
    Serbia; Slovenia
Yurchak, A. 103

Zhao, Yuezhi 224
Zhovtis, Evgeny 284, 286, 292
Zhukov, S. 252
Zielińska, E. 97
*Zigeuner see* Roma
Zimmermann, Warren 169
Zizek, Slavoj 159
Zoon, I. 133